Complexity and Organization

Since the mid-1990s, complexity-based thinking has exerted increasing, yet somewhat controversial, influence over management theory and practice. This has in some part been due to the influence of a number of high-profile articles and the not inconsiderable hype which accompanied them. Another feature of the subject's development has been the diversity of the origins of the thinking and the claims which have been made for it in terms of managerial and organizational implications.

Complexity and Organization is the first text to bring this thinking together, presenting some of the most influential writing in the field and showing how the subject has emerged, developed and continues to influence managerial thinking. Seminal contributions to the field have been brought together in a single volume, allowing readers to access what might otherwise appear a very diffuse literature. Moreover, the editors, who represent some of the leading thinkers and writers in this field, have combined these readings with a unique commentary, not only indicating the significance of the articles but also teasing out the subtle differences and similarities between them. These commentaries take the form of a discussion between the editors, debating the contribution that each reading has made to the field and the influence it has had on management thinking.

Providing a unique overview, this informative and thought-provoking Reader will be an essential resource for anyone interested in complexity-based approaches.

Robert MacIntosh began his academic career as a researcher at the University of Strathclyde and completed his PhD in engineering before moving to a post in the Business School at the University of Glasgow. In 2004, he returned to Strathclyde where he is now a Professor in the Business School.

Donald MacLean is a Professional Research Fellow at the University of Glasgow. He is a faculty member of the Complexity and Management Centre of the University of Hertfordshire, a member of the faculty of the Institute of Directors in Scotland and an associate of the Glasgow Centre for Population Health.

Ralph Stacey is Professor of Management and Director of the Complexity and Management Centre at the Business School of the University of Hertfordshire.

Douglas Griffin is Associate Director of the Complexity and Management Centre at the Business School of the University of Hertfordshire. He is also an independent consultant.

Complexity and Organization

Readings and conversations

Edited by

Robert MacIntosh, Donald MacLean, Ralph Stacey and Douglas Griffin

Routledge
Taylor & Francis Group

LONDON AND NEW YORK

First published 2006
by Routledge
2 Park Square, Milton Park, Abingdon, Oxon OX14 4RN

Simultaneously published in the USA and Canada
by Routledge
270 Madison Ave, New York, NY 10016

Routledge is an imprint of the Taylor & Francis Group, an informa business

© 2006 Selection and editorial matter, Robert MacIntosh, Donald MacLean, Ralph Stacey
and Douglas Griffin; individual readings, their contributors (as specified in the
acknowledgements page).

Typeset in Perpetua and Bell Gothic by
Keystroke, Jacaranda Lodge, Wolverhampton
Printed and bound in Great Britain by
TJ International Ltd, Padstow, Cornwall

British Library Cataloguing in Publication Data
A catalogue record for this book is available from the British Library

Library of Congress Cataloging in Publication Data
Library of Congress Cataloging-in-Publication Data
Complexity and organization : readings and conversations / [edited by] Robert MacIntosh . . . [et al.].
    p. cm.
Includes bibliographical references and index.
ISBN 0–415–35240–1 (hard cover) – ISBN 0–415–35241–X (soft cover) 1. Management.
2. Organization. 3. Complex organizations–Management. 4. Complexity (Philosophy)
I. MacIntosh, Robert.
HD31.C6184 2006
658.4–dc22
2005018893

ISBN10: 0–415–35240–1 (hbk)
ISBN10: 0–415–35241–X (pbk)

ISBN13: 978–0–415–35240–6 (hbk)
ISBN13: 978–0–415–35241–3 (pbk)

Contents

About the Editors

Robert MacIntosh began his academic career as a researcher at the University of Strathclyde and completed his PhD in engineering before moving to a post in the Business School at the University of Glasgow. His main research interests lie in the area of strategic change. He has researched the application of complexity thinking to managerial and organizational issues for a number of years and has published on these topics. He has performed funded research for a range of funding bodies, is sub-theme chair in the European Group for Organization Studies and is a member of the Council for the British Academy of Management. At the moment he is working on a range of projects with the National Health Service in Glasgow. He lives in Glasgow with his wife Anne and their children Euan, Eilidh and Eva. He is happiest when he is at home and in their company. Undermining his credibility as a management researcher, however, is his status as a shareholder in Aberdeen Football Club – not the wisest investment decision, but one filled with hope!

Donald MacLean received his PhD from the University of Cambridge and spent ten years working in the optoelectronics industry and a further fifteen lecturing in strategic management. He is now a Professorial Research Fellow at the University of Glasgow. His interests lie in the development of alternative conceptions of the process, purpose and nature of organization and management. He is a faculty member of the Complexity and Management Centre of the University of Hertfordshire, a member of the faculty of the Institute of Directors in Scotland and an associate of the Glasgow Centre for Population Health. He lives with his wife and two sons, near Oban, on the West Coast of Scotland.

Ralph Stacey is Professor of Management and Director of the Complexity and Management Centre at the Business School of the University of Hertfordshire. He is the author of a number of books and articles that have been translated into other languages. These include *Strategic Management and Organisational Dynamics* (Pitman, 4th edition, 2003), *Complex Responsive Processes in Organisations* (Routledge 2001) and *Complexity and Group Processes: a radically social understanding of the* *individual* (Routledge 2003). He is co-author of *Complexity and Management: fad or radical challenge to systems thinking* (Stacey, Griffin and Shaw, Routledge 2000). He is a Member of the Institute of Group Analysis.

Douglas Griffin is an independent consultant, Visiting Professor at the Business School of the University of Hertfordshire and Associate Director of the Complexity and Management Centre. He has worked as an independent organization consultant since the mid-1980s and has also been employed with 3M Germany in strategic personnel development and organizational learning services. His current research interests are in the cultural and ethical implications of taking analogies from the complexity sciences to challenge our understanding of social interaction and organizational change.

Acknowledgements

The editors would like to thank all those who helped to bring this project about. The idea of creating a Reader for complexity writing in organizations had been in circulation for some time. Jacqueline Curthoys prompted us to move the project forward and, critically, she suggested that collaboration between Glasgow and Hertfordshire might produce a far more authoritative text – we feel sure that she was right, though you must judge this for yourself. In addition, Emma Joyes has kept the project on track, providing invaluable advice on formatting and finishing the manuscript. Also, we are indebted to Cherisse McLaren at Glasgow University for patiently transcribing our commentaries on the readings in each part.

We would like to offer our sincere thanks to the authors of the pieces gathered together in this Reader. We greatly enjoyed rereading the articles and are grateful for the opportunity to reprint them here. In particular, we would like to thank Jeffrey Goldstein for helping us with securing copyright on his article here. This was a complicated process and we are grateful for his persistent and conscientious approach to dealing with something that was really our problem, not his.

The publishers would like to thank the following for permission to reprint their material:

Berrett-Koehler Publishers Inc., 235 Montgomery Street, Suite 650, San Francisco, CA 94104–2916

    Wheatley, M. (1992/1999) Chaos and the Strange Attractor of Meaning, in *Leadership and the New Sciences: discovering order in a chaotic world*, 2nd edition, Chapter 7: 114–134. Berrett-Koehler, San Francisco, CA.

Emerald Group Publishing Limited, 60/62 Toller Lane, Bradford, West Yorkshire, BD8 9BY

    Stacey, R. (2003) Learning as an Activity of Interdependent People, *The Learning Organization*, 10 (6): 325–331.

John Wiley and Sons Ltd, The Atrium, Southern Gate, Chichester, West Sussex, PO19 8SQ

> Levy, D. (1994) Chaos Theory and Strategy: theory, application and managerial implications, *Strategic Management Journal*, 15: 167–178.

> MacIntosh, R. and MacLean, D. (1999) Conditioned Emergence: a dissipative structures approach to transformation, *Strategic Management Journal*, 20: 297–316.

> Stacey, R. (1995) The Science of Complexity: an alternative perspective for strategic change processes, *Strategic Management Journal*, 16: 477–495.

Michael Lissack and Jeffrey Goldstein

> Goldstein, J. (2000) Emergence: a construct amid a thicket of conceptual snares, *Emergence*, 2(1): 5–22.

Sage Publications Ltd, 1 Oliver's Yard, 55 City Road, London, EC1Y 1SP

> Chia, R. (1998) From Complexity Science to Complex Thinking: organization as simple location, *Organization*, 5 (3): 341–370.

> Griffin, D., Shaw, P. and Stacey, R. (1998) Speaking of Complexity in Management Theory and Practice, *Organization*, 5, (3): 315–339.

> Tsoukas, H. and Hatch, M. J. (2001) Complex Thinking, Complex Practice: the case for a narrative approach to organizational complexity, *Human Relations*, 54 (8): 879–1013.

Tribune Media Services, Suite 1400, 435 N. Michigan Avenue, Chicago, IL 60611

> Pascale, R. T. (1999) Surfing the Edge of Chaos, *Sloan Management Review*, Spring: 83–94.

Walter de Gruyter GMBH & Co. KG, Postfach 30 34 31, 10728, Berlin

> Allen, P. (1998) Evolving Complexity in Social Science, in G. Altmann and W. A. Koch (eds) *Systems: new paradigms for the human sciences*, Walter de Gruyter, New York.

INTRODUCTION

This book has its roots in the difficult experience of trying to introduce people, often students or would-be students, to the subject of complexity theory as it applies to organizations and management. Each of us has spent over a decade immersing ourselves in this new, and rapidly emerging, body of research. There is much that is promising, exciting, provocative and challenging when looking at familiar problems from a complexity perspective. Yet, we have each found that the further we travel on our voyage of discovery, the harder it becomes to summarize the field for newcomers.

In a number of settings, with managers or students, in formal taught courses or in informal conversation, one question remains decidedly difficult to answer. Excited by the prospect of a radical new approach to organizing and managing, potential friends, collaborators, students or clients ask: 'So, where can I find out more about complexity and organizations?' Typically, the conversation then stumbles and stutters. The possibility of buying a book might be discussed, but these range in both quality and accessibility. The thought might occur that reading a few academic articles would help, but the problem then becomes one of selection – let alone copyright. For us, the genesis of this book can be found in multiple experiences of such conversations over recent years.

Our intention in this book is to offer a more structured way of engaging with a subject area whose breadth can seem overwhelming. We have selected the term complexity but any literature search might throw up a range of related labels: chaos theory, complexity theory, complex adaptive systems, complexity thinking, etc. Such diversity is itself an indicator that we are dealing with a reasonably new field. Applications of complexity thinking to organizations and management processes are even newer (the earliest article in this Reader dates from 1994). As with the developmental phase of any subject, the early years are marked by a range of related but often contradictory views and difficulties over things that more established topics take for granted e.g. terminology and definitions.

Most people are aware of developments in complexity thinking without necessarily realizing that this is the case. Edward Lorenz's work using computer simulations to study the behaviour of weather systems seems an unlikely route to international stardom. Yet, most people have heard of the Butterfly Effect.[1] When questioned further about the Butterfly Effect, few can tell you who did the research, or the scientific basis of the phrase's meaning. Though difficult to articulate, notions of little things leading to big things and unpredictability spring to mind. Moving beyond this intuitive understanding to a position of greater conceptual clarity is where the real challenge lies.

Lorenz's work points to the possibility that infinitesimally small changes can have profound effects over time because complex systems are highly sensitive to initial conditions. Yet, as Nobel Laureate Ilya Prigogine points out, 'although we may know the initial conditions to an infinite number of decimal points, the future remains impossible to forecast'.[2] This is because a number of the concepts described in the readings in this book operate in concert. Peter Allen argues that any system which has within itself the capacity to respond to its environment in more than one way is complex.[3] Thus, complex systems tend to *self-organize*, producing new *emergent* ordered states. There is a paradigm shift in emphasis from systems which remain in equilibrium to systems which operate in *far from equilibrium* states. In these highly unstable states, processes of *positive feedback* can turn tiny changes into 'gigantic structure breaking waves'.[4] During such episodes, systems self-organize 'to produce a different pattern, without any blueprint'.[5] Excitement about this body of work stems from a fundamental challenge to much of the mechanistic and reductionist thinking which influences the ways in which we conceptualize the very nature of management and organization.

Applying these concepts to management and organization does introduce an added problem since complexity thinking began in the natural sciences, yet organizational usage of the concepts involves a translation to social science settings. In the Reader, we have grouped the readings into three parts. The first grouping takes complexity concepts and applies them directly to organizational issues. The articles selected show that this yields many insights, but raises other questions. The second group of readings offers various authors' attempts to categorize and define types of systems, bodies of research, etc. These categorizing articles are helpful in the sense that they are trying to offer a structure to a new, diverse field of study. The final group of readings places greater emphasis on the social nature of organizations. Though great theoretical insights have been gained by the study of chemical reactions, human systems bring their own complexities. Issues such as agency feature more heavily in this final group of readings than in those from Parts One and Two. Within each of these groups, we have selected what we believe to be a representative cross-section of articles. There were many other articles that we could have selected but didn't. Each part of the book does, however, close with a list of those authors and articles mentioned in the editors' conversation. Our hope is that this Reader will mark the start of your own voyage of discovery and that you might then follow up on those lines of enquiry which seem most relevant and inspiring to you.

Of course, no individual article or chapter could hope to deal effectively with the breadth of the challenges alluded to above. Nevertheless, we believe that in considering a collection of readings such as those in this book, there is something of a cumulative effect. Patterns can be observed, distinctive positions are being developed. Different assumptions underpin the work of different authors. In this book, we include what we believe to be a representative spectrum of work. Each reading, however, throws up a set of very similar questions relating to a fairly narrow range of concepts. In rereading these articles we found ourselves in deep discussion about the nature of emergence and self-organization, whether the question of agency was being treated seriously, whether the work was metaphorical or literal in its use of complexity thinking. These questions seemed familiar to us because they had been asked many times before, by many audiences. In part, they perhaps explain the difficulties of introducing new students to the field. The readings in themselves are interesting and each makes its own contribution. Taken collectively, however, they point to a set of questions that we have been grappling with for a number of years. In response, we have chosen to close each of the three parts with a transcript of our own conversation about the readings. This may seem a little self-indulgent, and perhaps it is. Our intention, however, was to begin to help readers of this book to engage with the literature in an active way.

At the start of each part, we briefly discuss our thinking in selecting particular articles and highlight some questions that it may be helpful to hold in mind whilst reading each individual article. The commentary at the end of each part then offers you some view of our reactions to the readings. We hope that this might achieve two things. First, it might offer some reassurance that these are difficult issues. Second, it might prompt you to agree or disagree with some or all of what you read. For us, the readings are a means of provoking a deeper conversation about a set of key questions. These questions are already live for us; we hope that in reading the articles and conversations in this book, they may come alive for you.

Notes

1   Edward Lorenz gave a talk at the December 1972 meeting of the American Association for the Advancement of Science in Washington, DC, entitled 'Predictability: does the flap of a butterfly's wings in Brazil set off a tornado in Texas?'
2   Prigogine, I. (1989) The Philosophy of Instability, *Futures*, 21(4): 396–400, at p. 400.
3   Allen, P. (2001) A Complex Systems Approach to Learning in Adaptive Network, *International Journal of Innovation Management*, 5(2): 149–180, at p. 150.
4   Prigogine, I. and Stengers, I. (1984) *Order out of Chaos: man's new dialogue with nature*, Bantam, New York, p. xvii.
5   Stacey, R. D. (2003) *Strategic Management and Organisational Dynamics: the challenge of complexity*, 4th edn, FT Prentice Hall, Harlow, p. 226.

PART ONE

Chaos theory and dissipative structures: direct applications of complexity thinking

EDITORS' INTRODUCTION AND COMMENTARY

In this first part, we consider a range of articles that draw on concepts such as chaos theory and dissipative structures from the natural sciences. We have selected five articles that we feel epitomize attempts to translate concepts directly from the natural to the social sciences and to ponder, to varying degrees, the implications of so doing.

All the readings in this part were originally published in the 1990s and some of them were influential in bringing complexity-based thinking to a wider audience. It is worth noting that the articles selected used different outlets to target different audiences. This, in part, is reflected in the differing styles of writing that they employ. In some senses, the earlier readings in this part might be seen as pioneering. However, we would not wish to give the impression that the direct translation of natural science concepts to managerial and organizational settings was restricted to a particular point in time. This approach continues to be seen in other current work.

The five readings cover related intellectual territory using similar terminology, concepts and root theories. In reading, and perhaps rereading, them it might be helpful to hold a number of questions in one's mind to help tease out similarities and differences across the set.

First, one might ask which tradition(s) each piece pursues. As we have already mentioned, there are different stylistic traditions being followed. Three of the articles appeared in the *Strategic Management Journal*, which is a traditional and highly scholarly academic outlet. These readings share a tendency to lay out prior work and relate complexity-based concepts to broader debates in the strategy literature. At the other end of the spectrum, Margaret Wheatley's best-selling book adopts a completely different tone. There are also intellectual traditions and trajectories running through the readings. For example, the MacIntosh and MacLean article and the Stacey article are both to some extent adopting a systems theory view of the world, whereas the Levy article focuses on a more mathematical treatment of chaos theory.

Next, one might ask the seemingly simple question of what each reading views as 'the organization'. Pascale and Wheatley talk of living systems, leading the reader to conceptualize the organization as a kind of organism. In contrast, Levy treats the organization as something of a black box, because his interests lie with chains of organizations connected as customers and suppliers. Stacey identifies both a formal and an informal organization. Leading on from a view of what constitutes the organization itself are issues about the extent and nature of managerial control. Again, these five readings offer very different views of the mechanisms through which control can or cannot be exerted and the extent to which management in the traditional sense is possible at all. The answers to these questions centre on usage of a range of key concepts such as simple rules, self-organization and emergence.

Human agency is at the heart of the distinction between the natural sciences (where many of these concepts were first developed) and the social sciences (where these concepts are being applied to organizations, strategy, supply chains, innovation, etc.). The issue of human agency is addressed to varying degrees in this first set of readings. For some, it is a key problem and requires further development of the underpinning theory. For others, the issue of agency seems to represent no problem at all and concepts are applied in social settings just as they would be in their natural science counterparts.

Finally, it is worth adopting a somewhat cynical stance and asking what, if any, new insights these readings offer. We will return to these questions in our discussion that follows the readings. At this stage, however, we would argue that whilst there is much that is new, exciting and radical in these readings, their real contribution emerges from their combined effect as a sort of sensitizing device. Taken as a set, they represent a new body of work that challenges much of what we have traditionally thought about the nature of organizations, the role (if any) of management, the sources of creativity and novelty, etc. These are key topics for those working in, or studying, organizations and the readings therefore not only merit our attention in their own right but also signal subsequent developments in a radical new line of thinking about organization and management.

David Levy

CHAOS THEORY AND STRATEGY: THEORY, APPLICATION, AND MANAGERIAL IMPLICATIONS

From *Strategic Management Journal* 1994, 15: 167–178. Copyright © 1994 by John Wiley & Sons Ltd. Reproduced with permission of the copyright owner. Further reproduction prohibited without permission.

Abstract

This paper argues that chaos theory provides a useful theoretical framework for understanding the dynamic evolution of industries and the complex interactions among industry actors. It is argued that industries can be conceptualized and modeled as complex, dynamic systems, which exhibit both unpredictability and underlying order. The relevance of chaos theory for strategy is discussed, and a number of managerial implications are suggested. To illustrate the application of chaos theory, a simulation model is presented that depicts the interactions between a manufacturer of computers, its suppliers, and its market. The results of the simulation demonstrate how managers might underestimate the costs of international production. The paper concludes that, by understanding industries as complex systems, managers can improve decision making and search for innovative solutions.
[. . .]

Introduction

One of the enduring problems facing the field of strategic management is the lack of theoretical tools available to describe and predict the behavior of firms and industries. For example, even if we know that oligopolistic industries are likely to experience periods of stability alternating with periods of intense competition, we do not know when they will occur or what will be the outcome. Similarly, it is almost impossible to predict the impact of the advent of a new competitor or technology in an industry. The fundamental problem is that industries evolve in a dynamic way over time as a result of complex interactions among firms, government, labor, consumers, financial institutions, and other elements of the environment. Not only does industry structure influence firm behavior, but firm behavior in turn can alter the structure of an industry and the contours of competition. Existing theoretical models, however, tend to assume relatively simple linear relationships without feedback. Indeed, many strategic theories attempt to classify firms and industries and to describe appropriate strategies for each class; examples include the Boston Consulting Group matrix for resource allocation and Bartlett's classification of international strategies (Bartlett and Ghoshal, 1989). Although these models are based on recurrent patterns that we recognize in the real world, there are usually far too many exceptions for the models to have much predictive value.

Chaos theory, which is the study of nonlinear dynamic systems, promises to be a useful conceptual framework that reconciles the essential unpredictability of industries with the emergence of distinctive patterns (Cartwright, 1991). Although chaos theory was originally developed in the context of the physical sciences, Radzicki (1990) and Butler (1990) amongst others have noted that social, ecological, and economic systems also tend to be characterized by nonlinear relationships and complex interactions that evolve dynamically over time. This recognition has led to a surge of interest in applying chaos theory to a number of fields, including ecology (Kauffman, 1991), medicine (Goldberger, Rigney and West, 1990), international relations (Mayer-Kress and Grossman, 1989), and economics (Baumol and Benhabib, 1989; Kelsey, 1988).[1] Despite the apparent applicability of chaos theory to the field of business strategy, there has been surprisingly little work in this area.

This paper introduces readers to chaos theory, and discusses its relevance to the social sciences in general and to aspects of strategy in particular, including planning and forecasting, and the impact of change on firms and industries. The application of chaos theory to a business situation is illustrated using a simulation model of an international supply chain. The model, which is based on the author's research into the supply chain of a California-based computer company, depicts the complex interactions between the firm, its suppliers, and its markets. The simulation results illustrate the managerial implications of applying chaos theory to strategic management. The model demonstrates how small disruptions to the supply chain interact to make the chain highly volatile, imposing significant costs on the organization. Although forecasting is very difficult in the supply chain, distinct patterns emerge which are useful for managers. The simulation also shows that by understanding the supply chain as a complex dynamic system, it is possible to identify managerial approaches that lower the cost of operating the supply chain.

An introduction to chaos theory

Chaos theory is the study of complex, nonlinear, dynamic systems. The field was pioneered by Lorenz (1963), who was studying the dynamics of turbulent flow in fluids. Although we all recognize the swirls and vortices that characterize turbulent flow, the complexities of turbulent flow have confounded mathematicians for years. A similar problem afflicts someone who is trying to calculate the path of an object in the gravitational pull of two or more bodies. While we can use simple Newtonian equations to predict the orbits of planets around the sun with a high degree of accuracy, the mathematics involved in the case of two or more 'suns' become intractable. The problem can be illustrated on a terrestrial level by observing the motion of a simple toy, a metal ball suspended over two or more magnets. The ball will trace a series of patterns that never exactly repeat themselves, and yet are not totally random.

The paradox here is that the motion of the metal ball is driven by the same Newtonian equations as the well understood case of a single gravitational attractor. If we knew precisely the original location, speed, and direction of the ball, we ought to be able to predict its path with a reasonable degree of accuracy. How is it that deterministic systems can give rise to unpredictability? The explanation is that tiny variations in the motion of the ball are magnified every time it swings by one of the magnets. It is a combination of this divergence and the repeated interactions that give rise to 'chaotic' behavior. Mathematically, chaotic systems are represented by differential equations that cannot be solved, so that we are unable to calculate the state of the system at a specific future time 't'.

At the limit, chaotic systems can become truly random. A toss of a coin or the roll of a die are, in theory, deterministic systems, but yield more or less random outcomes. Not only is it impossible to toss a coin twice in exactly the same way, but on each toss the coin is subject to slightly different air currents, themselves a result of turbulent air flow (Ford, 1983).

To overcome the problem of intractable differential equations, researchers usually model systems as discrete difference equations, which specify what the state of the system will be at time 't + 1' given the state of the system at time 't.' Computer simulations can then be used to see how the system evolves over time.

One of the major achievements of chaos theory is its ability to demonstrate how a simple set of deterministic relationships can produce patterned yet unpredictable outcomes. Chaotic systems never return to the same exact state, yet the outcomes are bounded and create patterns that embody mathematical constants (Feigenbaum, 1983). It is the promise of finding a fundamental order and structure behind complex events that probably explains the great interest chaos theory has generated in so many fields.

Chaos theory and the social sciences

Proponents of chaos theory enthusiastically see signs of it everywhere, pointing to the ubiquity of complex, dynamic systems in the social world and the resemblance between patterns generated by simulated nonlinear systems and real time series of stock exchange or commodity prices. From a theoretical perspective, chaos theory is congruous with the postmodern paradigm, which questions deterministic positivism as it acknowledges the complexity and diversity of experience. While postmodernism has had a profound influence on many areas of social science and the humanities, it has been neglected by organization theorists until very recently (Hassard and Parker, 1993).

Despite its attractions, the application of chaos theory to the social sciences is still in its infancy, and there are those who think that expectations are too high (Baumol and Benhabib, 1989). Although real life phenomena may resemble the patterns generated by simple nonlinear systems, that does not mean that we can easily model and forecast these phenomena; it is almost impossible to take a set of data and determine the system of relationships that generates it (Butler, 1990). In fact, there is considerable debate in the economics and finance literature about how one tests a data series to determine if it is chaotic or simply subject to random influences (Brock and Malliaris, 1989; Hsieh, 1991). Moreover, it is important to recognize that many systems are not chaotic, and that systems can oscillate between chaotic and nonchaotic states. Chaos theory is perhaps better seen as an extension of systems theory (Katz and Kahn, 1966; Thompson, 1967) into the realm of nonlinear dynamics rather than as a total paradigm shift.

It is possible that the application of chaos theory to social science has been constrained by the fact that it has developed in relation to physical systems, without taking into account fundamental differences between physical and social science. In the social world, outcomes often reflect very complex underlying relationships that include the interaction of several potentially chaotic systems: crop prices, for example, are influenced by the interaction of economic and weather systems. The search for a simple set of equations to explain complex phenomena may be a futile attempt to construct grand 'meta-theory,' a project that is rejected in the post-modern paradigm. The application presented here uses a different approach: field study research is used to derive a set of relationships among variables and the influence of external systems is modeled probabilistically, a method suggested by Kelsey (1988).

Social and physical systems also differ in the source of unpredictability. In the physical world, unpredictability arises due to many iterations, nonlinearity, and our inability to define starting conditions with infinite precision. In the social world, far less accuracy is possible in defining starting conditions, and the specification of the system structure itself is much less precise.

A final difference is that physical systems are shaped by unchanging natural laws, whereas social systems are subject to intervention by individuals and organizations. Investigations of economic time series by chaos theorists have usually assumed that relationships among economic actors are fixed over time. In reality, methods of stabilizing the economy have changed from the use of the gold standard and balanced budgets to Keynesian demand management and, later, to monetarist controls. Human agency can alter the parameters and very structures of social systems, and it is perhaps unrealistically ambitious to think that the effects of such intervention can be endogenized in chaotic models.[2] Nevertheless, chaotic models can be used to suggest ways that people might intervene to achieve certain goals. The application presented here, for example, shows how management can reduce the volatility of the supply chain to improve performance.

Relevance of chaos theory to strategy

To understand the relevance of chaos theory to strategy, we need to conceptualize industries as complex, dynamic, nonlinear systems. Firms interact with each other and with other actors in their environment, such as consumers, labor, the government, and financial institutions. These interactions are strategic in the sense that decisions by one actor take into account anticipated reactions by others, and thus reflect a recognition of interdependence. Although interfirm behavior has been modeled formally in economics and business strategy using game theory (Camerer, 1991), these models tend to presume the emergence of equilibrium and do not adequately reflect industry dynamics. As Porter (1990) emphasizes, the evolution of industries is dynamic and path dependent: corporate (and country-level) capabilities acquired during previous competitive episodes shape the context for future competitive battles. Moreover, the accumulation of competitive advantage can be self-reinforcing, suggesting at least one way in which industries are nonlinear. If industries do behave as chaotic systems, a number of implications for strategy can be drawn.

Long-term planning is very difficult

In chaotic systems, small disturbances multiply over time because of nonlinear relationships and the dynamic, repetitive nature of chaotic systems. As a result, such systems are extremely sensitive to initial conditions, which makes forecasting very difficult. This is a problem that has confronted meteorologists trying to model the weather: the fundamental problem is trying to use finite measurements in an infinite world. A related problem is that as systems evolve dynamically, they are subject to myriad small random (or perhaps chaotic) influences that cannot be incorporated into the model.

Formulating a long-term plan is clearly a key strategic task facing any organization. People involved in planning, whether in business, economics, or some other area, have always known that models are always just models, that forecasts are uncertain, and that uncertainty grows over time. Nevertheless, our conventional understanding of linear models and the influence of random errors would lead us to think that better models and a more accurate specification of starting conditions would yield better forecasts, useful for perhaps months if not years into the future. Chaos theory suggests otherwise: the payoff in terms of better forecasts of building more complex and more accurate models may be small. Similarly, we cannot learn too much about the future by studying the past: if history is the sum of complex and nonlinear interactions among people and nations, then history does not repeat itself. Concerning urban planning, Cartwright (1991) has noted that we have to acknowledge that 'a complete understanding of some of the things we plan may be beyond all possibility.'

The notion that long-term planning for chaotic systems is not only difficult but essentially impossible has profound implications for organizations trying to set strategy based on their anticipation of the future. Rather than expend large amounts of resources on forecasting, strategic planning needs to take into account a number of possible scenarios. Moreover, too narrow a focus on a firm's core products and markets might reduce the ability of the organization to adapt and be flexible in the face of change. The proliferation of joint ventures and the acquisition by large firms of stakes in entrepreneurial enterprises can perhaps be understood as attempts to keep a foothold in a number of potential scenarios in the face of uncertainty and accelerating change.

Industries do not reach a stable equilibrium

The traditional approach to understanding the influence of industry structure on firm behavior and competitive outcomes has been derived from microeconomics, with its emphasis on comparative statics and equilibrium. More recent applications of game theory have attempted to account for interactions among small numbers of firms (usually two), yielding predictions about, for example, investments in R&D or plant capacity to seize first-mover advantages. Even the most complex game theoretic models, however, are only considered useful if they predict an equilibrium outcome. By contrast, chaotic systems do not reach a stable equilibrium; indeed, they can never pass through the same exact state more than once. If they did, they would cycle endlessly through the same path because they are driven by deterministic relationships. The implication is that industries do not 'settle down' and any apparent stability, for example in pricing or investment patterns, is likely to be short lived.

Chaos theory also suggests that changes in industry structures can be endogenous. Corporate decisions to enter or exit the market, or to develop new technologies, alter the very structure of the industry, which in turn influences future firm behavior. One of the most provocative and controversial elements of chaos theory is that chaotic systems can spontaneously self-organize into more complex structures (Allen, 1988). The notion has been applied to biological evolution (Laszlo, 1987) as well as to economic systems (Mosekilde and Rasmussen, 1986). In the context of business strategy, the concept could potentially be applied to the evolution of complex organizational relationships such as long-term contracts and technical cooperation with suppliers, and hybrid forms of organizational control such as joint ventures. Chaos theory suggests that new, more complex organizational forms will appear more frequently than if they were simply the result of random mutations.

Dramatic change can occur unexpectedly

Traditional paradigms of economics and strategy, which are generally based upon assumptions of linear relationships and the use of comparative static analysis, lead to the conclusion that small changes in parameters should lead to correspondingly small changes in the equilibrium outcome. Chaos theory forces us to reconsider this conclusion. Large fluctuations can be generated internally by deterministic chaotic systems. Models of population growth based on the logistic difference equation illustrate how sudden, large changes in population levels can arise from the dynamics of the system rather than from the influence of external shocks (Radzicki, 1990).[3] Similarly, if economic systems are chaotic then we do not need to search for wars or natural disasters to account for economic depressions or a crash in the stock market.

The size of fluctuations from one period to the next in chaotic systems has a characteristic probability distribution (Bak and Chen, 1991). Under this distribution, large fluctuations occur more frequently than under the normal distribution, suggesting that managers might underestimate the potential for large changes in industry conditions or competitors' behavior.

Small exogenous disturbances to chaotic systems can also cause unexpectedly large changes. The implication for business strategy is that the entry of one new competitor or the development of a seemingly minor technology can have a substantial impact on competition in an industry. An example that comes to mind is the way Dell's mail order strategy in the personal computer industry forced other companies to reduce their prices and reexamine their traditional high-cost sales and service channels.

Short-term forecasts and predictions of patterns can be made

Although the unpredictability and instability of chaotic systems has been emphasized, there is also a surprising degree of order in chaotic systems. Short-term forecasting is possible because in a deterministic system, given the conditions at time 't,' we can calculate the conditions at time 't + 1.' A carefully constructed simulation model of a complex system with accurately specified starting conditions can yield useful forecasts at least for several time periods. Weather forecasts based on sophisticated computer models using measurements from thousands of points around the globe do provide useful forecasts for a few days, which is usually sufficient for purposes such as hurricane warnings. If we imagine that strategic decisions in companies are made on a monthly or even annual cycle, then industry simulation models might be able to make useful predictions over a time horizon of several months or possibly years.

Another feature of chaotic systems that lends them a degree of order is that they are bounded: outcome variables such as pricing or investments in new capacity fluctuate within certain bounds that are determined by the structure of the system and its parameters but not its initial conditions. In the context of business strategy these bounds might be set by feedback loops such as the entrance of new firms or antitrust action by the government in response to monopolistic conditions.

Although we cannot forecast the precise state of a chaotic system in the longer term, chaotic systems trace repetitive patterns which often provide useful information. According to Radzicki (1990), deterministic chaos 'is characterized by self-sustained oscillations whose period and amplitude are nonrepetitive and unpredictable, yet generated by a system devoid of randomness.' For example, while we do not know exactly where or when tornadoes and hurricanes will strike, we do know what conditions lead to their occurrence, when and where they are most frequent, and their likely paths. In a similar way, we know that oligopolistic industries tend to alternate between periods of intense competition and periods of more cooperative behavior, though we do not know when an industry will make the transition from one state to another. To give a third example, we know that the economy cycles through recessions and booms, though we cannot predict very well the depth or duration of a particular recession (Butler, 1990). Observing patterns is especially useful if we can associate different phases of the system with other characteristics: for example, there is a strong relationship between business cycles and other variables such as demand, interest rates, the availability of credit, vendor lead times, and the tightness of the labor market.

An intriguing aspect of the patterns traced by chaotic systems is that they are independent of scale; in other words, similar patterns are traced by a system whatever horizon is used to view it. Economic time series often appear to display this property. Stock prices, for example, display a remarkably similar pattern whether one observes daily changes over 1 year or minute-by-minute changes over a day. These images of patterns within patterns are termed fractals when they are generated by chaotic systems. In the natural world, fractals can be found in many phenomena, from the shape of coastlines to ice crystals. The implications for business strategy are not entirely clear. One interpretation is that previous experiences in an industry are likely to recur on a much larger scale. A second interpretation is that similar patterns of behavior might be expected whether one examines competition between countries, between firms in an industry, or even between departments in a firm.

Guidelines are needed to cope with complexity and uncertainty

'Strategy' can refer to a set of guidelines that influence decisions and behavior. It is the complexity of strategic interactions, whether in chess, soccer, or in business, that makes it essential to adopt simplifying strategies to guide decisions; even the most powerful computers are unable to track all possible moves and counter-moves in a chess game. General Electric's well-known strategy of being number one or number two in every industry in which it participates is a simple example of a guideline which may be generally useful but is not always optimal in every situation. We need general guidelines because it is impossible to specify the optimal course of action for every possible scenario.

It is important to distinguish the guidelines and patterns of behavior that constitute strategy from the underlying rules of the game. In a game of chess, for example, knowing the rules for playing the game does not necessarily give one insights into strategies for successful play. One can only learn these strategies after experiencing the complexities of interactions on the chess board. Indeed, because of the complexity of strategic interactions, one does not always know why a particular strategy is successful.

While the complexity of industry systems dictates the need for broad strategies, the dynamic nature of chaotic systems mandates that strategies adapt. As industry structures evolve and competitors change their strategies, a firm clearly needs to change its own guidelines and decision rules. The problem here is that there is no simple way of deriving optimal strategies for a given system. Indeed, in a complex system the best strategies might achieve goals indirectly and even appear counter-intuitive. The best way to improve quality is not necessarily to check every product several times: it may be to improve labor relations and thus gain labor's cooperation in finding ways to reduce defects. IBM's decision in 1981 to let other 'clone' manu-facturers use the DOS operating system for personal computers helped competitors but also indirectly helped IBM to build market share by creating the industry standard.

In order to understand indirect or counter-intuitive means to an end, a system needs to be understood as a whole. If systems are very complex, then simulation models might prove helpful in finding the most effective way to achieve a goal. The example discussed later in this paper illustrates how the best way to cut inventory in a supply chain might be to reduce disruptions to the chain rather than shorten lead times.

Simulation of an international supply chain

The supply chain as a complex dynamic system

The simulation of an international supply chain demonstrates how chaos theory can be applied to the understanding of a real managerial issue. The example is drawn from the author's research into the costs of a personal computer company called California Computer Technology (CCT).[4] Following Eisenhardt (1989), a case approach was used to build and test theory in an iterative manner.

The research led to a conceptualization of the supply chain as a complex, dynamic, nonlinear system. The system is subject to external disruptions, and the stages of the chain are linked by flows of goods and information, with time lags and feedback mechanisms. The complexity of interactions along the supply chain is such that one cannot easily predict how the system will operate under various conditions, but a computer model of these processes can simulate the outcome (Lant and Mezias, 1990; Morecroft 1984). Figure 1 is a simplified representation of CCT's supply chain, showing in schematic form the flows of goods and infor-mation within the model. Solid lines represent flows of goods, dotted lines flows of information.

In reality, supply chains are often much more complex than this. CCT, for example, has hundreds of vendors, three production sites, and distributors and warehouses in many countries. Corporate headquarters functions interact with vendors, the field sales organization, and the production sites. Nevertheless, the diagram does capture the essence of the supply chain. Materials move along the chain in one direction, gaining value at each stage. Information is exchanged in both directions among the organizations along the chain. This simple representation is very useful in analyzing the potential sources of coordination costs in a supply chain and the impact of geographically separating stages of the chain. It is also valuable as a tool for designing strategies that improve the performance of a supply chain.

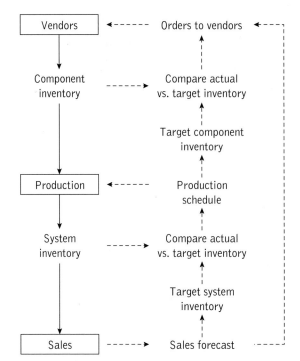

Figure 1 A model of CCT's supply chain

There are two important dimensions to this system, uncertainty and time relationships. Rather than performing as a stable, ready state system, each stage of the chain is potentially subject to disruptions, or 'shocks.' Demand fluctuates in an unpredictable way, production problems can affect output and suppliers do not always deliver on time. When demand and production are rising, delivery and production problems are more likely. As a result of the uncertainty at each stage, flows of materials and finished systems fluctuate in volume, and inventories need to be adjusted to cope with the uncertainty. The linkages themselves are also subject to disruption. Shipments and communication can be delayed, and information can be misunderstood.

A second important dimension of the supply chain system is the time relationship among the stages. As a result of the time lags in communication, production, and distribution, a disruption to one element generates a sequence of changes in other parts of the system. For example, demand fluctuations cause changes in sales forecasts, production schedules, and orders to vendors. Disruptions originating in any one part of the system, in effect, propagate forwards and backwards along the chain. Disruptions can interact: for example, a production problem could occur in a month when demand was unexpectedly high, causing some demand to go unmet.

A number of researchers investigating aspects of the supply chain have recently turned to simulation models, most of which attempt to find cost-minimizing solutions using linear or nonlinear programming (e.g., Breitman and Lucas, 1987; Cohen and Lee, 1989; Hodder and Jucker, 1985: Hodder and Dincer, 1986). These models do not, however, deal adequately with uncertainty in a dynamic, multiperiod setting.

The simulation model developed for this study is described in more detail in the Appendix and in Levy (1992). The model assumes a set of decision rules and linkages among the stages of the supply chain, which are used to determine the production plan and other variables each month. Each stage of the supply chain is subject to random fluctuations, and the chain evolves in a dynamic fashion from month to month.

Results and implications

Figure 2 shows simulated inventory levels over a period of 100 months based on a version of the model representing production in Singapore for the U.S. market, which entails 30 days' shipping time. Inventory levels are expressed as a proportion of monthly demand, and negative values indicate that demand cannot be met from inventory that month.

The most obvious feature of the graph is the volatility of inventory levels. These large fluctuations illustrate well how relatively small disruptions to the supply chain can interact with organizational decision processes and lead times in the system to produce large and unpredictable outcomes. CCT's managers did not expect this volatility, because the strategic decision to source from Singapore was taken using cost estimates that assumed a stable supply chain. In fact, the instability of the chain imposed substantial unexpected costs on CCT, primarily related to the expense of

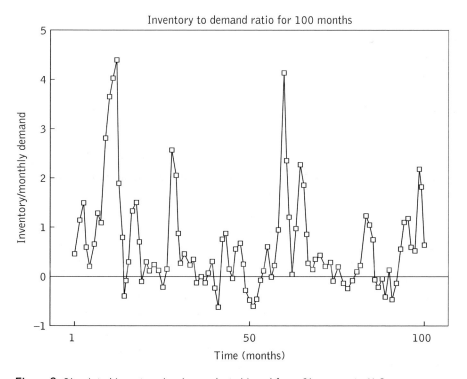

Figure 2 Simulated inventory levels, product shipped from Singapore to U.S.

using air-freight to expedite shipments, the opportunity cost of lost sales, and the cost of holding excess inventories. In addition, CCT incurred expenses relating to the communication and managerial time needed to manage the unstable supply chain. These costs were all underestimated because managers did not appreciate the impact of complex interactions along the supply chain, and tended to treat each disruption as a one-time event.

The simulation does reveal some patterns within the fluctuating inventory levels. Peak inventory levels are reached, on average, every 5 months, though the number of months between peaks varies from 2–7 months; the system is clearly aperiodic. Moreover, there is a relationship between the average time between peak inventory levels and shipping time: when production is available for sale the same month (representing production in the U.S. for the U.S. market), average time between peak inventory levels fall to around 4 months. Note also that inventory levels are less volatile and that peaks are lower, as would be expected when delivery times are shorter [see Figure 3].

As well as illustrating the volatility of the supply chain and its associated costs, the model can be used to guide decisions concerning production location, sourcing, and optimum inventory levels. Used for this purpose, the simulation model demonstrates how complex systems need to be understood as a whole, and how goals can be achieved through indirect and nonobvious means. For example, the simulation model enables the cost of offshore sourcing to be estimated in terms of the incremental inventory needed to maintain demand fulfillment at some specified

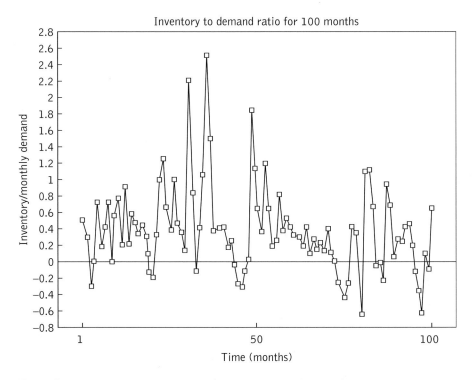

Figure 3 Simulated inventory levels, product made and sold in U.S.

level. It was estimated that in order to maintain an average level of 95 percent demand fulfillment when sourcing from Singapore rather than California for the U.S. market, average system inventory levels would have to increase by more than 2 months of sales.

The underlying order in the supply chain system can be glimpsed in Figure 4. The X-axis shows the value of a parameter representing the standard deviation of the monthly percentage change in demand, a measure of demand instability. The range of values was chosen to reflect the instability observed for CCT's products. The Y-axis shows the average proportion of demand that could not be fulfilled over 100 iterations of a 36-month period.

There appears to be a threshold beneath which demand instability does not have a significant effect; in this region, the system does not exhibit chaos. Once the instability parameter approaches 0.1, the proportion of demand unfulfilled begins to rise rapidly but smoothly and exceeds 10 percent of demand for products with the most unstable demand.

While the simulation model illustrates the costs and difficulties of an unstable supply chain, it also suggests approaches to solving these problems. The simulation model could be used to determine optimal inventory levels for different products and components and to identify those which need to be manufactured locally, based on the level of volatility associated with them. Although CCT's managers had always been aware that unstable products should be produced locally, they tended to underestimate these costs. The simulation provided a tool to analyze more precisely which products were stable enough for offshore manufacture.

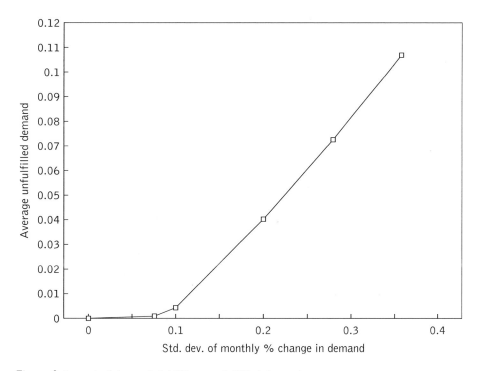

Figure 4 Impact of demand stability on unfulfilled demands

Another approach, using the insight gained from Figure 4 above, would be for managers to attempt to improve the accuracy of sales forecasting in order to reduce the cost of offshore manufacture. Similarly, managers could try to reduce disruptions to the supply chain from other sources, by working with suppliers to improve quality and reduce lead times, and by reducing the occurrence of internal production problems. Volatility can also be reduced by intervening at the boundaries of the system to change its structure. CCT, for example, has participated in the widely observed trend toward fewer suppliers. Using these techniques, management could simplify and stabilize the system, possibly making it nonchaotic.

It should be noted that the approaches to managing complex systems described above constitute key elements of lean production (Womack, Jones, and Roos, 1990). Lean production can thus be conceptualized as a way to simplify and reduce the variance of complex dynamic supply chain systems, making their behavior more predictable. Indeed, this research suggests that, contrary to the prevailing notion that lean production methods constrain international production (Hoffman and Kaplinsky, 1988; Jones and Womack, 1985), lean production could actually facilitate international operations by reducing volatility along the supply chain.

Conclusions

Chaos theory is a promising framework that accounts for the dynamic evolution of industries and the complex interactions among industry actors. By conceptualizing industries as chaotic systems, a number of managerial implications can be developed. Long-term forecasting is almost impossible for chaotic systems, and dramatic change can occur unexpectedly; as a result, flexibility and adaptiveness are essential for organizations to survive. Nevertheless, chaotic systems exhibit a degree of order, enabling short-term forecasting to be undertaken and underlying patterns can be discerned. Chaos theory also points to the importance of developing guidelines and decision rules to cope with complexity, and of searching for nonobvious and indirect means to achieving goals.

The simulation model presented here demonstrates that chaos theory has practical application to issues of business strategy. The simulation illustrates how management can underestimate the impact of disruptions to an international supply chain, generating substantial unanticipated costs. It also demonstrates how management might intervene to reduce the volatility of the supply chain and improve its performance, by reducing the extent of disruptions and changing the structure of the supply chain system.

APPENDIX

The supply chain was simulated using a spreadsheet model, with columns representing the variables in the system, and rows representing successive months. In order to model the stochastic nature of the supply chain, a simulation package called 'RISK' was used, which allows a variety of probability distributions to be assigned to each cell of the spreadsheet. Actual data and decision criteria from CCT were used to determine the structure of the model and the range of values to be used for various parameters. For example, monthly bookings data revealed that the level of bookings each month could be modeled by taking the previous month's demand plus a percentage change that was a normally distributed random variable with mean zero.

Three sets of input parameters were used for the model. The first set represents the level of disruptions affecting demand, supplier deliveries, and production. The second set represents the target levels of system and component inventories. The standard values for these were set at half a month's sales for systems, excluding any inventory in transit, and 1 week's production for components. The third group of input parameters represents the impact of distance on shipping time for finished goods, and of different vendor lead times. The main output variables of the system were the levels of system and component inventories and the level of demand fulfillment. Using these parameters, the model simulates a 36-month time period. The model begins at time zero with a nominal level of demand and production of 100 units, but these values evolve over time. The simulation package enables the spreadsheet to be recalculated a specified number of times. On each iteration, the entire 36-month spreadsheet is recalculated with a new set of random numbers. A large number of iterations can thus be used to build up a probability distribution for these output variables and to calculate a mean (expected) value. The results presented here were obtained using one hundred iterations for each simulation. Each simulation of 100 iterations was run using a different set of input parameters. A list of variables recalculated on a monthly basis is given in the Appendix.

Three main performance measures were captured as output variables. Average system and average component inventory levels over 100 iterations of the 36-month period were expressed in terms of months' sales. Demand fulfillment was measured by summing the total number of units of demand which could not be met due to inadequate inventory, and dividing this total by total demand to give a ratio indicating unfulfilled demand.

The effect of distance on shipping times and of different vendor lead times was modeled by using different versions of the basic model. The simulations used for this paper used a version in which production in Singapore is available for sale in the U.S. the following month (i.e., 30 days to ship and clear customs) and vendor lead times are 60 days.

Variables recalculated on monthly basis for simulation model

ACTUAL DEMAND:	Demand for systems each month was equal to the previous month's demand plus a random percentage change.
ACTUAL SALES:	Sales of systems each month were equal to demand unless constrained by lack of inventory.
SALES FORECAST:	The best sales forecast for the next month was the previous month's demand, as no trend was built into demand fluctuations.

ENDING COMP. INV.:	The level of component (or material) inventory each month was the level of the previous month plus deliveries from vendors less whatever was consumed in production.
TARGET COMP. INV.:	The target level of component inventory was adjusted each month to equal a proportion of the current sales forecast.
ORDERS TO VENDORS:	Orders to vendors were based on the sales forecast, the production schedule for the following month, and a comparison of actual with target component inventory levels.
DEL. FROM VENDORS:	Deliveries each month equalled orders placed 1 or 2 months previously, depending on the version, less a random percentage.
ENDING SYSTEM INV:	System inventory at the end of each month was equal to the inventory the previous month less sales plus production the same or the previous month, depending on the model version.
TARGET SYSTEM INV:	The target level of system inventory was adjusted each month to equal a proportion of the current sales forecast.
PRODUCTION PLAN:	The production plan for the following month was based on the sales forecast, adjusted for the difference between actual and planned system inventory.
ACTUAL PRODUCTION:	System production each month was equal to the production plan of the previous month, less a random percentage, and constrained by the availability of material inventory.
UNFUL. DEMAND:	Unfulfilled demand equalled monthly demand less monthly sales.

Notes

1   See also special issues of *Journal of Economic Theory*, 40(1), 1986, and *Journal of Economic Behavior and Organization*, 8(3), 1987.

2   To some extent, the distinction between endogenous and exogenous variables in a model is one of convenience; a factor that is exogenous in a simple model might become endogenous in a more complex and comprehensive one. Exogenous factors can be included as random variables in chaotic systems for modeling purposes (Kelsey, 1988).

3   The logistic difference equation has the form: $P_{t+1} = P * R * (1 - P_1)$

P, a fraction between 0 and 1, represents the population level as a proportion of the maximum carrying capacity of the environment. R is the growth rate from one cycle to the next. Population growth is constrained by the factor $1 - P_1$ which can be understood as a resource constraint.

4   The name of the company has been disguised to protect proprietary information.

References

Allen, P. M. (1988). 'Dynamics models of evolving systems', *System Dynamics Review*, 4, Summer, pp. 109–130.

Bak, P. and K. Chen (1991). 'Self-organized criticality', *Scientific American*, **264**(1) pp. 46–53.

Bartlett, C. A. and S. Ghoshal (1989). *Managing across Borders: The Transnational Solution*. Harvard Business School Press, Boston, MA.

Baumol, W. and J. Benhabib (1989). 'Chaos: Significance, mechanism, and economic applications', *Journal of Economic Perspectives*, **3**, pp. 77–105.

Breitman, R. L. and J. M. Lucas (1987). 'PLANETS: A modeling system for business planning', *Interfaces*, **17**(1), pp. 94–106.

Brock, W. and A. Malliaris (1989). *Differential Equations, Stability and Chaos in Dynamic Systems*. North-Holland, New York.

Butler, A. (1990). 'A methodological approach to chaos: Are economists missing the point?', *Federal Reserve Bank of St. Louis* **72**(13), pp. 36–48.

Camerer, C. F. (1991). 'Does strategy research need game theory?', *Strategic Management Journal*, **12**, Winter Special Issue, pp. 137–153.

Cartwright, T. J. (1991). Planning and chaos theory', *Journal of the American Planning Association*, **57**(1), pp. 44–56.

Cohen, M. A. and H. L. Lee (1989). 'Resource deployment analysis of global manufacturing and distribution networks', *Journal of Manufacturing and Operations Management*, **2**, pp. 81–104.

Eisenhardt, K. M. (1989). 'Building theories from case study research', *Academy of Management Review*, **14**(4), pp. 532–550.

Feigenbaum, M. J. (May 1983). Universal behavior in nonlinear systems', *Physica*, **7**, pp. 16–39.

Ford, J. (April 1983). 'How random is a coin toss?' *Physics Today*, **36**, pp. 40–47.

Goldberger, A. L., D. R. Rigney and B. J. West (February 1990). 'Chaos and fractals in physiology', *Scientific American*, **263**, pp. 43–49.

Hassard, J. and M. Parker (eds.) (1993). *Postmodernism and Organizations*. Sage, Thousand Oaks, CA.

Hodder, J. E. and M. C. Dincer (1986). 'A multifactor model for international facility location and financing under uncertainty', *Computers and Operations Research*, **13**(5), pp. 601–609.

Hodder, J. E. and J. V. Jucker (1985). 'International plant location under price and exchange rate uncertainty', *Engineering Costs and Production Economics*, **9**, pp. 225–229.

Hoffman, K. and R. Kaplinsky (1988). *Driving Force*. Westview Press, Boulder, CO.

Hsieh, D. A. (1991). 'Chaos and nonlinear dynamics: Application to financial markets', *Journal of Finance*, **46**(5), pp. 1839–1877.

Jones, D. T. and J. P. Womack (1985). 'Developing countries and the future of the automobile industry', *World Development*, **13**(3), pp. 393–407.

Katz, D. and R. L. Kahn (1966). *The Social Psychology of Organizations*. John Wiley and Sons, Chichester.

Kauffman, S. A. (1991). 'Antichaos and adaptation', *Scientific American*, **265**(2), pp. 78–84.

Kelsey, D. (1988). 'The economics of chaos or the chaos of economics', *Oxford Economic Papers*, **40**, pp. 1–31.

Lant, T. K. and S. J. Mezias (1990). 'Managing discontinuous change: A simulation study of organizational learning and entrepreneurship', *Strategic Management Journal*, Summer Special Issue, **11**, pp. 147–179.

Laszlo, E. (1987). *Evolution: The Grand Synthesis*. Shambhala, Boston, MA.

Levy, D. (1992). 'The costs of coordinating international production'. DBA Dissertation, Harvard University Graduate School of Business Administration.

Lorenz, E. N. (March 1963). 'Deterministic non-periodic flow', *Journal of the Atmospheric Sciences*, **20**, pp. 130–141.

Mayer-Kress, G. and S. Grossman (1989). 'Chaos in the international arms race', *Nature*, **337**, pp. 701–704.

Morecroft, J. D. (1984). 'Strategy support models', *Strategic Management Journal*, **5**(3), pp. 215–229.

Mosekilde, E. and S. Rasmussen (1986). 'Technical economic succession and the economic long wave', *European Journal of Operational Research*, 25, pp. 27–38.

Porter, M. E. (1990). *The Competitive Advantage of Nations*. Free Press, New York.

Radzicki, M. J. (1990). 'Institutional dynamics, deterministic chaos, and self-organizing systems', *Journal of Economic Issues*, **24**(1), pp. 57–102.

Sterman, J. D. (1989). 'Deterministic chaos in an experimental economic system', *Journal of Economic Behavior and Organization*, **12**(29), pp. 1–28.

Thompson, J. D. (1967). *Organizations in Action*. McGraw-Hill, New York.

Womack, J. P., D. T. Jones and D. Roos (1990). *The Machine that Changed the World*. Rawson Macmillan, New York.

Robert MacIntosh and Donald MacLean

CONDITIONED EMERGENCE: A DISSIPATIVE STRUCTURES APPROACH TO TRANSFORMATION

From *Strategic Management Journal* 1999, 20: 297–316. Copyright © 1999 by John Wiley & Sons Ltd. Reproduced with permission of the copyright owner. Further reproduction prohibited without permission.

Abstract

This paper presents a novel framework for the management of organizational transformation, defined here as a relatively rapid transition from one archetype to another. The concept of dissipative structures, from the field of complexity theory, is used to develop and explain a specific sequence of activities which underpin effective transformation. This sequence integrates selected concepts from the literatures on strategic change, organizational learning, and business processes; in so doing, it introduces a degree of prescriptiveness which differentiates it from other managerial interpretations of complexity theory. Specifically, it proposes a three-stage process: first, the organization 'conditions' the outcome of the transformation process by articulating and reconfiguring the rules which underpin its deep structure; second, it takes steps to move from its current equilibrium; and, finally, it moves into a period where positive and negative feedback loops become the focus of managerial attention. The paper argues that by managing at the level of deep structure in social systems, organizations can gain some influence over self-organizing processes which are typically regarded as unpredictable in the natural sciences. However, the paper further argues that this influence is limited to archetypal features and that detailed forms and behaviors are emergent properties of the system. Two illustrative case vignettes are presented to give an insight into the practical application of the model before conclusions are reached which speculate on the implications of this approach for strategy research.

[. . .]

Introduction

The historical division of strategy into content and process is of growing concern to scholars and practitioners of strategy (Schendel, 1992). The first represents the view of strategy which focuses on the development of competitive superiority through the reconfiguration of resources, competencies, and linkages. The second approach is primarily concerned with the management processes which underpin strategic change and innovation.

Whilst the need for meaningful reconciliation of strategy formulation and implementation is broadly agreed (Pettigrew, 1992), it nevertheless presents major challenges: the content-driven approach – which remains largely dominated by notions of equilibrium and control – does not sit comfortably with the assumptions of dynamism and emergence associated with the process school. A combination of this and other tensions which we will introduce produces the kind of paradoxical landscape which we are encouraged to explore in search of novel ways of conceptualizing important issues and problems (Van de Ven and Poole, 1988; Abrahamson, 1991).

It was in attempting to reconcile some difficult elements of choice and change that we encountered complexity theory. The specifics will be laid out in the course of this paper, but we should like to make it clear at the outset that the paper's structure, and the somewhat positivist assumptions that it may suggest, should not be interpreted as reflecting the way in which the research was actually conducted. Although our presentation attempts to lay out a literature review, construct a model, and then report on its application, the reality of our work was somewhat different (as detailed later in the paper).

In practice we experienced a good deal more by way of hindsight and dead-end streets than the sequence of our delivery would suggest. We did not consciously set out with the view of applying complexity theory – it simply became our established template as a number of influences operated over the period of the research. We nevertheless believe that we have arrived at a rich, if somewhat personal, understanding of strategic change which addresses the challenge of integrating strategy, process and content. At this stage we feel it would be more fruitful to attempt to convey our understanding in the form of a model than to synthesize a self-consistent account of what happened. As such, we will begin by examining the existing strategy literature before developing our model and relating its application through case study accounts.

Strategic change

As stated in the Introduction, research in strategy falls loosely into two domains: content and process (Schendel, 1992).

The former is strongly influenced by concepts developed in the field of economics. Accordingly, the debate tends to center around management activities which aim to achieve a predetermined, optimum, and rationally derived set of objectives, with profit maximization traditionally foremost. Within this school one can discern three main streams. First there is the strategy–structure–performance contingent which is mainly concerned with the scale, scope, and form of corpora-tions (Chandler, 1962; Rumelt, 1982). Second there is a counterpart which grew out of work at Harvard on industrial organization, the most influential of which is Michael Porter's development of the structure–conduct–performance model (Bain, 1956) into his influential theories of position and market power (Porter, 1980, 1985). The third and final stream can be traced back to the late 1950s (Penrose, 1959; Chandler, 1962; Selznick, 1957) and has been developed by various authors in the 1980s (Rumelt, 1984; Barney, 1991; Wernerfelt, 1984) into what has become termed the resource-based view. This stream of research has been popularized by Prahalad and Hamel in the form of Core Competencies (Prahalad and Hamel, 1990).

A detailed discussion of developments in these three areas and their implications would be inappropriate here; however, some general considerations do have a bear-ing on the substance of our case. On the one hand, the three approaches are, to some extent at least, united by origin. The modernist paradigm from which they spring for the most part binds them together through assumptions of economic rationality and Newtonian conceptions of equilibrium and stability. On the other hand, it is noteworthy that, at the present time, the focus would appear to be moving some-what from the demand side to the supply side, with the increasing recognition of the importance of key organizational attributes and resources.

In particular, a growing concern with intangible resources such as tactic knowledge (Nonaka, 1991; Spender, 1996), learning (Argyris, 1990), strategic intent (Hamel and Prahalad, 1989), and intelligence (Penrose, 1959) may signal a movement towards a model of firm behavior which draws on a more evolutionary view of economics (Nelson and Winter, 1982). This may accord with exhortations to adopt a more dynamic perspective (Porter, 1991); it is certainly true that key protagonists of the resource-based view are also issuing calls for a 'new paradigm' which must entail a break from the entrenched limitations of current mindsets (Hamel and Prahalad, 1996). We would argue that this 'movement' on the part of resource-based scholars is towards a process perspective and that the new paradigm which is sought is essentially one which reintegrates process and content.

The process-driven school is more eclectic in its make-up and origins, with influences from biology, psychology, sociology, systems dynamics, and evolutionary economics amongst others. The unifying factor among these diverse influences is the suspicion that economic rationality is not the primary determinant of strategic behavior (March and Simon, 1958). Rather, the focus of this school is the extent to which strategy and change are dominated by events and activities which typically emerge from a wide variety of influences.

As with its strategy content counterpart, the process school has internal divisions. In the main, these are manifest as two broad streams (Pettigrew, 1992). First there are the researchers who are primarily concerned with the way in which strategic decisions are made. In contrast with the content school, the focus of this work is not on what constitutes an optimum decision, but how cognitive and social phenomena such as bounded rationality, politics, and chance influence the decision process in organizations (see Cyert and March, 1963; Pettigrew, 1973; Cohen, March, and Olson, 1972; Mintzberg, 1978, 1994; Pfeffer, 1981; Quinn, 1980).

The second main stream of strategy process research is focused on the management of strategic change. That is to say, that in the context of the content–process split, it is focused on implementation. In addition to a growth in popular prescriptive works (e.g., Peters and Waterman, 1982; Kanter, 1983) there emerged a body of academic work which aimed to draw attention to strategy implementation issues in an attempt to tackle implementation failure (Pettigrew, 1992).

This work (e.g., Johnson, 1987; Pettigrew and Whipp, 1991; Mintzberg, 1994) varies in terms of implications ranging from notions of organizational culture and cultural fit as important inputs to an improved choice process, through participation and flexibility to views of strategic behavior as a phenomenon which emerges in an unpredictable way from the networks of influence and interaction in the organization. Thus one sees evidence of attempts to improve failure rates with solutions which range from design-for-implementation to facilitation of emergence. Quinn's notion of logical incrementalism (Quinn, 1980) incorporates elements of design at a broad level with some of the flexibility of the emergent approach and in so doing, one could argue, comes closer to closing the content–process split than many of his peers.

As the term would suggest, the literature on strategic change deals with implementation on a variety of dimensions and timescales. Mintzberg and Westley (1992) classify changes according to their nature and context within the organization. The former addresses the extent of adjustment to the direction and state of the organization at the conceptual and 'concrete' levels, whilst the latter refers to the scope of the change in question, from incremental through to all-encompassing or revolutionary. A similar scheme is used by Greenwood and Hinings (1996), who describe change on two dimensions: the first, essentially a question of pace, deals with whether the change is evolutionary or revolutionary, whilst the second is concerned with whether the change is convergent or radical.

This latter issue capitalizes on the concept of archetypes. For some authors, use of the term denotes subscription to a belief that the relationship between structure and process is manifest in a finite number of possible types or configurations with distinctive behavioral implications (e.g., Miles and Snow, 1978; Mintzberg, 1983; Miller and Friesen, 1984). Greenwood and Hinings (1988, 1993) add the concept of 'interpretative schemes' to emphasize the cognitive dimension of archetypal behavior.

The concept of archetypes is important here for a number of reasons. We are primarily concerned with change which is radical, all-encompassing, and rapid. The concept of switching from one archetype to another (Greenwood and Hinings, 1988) is a useful way of capturing the essence of the transformation process which has been described in different ways by a variety of authors (see Miller, 1982; Abernathy and Clarke, 1985; Pettigrew, 1985; Nadler and Tushman, 1989). We have chosen to work with the concept of archetypes rather than the more familiar notion of culture (e.g., Schein, 1985) or paradigm (Kuhn, 1962; Pascale, 1990) because our framework describes transitions between discrete and distinct organizational forms as opposed to movement along a continuum. Also, Greenwood and Hinings' definition of an archetype as a 'set of structures and systems that reflects a single interpretative scheme' suggests a level of detail which is consistent with our prescribed sequence of interventions; i.e., the elements of their definition represent the focal points of our model.

It is clear that in many respects the content and process views of strategy are complementary if taken as a set or incomplete if treated as individual elements. If one likens the issue to a journey, the content approach has a clear destination but the means of transport is indeterminate whereas with the process approach the transport is known and in motion, but the journey is something of a 'mystery tour'.

One could argue that if a complete theory of strategy is in fact needed, why not just use the two approaches as appropriate, as is indeed the practice in many institutions? It is our belief, however, that an overall framework which transforms and reconciles the mutually contradictory assumptions of each approach would constitute a significant step forward, in both practical and scholarly terms.

Moreover, we feel that the need to reintegrate process and content is essentially the same need as that which relates to calls for a more dynamic view of strategy. It is unsurprising therefore that in our view the means to effecting the kind of synthesis to which we refer lies in the explicit use of time and sequencing as a dimension. This approach, borrowed in our case from the natural sciences, will allow temporal coexistence of spatially contradictory explanations. Before laying out our approach and a brief review of the theories on which it is based, we will conclude this section by explaining why we feel that the timing is right for such a development.

The need for a proven approach to the management of corporate renewal is becoming increasingly evident in most sectors of today's developed economy. Some attribute the current preoccupation with strategic innovation to attempts to come to terms with a new era of industrial organization along post-Fordist, information-intensive lines (Best, 1990; Storper and Scott, 1992) described variously as flexible specialization (Piore and Sable, 1984) or mass customization (Pine, 1993). Another view is that we are experiencing a short-term adjustment to the globalization of markets and the influence of powerful new technologies (Staber and Sharma, 1994). Both explanations acknowledge the increasing importance with which organizations view the role of innovation and the management technologies required to foster it.

These pressures are perhaps responsible for the growing literature on transformation and strategic innovation in an organizational context. Institutional theory has provided powerful insights into how new structures and processes are absorbed from the environmental context and become legitimate, persistent features of the organization (Zucker, 1977; Powell and DiMaggio, 1991). More recently, work has focused on how change can occur through deinstitutionalization (Oliver, 1992; Greenwood and Hinings, 1996) and on structurationist conceptions of managerial agency (Whittington, 1992). Insights from population ecology have highlighted the difficulties of change at the level of groups of organizations (Hannan and Freeman, 1977) whilst evolutionary theories (Nelson and Winter, 1982; Hodgson, 1993; Baum and Singh, 1994; Barnett and Burgleman, 1996) have drawn attention not only to selection pressures but also to the processes by which variety is created and the importance of initial conditions and genetic traits and routines. Knowledge management (Spender and Grant, 1996; Moingeon and Edmonson, 1996) is combining elements of the above with resource-based thinking and learning theory in pursuit of a dynamic view of strategy that befits the 'knowledge age'.

Such endeavors have not explicitly addressed the split between content and process in strategy, though their dynamic focus has to some extent caused a blurring of the boundaries. We would argue, however, that content and process have to be reintegrated in a way that is meaningful for both academics and practitioners and that in essence this means provision of a framework that offers guidance on what decisions to make, how to make them, and how to act upon them to realize aims. In short, it has to combine academic validity with business logic (Beer and Eisenstat, 1996; Beer et al., 1990). It is for this reason that we have turned to complexity theory.

We should state that we are not claiming to have developed a grand new dynamic theory of strategy; rather we are proposing an overarching framework based on the new science of complexity. We argue that it provides some justification for integrating specific elements of existing theories into a dynamic whole and thus provides a template for the management of transformation.

Complexity theory

In the natural sciences, the past two or three decades have witnessed a growing interest in what has been billed as an alternative to the classical perspective. The Nobel prize-winning work of Belgian physicist Ilya Prigogine and colleagues, in the field of nonequilibrium thermodynamics (Prigogine and Stengers, 1984), sought to explain the existence and development of order in the world – as opposed to the ongoing deterioration and rundown of systems implied by the second law of thermodynamics.

Rather than viewing the world as essentially static, with equilibrium only occasionally disturbed, Prigogine regards the world as dynamic and characterized by systems in which normal Newtonian laws may apply, but only in a minority of situations. That is to say that, whilst such systems can exist in equilibrium, change and transformation are associated with nonequilibrium conditions, which are subject to a different set of laws. The evolution of nonequilibrium systems is influenced by a combination of a complex network of nonlinear system relationships and random developments, which combine to create new system configurations in a way which is largely indeterminate. In extreme cases, the system can be so far from equilibrium that the structure breaks down and the system becomes chaotic. In such circumstances, the operation of simple rules in conjunction with nonlinear processes (i.e., the action of positive feedback on small and possibly random events) can give rise to the emergence of new, qualitatively different, structures. Since Prigogine's work focused on phenomena such as phase transitions in matter, his work is characterized by descriptions of systems moving progressively further from equilibrium to the point where a 'descent into chaos' ensues and the system structures are broken down. At this point the system becomes open to its environment, importing energy and exporting entropy (a measure of disorder) as a new structure takes shape in accordance with the operations of a set of simple order-generating rules. Since, in physics, heat is the most entropic form of energy, the system is said to be dissipative, in that the entropy exportation is characterized by heat loss. The system is thus termed a 'dissipative structure'.

In biology, the search for an explanation of the complexity of living systems focused attention on processes of adaptation and the conditions under which new order is created. In this field, attention is focused not on the emergence of order from chaos, but on the continual adaptation of systems on 'the edge of chaos' (Kauffmann, 1993, 1995). Again, explanations of complex structures developing around the repeated application of simple rules relies on concepts such as non-linearity, interconnectedness and far-from-equilibrium conditions (Kauffmann, 1993). In the mid-1980s the Santa Fe institute was established in New Mexico, bringing together researchers from a variety of disciplines including physics, biology economics, and computer science with a view to developing and applying the 'new science of complexity' (Waldrop, 1992). This process whereby a new order spontaneously emerges out of a chaotic state is sometimes referred to as self-organization (Kauffmann, 1993; Coveney and Highfield, 1995).

Whilst the exact form of such emergent structures cannot be predicted, the range of broad possibilities is to some extent contained within the set of simple rules which was applied to generate the new order. Mathematical modeling of the repeated application of simple rules in a variety of contexts has given rise to the visual representation of order creation through the intricate patterns of fractals (Mandelbrot, 1977; Coveney and Highfield, 1995).

Although different in their focal points, the various applications of complexity theory demonstrate the central concepts around which the subject is organized, namely the operation of nonlinear feedback on generative rules in densely inter-connected, nonequilibrium systems. The dynamics and evolution of such a system are influenced by the operation of any number of positive and negative feedback loops within the system. Some signals are amplified and others damped down so that the initial configuration and conditions determine the future unfolding of the system's behavior. The potential importance of even the faintest of signals to the subsequent chain of events in such far-from-equilibrium conditions means that at a given time a system's future may unfold in any one of a number of possible directions for a given level of energy input. This point at which multiple, equally probable trajectories extend into the future is associated with high levels of uncertainty and instability. It is the contrast between the above characteristics and those of more simple, mechanistic counterparts which has given rise to application of the term 'complex' in relation to nonequilibrium systems.

The development of complexity theory, as it has been popularly titled, is regarded by some as signaling the arrival of a new scientific paradigm in the Kuhnian sense (Kuhn, 1962). Jantsch was among the first to see applications in social science in general and in management in particular (Jantsch, 1980). In terms of organ-ization, the world is a myriad of self-organizing, interacting and co-evolving systems and subsystems. This gives rise to an essentially dynamic system in which change and innovation become key features of organizational life. The apparent fit between complexity theory and the practical manifestation of many of the themes which this paper introduced in the review of strategic change first led us to explore its application to the management of organizational transformation.

Dissipative structures and organizations

In the previous section, two broad subthemes within complexity theory were introduced. On the one hand was the concept of 'dissipative structures,' with the implied sequence of stability giving way to chaos out of which new order emerges; on the other was the 'edge of chaos' view, in which living systems are conceptualized as constantly adapting and self-organizing in a zone which, although far from equilibrium, stops short of the 'descent into chaos'.

If one accepts the notion that systems are not only complex and adaptive, but that their complexity and adaptiveness can themselves change, then one can see different implications for the evolution of organizations. On the one hand, organizations might be relatively stationary on a spectrum from simple static through to complex adaptive with innovative organizations existing more towards the latter extreme, perhaps on the 'edge of chaos.' On the other hand, organizations might move about this spectrum, or possibly through a cycle, where adaptedness gradually displaces adaptiveness and complexity gives way to complication. In this 'dissipative structures' perspective, organizations are likely to go through cycles of evolution and revolution: from stable order into chaos out of which emerges a new dynamic order which in turn eventually congeals and so on. The paper now looks briefly at the organizational counterparts of these two models before detailing our interpretation of dissipative structures which forms the basis of the remaining sections.

Recent years have seen a steady trickle of papers on applications of complexity theory in the management literature. In broad (and perhaps somewhat crude) terms, such work can be categorized according to whether it subscribes to the 'edge of chaos' or 'dissipative structures' frameworks which, although overlapping, typically emphasize different conceptual themes as detailed above. This polarization is akin to the issue of evolutionary vs. revolutionary change developed by Miller (1982) and others, as discussed earlier in this paper.

The 'edge of chaos' viewpoint tends to focus on issues such as instability, interconnectedness, and self-organization which is spontaneous and unpredictable. In a previous issue of this journal, Stacey elaborated some of the managerial implications associated with this view (Stacey, 1995). Brown and Eisenhardt further argue that innovative organizations exist on the 'edge of chaos' and thus avoid the chaos and upheaval implied by the dissipative structures view (Brown and Eisenhardt, 1997).

In contrast with 'edge of chaos' interpretations, management writings based on 'dissipative structures' have a somewhat broader focus: some authors are concerned with modeling organizations using chaos theory either by simulation (Levy, 1994) or analogy (Thietart and Forgues, 1997) whilst others present more detailed examinations of the ways in which order can emerge from chaos through the interaction of rules, deep structures, and organizational processes (Drazin and Sandelands, 1992; Gersick, 1991; Leifer, 1989).

Work on the application to social systems of a 'dissipative structures' framework to organizational transformation appears to predate its 'edge of chaos' counterpart, and is traceable back to the work of Prigogine (Prigogine and Stengers, 1984) and, more directly, to Jantsch (1980). Smith and Gemmill (1991) have applied the concept to change in small groups and to organizations in general (Gemmill and Smith, 1985; Smith, 1986), the latter also being the subject of Leifer's work (Leifer, 1989). This work shares a reliance on a view in which organizations undergoing transformation experience a common set of related events. First, the organization is moved out of its normal equilibrium state, due either to internal or external fluctuations; whilst in nonequilibrium conditions, it experiences a breakdown of its existing structures and some symmetry-breaking event which serves to irreversibly sever the possibility of reconstructing them; there follows a period of experimentation during which the organization selects a new form of behavior which 'aligns' with its deep structure and order emerges in the system as the new behavior 'resonates' across subsystem boundaries.

The concept of deep structure is important in distinguishing dissipative structures thinking from its edge-of-chaos counterpart. Whilst it appears to play no role in the latter, dissipative structures rely on it as a quasi-permanent, invisible substructure which remains largely intact whilst manifest, observable structures break down. As such it forms the basis for the self-referencing processes which occur during self-organization (see Smith, 1986, for a more detailed discussion).

Our work develops the above concepts though our resulting framework differs in some fundamental and important ways. We largely adopt the sequence presented above, though we adopt a more prescriptive position and detail managerial interventions associated with each stage – in our case presented as a three-stage sequence. In particular, we make use of the concept of deep structure but we link it explicitly to organizational rules; i.e., we propose that the deep structure of organization can be expressed as a set of simple 'rules' which comprise organizing principles and business logic. As is described later in the paper, these rules are surfaced, reframed, and enacted as a key part of the transformation sequence; as such the prescriptive aspect of our process is based on 'management' of deep structure, or organizational rules which remain visible during the 'chaotic' period of a transformation process.

Most importantly, perhaps, we use the above differences to justify an approach to transformation in which limited influence over the outcomes of so-called self-organization is obtained by focusing on deep structure. In so doing, we accept the possibility but reject the necessity of 'pure' self-organization in social systems and, thereby, clearly differentiate our work from the majority of other writers concerned with organizational applications of complexity theory.

We have adopted the dissipative structures approach since it is better suited to dealing with the kind of radical transformation with which we are concerned. We also feel that it fits well with much current thinking on strategic change and it offers a route to integrating process and content in a dynamic framework. We will attempt to show this using the example below. We will first present a simple transformation trajectory set in the terminology of dissipative structures and then attempt to relate our description to the more recent management literature discussed earlier in the paper.

Consider the case of an organization which is stagnant, underperforming and facing increasing pressure to improve its situation. In the most simple case, it is faced with two equally probable trajectories where there is either a successful response to the situation or performance continues to decline (see Figure 1). The decision point

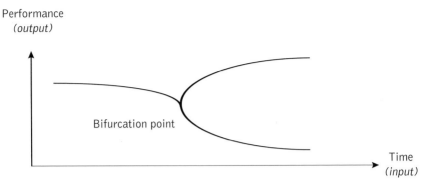

Figure 1 The bifurcation diagram (adapted from Leifer, 1989)

is termed the bifurcation point and could be interpreted as a crisis brought about by the failure of the organization's current systems to cope with the internal or external situation. In a successful response, the system becomes open, blurring its boundaries with the environment in a bid to import the energy required to sustain future growth and export the entropy or disorder which has arisen from its over-whelmed control systems. This net release of disorder into the environment gives rise to the term 'dissipative' as the organization is essentially absorbing useful energy and expelling the useless energy caused mainly by relatively inefficient conversion processes. The inefficiency of these conversion processes is associated with the breakdown of old mechanisms and the experimentation of emerging ones seeking to establish dynamic (as opposed to static) efficiency in order to cope with the new, unstable conditions.

Before the bifurcation point the organization is, for the most part, in equilibrium with its environment, having adapted itself to its institutional context (Powell and DiMaggio, 1991; Zucker, 1977) with a well defined archetypal form (Miller and Friesen, 1984; Greenwood and Hinings, 1993). As it proceeds towards the bifurca-tion point, deinstitutionalizing pressures begin to mount (Oliver, 1992; Greenwood and Hinings, 1996), taken-for-granted assumptions are increasingly questioned, and new interpretative schemes (Greenwood and Hinings, 1988) or mental models (Senge, 1990) emerge as entropy increases and organizational coherence is stretched. These deinstitutionalizing pressures increase entropy (Oliver, 1992), weakening existing structures and promoting instability.

At the bifurcation point, organizational equilibrium is destroyed and a chaotic period ensues. During this time, individual and collective learning (Senge, 1990) occurs as the organization experiments with new ways of doing things – by developing and applying new rules associated with both the old and alternative, new interpretative schemes. A variety of influences such as external pressures, internal politics, and random couplings combine as a new archetype attempts to establish itself in the face of resistance from defensive routines (Argyris, 1990).

As the chaos subsides, the new archetype begins to take shape, but negative feedback exerts continuous pressure to revert to the previous archetype. Switching or schizoid behavior ensues (Greenwood and Hinings, 1988) but, in the case of a successful transformation, the new archetype eventually prevails. Generative learning continues until institutional pressures and inertia cause adaptive learning to dominate. Eventually the organization becomes adapted to the point where it begins to stagnate again and the cycle repeats. As such, the cycle is reminiscent of the concept of punctuated equilibrium (Tushman and Anderson, 1986; Gersick, 1991) but, as is argued below, it affords a more detailed examination of discontinuous change.

Conditioned emergence

Applying the concepts of complexity theory, dissipative structures, self-organization, and bistable states to the organizational context, we have amended the bifurcation diagram shown in Figure 1 to provide a more realistic view of how organizations behave in the face of declining performance. In the amended bifurcation diagram (see Figure 2), declining performance eventually precipitates a crisis, causing the organization to move to far-from-equilibrium conditions, at the bifurcation zone, where feedback mechanisms will eventually determine the trajectory followed. In the remainder of this section we will further explain the two trajectories in the amended bifurcation diagram, then focus on the role of conditioning in influencing the trajectory followed.

The two trajectories shown in Figure 2 represent different reactions to the crisis: one where a new archetype is adopted and the other where the old archetype is maintained. It is worth stressing that we are using the notion of archetypes merely to signal a transformation having taken place and not for the purposes of producing a typology of archetypes as has been done elsewhere (see, for example, Miller and Friesen, 1984). Trajectory [1] represents a typical managerial response to the crisis, where energy and attention are focused on resolving the performance problem. This often involves raising the level of control, which might be characterized as pushing the old systems harder, but does not involve a change in archetype. In the short term, such a response will often improve performance. However, if the problem arose from a mismatch between the organization's systems, routines and procedures, and the environment in which they operate, this short-term response is unlikely to have addressed the underlying issues. In the longer term, the

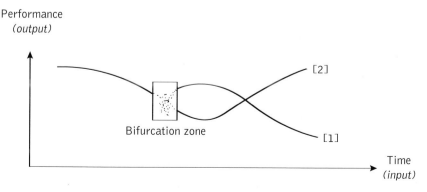

Figure 2 Amended bifurcation diagram

organization's performance will continue to decline as the current archetype persists.

The alternative is to pursue long-term success by changing archetype and following trajectory [2]. While this provides the longer-term benefits that any transformation program aims to deliver, the organization must accept a dip in performance as it learns to adopt a new archetype and experiments with ways of dealing with the conditions it encounters far from the old equilibrium.

In reality, the prospect of immediate gains in the face of a looming crisis will tend to force most candidates for transformation onto trajectory [1]. Those organizations which do embark on trajectory [2] will experience switching pressure to revert to the old archetype as individuals within the organization realize that performance, in the short term at least, is getting worse, not better. This is simply a statement of the known difficulties of strategic change viewed through the lens of complexity theory and dissipative structures. The justification for taking this particular view is that it informs the specific sequence we have developed to reduce the risk of erroneously embarking on, or switching to, trajectory [1].

We have created a framework for Conditioned Emergence with a specific sequence of three stages which we believe characterize successful transformation programs (i.e., managed progression along trajectory [2] resulting in the adoption of a new archetype). The emphasis is on early conditioning as a means of influencing the order which emerges from the transformation process. The conditioned emergence sequence is as follows:

Stage 1: Conditioning

A central feature of complexity theory is the emergence of order through the repeated application of simple rules. Prior to undertaking a transformation from one archetype to another, the organization must identify the deep structure and rules which underpin its current archetype, in much the same way that Senge (1990) highlights the importance of surfacing assumptions and sharing mental models. The deep structure and rules are often barely articulated views on what the organization represents and how it operates, e.g., the kind of business which is taken on or the type of people recruited. As such these rules relate to issues of both content and process and must be moved from the tacit to the codified domain. The organization can then formulate a new deep structure which may involve some, but not all, of the old rules alongside some new ones. Again these new rules may be process oriented (e.g., the way things are done), content oriented (what kind of business is conducted), or both. The old rules which are rejected are usually defensive routines which might impede any significant change and these are outlawed by consensus. The new rules are typically a mixture of primary rules (about what should be done) and secondary rules (about how the rules themselves should be maintained and updated).

Stage 2: Creating far-from-equilibrium conditions

Having done the conditioning work, the organization must now move to far-from-equilibrium conditions in order to create the space for the new deep structure to take hold. The onset of a crisis, either real or precipitated, should involve a fundamental change in the codified domain, radically altering the way in which things are done. A typical mechanism for achieving this would be a major restructuring exercise. While the organization resides in such unfamiliar territory it typically becomes more open, often developing a capacity to import energy and export entropy. During this period, a new order based on the new deep structure will seek to impose itself. Again, this order will reflect both content and process aspirations as broadly defined by the rules.

Stage 3: Managing the feedback processes

As the new archetype begins to emerge, positive and negative feedback must be applied as appropriate. Traces of the old archetype will inevitably remain and there will be pressure to apply negative feedback to restore the old equilibrium. During this stage, the key managerial task is to look for small signals consistent with the new deep structure agreed in stage 1. Positive feedback, applied to these signals, provides the multiplier effect which causes the nonlinear development of new systems. Anything which reinforces the new rules should be encouraged in order that the effects may be amplified, allowing the new archetype to take hold. During this stage the organization will be somewhat unstable as the two trajectories compete with each other; this will be particularly true at the outset since, according to Figure 2, it will appear obvious that reverting to discarded practices will realize short-term performance gains.

We believe that the pattern of events represented in this sequence offers some important insights into the process of successful organizational transformation. Consistent with the concepts of complexity theory and self-organization presented earlier, we believe that the eventual outcome of a transformation program is extremely sensitive to the initial conditions under which the transformation is undertaken. However, our model of conditioned emergence differs significantly from those used in the natural sciences in that we do not believe that the process of self-organization has to be spontaneous, random, and unpredictable.

We believe that the key difference in applying complexity theory and dissipative structures to organizations as opposed to organisms is that organizations have the capacity to bring about a change in archetype through consciously creating the conditions in which successful transformation can occur. Those within the organization can, to some extent, choose the primary rules which govern the deep structure. Furthermore, they know the status of these rules at any given point in time and are able to define secondary rules which specify how the rules will be developed and maintained in the future.

Two criteria appear to be key to the onset of successful self-organization: on the one hand the system must promote experimentation, error and introspection whilst on the other hand being far from equilibrium, fluid, open to its surroundings, etc. The conditioned emergence model is an attempt to ensure that both of these criteria are met. An obvious counter-argument is that issues such as power and politics can stop transformation occurring. While this is undeniably true, the conditioned emergence model does attempt to deal with this by moving some of these issues from the tacit to the codified domain then moving far enough from current equilibrium conditions that old power and political structures are less able to operate effectively.

In the conditioned emergence model the focus is on redesigning the deep structure as opposed to the operational systems and procedures. By working with rules governing the deep structure we believe it is possible to determine the characteristics of the new archetype without necessarily prescribing its exact form. The form comes through the repeated application of the deep structure rules and is random only within bounded limits. This places a particular focus on managing the process rather than the content of the transformation. We will now examine some managerial technologies to see how they might be used to operationalize the conditioned emergence model.

Organizational learning [OL]

There are many traits in the field of OL which are consistent with the processual model of strategic change. The initial work by Argyris and Schon (1978), Hedberg (1981), and Pedler, Burgoyne, and Boydell (1990), which has since been popularized by Senge (1990), does not sit comfortably with the Newtonian rationality of optimal designs for business processes. Following Kolb's view of individual learning as the process whereby knowledge is created through the transformation of experience (Kolb, Rubin, and McIntyre, 1971), Argyris and Schon argue that learning is demonstrated by new, and replicable, behavior. If learning means reacting to the same stimulus in new ways, proponents of OL claim that most organizations suppress learning by reacting to different stimuli in the same way. Argyris explains this behavior as the organization reacting to new situations by habitually enacting defensive routines (Argyris, 1990) which are widely accepted, if often inappropriate, responses that were extremely successful at some stage in the past.

Routines are an important part of organizational life and to some extent act as the organization's memory or the repository of past learning. They become dangerous when repeated use of the same routine institutionalizes it to the point where it is applied even when the environment is radically different. Argyris uses another useful concept to distinguish between different types of learning, which he labels single and double loop learning (Argyris, 1992). An example of single loop learning might be the refinement of an existing routine whereas double loop learning would involve fundamentally questioning the assumptions underpinning a particular routine and perhaps introducing a completely new one. However, routines also offer ways of capturing, codifying, and sharing information on procedures and best practice. This introduces a tension between the need to codify current learning and the tendency to produce new defensive routines. Leavitt and March (1988) highlight this tension, commenting on the irony that long-term survival requires organizations to avoid competency traps by periodically stepping out of smooth-running routines which have been created and reinforced by past successes. Innovation lies in the exceptions, not the routines, but there is a risk associated with this.

In the strategic management literature, the resource-based view is increasingly focusing on the importance of intelligence (Penrose, 1959). Prahalad and Hamel (1990) state that an organization's capacity to improve existing skills and learn new ones offers the most defensible competitive advantage of all. Barney (1986) focuses specifically on tacit knowledge as the key feature of an organization's competitive advantage. However, there is a substantial difference between acknowledging the importance of learning processes and putting the theory into practice. As Wheatley observes (interviewed in *Training and Development*, 1994), how many of us today would risk reading even a work-related book during business hours?

The field of OL is attempting to provide organizations with the tools to proactively manage these learning processes and their tacit knowledge base but the theory of OL is still at an embryonic stage, particularly in relation to the distinction(s) between individual and collective learning (Kim, 1993). There is a limited amount of work which is immediately transferable from the conceptual to the practical domain. However, OL techniques would appear well suited to the conditioning stage of the conditioned emergence model in that they offer a structure by which to understand and manipulate the deep structure and rules which define an organization's archetype.

Business process reengineering

The second management technology we will examine is business process re-engineering (BPR). In recent years, new entrants to many markets, with the benefits of greenfield sites, have been using information technology (IT) to enable powerful new ways of doing business. In the last decade IT has tended not to produce spectacular performance improvements despite large capital investments. In the U.S. service sector IT investment per white collar worker has more than doubled to $12,000 per annum while productivity has only increased by approximately 0.5 per cent per annum (Roach, 1991). It is claimed that this is because IT has traditionally been used to hasten work, not transform it (Davenport, 1993).

BPR emerged in the early 1990s as a management technique which used the power of IT to enable new ways of managing and operating businesses. The main proponents of BPR claim that organizations adopted functional structures which were appropriate when they were originally introduced but which artificially sub-divide business processes so that no one is responsible for the performance of the complete process (Hammer, 1990; Davenport and Short, 1990; Hammer and Champy, 1993). Initial BPR work focused on operational business processes such as product design and order fulfilment but more recently managerial processes have also been considered (Champy, 1995).

BPR's popularity has been chronicled in a number of surveys which have been conducted to assess the level of interest in BPR. Following the emergence of the approach, large numbers of organizations undertook business process applications under the broad heading of BPR projects. A series of surveys showed high levels of BPR activity in North America, Europe and the United Kingdom (see Cafasso, 1993; Pearson and Skinner, 1993; Preece and Edwards, 1993; CSC Index, 1994; Harvey, 1994; Pitney Bowes Management Services, 1995; Sockalingham and Doswell, 1996). While the statistics vary from survey to survey, there has undoubtedly been a high level of interest in the concepts and large numbers of organizations that have attempted to implement them.

As data became available on these implementations, it has become increasingly clear that translating the concepts into practice is far from straightforward. Failure rates in the region of 70 per cent are regularly reported for BPR projects, even by proponents of the approach (see Rothschild, 1992; CSC Index, 1994). In addition, it has been claimed that firms implementing BPR projects reduced their staffing levels by an average of 21 per cent in the areas affected by the project (CSC Index, 1994). While the blame for this has been attached to the business processes concept, such job losses may simply be an extension of the seemingly inexorable trend of doing more with less. During the period 1969–91 the United Kingdom's manufacturing output rose by 10 per cent, while the number of workers was halved (*Accountancy Age*, 1997).

It is now widely accepted that the majority of business process projects fail to live up to expectations, although there are some surveys which show more encouraging results (Sockalingham and Doswell, 1996). Davenport (1995) has stated that he believes the issue of failure rates to be a red herring. Indeed, BPR might be thought of as following an established pattern of poor implementation; a recent survey indicated that 85 per cent of companies using TQM had been disappointed with the results (Oates, 1993).

Perhaps in response to these high failure rates, there has been a change in the language used to describe the BPR. In his recent work, Hammer claims that he was wrong to focus on the radical nature of the change required and that he should have emphasized the move to a process, as opposed to task-centered mode of operation (Hammer, 1996). BPR has tended to focus on the systems and procedures of work and is a powerful tool for breaking with historical working practices. As such it is a useful mechanism for creating far-from-equilibrium conditions as discussed in stage 2 of the conditioned emergence model. It may also provide some new rules to do with a process-oriented organizational structure and a customer focus which may affect the deep structure of the organization. We believe that BPR's focus on codified as opposed to tacit knowledge means that the new process-oriented structure may be successfully used for a short period but in the longer term elements of the old processes and old behaviors will reemerge.

Illustrative case studies

We have proposed conditioned emergence as a three-stage model for successful transformation and identified OL and BPR as appropriate managerial technologies for the first and second stages of the model. We now present some illustrative case study material to develop a deeper understanding of how the model translates into practice. We begin by presenting an account of an extended transformation program which we conducted with a Scottish food-manufacturing company and we then present a short historical review of the transformation achieved by the Rover Group in recent years. These accounts are not presented as definitive empirical evidence in support of conditioned emergence. Rather, it is hoped that their inclusion might provide a richer understanding of the pattern implied by conditioned emergence.

The first example involves a well-established food-manufacturing company located in the west of Scotland. Founded in the early part of this century, the company is now run by the third generation of owner-managers and employs approximately 250 people.

The company operates in mature markets, with demand for many of its traditional products experiencing a decline. Although buoyant for much of its existence, recent years had brought a downturn in company performance. Organized along traditional command-and-control lines, management processes and structures had remained largely unchanged for several decades and the organization had struggled to respond to a worsening competitive climate which had seen a number of its major competitors disappear in the past 3 years. One of the company's most significant problems had been its failure to introduce new products in recent years. Consequently, business orders had been secured on the basis of price or historical relationships and margins had shrunk to the point where long-term viability was in question.

Originally, we were contacted with a view to helping the company address some of the problems outlined above. The directors of the company stated a wish to see the company not only perform better, but undergo radical transformation and develop a progressive approach to management. They were firmly of the view that they did not want a 'quick-fix', consultancy-driven approach, preferring lower-key, process-oriented help that would encourage individual and collective initiatives and leave the company able to sustain its own continued development.

Our interaction with the transformation process therefore took the form of intermittent site visits along with hosting off-site meetings, workshops, etc. over a period of approximately 18 months. The program of activities was supported by a local economic development agency which had an interest in assessing a novel form of management development. However, the bulk of the funding and resources were provided by the company itself. Essentially the program represented a test of the conditioned emergence model along action-research lines (Easterby-Smith, Thorpe, and Lowe, 1991); i.e., the program required our involvement on issues of process and to some extent constituted a form of experimental intervention. We made no direct contribution to issues of content, though of course our involvement in process issues may have had some influence on emergent content.

The owners of the organization were aware of the risks of this approach but were of the view that some radical action was required and felt that our approach was appropriate in the circumstances. From a research standpoint we are of the opinion that such process interventions are entirely consistent with the nature of the conditioned emergence model in that we are attempting to investigate an approach which combines strategy process with a degree of prescription more normally associated with the content school. Our focus on process, coupled with the organization's concern for content in the form of business results, allowed for the kind of marriage of academic research and business logic described by Beer and Eisenstat (1996) and mentioned in the literature review of this paper.

Following the structure of the model, we will now attempt to summarize the key events in what transpired to be an 18-month program.

Stage 1: Conditioning

According to the model, this is the stage at which the 'conditioning' in conditioned emergence occurs. The organization conditioned itself for the forthcoming trans-formation process by identifying its current rules, constructing new rules and outlawing the use of particular defensive routines which might inhibit progress. To promote this process we made extensive use of organizational learning techniques (see Senge, 1990).

We used a combination of theory sessions, seminars, workshops, and computer profiling to help the organization identify its current rules. Individuals were encouraged to articulate their assumptions about the business, their roles in it, and their aspirations for both. The construction of the new rules was initiated in teams comprising all the senior and middle managers. An iterative process of comparing responses led to the development of a corporate view of the organization's current rules.

From an agreement of the current rules, the organization began to develop a shared view of what it might become and what kind of behaviors and attitudes would be required to get it there. In essence, this part of the exercise amounted to the construction of a new set of desired operating rules for the company and visualization of an alternative archetype.

It was widely recognized that operationalizing these rules on a day-to-day basis would be problematic as the rigors of continued business operation inevitably locked the organization into existing practices. Outdoor simulations were used to allow the management team to experience the operation of defensive routines in unfamiliar situations. Having experienced defensive routines at the behavioral level, workshops and brainstorming were used to identify organizational equivalents of these defensive routines. These defensive routines were then outlawed by consensus.

Interestingly, our initial process design included a harmonization process intended to develop a single set of new rules from those produced by the various teams involved. In practice this proved to be unnecessary as we found that the rules produced by different teams were broadly similar. Our first conclusion was that the similarities reflected a particularly uniform culture within the organization, con-sistent with its level of maturity. However, subsequent analysis revealed that the similarities extended beyond the company to the large number of teams we have dealt with from other organizations. This may point to some prescriptive feature of the process interventions we apply, or perhaps to the existence of team archetypes. New rules tend to be more aspirational and generic in nature, typically identifying desirable behaviors, etc. Old rules and defensive routines are usually far more context specific in that they often relate to particular instances in an organization's history which have significantly influenced its development.

By the end of this stage the broad scope of the feedback processes had been determined; positive feedback would be applied to amplify actions consistent with the new rules, and the management team would intervene to stifle attempts to enact the outlawed defensive routines. The next stage in the process would require movement away from organization's current equilibrium to enable the redefined rule set to guide the emergence of a new archetype.

Stage 2: Creating far-from-equilibrium conditions

This stage is typically where prescriptive managerial intervention on content issues occurs, and maximum organizational discomfort is felt as current equilibria are destroyed. In the conditioned emergence model, this phase centers around the bifurcation zone, beyond which a range of possible archetypal trajectories extend into the future.

In the case study, this area proved to be the most problematic. This is perhaps unsurprising in that it sets in motion the departure from existing practices, removing many of the reference points on which negative feedback would traditionally operate.

The first approach was to restructure the organization, creating two separate units serving different markets. The organization considered this too risky and opted to introduce a cross-functional team structure, overlaid on the existing organizational arrangements. Three project teams were put in place, each one charged with effecting major performance improvements in selected areas of the business. Each one could be described as strategic in scope; indeed, one team had a particular remit to restructure the company in the medium term, using BPR technologies. Each team was intended as a far-from-equilibrium zone and all activities relating to the projects were managed in accordance with the new rules. After a promising start, in which the teams made a number of incremental improvements in their respective areas, progress gradually ground to a halt as old practices overwhelmed new activities. We considered two possible explanations of this: either we had been unsuccessful in effecting a sufficient departure from the current equilibrium, or feedback mechanisms had restored the old rules. It is perhaps worth observing that in this instance feedback on both the old and the new rules operated through the same channel, namely the managers. For example, one of the old rules which had been identified and then outlawed was that machine breakdowns which interrupted production were resolved by director-level intervention. The corresponding new rule was that the management team would resolve such problems without the assistance of directors. In the early stages of this phase, delivery deadlines resulted in pressure to enact the old rule and solve the immediate problem. Any managerial feedback which encouraged the usage of the old rule set to solve immediate problems automatically resulted in decreased usage of the new rules.

To a large extent, which of the two possible effects was the actual source of failure was overshadowed by the fact that the existing archetype had reasserted itself, thus requiring a second attempt to create far-from-equilibrium conditions. In the second attempt, a more dramatic restructuring along business process lines was initiated and the project teams relaunched. This attempt also failed, though more quickly than its predecessor. The new organizational structure was accepted in principle then rejected in practice by some members of the board of directors.

The third attempt was finally successful and the organization became more 'open'. Taking soundings from a range of associates in financial and business spheres, the company formed a clear view that decisive action was overdue and an air of impending crisis began to emerge. A new structure was adopted and there were departures at the managerial level, including one of the directors. At this point, the teams spontaneously reactivated themselves and began to tackle the projects with renewed vigor. The production area was reorganized and, according to representatives from the company, there existed a general conviction that the organization was in upheaval. The key lesson for us was that sustainable experimentation and reconfiguration were only possible following a dramatic break from the organization's established equilibrium. This achieved, feedback mechanisms would determine whether the reconfiguration was permanent or temporary.

Stage 3: Managing the feedback processes

In the final stage of the conditioned emergence model, feedback is applied to amplify actions consistent with the new rules and archetype. Feedback must also be used to damp actions or behaviors which belong to the old rules and archetype.

The new rules are reasonably visible in the organization, being displayed in the boardroom and some offices. The example of resolving production problems, quoted earlier, illustrates one feedback mechanism which was used to encourage the new rules and discourage reverting to the old archetype. The managing director, who would historically intervene to resolve most production problems, now displays the organization's new rules on the overalls he wears when on the shopfloor. These rules clearly state that he should not intervene in such matters when on the shopfloor. Our assessment is that the organization is now moving beyond the bistable state with the new archetype beginning to take hold. A number of small signals indicate that the organization has changed and their financial performance is beginning to improve as they develop new products and break into markets which had long eluded them.

Interestingly, the 'openness' referred to in the account of stage 2 has been followed by what appears to be a qualitative change in the company's operating environment. It is now active in new and different markets (e.g., large multiple retailers), has redefined its supply base and has a growing network of associated businesses. The new archetype represents a new set of organizational arrangements, structured around business processes as opposed to the functionally based, command and control organization which had represented the old archetype. The organization is now less inward looking and is more proactive in its relationship with other parts of the supply chain. Innovation and organizational learning are now regarded as key priorities within the company. In practical terms the directors and managers are being encouraged to gain new skills which are consistent with this new archetype. This is partially driven by the higher demands placed on the company by some major new accounts which have recently been won. The management team is being made more accountable for its performance against key competitive criteria whilst also being afforded greater freedom to achieve its targets.

At the time of writing our involvement in the transformation program is coming to an end and our role is changing to that of periodic observers. We believe that it may be too early to claim that the organization has effected an irreversible switch in archetypes. Whilst evidence of old behavior and rules appears to be declining, there are occasional tendencies for individuals to revert to pre-transformation practices. These are perhaps most evident when applying old rules which have been incorporated into the new archetype. These old rules may well have strong habitual associations with other old but outlawed rules (defensive routines) indicating that it is difficult to operate some old rules whilst suppressing others. This possibility is supported by the fact that old behaviors are most evident in areas of the company where old operating rules are most active, such as finance (e.g., pricing products). An alternative explanation is that these areas do not have the same degree of external connection with the company's redefined operating environment. As long as such isolated tendencies exist, one cannot discount the possibility of their extension and reestablishment during some period of instability. However, in our judgement, this is becoming increasingly unlikely and the new archetype is continuing to flourish.

For our second illustrative case study we examine the experiences of the Rover Group. Although Rover did not explicitly follow the conditioned emergence model, discussions with those in the organization have led us to believe that their experience is consistent with the overall pattern implied by it. Until comparatively recently, Rover represented all that was bad about manufacturing in the United Kingdom. The publicity they received during the 1970s and early 1980s was generally for poor-quality products (Done, 1993) and strained industrial relations (Goodhart, 1993). The last decade has seen a distinct upturn in Rover's fortunes, with a string of successful new products from Land Rover's Discovery to the revival of the MG brand with the critically acclaimed MGF. In managerial terms they have adopted a number of techniques including Total Quality, concurrent engineering, OL and BPR.

A former Chief Executive of the Rover Group points to the company's Total Quality initiative in 1986 as the genesis of the transformation process (Towers, 1996). A company-wide survey undertaken at that time might be interpreted as part of the conditioning process to identify existing attitudes and rules. The survey revealed a wealth of creative talent amongst the employees, which was only being utilized outside the workplace. The company identified learning as a fundamentally important activity for its employees and began to look for ways in which to stimulate learning within the organization. Again, this might be viewed as creating a new set of rules for the organization based around innovation and learning processes. Rover Learning Business was established in 1989 as a wholly owned subsidiary with specific responsibility to develop education and training programs for the Rover Group (Farish, 1994). In May 1990, the company made a further commitment to these new rules with the Rover Employees Assisted Learning (REAL) scheme, which offered all employees £100 per year to spend on any form of training (Bower, 1994). With anything from ballroom dancing to golf lessons being funded, the organization took a leap of faith that encouraging employees to learn in any subject area would have a positive impact on their willingness to learn in the business context.

Any one of a number of significant changes experienced by Rover during the 1980s could be viewed as having created far-from-equilibrium conditions (e.g., changes in ownership, new working practices and organizational structure). During the 1990s Rover used BPR to great effect in breaking down historical working procedures and now operates with a substantially different, more process-oriented, organizational structure (Harvey, 1994). However, we believe that it is no coincidence that their successful reengineering efforts were preceded by the application of OL techniques. Rover Learning Business was established the year before the term BPR had even been coined.

Discussions with the organization have led us to believe that the management team was successful in continuing to apply feedback signals which encouraged behaviors consistent with the new rules, while inhibiting use of the old rules.

Concluding remarks

In developing the conditioned emergence model we have made assumptions and observations which are at least different from, and in some cases contrary to, corresponding observations made by others working in the field. We have therefore chosen to examine the contribution of conditioned emergence to the integration of strategy process and content under a dynamic framework – the issue on which we opened the paper – before closing with a series of detailed questions arising from each of the stages in our model.

Conditioned emergence employs a specific sequence to introduce time as a dimension in organizational transformation and encourages planning at the level of deep structure and processes, whilst allowing emergence at the level of particular outcomes. Our model builds upon some established concepts yet contravenes others. We have argued in favor of a long-term view of strategy but focus on deep structure and the rules which underpin it. We have used the concept of emergence but introduce an element of coherence and collective intention through managing at the deep structural level. We have accepted that issues of content are important but propose that they should be managed at the level of the rules which generate outcomes rather than at the level of the outcomes themselves. We recognize the importance of positioning since an organization can be thought of as part of a co-evolving network of mutually interacting entities. However, we acknowledge the central role of resources in organizational transformation because the self-organizing processes which we describe involve self-referencing in relation to the organization's deep structure. Our model also addresses the issue of dynamism through the use of sequencing and feedback mechanisms. We have considered the nature and purpose of positive feedback in far-from-equilibrium conditions but also accept the role of negative feedback and the natural drive towards stability associated with single loop learning. Indeed, our sequence depicts a change in emphasis, from one form of feedback to the other, over time.

Our research has led us to question the continued validity of strategy as it is currently conceived. Viewed in the context of our model, we believe that many of the dichotomies with which the strategy literature seems to be increasingly concerned (e.g., static vs. dynamic, process vs. content, positioning vs. resources, planning vs. emergence) could be symptomatic of the decreasing relevance of current conceptions of strategy in the so-called 'knowledge age'. We believe strategy researchers should now concern themselves with the management of deep structure, instability and feedback loops as more general headings for the three stages of the conditioned emergence model. However, there are a number of interrelated areas for further research under each of these headings.

Management of deep structure

We have already highlighted that there are differing interpretations of complexity theory being applied to organizational problems. Conditioned emergence utilizes the concept of dissipative structures and implies that organizations move through a cycle of gradual evolution, stagnation, radical upheaval, and self-organization. As an organization evolves through repetition of this cycle, we believe that awareness of its accumulated learning, as reflected in its relatively stable deep structure, provides a degree of irreversibility to the evolutionary process. The edge of chaos view, as an alternative interpretation of complexity theory, proposes that organizations are capable of perpetually reconfiguring themselves to meet changing needs as self-organizing processes facilitate the emergence of a new order. Whilst we acknowledge that this is an attractive proposition we remain unconvinced of its validity in an organizational setting. For us, there appears to be some contradiction between the notion of naturally occurring self-organizing processes and the implied need for some managerial intervention to position organizations on the edge of chaos. It would appear that the different interpretations of complexity theory operate with different assumptions about organizations; further research is needed to clarify the nature and implications of these differing assumptions.

Management of instability

A key question arising from our work is whether the periodic upheaval it implies can be predicted (or indeed precipitated) by managerial intervention. Research to identify a range of indicators which might signal the onset, nature, and magnitude of instability would be extremely valuable and might in turn clarify the types of management interventions which would be required to deliberately trigger instability. Having dealt with the onset of instability, self-organization raises further questions. It is traditionally viewed as an unpredictable process where eventual outcomes are highly sensitive to random events and initial conditions. In self-organization, new order emerges from the repeated application of rules and conditioned emergence implies an element of control through development and management of the rule set. We have argued that it is possible to influence the outcome of self-organizing processes because in organizations as opposed to organisms there is an element of choice in terms of which rules to enact and which to discard. The influence of cognitive processes, awareness and choice in surfacing and shaping the rule set(s) raises interesting questions which link to another concern with the model as presented here; i.e., is the bistablility in our model a limiting case which is generally a multistable phenomenon characterized by lower degrees of archetypal uniformity when there is less overt management of deep structure and rules?

Management of feedback loops

We have identified feedback mechanisms as having an important impact on which rules are enacted. However, this has been an area of some conceptual difficulty for us. Amplifying behaviors consistent with the new rules could be viewed as positive feedback to encourage the nonlinear effects often associated with complexity theory and self-organization. However, at the deep structural level, the same actions could be viewed as negative feedback to ensure convergence on the new rules. This introduces the possibility of different organizational strata (e.g., deep structure and manifest structure) being subject to varying levels and types of stability and feedback. Further research is needed to investigate linkages between types of feedback, time lag effects and archetypal structures, perhaps reexamining previous work on classification systems and archetypes using the concepts of rules.

We believe that the concept of dissipative structures as presented in this paper is pointing towards a new conceptualization of strategy, which we believe addresses Jantsch's call for 'an end to the dualism between the planner and the planned'.

References

Abernathy, W. J. and K. B. Clarke (1985). 'Innovation: Mapping the winds of creative destruction', *Research Policy*, **14**, pp. 3–22.

Abrahamson, E. (1991). 'Managerial fads and fashions: The diffusion and rejection of innovations', *Academy of Management Review*, **16**(3), pp. 586–612.

Accountancy Age (20 February 1997). 'UK: The rights and wrongs of BPR', p. 18.

Argyris, C. (1990). *Overcoming Organizational Defenses: Facilitating Organizational Learning.* Prentice-Hall, Englewood Cliffs, NJ.

Argyris, C. (1992). *On Organizational Learning.* Blackwell, Cambridge, MA.

Argyris, C. and D. A. Schon (1978). *Organizational Learning: A Theory of Action Perspective.* Addison-Wesley, Reading, MA.

Bain, J. (1956). *Barriers in New Competition: Their Character and Consequences in Manufacturing Industries.* Harvard University Press, Cambridge, MA.

Barnett. W. P. and R. A. Burgleman (1996). 'Evolutionary perspectives on strategy', *Strategic Management Journal*, Summer Special Issue, **17**, pp. 5–19.

Barney, J. (1986). 'Organizational culture: Can it be a source of sustained competitive advantage?', *Academy of Management Review*, **11**, pp. 656–665.

Barney, J. (1991). 'Firm resources and sustained competitive advantage', *Journal of Management*, **17**, pp. 99–120.

Baum, J. A. C. and J. V. Singh (eds.) (1994). *Evolutionary Dynamics of Organizations*. Oxford University Press, New York.

Beer, M. and R. A. Eisenstat (1996). 'Developing an organization capable of implementing strategy and learning', *Human Relations*, **49**(5), pp. 597–619.

Beer, M., R. A. Eisenstat and B. Spector (1990). 'Why change programs don't produce change', *Harvard Business Review*, **68**(6), pp. 158–166.

Best, M. H. (1990). *The New Competition*. Polity Press, Cambridge, U.K.

Bower, D. G. (1994). 'Unleashing the potential of people', *Journal of European Industrial Training*, **18**(7), pp. 30–36.

Brown, S. L. and K. M. Eisenhardt (1997). 'The art of continuous change: Linking and time-paced evolution in relentlessly shifting organizations', *Administrative Science Quarterly*, **42**, pp. 1–34.

Cafasso, R. (15 March 1993). 'Rethinking re-engineering', *Computerworld*, pp. 102–105.

Champy, J. (1995). *Re-engineering Management*. HarperCollins, London.

Chandler, A. D., Jr. (1962). *Strategy and Structure: Chapter in the History of the Industrial Enterprise*. MIT Press, Cambridge, MA.

Cohen, M. D., J. G. March and J. P. Olsen (1972). 'A garbage-can model of organizations choice', *Administrative Science Quarterly*, **17**, pp. 1–25.

Coveney, P. and R. Highfield (1995). *Frontiers of Complexity*. Faber & Faber, London.

CSC Index (1994). *State of Re-engineering Report*. CSC Index, Cambridge, MA.

Cyert, R. M. and J. G. March (1963). *A Behavioral Theory of the Firm*. Prentice-Hall, Englewood Cliffs, NJ.

Davenport, T. H. (1993). *Process Innovation*. Harvard Business School Press, Boston, MA.

Davenport, T. H. (March 1995). 'Re-engineering perceptions', *Informationweek*, Issue 518, p. 90.

Davenport, T. H. and J. E. Short (1990). 'The new industrial engineering: Information technology and business process redesign', *Sloan Management Review*, Summer, pp. 11–27.

Done, K. (7 April 1993). 'Road map to Rover's return', *Financial Times*, p. 19.

Drazin, R. and L. Sandelands (1992). 'Autogenesis: A perspective on the process of organising', *Organization Science*, **3**(2), pp. 231–249.

Easterby-Smith, M., R. Thorpe and A. Lowe (1991). *Management Research: An Introduction*. Sage, London.

Farish, M. (25 March 1994). 'Back to the school desk with Rover', *Financial Times, Engineering Review*, p. 7.

Gemmill, G. and C. Smith (1985). 'A dissipative structure model of organization transformation', *Human Relations*, **38**(8), pp. 751–766.

Gersick, C. J. G. (1991). 'Revolutionary change theory: A multilevel exploration of the punctuated paradigm', *Academy of Management Review*, **32**, pp. 274–309.

Goodhart, D. (7 January 1993). 'Scanlon admits damage done by unions', *Financial Times*, p. 16.

Greenwood, R. and C. R. Hinings (1988). 'Organizational design types, tracks and the dynamic of strategic change', *Organization Studies*, **9**(3), pp. 293–316.

Greenwood, R. and C. R. Hinings (1993). 'Understanding strategic change: The contribution of archetypes', *Academy of Management Journal*, **36**(5), pp. 1052–1081.

Greenwood, R. and C. R. Hinings (1996). 'Understanding radical organizational change: Bringing together the old and the new institutionalism', *Academy of Management Review*, **21**(4), pp. 1022–1054.

Hamel, G. L. and C. K. Prahalad (1989). 'Strategic intent', *Harvard Business Review*, **67**(3), pp. 63–76.

Hamel, G. L. and C. K. Prahalad (1996). 'Competing in the new economy: Managing out of bounds', *Strategic Management Journal*, **17**(3), pp. 237–242.

Hammer, M. (1990). 'Re-engineering work: Don't automate, obliterate', *Harvard Business Review*, **68**(4), pp. 104–112.

Hammer, M. (1996). *Beyond Re-engineering: How the Process-Centred Organisation Is Changing Our Work and Our Lives*. HarperCollins Business, London.

Hammer, M. and J. Champy (1993). *Re-engineering the Corporation: A Manifesto for Business Revolution*. Nicholas Brealey, London.

Hannan, M. and J. Freeman (1977). 'The population ecology of organizations', *American Journal of Sociology*, **82**, pp. 929–964.

Harvey, D. (1994). *Re-engineering: The Critical Success Factors*. Business Intelligence, London.

Hedberg, B. (1981). 'How organizations learn and unlearn'. In P. Nystrom and W. Starbuck (eds.), *Handbook of Organizational Design*. Oxford University Press, New York, pp. 1–27.

Hodgson, G. M. (1993). *Economics and Evolution*. Polity Press, Cambridge, U.K.

Jantsch, E. (1980). *The Selforganizing Universe*. George Braziller, New York.

Johnson, G. (1987). *Strategy and the Management Process*. Basil Blackwell, Oxford.

Kanter, R. M. (1983). *The Change Masters: Corporate Entrepreneurs at Work*. Simon & Schuster, New York.

Kauffman, S. A. (1993). *The Origins of Order: Self Organisation and Selection in Evolution*. Oxford University Press, Oxford.

Kauffman, S. A. (1995). *At Home in the Universe*. Penguin, London.

Kim, D. (1993). 'The link between individual and organizational learning', *Sloan Management Review*, Fall, pp. 37–50.

Kolb, D. A., I. M. Rubin and J. M. McIntyre (1971). *Organizational Psychology: An Experiential Approach*. Prentice-Hall, Englewood Cliffs, NJ.

Kuhn, T. S. (1962). *The Structure of Scientific Revolutions*. University of Chicago Press, Chicago, IL.

Leavitt, B. and J. G. March (1988). 'Organizational learning', *Annual Review of Sociology*, **14**, pp. 319–340.

Leifer, R. (1989). 'Understanding organizational transformation using a dissipative structures model', *Human Relations*, **42**(10), pp. 899–916.

Levy, D. (1994). 'Chaos theory and strategy: Theory application and managerial implications', *Strategic Management Journal*, Summer Special Issue, **15**, pp. 167–178.

Mandelbrot, B. (1977). *Fractals: Form, Chance and Dimension*. Freeman, San Francisco, CA.

March, J. G. and H. A. Simon (1958). *Organizations*. Wiley, New York.

Miles, R. and C. Snow (1978). *Organization Strategy, Structure, and Processes*. McGraw-Hill, New York.

Miller, D. (1982). 'Evolution and revolution: A quantum view of structural change in organizations', *Journal of Management Studies*, **19**(2), pp. 131–151.

Miller, D. and P. Friesen (1984). *Organizations: A Quantum View*. Prentice-Hall, Englewood Cliffs, NJ.

Mintzberg, H. (1978). 'Patterns in strategy formulation', *Management Science*, **24**(9), pp. 934–948.

Mintzberg, H. (1983). *Structures in Fives: Designing Effective Organizations*. Prentice-Hall, Englewood Cliffs, NJ.

Mintzberg, H. (1994). *The Rise and Fall of Strategic Planning*. Prentice-Hall, Englewood Cliffs, NJ.

Mintzberg, H. and F. Westley (1992). 'Cycles of organizational change', *Strategic Management Journal*, Winter Special Issue, **13**, pp. 39–59.

Moingeon, B. and A. Edmonson (eds.) (1996). *Organizational Learning and Competitive Advantage*. Sage, London.

Nadler, D. A. and M. L. Tushman (1989). 'Organizational frame bending: Principles for managing re-orientation', *Academy of Management Executive*, **3**(3), pp. 194–204.

Nelson, R. R. and S. G. Winter (1982). *An Evolutionary Theory of Economic Change*. Belknap Press, Cambridge, MA.

Nonaka, I. (1991). 'The knowledge-creating company', *Harvard Business Review*, **69**(6), pp. 96–104.

Oates, D. (1993). 'Buzzwords: Learning the language of business', *Accountancy*, **112**(1200), p. 38.

Oliver, C. (1992). 'The antecedents of deinstitutionalization', *Organizational Studies*, **13**(4), pp. 563–588.

Pascale, R. T. (1990). *Managing on the Edge*. Simon & Schuster, New York.

Pearson, J. R. W. and C. Skinner (1993). *Business Process Re-engineering in the U.K. Financial Services Industry: The First Research into BPR Programmes in U.K. Financial Services*. University of Bristol Press, Bristol.

Pedler, M., J. Burgoyne and T. Boydell (eds.) (1990). *Self-development in Organizations*. McGraw-Hill, London.

Penrose, E. (1959). *A Theory of Growth of the Firm*. Blackwell, Oxford.

Peters, T. J. and R. H. Waterman (1982). *In Search of Excellence*. Harper & Row, New York.

Pettigrew, A. M. (1973). *Politics of Organisational Decision Making*. Tavistock, London.

Pettigrew, A. M. (1985). *The Awakening Giant*. Basil Blackwell, Oxford.

Pettigrew, A. M. (1992). 'The character and significance of strategy process research', *Strategic Management Journal*, Winter Special Issue, **13**, pp. 5–16.

Pettigrew, A. M. and R. Whipp (1991). *Managing Change for Comprehensive Success*. Basil Blackwell, Oxford.

Pfeffer, J. (1981). *Power in Organizations*. Pitman, Marshfield, MA.

Pine. B. J., II (1993). *Mass Customization: The New Frontier in Business Competition*. Harvard Business School Press, Boston, MA.

Piore, J. M. and C. Sabel (1984). *The Second Industrial Divide: Possibilities for Prosperity*. Free Press, New York.

Pitney Bowes Management Services (May 1995). 'Re-engineering among the *Fortune* 500: Focus on change management', *Cases in Business Process Re-engineering*, **14**, pp. 12–14.

Porter, M. E. (1980). *Competitive Strategy*. Free Press, New York.

Porter, M. E. (1985). *Competitive Advantage: Creating and Sustaining Superior Performance*. Free Press, New York.

Porter, M. E. (1991). 'Towards a dynamic theory of strategy', *Strategic Management Journal*, Winter Special Issue, **12**, pp. 95–117.

Powell, W. W. and P. J. DiMaggio (eds.) (1991). *The New Institutionalism in Organizational Analysis*. University of Chicago Press, Chicago, IL.

Prahalad, C. K. and G. Hamel (1990). 'The core competence of the corporation', *Harvard Business Review*, **68**(3), pp. 79–93.

Preece, I. and C. Edwards (1993). 'A survey of BPR activity in the U.K.', working paper, Version 2.4, Ref: BPR-Ian/2, School of Management, Cranfield University.

Prigogine, I. and I. Stengers (1984). *Order out of Chaos: Man's New Dialogue with Nature.* Bantam, New York.

Quinn, J. B. (1980). *Strategies for Change: Logical Incrementalism.* Irwin, Homewood, IL.

Roach, S. S. (1991). 'Services under siege: The restructuring imperative', *Harvard Business Review*, **69**(5), pp. 83–91.

Rothschild, M. (7 December 1992). 'How to be a high IQ company', *Forbes* (issue supplement), pp. 17–18.

Rumelt, R. P. (1982). 'Diversification strategy and profitability', *Strategic Management Journal*, **3**(4), pp. 359–369.

Rumelt, R. P. (1984). 'Towards a strategic theory of the firm'. In R. B. Lamb (ed.), *Competitive Strategic Management*. Prentice-Hall, Englewood Cliffs, NJ, pp. 556–570.

Schein, E. H. (1985). *Organizational Culture and Leadership*. Jossey-Bass, San Francisco, CA.

Schendel, D. (1992). 'Introduction to the Winter 1992 Special Issue on Fundamental Themes in Strategy Process Research', *Strategic Management Journal*, Winter Special Issue, **13**, pp. 1–3.

Selznick, P. (1957). *Leadership in Administration: A Sociological Interpretation*. Harper & Row, New York.

Senge, P. (1990). *The Fifth Discipline: The Art and Practice of the Learning Organisation*. Currency/Doubleday, New York.

Smith, C. (1986). 'Transformation and regeneration in social systems: A dissipative structure perspective', *Systems Research*, **3**(4), pp. 203–213.

Smith, C. and G. Gemmill (1991). 'Change in the small group: A dissipative structure perspective', *Human Relations*, **44**(7), pp. 697–715.

Sockalingham, S. and A. Dowsell (1996). 'Business process re-engineering in Scotland: Survey and comparison', *Business Change and Re-engineering*, **3**(4), pp. 33–44.

Spender, J. C. (1996). 'Competitive advantage from tacit knowledge? Unpacking the concept and its strategic implications'. In B. Moingeon and A. Edmonson (eds.), *Organisational Learning and Competitive Advantage*. Sage, London, pp. 56–73.

Spender, J. C. and R. M. Grant (1996). 'Knowledge and the firm: Overview', *Strategic Management Journal*, Winter Special Issue, **17**, pp. 5–9.

Staber, U. and B. Sharma (1994). 'The employment regimes of industrial districts: Promises, myths and realities', *Industrielle Beziehungen*, **1**(4), pp. 321–345.

Stacey, R. (1993). *Strategic Management and Organisational Dynamics*. Pitman, London.

Stacey, R. (1995). 'The science of complexity: An alternative perspective for strategic change processes', *Strategic Management Journal*, **16**(6), pp. 477–495.

Storper, M. and A. J. Scott (eds.) (1992). *Pathways to Industrialisation and Regional Development*. Routledge, London.

Thietart, R. A. and B. Forgues (1997). 'Action, structure and chaos', *Organizational Studies*, **18**(1), pp. 119–143.

Towers, J. (June 1996). 'Who needs learning?', *Manufacturing Engineer*, pp. 144–146.

Training and Development (May 1994). 'The future of workplace learning and performance', **48**(5), pp. 36–47.

Tushman, M. L. and P. Anderson (1986). 'Technological discontinuities and organizational environments', *Administrative Science Quarterly*, **31**(3), pp. 439–465.

Van de Ven, A. and M. S. Poole (1988). 'Paradoxical requirement for a theory of change'. In R. E. Quinn and K. S. Cameron (eds.), *Paradox and Transformation: Towards a Theory of Change in Organization and Management*. Ballinger, Cambridge, MA, pp. 19–63.

Waldrop, W. M. (1992). *Complexity: The Emerging Science at the Edge of Order and Chaos*. Touchstone, New York.

Wernerfelt, B. (1984). 'A resource-based view of the firm', *Strategic Management Journal*, **5**(2), pp. 171–181.

Whittington, R. (1992). 'Putting Giddens into action: Social systems and management agency', *Journal of Management Studies*, **29**(6), pp. 693–712.

Zucker, L. G. (1977). 'The role of institutionalization in cultural persistence', *American Sociology Review*, **42**, pp. 726–743.

Richard T. Pascale

SURFING THE EDGE OF CHAOS

From *Sloan Management Review* 1999, Spring: 83–94. Copyright © 1999 by MIT Sloan Management Review. All rights reserved.

[. . .]

Every decade or two during the past one hundred years, a point of inflection has occurred in management thinking. These breakthroughs are akin to the S-curves of technology that characterize the life cycle of many industrial and consumer products: Introduction → Acceleration → Acceptance → Maturity. Each big idea catches hold slowly. Yet, within a relatively short time, the new approach becomes so widely accepted that it is difficult even for old-timers to reconstruct how the world looked before.

The decade following World War II gave birth to the "strategic era." While the tenets of military strategy had been evolving for centuries, the link to commercial enterprise was tenuous. Before the late 1940s, most companies adhered to the tenet "make a little, sell a little, make a little more." After the war, faculty at the Harvard Business School (soon joined by swelling ranks of consultants) began to take the discipline of strategy seriously. By the late 1970s, the array of strategic concept (SWOT analysis, the five forces framework, experience curves, strategic portfolios, the concept of competitive advantage) had become standard ordnance in the management arsenal. Today, a mere twenty years later, a grasp of these concepts is presumed as a threshold of management literacy. They have become so familiar that it is hard to imagine a world without them.

It is useful to step back and reflect on the scientific underpinnings to this legacy. Eric Beinhocker writes:

> The early micro-economists copied the mathematics of mid-nineteenth century physics equation by equation. ["Atoms"] became the individual,

"force" became the economists' notion of "marginal utility" (or demand), "kinetic energy" became total expenditure. All of this was synthesized into a coherent theory by Alfred Marshall – known as the theory of industrial organization.[1]

Marshall's work and its underpinnings in nineteenth-century physics exert a huge influence on strategic thinking to this day. From our concept of strategy to our efforts at organizational renewal, the deep logic is based on assumptions of deterministic cause and effect (i.e., a billiard ball model of how competitors will respond to a strategic challenge or how employees will behave under a new incentive scheme). And all of this, consistent with Newton's initial conceptions, is assumed to take place in a world where time, space (i.e., a particular industry structure or definition of a market), and dynamic equilibrium are accepted as reasonable underpinnings for the formulation of executive action. That's where the trouble begins. Marshall's equilibrium model offered appropriate approximations for the dominant sectors of agriculture and manufacturing of his era and is still useful in many situations. But these constructs run into difficulty in the far-from-equilibrium conditions found in today's service, technology, or communications-intensive businesses. When new entrants such as Nokia, Amazon.com, Dell Computer, or CNN invade a market, they succeed despite what traditional strategic thinkers would write off as a long shot.

During the 1980s and 1990s, performance improvement (e.g., total quality management, *kaizen*, just-in-time, reengineering) succeeded the strategic era. It, too, has followed the S-curve trajectory. Now, as it trails off, an uneasiness is stirring, a feeling that "something more" is required. In particular, disquiet has arisen over the rapidly rising fatality rates of major companies. Organizations cannot win by cost reduction alone and cannot invent appropriate strategic responses fast enough to stay abreast of nimble rivals. Many are exhausted by the pace of change, and their harried attempts to execute new initiatives fall short of expectations.

The next point of inflection is about to unfold. To succeed, the next big idea must address the biggest challenge facing corporations today – namely, to dramatically improve the hit rate of strategic initiatives and attain the level of renewal necessary for successful execution. As in the previous eras, we can expect that the next big idea will at first seem strange and inaccessible.

Here's the good news. For well over a decade, the hard sciences have made enormous strides in understanding and describing how the living world works. Scientists use the term "complex adaptive systems" ("complexity" for short) to label these theories. To be sure, the new theories do not explain everything. But the work has identified principles that apply to many living things – amoebae and ant colonies, beehives and bond traders, ecologies and economies, you and me. [. . .]

For an entity to qualify as a complex adaptive system, it must meet four tests. *First*, it must be composed of many agents acting in parallel. It is not hierarchically controlled. *Second*, it continuously shuffles these building blocks and generates multiple levels of organization and structure. *Third*, it is subject to the second law of thermodynamics, exhibiting entropy and winding down over time unless replenished with energy. In this sense, complex adaptive systems are vulnerable to death. *Fourth*, a distinguishing characteristic, all complex adaptive systems exhibit a capacity for pattern recognition and employ this to anticipate the future and learn to recognize the anticipation of seasonal change.

Many systems are complex but not adaptive (i.e., they meet some of the above conditions, but not all). If sand is gradually piled on a table, it will slide off in patterns. If a wave in a stream is disturbed, it will repair itself once the obstruction is removed. But neither of these complex systems anticipates and learns. Only living systems cope with their environment with a predictive model that anticipates and pro-acts. Thus, when the worldwide community of strep bacteria mutates to circumvent the threat of the latest antibiotic (as it does rather reliably within three years), it is reaffirming its membership in the club of complexity.

Work on complexity originated during the mid-1980s at New Mexico's Santa Fe Institute. A group of distinguished scientists with backgrounds in particle physics, microbiology, archaeology, astrophysics, paleontology, zoology, botany, and economics were drawn together by similar questions.[2] A series of symposia, underwritten by the Carnegie Foundation, revealed that all the assembled disciplines shared, at their core, building blocks composed of many agents. These might be molecules, neurons, a species, customers, members of a social system, or networks of corporations. Further, these fundamental systems were continually organizing and reorganizing themselves, all flourishing in a boundary between rigidity and randomness and all occasionally forming larger structures through the clash of natural accommodation and competition. Molecules form cells; neurons cluster into neural networks (or brains); species form ecosystems; individuals form tribes or societies; consumers and corporations form economies. These self-organizing structures give rise to emergent behavior (an example of which is the process whereby prebiotic chemicals combined to form the extraordinary diversity of life on earth). Complexity science informs us about organization, stability, and change in social and natural system. "Unlike the earlier advances in hard science," writes economist Alex Trosiglio, "complexity deals with a world that is far from equilibrium, and is creative and evolving in ways that we cannot hope to predict. It points to fundamental limits to our ability to understand, control, and manage the world, and the need for us to accept unpredictability and change."[3]

The science of complexity has yielded four bedrock principles relevant to the new strategic work:

1   Complex adaptive systems are at risk when in equilibrium. Equilibrium is a precursor to death.[4]

2   Complex adaptive systems exhibit the capacity of self-organization and emergent complexity.[5] Self-organization arises from intelligence in the remote clusters (or "nodes") within a network. Emergent complexity is generated by the propensity of simple structures to generate novel patterns, infinite variety, and often, a sum that is greater than the parts. (Again, the escalating complexity of life on earth is an example.) [. . .]

3   Complex adaptive systems tend to move toward the edge of chaos when provoked by a complex task.[6] Bounded instability is more conducive to evolution than either stable equilibrium or explosive instability. (For example,

fire has been found to be a critical factor in regenerating healthy forests and prairies.) One important corollary to this principle is that a complex adaptive system, once having reached a temporary "peak" in its fitness landscape (e.g., a company during a golden era), must then "go down to go up" (i.e., moving from one peak to a still higher peak requires it to traverse the valleys of the fitness landscape). In cybernetic terms, the organism must be pulled by competitive pressures far enough out of its usual arrangements before it can create substantially different forms and arrive at a more evolved basin of attraction.

4   One cannot direct a living system, only disturb it.[7] Complex adaptive systems are characterized by weak cause-and-effect linkages. Phase transitions occur in the realm where one relatively small and isolated variation can produce huge effects. Alternatively, large changes may have little effect. (This phenomenon is common in the information industry. Massive efforts to promote a superior operating system may come to naught, whereas a series of serendipitous events may establish an inferior operating system — such as MS-DOS — as the industry standard.)

Is complexity just interesting science, or does it represent something of great importance in thinking about strategic work? As these illustrations suggest, treating organizations as complex adaptive systems provides useful insight into the nature of strategic work. In the following pages, I will (1) briefly describe how the four bedrock principles of complexity occur in nature, and (2) demonstrate how they can be applied in a managerial context. In particular, I use the efforts underway at Royal Dutch/Shell to describe an extensive and pragmatic test of these ideas.

The successes at Shell and other companies described here might be achieved with a more traditional mind-set (in much the same way as Newton's laws can be used to explain the mechanics of matter on earth with sufficient accuracy so as to not require the General Theory of Relativity). But the contribution of scientific insight is much more than descriptions of increasing accuracy. Deep theories reveal previously unsuspected aspects of reality that we don't see (the curvature of space-time in the case of relativity theory) and thereby alter the fabric of reality. This is the context for an article on complexity science and strategy. Complexity makes the strategic challenge more understandable and the task of strategic renewal more accessible. In short, this is not a polemic against the traditional strategic approach, but an argument for broadening it.

Stable equilibrium equals death

An obscure but important law of cybernetics, the law of requisite variety, states: For any system to survive, it must cultivate variety in its internal controls. If it fails to do so internally, it will fail to cope with variety successfully when it comes from an external source.[8] Here, in the mundane prose of a cybernetic axiom, is the rationale for bounded instability.

A perverse example of this axiom in action was driven home by the devastating fires that wiped out 25 percent of Yellowstone National Park in 1992. For decades, the National Park Service had *imposed* equilibrium on the forest by extinguishing fires whenever they appeared. Gradually, the forest floor became littered with a thick layer of debris. When a lightning strike and ill-timed winds created a conflagration that could not be contained, this carpet of dry material burned longer and hotter than normal. By suppressing natural fires for close to 100 years, the park service had prevented the forest floor from being cleansed in a natural rhythm. Now a century's accumulation of deadfall generated extreme temperatures. The fire incinerated large trees and the living components of top soil that would otherwise have survived. This is the price of enforced equilibrium.

The seductive pull of equilibrium poses a constant danger to successful established companies. Jim Cannavino, a former IBM senior executive, provides an anecdote that speaks to the hazards of resisting change. In 1993, Cannavino was asked by IBM's new CEO, Lou Gerstner, to take a hard look at the strategic planning process. Why had IBM so badly missed the mark? Cannavino dutifully examined the work product – library shelves filled with blue binders containing twenty years of forecasts, trends, and strategic analysis. "It all could be distilled down to one sentence," he recounts.

> "We saw it coming" – PC open architecture, networking intelligence in microprocessors, higher margins in software and services than hardware; it was all there. So I looked at the operating plans. How did they reflect the shifts the strategists had projected? These blue volumes (three times as voluminous as the strategic plans) could also be summarized in one sentence: "Nothing changed." And the final dose of arsenic to this diet of cyanide was the year-end financial reconciliation process. When we rolled up the sector submissions into totals for the corporation, the growth opportunities never quite covered the erosion of market share. This shortfall, of course, was the tip of an iceberg that would one day upend our strategy and our primary product – the IBM 360 mainframe. But facing these fundamental trends would have precipitated a great deal of turmoil and instability. Instead, year after year, a few of our most senior leaders went behind closed doors and raised prices.[9] [. . .]

While equilibrium endangers living systems, it often wears the disguise of an attribute. Equilibrium is concealed inside strong values or a coherent, close-knit social system, or within a company's well-synchronized operating system (often referred to as "organizational fit"). Vision, values, and organizational fit are double-edged swords.

Species are inherently drawn toward the seeming oasis of stability and equilibrium – and the further they drift toward this destination, the less likely they are to adapt successfully when change is necessary. So why don't all species drift into the thrall of equilibrium and die off? Two forces thwart equilibrium and promote instability: (1) the threat of death, and (2) the promise of sex.

The Darwinian process, called "selection pressures" by natural scientists, imposes harsh consequences on species entrapped in equilibrium. Most species, when challenged to adapt too far from their origins, are unable to do so and gradually disappear. But from the vantage point of the larger ecological community, selection pressures enforce an ecological upgrade, insofar as mutations that survive offer a better fit with the new environment. Natural selection exerts itself most aggressively during periods of radical change. Few readers will have difficulty identifying these forces at work in industry today. There are no safe havens. From toothpaste to camcorders, pharmaceuticals to office supplies, bookstores to booster rockets for space payloads, soap to software, it's a Darwinian jungle out there, and it's not getting easier. [. . .]

As a rule, a species becomes more vulnerable as it becomes more genetically homogeneous. Nature hedges against this condition through the reproductive process. Of the several means of reproduction that have evolved on the planet, sex is best. It is decisively superior to parthenogenesis (the process by which most plants, worms, and a few mammals conceive offspring through self-induced combination of identical genetic material).

Sexual reproduction maximizes diversity. Chromosome combinations are randomly matched in variant pairings, thereby generating more permutations and variety in offspring. Oxford's evolutionary theorist, William Hamilton, explains why this benefits a species. Enemies (i.e., harmful diseases and parasites) find it harder to adapt to the diverse attributes of a population generating by sexual reproduction than to the comparative uniformity of one produced by parthenogenesis.[10]

How does this relate to organizations? In organizations, people are the chromosomes, the genetic material that can create variety. When management thinker Gary Hamel was asked if he thought IBM had a chance of leading the next stage of the information revolution, he replied:

> I'd need to know how many of IBM's top 100 executives had grown up on the west coast of America where the future of the computer industry is being created and how many were under forty years of age. If a quarter or a third of the senior group were both under forty and possessed a west coast perspective, IBM has a chance.[11]

Here's the rub: The "exchanges of DNA" attempted within social systems are not nearly as reliable as those driven by the mechanics of reproductive chemistry. True, organizations can hire from the outside, bring seniors into frequent contact with iconoclasts from the ranks, or confront engineers and designers with disgruntled customers. But the enemy of these methods is, of course, the existing social order, which, like the body's immune defense system, seeks to neutralize, isolate, or destroy foreign invaders. "Antibodies" in the form of social norms, corporate values, and orthodox beliefs nullify the advantages of diversity. An executive team may include divergent interests, only to engage in stereotyped listening (e.g., "There goes Techie again") or freeze iconoclasts out of important informal discussions. If authentic diversity is sought, all executives, in particular the seniors, must be more seeker than guru.

Disturbing equilibrium at Shell

In 1996, Steve Miller, age fifty-one, became a member of Shell's committee of managing directors – the five senior leaders who develop objectives and long-term plans for Royal Dutch/Shell.[12] The group found itself captive to its hundred-year-old history. The numbing effects of tradition – a staggering $130 billion in annual revenues, 105,000 predominantly long-tenured employees, and global operations – left Shell vulnerable. While profits continued to flow, fissures were forming beneath the surface.

Miller was appointed group managing director of Shell's worldwide oil products business (known as "Downstream"), which accounts for $40 billion of revenues within the Shell Group. During the previous two years, the company had been engaged in a program to "transform" the organization. Yet the regimen of massive reorganization, traumatic downsizing, and senior management workshops accomplished little. Shell's earnings, while solid, were disappointing to financial analysts who expected more from the industry's largest competitor. Employees registered widespread resignation and cynicism. And the operating units at the "coal face" (Shell's term for its front-line activities within the 130 countries where Downstream does business) saw little more than business as usual.

For Steve Miller, Shell's impenetrable culture was worrisome. The Downstream business accounted for 37 percent of Shell's assets. Among the businesses in the Shell Group's portfolio, Downstream faced the gravest competitive threats. From 1992 to 1995, a full 50 percent of Shell's retail revenues in France fell victim to the onslaught of the European hypermarkets: a similar pattern was emerging in the United Kingdom. Elsewhere in the world, new competitors, global customers, and more savvy national oil companies were demanding a radically different approach to the marketplace. Having observed Shell's previous transformation efforts, Miller was convinced that it was essential to reach around the resistant bureaucracy and involve the front lines of the organization, a formidable task given the sheer size of the operation. In addition to Downstream's 61,000 full-time employees, Shell's 47,000 filling stations employed hundreds of thousands, mostly part-time attendants and catered to more than 10 million customers every day. In the language of complexity, Miller believed it necessary to tap the emergent properties of Shell's enormous distribution system and shift the locus of strategic initiative to the front lines. He saw this system as a fertile organism that needed encouragement to, in his words, "send green shoots forth."

In an effort to gain the organization's attention (i.e., disturb equilibrium), beginning in mid-1996, Miller reallocated more than 50 percent of his calendar to work directly with front-line personnel. Miller states:

> Our Downstream business transformation program had bogged down largely because of the impasse between headquarters and the operating companies, Shell's term for its highly independent country operations. The balance of power between headquarters and field, honed during a period of relative equilibrium, had ground to a stalemate. But the forces for continuing in the old way were enormous and extended throughout

the organization. We were overseeing the most decentralized operation in the world, with country chief executives that had, since the 1950s, enjoyed enormous autonomy. This had been part of our success formula. Yet we were encountering a set of daunting competitive threats that transcended national boundaries. Global customers – like British Airways or Daimler Benz – wanted to deal with one Shell contact, not with a different Shell representative in every country in which they operate. We had huge overcapacity in refining, but each country CEO (motivated to maximize his own P&L) resisted the consolidation of refining capacity. These problems begged for a new strategic approach in which the task at the top was to provide the framework and then unleash the regional and local levels to find a path that was best for their market and the corporation as a whole.

Shell had tried to rationalize its assets through a well-engineered strategic response: directives were issued by the top and driven through the organization. But country heads successfully thwarted consolidation under the banner of host-country objections to the threatened closing of their dedicated refining capacity. Miller continues:

We were equally unsuccessful at igniting a more imaginative approach toward the marketplace. It was like the old game of telephone that we used to play when we were kids: you'd whisper a message to the person next to you, and it goes around the circle. By the time you get to the last person, it bears almost no resemblance to the message you started with. Apply that to the 61,000 people in the Downstream business across the globe, and I knew our strategic aspirations could never penetrate through to the marketplace. The linkages between directives given and actions taken are too problematic.

What made sense to Miller was to fundamentally alter the conversation and unleash the emergent possibilities. Midway through the process, Miller became acquainted with core principles of living systems and adopted them as a framework to provide his organization with a context for renewal.

Miller's reports in the operating companies were saying, "Centralization will only bog us down." "They were partly right," he acknowledges.

These are big companies. Some earn several hundreds of millions a year in net income. But the alternative wasn't centralization – it was a radical change in the responsiveness of the Downstream business to the dynamics of the marketplace – from top to bottom such that we could come together in appropriate groups, solve problems, and operate in a manner which transcended the old headquarters versus field schism. What initially seemed like a huge conflict has gradually melted away, I believe, because we stopped treating the Downstream business like a machine to be driven and began to regard it as a living system that needed to evolve.

Miller's solution was to cut through the organization's layers and barriers, put senior management in direct contact with the people at the grassroots level, foster strategic initiatives, create a new sense of urgency, and overwhelm the old order. The first wave of initiatives spawned other initiatives. In Malaysia, for example, Miller's pilot efforts with four initiative teams (called "action labs") have proliferated to forty. "It worked," he states,

> because the people at the coal face usually know what's going on. They see the competitive threats and our inadequate response every day. Once you give them the context, they can do a better job of spotting opportunities and stepping up to decisions. In less than two years, we've seen astonishing progress in our retail business in some twenty-five countries. This represents around 85 percent of our retail sales volume, and we have now begun to use this approach in our service organizations and lubricant business. Results? By the end of 1997, Shell's operations in France had regained initiative and achieved double-digit growth and double-digit return on capital. Market share was increasing after years of decline.

Austria went from a probable exit candidate to a highly profitable operation. Overall, Shell gained in brand-share preference throughout Europe and ranked first in share among other major oil companies. By the close of 1998, approximately 10,000 Downstream employees have been involved in this effort with audited results (directly attributed to the program) exceeding a $300 million contribution to Shell's bottom line.

Self-organization and emergent complexity

Santa Fe Institute's Stuart Kauffman is a geneticist. His lifetime fascination has been with the ordered process by which a fertilized egg unfolds into a new-born infant and later into an adult. Earlier Nobel Prize-winning work on genetic circuits had shown that every cell contains a number of "regulatory" genes that act as switches to turn one another on and off. Modern computers use sequential instructions, whereas the genetic system exercises most of its instructions simultaneously. For decades, scientists have sought to discover the governing mechanism that causes this simultaneous, nonlinear system to settle down and replicate a species.[13]

Kauffman built a simple simulation of a genetic system. His array of 100 light bulbs looked like a Las Vegas marquee. Since regulatory genes cause the cells (like bulbs) to turn on or off, Kauffman arranged for his bulbs to do just that, each independently of the other. His hypothesis was that no governing mechanism existed; rather, random and independent behavior would settle into patterns – a view that was far from self-evident. The possible combinations in Kauffman's arrangement of blinking lights was two (i.e., on and off), multiplied by itself 100 times (i.e., almost one million, trillion, trillion possibilities!).

When Kauffman switched the system on, the result was astonishing. Instead of patterns of infinite variety, the system always settled down within a few minutes to a few more or less orderly states. The implications of Kauffman's work are far-reaching. Theorists had been searching for the sequence of primordial events that could have produced the first DNA – the building block of life. Kauffman asked instead, "What if life was not just standing around and waiting until DNA happened? What if all those amino acids and sugars and gases and solar energy were each just doing their thing like the billboard of lights?" If the conditions in primordial soup were right, it wouldn't take a miracle (like a million decks of cards falling from a balcony and all coming up aces) for DNA to randomly turn up. Rather, the compounds in the soup could have formed a coherent, self-reinforcing web of reactions and these, in turn, generated the more complex patterns of DNA.[14] [. . .]

Emergent complexity is driven by a few simple patterns that combine to generate infinite variety. For example, simulations have shown that a three-pronged "crow's foot" pattern, if combined in various ways, perfectly replicates the foliage patterns of every fern on earth. Similar phenomena hold true in business. John Kao, a specialist in creativity, has observed how one simple creative breakthrough can evoke a cascade of increasing complexity.[15] "Simple" inventions such as the wheel, printing press, or transistor lead to "complex" offshoots such as automobiles, cellular phones, electronic publishing, and computing.

The phenomenon of emergence arises from the way simple patterns combine. Mathematics has coined the term "fractals" to describe a set of simple equations that combine to form endless diversity.[16] Fractal mathematics has given us valuable insight into how nature creates the shapes we observe. Mountains, rivers, coastline vegetation, lungs, and circulatory systems are fractal, replicating a dominant pattern at several smaller levels of scale. Fractals, in effect, act like genetic algorithms enabling a species to efficiently replicate essential functions.

One consequence of emerging complexity is that you cannot see the end from the beginning. While many can readily acknowledge nature's propensity to self-organize and generate more complex levels, it is less comforting to put oneself at the mercy of this process with the foreknowledge that we cannot predict the shape that the future will take. Emerging complexity creates not one future but many.

Self-organization and emergence at Shell

Building on (1) the principles of complexity, (2) the fractal-like properties of a business model developed by Columbia University's Larry Seldon,[17] and (3) a second fractal-like process, the action labs, Steve Miller and his colleagues at Shell tapped into the intelligence in the trenches and channeled it into a tailored marketplace response.[18]

Miller states:

> We needed a vehicle to give us an energy transfusion and remind us
> that we could play at a far more competitive level. The properties of
> self-organization and emergence make intuitive sense to me. The
> question was how to release them. Seldon's model gave us a sharp-edged
> tool to identify customer needs and markets and to develop our value

proposition. This, in effect, gave our troops the "ammunition" to shoot with – analytical distinctions to make the business case. Shell has always been a wholesaler. Yet the forecourt of every service station is an artery for commerce that any retailer would envy. Our task was to tap the potential of that real estate, and we needed both the insight and the initiatives of our front-line troops to pull it off. For a company as large as Shell, leadership can't drive these answers down from the top. We needed to tap into ideas that were out there in the ranks – latent but ready to bear fruit if given encouragement.

At first glance, Shell's methods look pedestrian. Miller began bringing six- to eight-person teams from a half-dozen operating companies from around the world into "retailing boot camps." The first five-day workshop introduced tools for identifying and exploiting market opportunities. It also included a dose of the leadership skills necessary to enroll others back home. Participants returned ready to apply the tools to achieve breakthroughs such as doubling net income in filling stations on the major north–south highways of Malaysia or tripling market share of bottled gas in South Africa. As part of the discipline of the model, every intention (e.g., "to lower fuel delivery costs") was translated into "key business activities" (or KBAs). As the first group went home, six more teams would rotate in. During the next sixty days, the first group of teams used the analytical tools to sample customers, identify segments, and develop a value proposition. The group would then return to the workshop for a "peer challenge" – tough give-and-take exchanges with other teams. Then it would go back again for another sixty days to perfect a business plan. At the close of the third workshop, each action lab spent three hours in the "fishbowl" with Miller and several of his direct reports, reviewing business plans, while the other teams observed the proceedings. At the close of each session, plans were approved, rejected, amended. Financial commitments were made in exchange for promised results. (The latter were incorporated in the country's operating goals for the year.) Then the teams went back to the field for another sixty days to put their ideas into action and returned for a follow-up session.

"Week after week, team after team," continues Miller,

> my six direct reports and I and our internal coaches reached out and worked directly with a diverse cross-section of customers, dealers, shop stewards, and young and mid-level professionals. And it worked. Operating company CEOs, historically leery of any "help" from head-quarters, saw their people return energized and armed with solid plans to beat the competition. The grassroots employees who participated in the program got to touch and feel the new Shell – a far more informal, give-and-take culture. The conversation down in the ranks of the organization began to change. Guerrilla leaders, historically resigned to Shell's conventional way of doing things, stepped forward to champion ingenious marketplace innovations (such as the Coca-Cola Challenge in Malaysia – a free Coke to any service-station customer who is not offered the full menu of forecourt services. It sounds trivial, but it

increased volume by 15 percent). Many, if not most, of the ideas come from the lower ranks of our company who are in direct contact with the customer. Best of all, we learned together. I can't overstate how infectious the optimism and energy of these committed employees was for the many managers above them. In a curious way, these front-line employees taught us to believe in ourselves again. [. . .]

As executives move up in organizations, they become removed from the work that goes on in the fields. Directives from the top become increasingly abstract as executives tend to rely on mechanical cause-and-effect linkages to drive the business: strategic guidelines, head-count controls, operational expense targets, pay-for-performance incentives, and so forth. These are the tie rods and pistons of "social engineering" – the old model of change. Complexity theory does not discard these useful devices but it starts from a different place. The living-systems approach begins with a focus on the intelligence in the nodes. It seeks to ferret out what this network sees, what stresses it is undergoing, and what is needed to unleash its potential. Other support elements (e.g., controls and rewards) are orchestrated to draw on this potential rather than to drive down solutions from above.

Miller was pioneering a very different model from what had always prevailed at Shell. His "design for emergence" generated hundreds of informal connections between headquarters and the field, resembling the parallel networks of the nervous system to the brain. It contrasted with the historical model of mechanical linkages analogous to those that transfer the energy from the engine in a car through a drive train to the tires that perform the "work."

Edge of chaos

Nothing novel can emerge from systems with high degrees of order and stability – for example, crystals, incestuous communities, or regulated industries. On the other hand, complete chaotic systems, such as stampedes, riots, rage, or the early years of the French Revolution, are too formless to coalesce. Generative complexity takes place in the boundary between rigidity and randomness.

Historically,[19] science viewed "change" as moving from one equilibrium state (water) to another (ice). Newtonian understandings could not cope with the random, near-chaotic messiness of the actual transition itself. Ecologists and economists similarly favored equilibrium conditions because neither observation nor modeling techniques could handle transition states. The relatively inexpensive computational power of modern computers has changed all that. Nonequilibrium and nonlinear simulations are now possible. These developments, along with the study of complexity, have enabled us to better understand the dynamics of "messiness."

Phase transitions occur in the realm near chaos where a relatively small and isolated variation can produce huge effects. Consider the example of lasers: while only a complex system and not an adaptive one, the infusion of energy into plasma excites a jumble of photons. The more the energy, the more jumbled they become.

Still more and the seething mass is transformed into the coherent light of a laser beam. What drives this transition, and how can we orchestrate it? Two determinants – (1) a precise tension between amplifying and damping feedback, and (2) (unique to mankind) the application of mindfulness and intention – are akin to rudder and sail when surfing near the edge of chaos.

Two factors determine the level of excitation in a system. In cybernetics, they are known as amplifying (positive) and damping (negative) feedback.[20] Damping feedback operates like a thermostat, which keeps temperatures within boundaries with a thermocouple that continually says "too hot, too cold." Amplifying feedback happens when a microphone gets too close to a loudspeaker. The signal is amplified until it oscillates to a piercing shriek. Living systems thrive when these mechanisms are in tension.

Getting the tension right is the hard part. Business obituaries abound with examples of one or the other of these feedback systems gone amok. IT&T under Harold Geneen or Sunbeam under "Chainsaw" Al Dunlap thrive briefly under stringent damping controls, then fade away owing to the loss of imagination and creative energy. At the opposite end, Value Jet thrives in an amplifying phase, adds more planes, departures, and staff without corresponding attention to the damping loop (operational controls, safety, reliability, and service standards).

Psychologists tell us that pain can cause us to change, and this is most likely to occur when we recontextualize pain as the means by which significant learning occurs. When the great Austro-American economist Joseph Schumpeter described the essence of free-market economies as "creative destruction," it could be interpreted as a characterization of the hazards near the edge of chaos. Enduring competitive advantage entails disrupting what has been done in the past and creating a new future. [. . .]

Hewlett-Packard's printer business was one of the most successful in its portfolio. Observing a downward spiral of margins as many "me too" printers entered the market, HP reinvented its offering. Today, HP's printers are the "free razor blade" – the loss leader in a very different strategy. To maintain scale, HP abandoned its high-cost distribution system with a dedicated sales force, opting instead for mass channels, partnering, and outsourcing to lower manufacturing costs. To protect margins, it targeted its forty biggest corporate customers and formed a partnership to deliver global business printing solutions – whether through low-cost, on-premise equipment, or networked technology. States Tim Mannon, president of HP's printer division: "The biggest single threat to our business today is staying with a previously successful business model one year too long."[21]

Shaping the edge of chaos at Shell

Shell moved to the edge of chaos with a multi-pronged design that intensified stress on all members of the Shell system.[22] First, as noted, Miller and his top team performed major surgery on their calendars and reallocated approximately half their time to teaching and coaching wave after wave of country teams. When the lowest levels of an organization were being trained, coached, and evaluated by those at the very top, it both inspired – and stressed – everyone in the system (including mid-level bosses who were not present). Second, the design, as we have seen, sent teams back to collect real data for three periods of sixty days (interspersed with additional workshop sessions). Pressure to succeed and long hours both during the workshops and back in the country (where these individuals continued to carry their regular duties along with project work) achieved the cultural "unfreezing" effects. Participants were resocialized into a more direct, informal, and less hierarchical way of working.

Miller states:

> One of the most important innovations in changing all of us was the fishbowl. The name describes what it is: I and a number of my management team sit in the middle of a room with one action lab in the center with us. The other team members listen from the outer circle. Everyone is watching as the group in the hot seat talks about what they're going to do and what they need from me and my colleagues to be able to do it. That may not sound revolutionary – but in our culture, it was very unusual for anyone lower in the organization to talk this directly to a managing director and his reports.
>
> In the fishbowl, the pressure is on to measure up. The truth is, the pressure is on me and my colleagues. The first time we're not consistent, we're dead meat. If a team brings in a plan that's really a bunch of crap, we've got to be able to call it a bunch of crap. If we cover for people or praise everyone, what do we say when someone brings in an excellent plan? That kind of straight talk is another big culture change for Shell.
>
> The whole process creates complete transparency between the people at the coal face and me and my top management team. At the end, these folks go back home and say, "I just cut a deal with the managing director and his team to do these things." It creates a personal connection, and it changes how we talk with each other and how we work with each other. After that, I can call up those folks anywhere in the world and talk in a very direct way because of this personal connectedness. It has completely changed the dynamics of our operations.

Disturbing a living system

An important and distinct property of living systems is the tenuous connection between cause and effect. As most seasoned managers know, the best-laid plans are often perverted through self-interest, misinterpretation, or lack of necessary skills to reach the intended goal.

Consider the war of attrition waged by ranchers and the U.S. Fish and Wildlife Service to "control" the coyote. A cumulative total of $3 billion (in 1997 dollars) has been spent during the past 100 years to underwrite bounty hunters, field a sophisticated array of traps, introduce novel morsels of poisoned bait, and interject genetic technology (to limit fertility of females) – all with the aim of protecting sheep and cattle ranchers from these wily predators. Result? When white men first appeared in significant numbers west of the Mississippi in the early 1800s, coyotes were found in twelve western states and never seen east of the Mississippi. However, as a direct result of the aggressive programs to eliminate the coyote, the modern day coyote is 20 percent larger and significantly smarter than his predecessor. The coyote is now found in forty-nine of the fifty states – including suburbs of New York City and Los Angeles. How could this occur? Human intervention so threatened the coyote's survival that a significant number fled into Canada where they bred with the larger Canadian wolf. Still later, these visitors migrated south (and further north to Alaska) and, over the decades, bred with (and increased the size of) the U.S. population. The same threats to survival that had driven some coyotes into Canada drove others to adapt to climates as varied as Florida and New Hampshire. Finally, the persistent efforts to trap or hunt or poison the coyote heightened selection pressures. The survivors were extremely streetwise and wary of human contact. Once alerted by a few fatalities among their brethren, coyotes are usually able to sniff out man's latest stratagem to do them harm. [. . .]

As the tale of the coyote suggests, living systems are difficult to direct because of these weak cause-and-effect linkages. The best laid efforts by man to intervene in a system, to do it harm, or even to replicate it artificially almost always miss the mark. The strategic intentions of governments in Japan, Taiwan, and Germany to replicate Silicon Valley provide one example. The cause-and-effect formula seemed simple: (1) identify a region with major universities with strong departments in such fields as microelectronics, genetics, and nuclear medicine and having a geography with climate and amenities suitable to attract professionals, and (2) invest to stimulate a self-reinforcing community of interests. But these and many similar efforts have never quite reached a critical mass. The cause-and-effect relationships proved unclear.[23] A lot depends on chance. One is wiser to acknowledge the broad possibilities that flow from weak cause-and-effect linkages and the need to consider the second- and third-order effects of any bold intervention one is about to undertake.

Disturbing a complex system at Shell

In today's fast-changing environment, Shell's Steve Miller dismisses the company's old traditional approach as mechanistic. "Top-down strategies don't win ballgames," he states. "Experimentation, rapid learning, and seizing the momentum of success is the better approach."[24]

Miller observes:

> We need a different definition of strategy and a different approach to generating it. In the past, strategy was the exclusive domain of top management. Today, if you're going to have a successful company, you have to recognize that the top can't possibly have all the answers. The leaders provide the vision and are the context setters. But the actual solutions about how best to meet the challenges of the moment, those

thousands of strategic challenges encountered every day, have to be made by the people closest to the action – the people at the coal face.

Change your approach to strategy, and you change the way a company runs. The leader becomes a context setter, the designer of a learning experience – not an authority figure with solutions. Once the folks at the grassroots realize they own the problem, they also discover that they can help create and own the answers, and they get after it very quickly, very aggressively, and very creatively, with a lot more ideas than the old-style strategic direction could ever have prescribed from headquarters.

A program like this is a high-risk proposition, because it goes counter to the way most senior executives spend their time. I spend 50 percent to 60 percent of my time at this, and there is no direct guarantee that what I'm doing is going make something happen down the line. It's like becoming the helmsman of a big ship when you've grown up behind the steering wheel of a car. This approach isn't about me. It's about rigorous, well-taught marketing concepts, combined with a strong process design, that enable front-line employees to think like business-people. Top executives and front-line employees learn to work together in partnership.

People want to evaluate this against the old way, which gives you the illusion of "making things happen." I encountered lots of thinly veiled skepticism: "Did your net income change from last quarter because of this change process?" These challenges create anxiety. The temptation, of course, is to reimpose your directives and controls even though we had an abundance of proof that this would not work. Instead, top executives and lower-level employees learn to work together in partnership. The grassroots approach to strategy development and implementation doesn't happen overnight. But it does happen. People always want results yesterday. But the process and behavior that drive authentic strategic change aren't like that.

There's another kind of risk to the leaders of a strategic inquiry of this kind – the risk of exposure. You're working very closely and intensely with all levels of staff, and they get to assess and evaluate you directly. Before, you were remote from them; now, you're very accessible. If that evaluation comes up negative, you've got a big-time problem. [. . .]

Finally, the scariest part is letting go. You don't have the same kind of control that traditional leadership is used to. What you don't realize until you do it is that you may, in fact, have more controls but in a different fashion. You get more feedback than before, you learn more than before, you know more through your own people about what's going on in the marketplace and with customers than before. But you still have to let go of the old sense of control.

Miller's words testify to his reconciliation with the weak cause-and-effect linkages that exist in a living system. When strategic work is accomplished through a "design for emergence," it never assumes that a particular input will produce a particular output. It is more akin to the study of subatomic particles in a bubble chamber. The experimenter's design creates probabilistic occurrences that take place within the domain of focus. Period. Greater precision is neither sought nor possible.

References

This article is drawn from R. Pascale, M. Millemann, and L. Gioja, *Surfing the Edge of Chaos: [The Laws of Nature and the New Laws of Business.* (London: Texere, 2000).]

1   E.D. Beinhocker, "Strategy at the Edge of Chaos," *McKinsey Quarterly*, number 1, 1997, p. 25.
2   For an entertaining treatment of this inquiry, see M.M. Waldrop, *Complexity* (New York: Simon & Schuster, 1992).
3   A. Trosiglio, "Managing Complexity" (unpublished working paper, June 1995), p. 3, and D. Deutsch, *The Fabric of Reality* (New York: Penguin, 1997), pp. 3–21.
4   See S. Kauffman, *At Home in the Universe* (New York: Oxford University Press, 1995), p. 21; and G. Hamel and C.K. Prahalad, "Strategic Intent," *Harvard Business Review*, volume 67, May–June 1989, pp. 63–76.
5   See Kauffman (1995), p. 205; and J.H. Holland, *Hidden Order* (Reading, Massachusetts: Addison-Wesley, 1995), p. 3.
6   See Kauffman (1995), p. 230; and M. Gell-Mann, *The Quark and the Jaguar* (New York: Freeman, 1994), p. 249.
7   See Gell-Mann (1994), pp. 238–239; and Holland (1995), pp. 38–39 and p. 5.
8   W. Ashby, *An Introduction to Cybernetics* (New York, Wiley, 1956).
9   R. Pascale, interviews with James Cannavino, May 1996.
10   See Gell-Mann (1994), p. 64 and p. 253; and S.J. Gould, *Full House* (New York: Crown Publishing, 1996), p. 138.
11   G. Hamel, "Strategy as Revolution," *Harvard Business Review*, volume 74, July–August 1996, pp. 69–82.
12   Information and quotations in this section are drawn from R. Pascale, interviews with Steve Miller, London, The Hague, and Houston, October 1997 through February 1998.
13   Kauffman (1995), pp. 80–86.
14   Waldrop (1992), p. 110.
15   J. Kao, *Jamming: The Art and Discipline of Business Creativity* (New York: HarperCollins, 1997).
16   I. Marshall and D. Zohar, *Who's Afraid of Schrodinger's Cat?* (New York, Morrow, 1997), p. 16, p. 19, pp. 153–158.
17   Seldon's work is unpublished. He considers it proprietary and solely for consulting purposes.
18   Information and quotations in this section are drawn from R. Pascale, interviews with Steve Miller, London, The Hague, and Houston, October 1997 through February 1998.
19   Gell-Mann (1994), pp. 228–230.
20   Waldrop (1992), pp. 138–139.
21   R. Hof, "Hewlett Packard," *BusinessWeek*, 13 February 1995, p. 67.
22   Information and quotations in this section are drawn from R. Pascale, interviews with Steve Miller, London, The Hague, and Houston, October 1997 through February 1998.

23 A. Saxenian, "Lessons from Silicon Valley," *Technology Review*, volume 97, number 5, July 1994, pp. 42–45.

24 Information and quotations in this section are drawn from: R. Pascale, interviews with Steve Miller, London, The Hague, and Houston, October 1997 through February 1998.

Ralph Stacey

THE SCIENCE OF COMPLEXITY: AN ALTERNATIVE PERSPECTIVE FOR STRATEGIC CHANGE PROCESSES

From *Strategic Management Journal* 1995, 16: 477–495. Copyright © 1995 by John Wiley & Sons Ltd. Reproduced with permission of the copyright owner. Further reproduction prohibited without permission.

Abstract

The two perspectives of strategy process most firmly established in the literature – strategic choice and ecology – assume the same about system dynamics: negative feedback processes driving successful systems (individual organizations or populations of organizations) toward predictable equilibrium states of adaptation to the environment. This paper proposes a third perspective, that of complex adaptive systems. The framework is provided by the modern science of complexity: the study of nonlinear and network feedback systems, incorporating theories of chaos, artificial life, self-organization and emergent order. Here system dynamics are characterized by positive and negative feedback as systems coevolve far from equilibrium, in a self-organizing manner, toward unpredictable long-term outcomes.
[. . .]

Introduction

Chakravarthy and Doz (1992) identify the principal challenge facing strategy process research as follows: to address the 'central evolutionary and transformational processes' through which organizations renew themselves, rather than simply focusing on single administrative systems. There are two well-established perspectives from which this strategy process challenge is most frequently viewed.

The first is that of strategic choice – a transformational process in which organizations adapt to environmental changes by restructuring themselves in an intentional, rational manner (Zajac and Kraatz, 1993; Fombrun and Ginsberg, 1990; Zajac and Shortell, 1989; Ginsberg, 1988; Thompson and Tuden, 1959). The second is that of ecology – an evolutionary process of competitive selection in which whole populations of organizations adapt to environmental change, given that individual organizational adaptation is blocked by institutional inertia and resource specificity (Hannan and Freeman, 1977). Despite the significant differences in terms of predicted outcome, however, both clearly make the same assumptions about system dynamics, namely, that successful systems (individual organizations/whole populations) are driven by negative feedback processes, toward predictable states of adaptation to the environment. The dynamics of success are therefore assumed to be a tendency toward equilibrium and thus stability, regularity and predictability.

These assumptions, which originate in Newtonian physics and Darwinian evolution (Parker and Stacey, 1994), are now being questioned at a fundamental level by developments in physics, biology, and mathematics. These developments can be grouped under the heading 'the science of complexity', a science which is concerned with the dynamical properties of nonlinear and network feedback systems (Gleick, 1987; Waldrop, 1992; Kauffman, 1991, 1992; Gell-Mann, 1994). The study of these systems has revealed that in order to produce creative, innovative, continually changeable behavior, systems must operate far from equilibrium where they are driven by negative and positive feedback to paradoxical states of stability and instability, predictability and unpredictability. The transformational process is one of internal, spontaneous self-organization amongst the agents of a system, pro-voked by instabilities, and potentially leading to emergent order. The evolutionary process is one of competitive selection which weeds out all systems incapable of spontaneous changeability. The dynamics of success then have to do with being kept away from equilibrium adaptation in states of instability, irregularity and unpredictability.

This paper suggests that the revolutionary new science of complexity may provide a framework for a third perspective on strategy process – one that pulls together, into a coherent whole, literature covering a number of views which do not currently command all that much attention from those researching the strategy process. The nature of this third perspective will be clarified by comparing how it and two well-established perspectives mentioned above deal with the following three closely interrelated issues:

1   The issue of *'systemic properties'* raised by the questions: what are the funda-mental properties of human systems that make them capable of transformation and renewal? Or to put it another way: what are the evolutionary and transformational processes that make organizations 'changeable'?

2   The *'intention vs. emergence'* issue raised by the questions: are new organizational states the outcome of prior shared intentions of the agents operating within them? Or do such states emerge from complex interactions between agents in the absence of prior shared intention? In other words: is it possible to determine the long-term future outcomes of a changeable system?

3   The '*free choice vs. determinism and constraint*' issue raised by the questions: are
     agents in a changeable system free to choose strategy and its outcomes? Or are
     their choices determined by the nature of their system and the environment
     it operates in?

Established perspectives on the three issues

Systemic properties

For the strategic choice school, the links between cause and effect are such that
individual organizations can themselves choose to reach equilibrium adaptation – it
is assumed that environmental changes are largely (but not totally) identifiable;
that organizations purposively and intendedly adapt to these environmental changes
through restructuring themselves; and that they do so in patterned, theoretically
predictable ways (Zajac and Kraatz, 1993). This school also assumes that a strategy/
environmental coalignment is desirable/needed and that organizations generally
manage to secure such an alignment (Zajac and Kraatz, 1993). Translating this
into the language to be used below to make comparisons, this means that organizations use negative feedback processes of formulating plans/policies and then
implementing them using monitoring forms of control.

   For the ecology school it is populations of organizations which adapt and the
negative feedback process of competitive selection ensures that this happens: a
particular environmental state is compatible with a limited number of particular
states of the organizational population and deviations from those states are weeded
out through competitive failure. The population of organizations is thus pulled
toward an equilibrium state.

   Clearly, both of these theories are assuming that organizations in their
environments are systems in which there are clear-cut links between specific causes
and specific effects. Negative feedback then ensures movement toward predictable
equilibrium states, where the dynamics are those of stable, regular behavior. In both
cases irregular behavior occurs because the environment bombards organizations
with events that agents within them have not foreseen (random shocks) or cannot
deal with. Any disorder is therefore the consequence of ignorance, inertia or
incompetence. The matter at issue between the two perspectives is simply the extent
of this ignorance, inertia, and incompetence – the strategic choice perspective
claims that it is not sufficient to block individual organizational ability to restructure
successfully and the ecology perspective holds the opposite view.

Intention vs. emergence

How each of the major perspectives deals with the issue of intention vs. emergence
follows from the assumptions they make about the extent of ignorance, inertia and
incompetence. From a strategic choice of perspective it is primarily the intention of
the dominant coalition in an individual organization which determines whether it

restructures or not, and whether that restructuring is successful or not – they are intendedly and bounded rational (Zajac and Kraatz, 1993). A population of organizations would then display patterns over time which are the aggregate of individual organizational intentions.

The ecology perspective, however, sees individual organizational outcomes as the product of an original intention as to institutional structure/resource endowment and subsequent competitive selection in the face of environmental change and organizational inertia. The long-term state of an individual organization thus emerges as far as the agents within it are concerned. But this emergent state is predictable – knowing the environmental change and knowing the institutional frameworks/resource endowments of the population of organizations, it is possible to predict who the survivors will be and what the population of organizations will be like.

Choice vs. determinism and constraint

From an ecology perspective, the evolution of an individual organization is fully determined by its initial institutional and resource choices, its inertia and the subsequent changes in its environment. According to strategic choice theory organizations are not so constrained by inertia, but success still requires that an organization be adapted to its environment – this implies some kind of deterministic relationship between the environment and the strategy/structure of an organization. Although environmental changes are assumed to be largely identifiable and unambiguous, choice remains a possibility because the environment–organization relationship allows for multiple equilibria – one cause has a limited number of potential effects from which it is assumed agents can choose (Zajac and Kraatz, 1993).

It can be seen from the above discussion that both the strategic choice and the ecology schools have in mind much the same kind of organization-in-its-environment system, with much the same dynamical properties, being driven by much the same kind of processes – they differ primarily in their views about organizational inertia and therefore in their prediction about individual organizational restructuring.

Alternative viewpoints

There are a number of other viewpoints in the management, economics, and sociology literatures which make assumptions about system dynamics that differ fundamentally from those of the two established perspectives discussed above.

Contradiction, paradox and nonequilibrium

When paradox (Hyman, 1987; Hampden-Turner, 1990; Quinn and Cameron, 1988) becomes the central focus then organizations are viewed as nonequilibrium systems with dynamics that are essentially disorderly, developing through political processes (Pettigrew, 1973, 1977, 1985; Pfeffer, 1981) in a dialectical manner (Pascale, 1990) and displaying one crisis after another (Miller, 1990). The contradictory nature of organizations makes it impossible for managers to establish a shared intention about comprehensive long-term outcomes in which their organization is adapted to its environment. Those outcomes partly emerge as far as the agents are concerned and partly they are the result of intentional choice (Mintzberg and Waters, 1985).

Spontaneous self-organization and creative destruction

Here, organizations are assumed to be systems, in turn part of larger environmental systems, that evolve through a process of creative destruction (Schumpeter, 1934) and spontaneous self-organization (Hayek, 1948). Such evolving systems are so complex that agents within them cannot intend their long-term futures. Instead, those futures emerge unpredictably from the interactions between agents in conditions of nonequilibrium and disorder. Individual free choice plays a vital role in the unpredictable, creative evolution of the system.

Irregularity and disorder as a systemic property

In sociology, structuration models (Giddens, 1979) present organizations as continuous feedback systems in which behavior unfolds or emerges from a dialectical process. The regularities in behavior come about because each successive piece of behavior is conditioned by the institutions within which it occurs (Weick, 1969/ 1979; Schein, 1985; Johnson, 1987), but each time around the choices of individuals can also make a difference in the sense that they can change the institutions. Irregularity and disorder can occur because of the nature of the system itself – individuals are free to disrupt institutions. Human systems are driven by feedback loops in which both free choice and constraint are present and the state systems occupy is the result of their detailed histories. The circular feedback nature of choice, action, and outcome leads to a complex connection between cause and effect (Forrester, 1958, 1961; Senge, 1990).

Positive feedback

Vicious (or virtuous) circles are immediately obvious examples of positive feedback loops in organizations (Gouldner, 1964; Merton, 1957; Arthur, 1988). Systems dynamicists (Forrester, 1958; Hall, 1976; Senge, 1990) have demonstrated that nonlinearity and positive feedback loops are fundamental properties of organizational life and that behavior patterns can emerge without being intended and in fact often emerge contrary to intention, producing unexpected and counter-intuitive outcomes. An example of this is Hall's (1976) study of the demise of the *Saturday Evening Post*. Hall showed how promotion expenditure taking the form of free trial subscriptions was having the intended effect of boosting sales volumes, but as the proportion of subscribers on free trials rose, average subscription rates plummeted with the unintended effect of cutting profits. When this was added to increased advertising rates leading to more than proportionate reductions in advertising volumes, the magazine was driven out of business. Apparently favorable policies in one area soon had amplifying adverse outcomes in other areas.

None of these alternative viewpoints commands anything like as much attention in the literature as the strategic choice or ecology perspectives, and this is even more true of management and consulting practice where the explicit emphasis is quite clearly on the strategic choice perspective. And each of the alternative viewpoints outlined above is based upon a fundamental assumption about organizational dynamics which is quite different from strategic choice / ecology perspectives. These differences are summarized in Table 1.

Two questions may be posed in relation to this comparison: is there any theoretical reason for putting the disparate viewpoints together into one coherent framework as an alternative to the two well-established perspectives? Is there any theoretical reason for adopting such an alternative perspective rather than the established ones?

This paper argues that the answer to these questions is 'yes.' The reason for this answer is that, although they were developed largely independently of each other, the alternative viewpoints listed above all turn out to deal with one aspect or another of the dynamics of a particular class of systems – nonlinear and network feedback systems, the subject area of the modern science of complexity. That science of complexity provides the theoretical framework for combining the above alternative viewpoints into a coherent perspective of strategy process, one which is arguably

Table 1 Fundamental assumptions on system dynamics made in different perspectives on the strategy process

Adaptation through choice	Adaptation through competitive selection	Alternative viewpoints
Clear-cut cause-and-effect links – predictability	Clear-cut cause-and-effect links – predictability	Clear-cut cause-and-effect links – but they are circular, leading to unexpected outcomes
Organizations intentionally seek adaptive equilibrium	Organizations are selected according to criteria of equilibrium adaptation	Organizations are nonequilibrium systems with disorderly dynamics
Long-term outcomes are intentional and chosen	Long-term outcomes determined by environment and inertia of organization	Long-term outcomes are partly emergent and partly intentional
Negative feedback drives system, i.e. individual organization	Negative feedback drives system, i.e. population of organizations	Complex nonlinear systems with positive and negative feedback. Spontaneous self-organization and creative destruction.

more comprehensive than either of the well-established perspectives. What is this 'science of complexity'?

Some insights from the science of complexity

The science of complexity is concerned with the fundamental logical properties of the behavior of nonlinear and network feedback systems, no matter where they are found. To date, most of the work in this field has been carried out in relation to systems in nature (the development of this science is described in Gleick, 1987; Waldrop, 1992; also see Prigogine and Stengers, 1984; and Nicolis and Prigogine, 1989, for self-organization), but there is a growing interest in applying the discoveries to social systems (e.g., Anderson, Arrow and Pines, 1988; Nonaka, 1988; Peters, 1991; Wheatley, 1992; Zimmerman, 1992; Stacey, 1991, 1992, 1993; Goldstein, 1994).

Nonlinear feedback systems

First, why should organizational theorists pay attention to the science of complexity? The answer is that organizations are nonlinear, network feedback systems and it therefore follows logically that the fundamental properties of such systems should apply to organizations.

Organizations are clearly feedback systems because every time two humans interact with each other the actions of one person have consequences for the other, leading that other to react in ways that have consequences for the first, requiring in turn a response from the first and so on through time. In this way an action taken by a person in one period of time feeds back to determine, in part at least, the next action of that person. Feedback systems are what they are because of the history they have experienced and that statement certainly applies to people and groups of people.

Furthermore, the feedback loops that people set up when they interact with each other, when they form a network, are nonlinear. This is because: the choices of agents in human systems are based on perceptions which lead to nonproportional over- and under-reaction; there are almost always many outcomes possible for any action; group behavior is more than simply the sum of individual behaviors; outcomes are usually stubbornly individual and often peculiar; and without doubt small changes often escalate into major outcomes. These are all defining features of nonlinear as opposed to linear systems and, therefore, all human systems are nonlinear feedback networks.

Given this conclusion it is reasonable to expect that two fundamental dynamical properties which have been identified in relation to nonlinear feedback systems and network feedback systems (e.g., cellular automata and complex adaptive systems) in general should apply to organizations in some way. These properties are

1   bounded instability; and
2   spontaneous self-organization and emergent order.

Bounded instability

Deterministic laws

All nonlinear feedback systems, including human organizations, can be expressed in terms of lawful rules and relationships: that is, such systems are deterministic in the same fundamental sense as Newton's laws or the laws of supply and demand in neoclassical economic theory.

In organizations such laws take the forms of decision rules and scripted relationships between people within an organization and with people across organizational boundaries – the 'institutions' referred to above in the discussion or Giddens' analysis. Agents in such a system have no choice but to move around the nonlinear feedback loops which these 'institutions' constitute and in that sense the system in which the agents operate is deterministic. Each time an agent goes around this loop, however, that agent is free to vary, ignore or alter the institutional arrangements – agents follow decision rules and behavioral scripts but those rules and scripts allow freedom of choice. So, agents can change the rules, schemas or scripts which govern their behavior, but they cannot remove the nonlinear feedback nature of their interactions, nor can they remove the consequence of that nonlinear feedback.

. . . may lead to stable outcomes

The outcome of any individual free choice, however, is determined not only by that agent's chosen intervention but also by the chosen interventions of other agents. When all the agents involved in the system accept a given set of rules and make their choices in accordance with those rules, then the whole system will eventually settle down into a state of regular behavior, that is, stable equilibrium. In other words, the system operates in a negative feedback manner to sustain regular predictable behavior – it is attracted to stable equilibrium adaptation to its environment when the rules are appropriate.

. . . or to unstable outcomes

On the other hand, if all the agents involved in a system keep changing the rules governing their behavior then no one will be able to rely on others. The system is then driven by amplifying, positive feedback along a predictable, explosively unstable equilibrium path – the system is attracted to unstable equilibrium.

So, as the contention level in a human system is raised, that system passes from a state in which it is attracted to stable equilibrium behavior to a state in which it is attracted to unstable behavior. The same kind of phenomenon applies to all nonlinear feedback systems wherever they are found, in nature or in mathematics – as some parameter (reflecting the speed with which energy or information moves through the system) is increased they pass from states of stable equilibrium to some explosively unstable state.

In the cases so far discussed a deterministic system leads to predictable, that is, determined outcomes. The profound insight coming from the science of complexity is that nonlinear feedback networks also have available to them a third state of behavior, a state which is neither stable nor unstable, but both at the same time.

. . . or to indeterminate outcomes: bounded instability

When a nonlinear feedback operates in a state poised at the edge of instability its behavior is paradoxically both stable and unstable at the same time: there is instability in the sense that specific behavior is inherently unpredictable over the long term, but there is also stability in the sense that there is qualitative structure to that behavior and also short-term outcomes are predictable. For example, the weather is unpredictable in specific terms over the long term, but we can say something about the next few days and the weather does display recognizable qualitative patterns of storm and sunshine. Or, to take an organizational example, we can detect archetypal, irregular patterns of fight, flight, and dependency behavior in groups of people when anxiety levels rise, but we cannot predict the specific course which those patterns will follow over any given time period.

Behavior at the edge of instability (or you could say the edge of stability) follows a random, inherently unpredictable path over time, but it does so within given limits – it is boundedly unstable. This behavior has been given names such as chaos; strange or fractal attractors; edge of chaos. For the purposes of this paper all of these terms are lumped together despite the fact that there are differences in their precise meanings. One of the key points as far as this paper is concerned is that all of these terms describe specific behavior that is inherently unpredictable over the long term but nevertheless has a recognizable pattern or structure. For most of the remainder of this paper the term bounded instability will be used to describe such behavior in the belief that it is the conceptual or philosophic content rather than the mathematical precision which is key to management and organizational theorizing. Another key point for the purposes of this paper is that it is both simple and complicated, both deterministic and probabilistic nonlinear feedback networks that can generate long-term outcomes which are indeterminate, that is, boundedly unstable.

The reason for this 'strange' behavior is that the system utilizes both positive and negative feedback, flipping autonomously from one to the other, rather than either negative feedback which can produce stability or positive feedback which produces instability. This state makes it possible for tiny changes – so tiny that it would be impossible to detect or measure them, to escalate into major qualitative alterations in the behavior of the system. This 'sensitive dependency on initial conditions' means that, for all practical purposes, links between specific causes and specific effects, between specific actions and specific outcomes, are lost in the complexity of what happens.

Prior shared intention?

When a nonlinear feedback system operates at the edge of instability, therefore, agents in that system cannot intend the long-term outcomes of their actions. Instead, those long-term outcomes emerge from the detailed interactions between the agents. Furthermore, new patterns of behavior that emerge fall within recognizable categories – they are similar to but never the same as previous patterns of behavior. In this sense history repeats itself but things are never the same. Although individual agents operate in a deterministic system (or a probabilistic one), they can quite easily exercise real choices that could have major impacts: they simply cannot know in advance whether a major impact will emerge and if so what it will be and hence they cannot intend the long-term outcomes of their next chosen actions. Choice is not restricted to a limited number of predictable equilibria – choice is truly open ended with unknowable outcomes.

Review of the argument so far

To summarize, perfectly deterministic nonlinear feedback networks may be attracted to one of a number of states.

When such systems are attracted to stable equilibrium, then there are clear-cut connections between cause and effect, so that conditions in the environment determine through the feedback laws what the long-term outcome is to be if the system is to be adapted – and it is perfectly possible for there to be a limited number of such adapted outcomes, as the strategic choice school assumes, because this is a nonlinear system. Individual agents could, therefore, make a difference by choosing one of these adapted equilibrium outcomes rather than another – they could intend the outcome of their actions but the range of such actions and outcomes are in effect prescribed within given limits by the environment if the system is to be adapted to its environment. The ecology school sees the same system dynamics but assumes that internal inertia prevents agents from implementing any choice they may make.

The two well-established perspectives therefore enable us to understand the development of organizations when they operate in stable equilibrium, where they can change in predictable ways, either repeating past behavior or selecting from a limited range of behaviors with foreseeable outcomes. In these circumstances, agents have to shift their system from one equilibrium position to another, selected from a limited number of feasible equilibria, and shifting from one equilibrium to another is difficult – the inertia forces operating on the system try to keep it in its existing equilibrium. This shift to a new, predictable equilibrium state is not the same as true innovation and creativity because that which is truly new is not already in the past or the present and cannot therefore be predicted. Creativity is rather associated with that endless variety of behavior arising from spontaneity.

It is at the edge, in bounded instability, that deterministic nonlinear systems become internally and spontaneously changeable – their behavior displays endless unpredictable variety in the sense that no behavior pattern is ever repeated exactly. When a system is in this state agents are constrained by their decision rules and behavioral scripts, but the choices they make within those constraints can have major consequences for the system because small changes can escalate into major qualitative changes in outcomes. When it is at the edge of instability, a system is far easier to change because small actions of agents within the system can escalate into major outcomes. Those outcomes, however, are not determinate: instead they emerge in the sense that they are surprising results, not of given environmental conditions, but of the undirected, self-organizing interactions between agents within and across system boundaries, who are together creating and recreating their environment. In other words, we have deterministic laws that lead to unpredictable, emergent outcomes. Disorder is not simply the result of inertia, incompetence or ignorance – it is a fundamental property of creative systems and it plays a vital role in that creativity. (A probabilistic feedback network, that is, one into which random shocks are introduced, has the same fundamental properties.)

This is not the kind of world that can be explained by either of the well-established perspectives of the strategy process. But it does seem to be very much the kind of world which each of the alternative viewpoints outlined above has in mind. The state of bounded instability that nonlinear feedback systems operating at the edge of stability are capable of generating quite clearly encompasses notions of inherent contradiction, feedback loops with a combination of free choice and constraint in which individuals can make a major difference, the operation of positive feedback, the idea of emergence and nonequilibrium concepts. All of these ideas can be brought together within a nonlinear feedback framework to construct a model of organizational dynamics. Furthermore, the concept of boundedly unstable behavior can be used to identify, in a more comprehensive way, the consequences of the notions of paradox, circular feedback loops, positive feedback processes and emergence.

Bounded instability and organizational dynamics

A nonlinear feedback framework for thinking about the strategy process would focus on the states to which an organization might be attracted: stability with either single or multiple equilibria; instability; or some state at the edge of instability. That latter state has been named bounded instability by some, chaos or the edge of chaos by others, and fractal or strange by yet others. There are differences in the precise meaning of all these terms but what they all share in common is that they describe a complex state of behavior which is both stable and unstable at the same time, in which connections between cause and effect disappear for practical purposes and in which therefore specific outcomes are unpredictable. What does all this mean in organizational terms?

All organizations consist of formal and informal systems and when we consider the stability and instability conditions of an organization's dynamics we need to distinguish between these two systems.

. . . stable equilibrium and the forces of integration

The formal system of an organization exists in the first place to carry out existing, repetitive, day-to-day activities as efficiently as possible and it must therefore function according to well-defined hierarchical structures and strictly applied rules and procedures. By its very nature an efficient formal system in an organization is not changeable – it is meant to resist change and sustain the status quo in the

Table 2 Assumptions on system dynamics: established perspectives compared to the alternative

Established perspectives	Alternative perspective
Cause-and-effect links can be identified so that actions can be selected according to long-term outcome. Inertia may or may not block implementation	Cause-and-effect links disappear so that actions cannot be selected according to long-term outcome
Organizations seek or are selected for adapted equilibrium	Agents within organizations sustain far-from-equilibrium conditions of conflict, ambiguity and dialog
Long-term outcomes are either intended by dominant coalitions within organizations or determined by competitive selection	Long-term outcomes emerge out of both spontaneous self-organization and competitive selection
Behavior driven by negative feedback	Behavior driven by both negative and positive feedback

interests of efficiency. The formal organization of any successful organization, innovative or otherwise, will therefore be orderly and stable. It is the powerful forces of integration, maintenance controls, as well as the need to adapt to the environment which pull the whole formal system of an organization toward stable equilibrium (Lawrence and Lorsch, 1967). Where this pull is reinforced by the informal system – a culture primarily satisfying the human desire for security, certainty, and conformity – then an organization as a whole will be attracted to stability. Negative feedback controls in both formal and informal systems will in effect generate behavior which is regular and predictable.

There is ample evidence of the existence and power of this attractor for organizational behavior. In the absence of strenuous effort to the contrary, organizations seem quite ready to slip into a stable bureaucratic state in which they carry on doing the same thing – the very point emphasized by the ecology school and well demonstrated in the studies by Pascale (1990) and Miller (1990).

. . . instability and the forces of division

At the same time as being pulled to stability, however, all organizations are also powerfully pulled in the opposite direction by the forces of division and decentralization (Lawrence and Lorsch, 1967). When the formal systems of an organization move too far in this direction, they become fragmented and unstable (Miller, 1990). As well as this, and even if the emphasis on decentralization does not go too far, there are more powerful forces pulling toward instability in the informal systems of an organization. Informal systems are a vehicle not only for securing conformity but also for satisfying human desires for excitement and innovation, isolation from their environment, aggression, and individuality. When informal systems are dominated by such behavior patterns they pull the entire organization to fragmentation and instability. This is what the attractor to instability means in organizational terms: positive feedback behavior such as political interaction and organizational defense mechanisms (Argyris, 1990) spread disorder through the system. This too is a powerful attractor in organizations – one to which many succumb (Miller, 1990). Again, the inability to escape from attraction to instability is the kind of inertia the ecology school refers to.

. . . chaos and paradox

The alternative to either stability or instability lies at the edge, in the border between them, where both negative and positive feedback, both stability and instability, operate at the same time to yield ever-changing emergent patterns of behavior which are unpredictable. In organizational terms this means that the formal systems operate in a stable way to secure efficient day-to-day operations while the informal system operates in a destabilizing manner to promote change. For an organization to be changeable its shadowy, invisible informal system – the shifting network of social and other informal contacts between people within an organization and across its boundaries – must operate in a state of bounded instability (Stacey, 1993).

This 'chaos' in the informal networks takes the form of opposing ways of behaving which are simultaneously present. For example, while some managers are operating in the formal organization using budgetary forms of control to keep the organization stable, others are operating at the same time in the informal networks to get around those budgetary controls, engaging in amplifying forms of political activity in which they try to undermine the status quo. Other examples of 'chaos' take the form of conflict, as when an organization experiences the clash of counter-cultures, the tensions of political activity, the contention and dialogue through which managers handle ambiguous strategic issues (Nonaka, 1988). There is 'chaos' when managers work in informal groups to learn and develop new strategies – the tensions they generate through the way they interact and exercise their power produce patterns of behavior that fall into recognizable categories, but are always different in specific terms.

Stability, instability or bounded instability?

As with all other nonlinear feedback systems, human organizations have open to them, in very broad terms, three alternative states of behavior: stability, instability, or bounded instability. The properties of these states in organizations are summarized in Table 3. Which leads to success? The answer depends upon the primary task.

'Sticking to the knitting'

Organizations exist because stakeholders want them to perform some primary task. That primary task may be about preserving traditions and beliefs, or providing safety and security from anxiety. In that case an organization operating in some stable equilibrium state is probably best able to perform the primary task. If the primary task of a commercial enterprise were to be that of doing better what it already does well, building on its existing strengths and 'sticking to the knitting,' then a stable

Table 3 The three attractors for organizations

	Formal system	Informal system
Stable equilibrium	Integrated hierarchy and bureaucracy. Negative feedback control systems	Conformist, risk-averse dependent culture. Strongly shared vision and culture
(Functioning formal systems supported by informal systems)		
Instability/randomness/ fragmentation	Too decentralized ineffective control systems	High cultural diversity, conflict, widespread political activity
(Malfunctioning formal systems aggravated by subversive informal systems)		
Bounded instability edge	Integrated hierarchy and bureaucracy. Negative feedback control systems	High cultural diversity, conflict, widespread political activity, dialog. Weakly shared vision, ambiguity, learning
(Functioning formal systems subverted and so changed by informal systems)		

equilibrium state is probably the one required for successful operation. For these purposes the two well-established perspectives of strategic choice and adaptation through competitive selection provide adequate frameworks for understanding the strategy process.

Innovation

However, where the primary task is that of generating new products and services, continually renewing and transforming, then both the stable equilibrium and the unstable equilibrium states are death. In both of these states, systems change repetitively, or they change from time to time in predictable ways, but they are not inherently changeable or continuously innovative. Such organizations cannot be producing anything truly new because that which is truly new is by definition not in the past or the present and so is unpredictable. To be internally and spontaneously changeable and innovative a nonlinear feedback system has to operate in 'chaos', at the edge of instability (Stacey, 1911 [1991]).

When stakeholders demand the new, only those organizations which are internally and spontaneously changeable – those operating at the edge – will survive selection by competition. The well-established perspectives apply when systems are not required to be innovative – then strategic choice may determine outcomes unless the organization is trapped by inertia, in which case it will be weeded out by competitive selection. However, when the requirement is for innovative organizations the strategic choice relates not to specific outcomes but to the kind of organizational dynamic – it has to be a choice to operate at the edge where long-term outcomes are unknowable. Competition then selects out both those that end up with an inappropriate specific outcome and those which have chosen not to operate at the edge.

Sustaining organizations at the edge of instability is far more difficult than giving in to the pull to either stability or instability. In these circumstances we would expect to find a population of organizations consisting of some which are stable in response to a stable primary task, successfully choosing their strategic outcomes; some choosing to operate at the edge of instability in response to a primary task to innovate, with some of these succeeding and others being weeded out by competitive selection; and yet others choosing to operate as stable systems despite a primary task of innovation and therefore gradually, or rapidly, being weeded out by competitive selection; and some succumbing to highly unstable disintegrating forces.

In such a population we will find organizational evidence for almost any specific hypothesis about the strategy process and organizational success, but we will only be able to make sense of it all by trying to understand the dynamics of whole systems.

The third perspective

A 'complex system' perspective is concerned with the dynamics of whole systems. At the individual organizational level it focuses the search for central evolutionary and transformational processes in the informal networks of organizations and the unstable, disorderly dynamics they generate. The application of the science of complexity to organizational life leads to the proposition that changeable organizations are those in which the informal feedback networks are sustained away from equilibrium in a state of bounded instability. The disorderly dynamics of contradiction, conflict, tension, and dialog provide the driving force for changeability.

Informal networks are generally established in rather random ways (Festinger, Schachter, and Back, 1950) depending on chance encounters and social proximity. Networks generally form around issues, and whether individuals are activated to join in a network around an issue often depends on chance. It is not so difficult to see how randomly formed informal networks, characterized by disorderly dynamics, might make an organization changeable in the sense of producing great variety in behavior patterns. But is there any reason to believe that this 'chaos' might produce coherent and useful patterns of behavior? The science of complexity has some insights that may well be of great use here.

Spontaneous self-organization and emergent order

Network feedback systems

Another way to conceive of a feedback system is in terms of a Boolean network (Kauffman, 1991, 1992). A Boolean network consists of a number of elements or cells. Each cell is connected to others, receiving inputs from some or all of those others and sending outputs to all or some of those others. What state each cell is in at any one moment – that is, what it is doing or outputting at any one time – depends upon the inputs it is receiving and the rules it follows to respond to those inputs. In other words the state of an individual cell changes from moment to moment according to the information or energy it receives and the rules it follows for converting these to action or outputs.

An example of a Boolean network

We can identify some fundamental properties of such a network by considering the following simple example. Suppose the network consists of a number of colored light-bulbs each of which can be switched either on or off. Suppose each bulb is assigned a rule which tells it whether it should be switched on or off. For example, one bulb may follow the rule that it will switch on if all the other bulbs to which it is connected are switched on. Or the rule could be that it will switch on as soon as two of those bulbs it is connected to are switched on. The bulb's response is thus determined by the inputs it receives according to a fixed 'decision-making' rule.

Suppose that each cell in the network is randomly connected to others and randomly assigned a different decision-making rule. Suppose also that we start off by randomly assigning on and off positions. We then sit back and watch how the behavior of the system – the pattern of light – unfolds. At each instant each bulb will examine the information on the state of the bulbs linked to it, and applying its decision-making rules to that information the bulb will switch on or off. As it does this it will of course affect the state of some other bulb, and that in turn will trigger a change in another, until eventually the consequences feed back to affect the first bulb. In this way the whole network of bulbs changes state at each moment in time and the behavior it displays will depend upon the way in which the bulbs are interconnected – the way in which the network is wired up.

Attraction to instability: randomness

When every element is wired up to every other then the whole system behaves randomly, never repeating a given pattern of on/off. Any tiny change in the initial pattern from which the system is started will lead to completely different subsequent patterns over time. It is hardly surprising, perhaps, that a system in which each element is connected to all others, each following randomly selected rules, should behave in a completely random way.

Attraction to stability: emergent order

However, when each bulb is connected to only two others and random switching rules are allocated to all the bulbs, the whole system soon settles down into a fixed orderly state in which there are stable patches of light.

The important point, then, is that random local rules of behavior can result in emergent order at a global level, and whether there is order or not depends upon the degree of connectedness between elements of the network. When the order emerges, it is a surprise, because there is nothing in all the random individual decision rules which determines it. Instead, the emergent patterns are a property of the system, of the interactions rather than the individuals.

Again, we have seen a feedback system which is attracted to stability when it is configured in one way and to random instability when it is configured in another.

When the interconnections between the elements in a network are sparse, then orderly, stable global behavior emerges from random local interactions and the system remains stuck in that behavior. As a richer pattern of interconnection is established the system becomes more changeable until, when everything is connected to everything else, the system becomes random, with patterns of behavior changing so fast that we can make little sense of them. Analysis of cellular automata – a system of cells interconnected by arbitrary decision rules in much the same way as Boolean networks – has also shown that these systems produce a simple stable behavior when connectivity is sparse and random patterns when connectivity is very rich.

At the edge: endless variety

However, just before such systems go completely random, at the edge of chaos, we find another form of behavior: coherent structures that grow, split apart, and recombine in different patterns in a never-ending way (Wolfram, 1986). What form these emergent patterns will take is unpredictable – the only way to find out is to run the system.

The work on Boolean networks and cellular automata has demonstrated that network systems consisting of random feedback connections at a local level can spontaneously produce emergent global order. When linkages are sparse, that order will take a frozen unchangeable form. However, when a rich pattern of interconnections is established, the system becomes changeable, with new forms continually emerging. If the interconnections become too rich, however, the system becomes so hyperactive that it becomes difficult to make any sense of it.

Feedback networks in organizations

This concept of a network connecting individual elements is of course already widely used in the management literature (Nohria and Eccles, 1992). The formal reporting structure of an organization is one kind of network in which the connections between one individual and another are centrally established, fixed, and clearly defined – there is nothing random about the interconnections between one person and another in formal organizational structures.

In the informal organization, however, we encounter what is to all intents and purposes a Boolean network. Each individual in an informal organization is linked to a number of other individuals both within his or her own organization and with individuals in others. These links are random in the sense that they come about through what largely amount to chance social encounters (Festinger *et al.*, 1950). When an individual is 'switched on' by some issue, that individual links up with others in his or her network, potentially 'switching them on' too. Some later issue may prompt the same individual to activate a different part of his or her network, and which part is activated may depend significantly on chance encounters (Mueller, 1986).

What the analysis of Boolean networks and cellular automata has shown is that such a process of random connections in a network can produce different forms of order – different patterns of behavior – depending upon the extent of connectivity across the network. Thus we would expect to find that stable organizations are those in which there are relatively few informal connections between people within and across organizational boundaries. But where an organization has an informal system in which there are rich, random patterns of connection in this informal network we would expect to find that such an organization produces great variety in behavior – it will be changeable. And that changeability will be directly related to how close behavior patterns are to chaotic ones. Limited random connectivity across a network produces emergent order that remains stable for lengthy periods but rich patterns of random connectivity produce a changing variety of emergent patterns.

Connectivity in networks

These findings on the relationship between the number of connections between the cells of a network and the changeability of the behavior which that network produces can be related to the research into strong and weak ties in the network systems of organizations. Granovetter (1973) demonstrated that organizations produced greater variety in behavior when the informal ties between people are weak rather than strong. Strong ties exist when people spend much time together, are emotionally involved, mutually confiding and provide reciprocal services. The effect of strong ties is to bind people together, making it likely that behavior will be repetitive and uniform. Weak ties, however, provide 'bridges' to other parts of a social system through which variety may be imported into a cluster of people held together by strong ties. Krackhardt (1992), however, argues that strong effective ties increase feelings of security and can thus make a group of people more likely to change: strong ties might then be associated with more variety in behavior than weak ties.

The analysis of Boolean networks suggests that it is the number of random ties rather than their individual strength or weakness that determines the variety in the behavior of a system. In Boolean network terms, a strong tie means that when cell or 'bulb' x turns on then so will y and vice versa; and a weak tie would be something along these lines: cell x turns on if w, y and z all also turn on, and y turns on only if z, m and u turn on. From this we can see that where the number of ties or connections is small, they are likely to be predominantly of the strong type, and where the number of connections is large the tendency will be for them to be of the weak type. Large numbers of ties imply weak ties and this means that the analysis of Boolean networks produces conclusions consistent with Granovetter's findings. The point, however, is that a large number of randomly distributed ties will include both the strong and the weak and it is the number and the randomness that are important rather than the strength or the weakness itself.

Implications for the strategy process: self-organization

Nonlinear dynamics and the analysis of Boolean networks and cellular automata suggest an alternative perspective for the strategy process: one that focuses on the informal feedback networks to be found in every organization in which individuals randomly establish linkages among themselves. The possibility of emergent order is a fundamental property of such feedback networks and changeability is also a fundamental property when the pattern of connectivity is rich enough. From this perspective the central evolutionary and transformational processes in organizations are ones of spontaneous self-organization, close to Hayek's notion (1948), which make an organization changeable and produce emergent new patterns of behavior in the manner postulaled by Giddens, Hayek, Schumpeter, and others.

The science of complexity leads to another proposition about changeable organizations: changeability becomes an internal property of an organization when its informal network system, consisting of self-organizing patterns of connections between people within and across its boundaries, is richly connected enough to operate on the edge of instability, where it produces ever-changing emergent patterns of behavior.

Discussion and conclusions

The established perspectives on the strategy process assume that it is possible to identify connections between specific causes and specific effects, specific actions and specific outcomes. This makes it legitimate to think about a human organization as a system in which some outsider (the consultant) or privileged insider (the leader) is able to make choices about the future direction and destination of the organization and then require others to follow a master plan. This is possible because the existence of cause-and-effect links means that the future is in the present and can be extracted by analysis or intuition.

The science of complexity demonstrates that for a system to be innovative, creative, and changeable it must be driven far from equilibrium where it can make use of disorder, irregularity, and difference as essential elements in the process of change. But far from equilibrium the links between cause and effect disappear because positive feedback enables a system to escalate many tiny changes into globally different behavior patterns. Sensitivity to initial conditions destroys identifiable links between individual actions and global outcomes. The state a system is in now is the result of every detail of its history, and what it will become can only be known if one knows every detail of its future development, and the only way one can do that is to let the development occur. The future of such a system is open and hence unknowable until it occurs.

It follows quite clearly that no expert outsider and no privileged insider can know what the destination or direction will be until it occurs. Thus no one can be in control. Individuals and groups of individuals in an organization can choose, plan, and control their next intervention but they cannot choose, plan, or control the long-term outcome of that intervention. Instead, long-term outcomes emerge from a process which is basically self-organizing. The only alternative is to allow an organization to give in to the powerful pull to equilibrium where all will be predictable – but that ultimately means death because significant change is so difficult. Competition – the selection of the fittest – weeds out all organizations that are allowed to move away from the edge of instability.

The science of complexity also provides a framework for bringing together into an alternative perspective a number of disparate ideas (paradox, circular causality, positive feedback, creative destruction, spontaneous self-organization, emergence) that are to be found outside the most well-established perspectives of the strategy processes. From this third perspective we deal with the three issues identified at the beginning of this paper in ways that are completely different from the well-established perspectives:

1   As far as 'systemic properties' are concerned, the alternative perspective focuses not on equilibrium but on a far-from-equilibrium paradox where the dynamics are both stable and unstable at the same time. This chaotic behavior is located in those informal networks which people spontaneously and randomly establish amongst themselves in a self-organizing manner and is activated when the pattern of connectivity is rich enough. Such informal networks may be engines of enquiry – the organizational instrument for exploring the space of possibilities.

2.   As far as 'choice vs. determinism and constraint' is concerned, the alternative perspective focuses on the possibility of open-ended choices available to agents made possible by chaotic dynamics, but constrained by the feedback structure of the system. Choice is possible not because there are a limited number of predictable equilibria, but because even though the system may be deterministic with regard to structure, it is open-ended with regard to outcome. Constraints do come from the tendency to inertia but this is not inevitable: the really important constraints are the self-organizing feedback structures people establish amongst themselves.

3   As far as the 'intention vs. emergence' issue is concerned, the alternative perspective focuses on processes of evolution and transformation taking the form of self-organizing network activities provoked by disorder, conflict, and disagreement. These processes produce emergent rather than intentional outcomes.

Implications for the research agenda

These conclusions form the basis for a somewhat different research agenda in the field of strategy process. Traditionally, the research questions posed are conditioned by the notion that strategic management should reduce the level of uncertainty, so diminishing the element of surprise in the development of an organization. The complexity theory framework, however, poses a different question: how do/should managers conduct themselves in the presence of irremovable, indeed desirable, uncertainty, surprise, unknowability, and open-endedness?

More specifically, the complexity theory framework puts long-term planning and strategic analysis into context. Analytical thinking and planning processes can only apply to repetitive, predictable activities since the ability to analyze and plan rests firmly on the existence of causal connections and predictability. Analysis and planning are processes required to build on existing strengths and do more efficiently what is already done well; that is, to repeat the past more and more efficiently. Essentially the same conclusion must apply to the notion of 'a shared vision' when that notion refers to some consensual picture of a future state – in changeable systems it is not possible to specify meaningful pictures of a future state, and any pictures which are specified cannot be connected back to the actions required to realize them because cause and effect links disappear. Furthermore, consensus around some picture of a future state removes the chaos which changeable systems must experience if they are to innovate. This leads to two questions: if they cannot plan and envision the future, what do managers actually do when they innovate, when they face the unknowable? Why do managers continue to prepare long-term plans and talk about shared visions in response to the need to innovate when these are not appropriate responses?

Self-organization and innovation

First, consider what managers actually do when they innovate. The processes required for creativity are those of intuition and reasoning by analogy, and the new insights these processes lead to are amplified through an organization when managers operate in informal networks to promote significant change. When they innovate, managers rely on self-organizing political and learning processes to produce an emerging, unfolding but unpredictable future. This can only happen when the informal networks are in a state of 'chaos,' that is, tension and conflict which generate dialogue. In such situations individuals and groups may learn and they may make a difference because tiny actions they take could escalate up through the system into major organizational changes – it is the positive feedback aspect of chaos that makes it possible for individuals to make a difference. There is no guarantee that this will happen, however, and the price is that the consequences of any individual intervention are unpredictable, indeed unknowable. Consequently new strategic direction, renewal, transformation, and innovation can only emerge. They must be negotiated in real time and cannot be arranged in advance.

The focus of research needs to be shifted firmly towards understanding the group dynamics of those spontaneously self-organizing political and organizational learning processes through which organizations innovate. The science of complexity suggests a focus on how random connections between people and the simple decision rules they use can lead to complex global patterns of behavior taking the form of new strategic direction and organizational renewal. Research work currently being done on networks and learning organizations is thereby put at the center of strategy process research. This research work should pay explicit attention to the positive role played by disorderly dynamics.

Defense against anxiety

Next, consider why managers continue to use planning processes. Planning and analysis are the processes of efficiency – they are required if an organization is to be able to carry out its repetitive day-to-day tasks. It follows that effective management is a paradox – managers must operate in a hierarchy using formal planning systems and analytical processes to conduct their business efficiently, but they must also operate in an informal network that seeks to undermine those hierarchies and systems in the interests of creativity and changeability. Understanding how this is done is a research program of great importance to strategic management.

But there is more to the use of planning processes and analytical techniques. It is clear that they are employed in circumstances in which a moment's reflection shows them to be inappropriate – they are processes which have for a long time been shown to be inapplicable to conditions of great uncertainty and yet they are used in just such circumstances. This suggests that managers use such routines and procedures to defend themselves against the anxiety which great uncertainty provokes; the literature on psychoanalytical approaches to organizations (Menzies, 1975; Jacques, 1955; Kets de Vries and Miller, 1984; Kets de Vries, 1980; Hirschhorn, 1990) therefore needs to be incorporated into strategic management thinking and the posing of research questions.

Leadership

The above conclusions have very important implications for the nature of leadership. Much of the research on leadership focuses on that type appropriate to conditions in which the leader can form some idea of where an organization is heading. But what does leadership mean when powerful figures in an organization may be able to choose, plan, and control the next interventions of large numbers of others but cannot choose, plan, or intend the long-term outcomes of those interventions? Research is required to understand more clearly how leaders affect and are affected by the informal networks of which they are a part, and what they need to do to encourage those networks to function in a manner which promotes conflict and dialog within boundaries.

To understand the kind of leadership required in turbulent times we need to understand more about the nature of the boundaries around the conflict, which is essential to organizational learning and how leaders may be able to manage those boundaries more effectively. More attention also needs to be paid to the notion of leadership which is located not simply in one person but shifts from person to person according to task needs or the emotional states of groups of people operating in informal networks (Bion, 1961). The causes and results of neurotic forms of leadership become particularly important here.

The complexity theory framework also has implications for the balance between strategy content and strategy process research. If futures are unknowable then it is impossible to select content areas that will be relevant for more than a rather short time period. The really fundamental questions and long-lasting 'answers' will relate to process.

Finally, the complexity perspective poses this question: how useful is the distinction between the tactical and the strategic in a world in which undetectable tiny actions can escalate into major outcomes, making it impossible to say in advance whether an action is tactical or strategic?

Implications for research methodology

The dominant frame of reference for research in management and organization is the reductionist one of testing hypothesized connections between a specific cause, usually in the environment, and a specific effect, usually in a part of the organization being studied. It is most usual to test these hypotheses using cross-sectional data on organizations obtained from statistics, public reports, questionnaires, and interviews.

The practical difficulties of this approach are of course well understood. First, the evidence and data collected to test hypotheses are based on what people in organizations say they do. It is now widely accepted, however, that behavior in organizations is driven by theories-in-use which often differ dramatically from espoused theories (Argyris and Schon, 1978) – people frequently say one thing and do another. It is also clear that behavior in organizations is determined to a significant extent by culture; that is, shared assumptions below the level of awareness on what to think and do and how to think and do it (Schein, 1985). The findings of cognitive psychology on how people make sense of the world by using partial mental models make it clear that managers use recipes, or causal maps, that they are usually unaware of (Johnson, 1987). The importance of tacit knowledge in the conduct of management has been established (Nonaka, 1991). This growing emphasis on what is tacit, below the level of awareness and contradictory, makes it unlikely that the straightforward application of questionnaire, public report, and interview data to the testing of hypotheses can be all that reliable.

In addition to these practical difficulties, there are also matters of principle. The reductionist approach of testing hypotheses about causality independently of each other assumes that the systems being studied are linear, or can be approximated by linear systems, or are nonlinear but are required to operate in states of stable equilibrium. From a complexity perspective, however, organizations are essentially nonlinear systems which cannot be approximated by any linear form and to be creative they have to operate far from equilibrium. For such systems it is extremely difficult to find the specific causes of specific effects. Even where it is possible to do so with hindsight, that provides little useful information about the future.

If innovative organizations are nonlinear feedback systems operating far from equilibrium then reductionist approaches to researching them are likely to produce seriously misleading conclusions. Cross-sectional tests of linear causal hypothesis will simply be interesting exercises in hindsight.

Instead, research will have to focus on the meanings of the irregular patterns of behavior observed and on reasoning about the kind of system those patterns are being generated by. Instead of looking for causes and effects it is necessary to look for patterns and their systemic implications.

The specific methods appropriate for this kind of research do exist but are relatively rarely applied to strategy process research – longitudinal studies, action science, the ethnographic approach, and clinical methods. Action science and ethnography are well known but some further clarification of the clinical method may be in order. Hirschhorn (1990) describes the clinical method as one which uses incidents, transcripts, and the researcher's own feelings to interpret events and assess both manifest and latent meanings. The goal is to find a common thread of meaning in a person's or a group's *particular* action and experience.

To summarize, in the dominant approach to management research we establish a theoretical causal hypothesis and then, adopting the role of uninvolved experimenter, we gather data to test the hypothesis – we formulate a general theoretical model and then seek to apply it directly to particular experience. In the alternative ethnographic and clinical approaches the researcher, having been educated both by acquiring theoretical models and by the experience of previous interventions in social systems, approaches a particular new experience without a specific model in mind – general theoretical models are abandoned as far as possible in the attempt to identify meaning in the new experience.

The method is one of gathering data from free-floating discussions and informal interpretation, avoiding the temptation to 'intellectualize'; that is, force experience into neat models and, by so doing, erect defenses against considering what the new experience itself might mean. The data gathered through free-floating discussion can be used to develop hypotheses to explain the specific experience being studied and these can then be tested with the people concerned. It is also important to remain aware of the fact that because this approach to research is primarily concerned with what is tacit and unconscious it will have to confront the defenses that we all, to one degree or another, use to defend ourselves against bringing the tacit and the unconscious into consciousness for fear of the anxiety it may unleash. For this reason the researcher needs to look for what is odd, contradictory, and paradoxical in what people say. Researchers need to be primarily concerned not with factual, concretely descriptive language, but with the metaphors and the images people use.

From a complexity perspective research will be unable to yield predictors of or prescriptions for long-term innovative success – research will have to focus on explanation instead, on hypotheses about whole systems, their dynamics, the conditions under which they will display different kinds of dynamic, and the relationship between the dynamic and innovative success.

Acknowledgements

The author would like to thank the following colleagues at the Business School of Hertfordshire University for the contributions they made in discussions to an earlier draft of this paper: Jerry Forester, Geraldine Healy, Bernard James, Al Rainnie, Keith Randle, Ivor Simpkin, and Ian Spurr.

References

Anderson, P. W., K. J. Arrow, and D. Pines (1988). *The Economy as an Evolving Complex System*, Addison-Wesley, Reading, MA.

Argyris, C. (1990). *Overcoming Organizational Defenses: Facilitating Organizational Learning*. Allyn & Bacon/Prentice-Hall, Boston, MA.

Argyris, C. and D. Schon (1978). *Organizational Learning: A Theory of Action Perspective*. Addison-Wesley, Reading, MA.

Arthur, W. B. (1988). 'Self-reinforcing mechanisms in economics'. In P. W. Anderson, K. J. Arrow and D. Pines (eds.), *The Economy as an Evolving Complex System*. Addison-Wesley, Reading, MA, pp. 9–32.

Bion, W. R. (1961). *Experiences in Groups and Other Papers*. Tavistock Publications, London.

Chakravarthy, B. S. and Y. Doz (1992). 'Strategy process research: Focusing on corporate self-renewal', *Strategic Management Journal*, Summer Special Issue, **13**, pp. 5–14.

Festinger, L., S. Schachter, and K. Back (1950). *Social Pressures in Informal Groups: A Study of a Housing Project*. Harper & Row, New York.

Fombrun, C. J. and A. Ginsberg (1990). 'Shifting gears: Enabling change in corporate aggressiveness', *Strategic Management Journal*, **11** (4), pp. 297–307.

Forrester, J. (1958). 'Industrial dynamics: A major breakthrough for decision-making', *Harvard Business Review*, **36** (4), pp. 37–66.

Forrester, J. (1961). *Industrial Dynamics*. MIT Press, Cambridge, MA.

Gell-Mann, M. (1994). *The Quark and the Jaguar*. Freeman, New York.

Giddens, A. (1979). *Central Problems in Social Theory*. Macmillan, London.

Ginsberg, A. (1988). 'Measuring and modelling changes in strategy: Theoretical foundations and empirical directions', *Strategic Management Journal*, **9** (6), pp. 559–575.

Gleick, J. (1987). *Chaos: The Making of a New Science*. Heinemann, London.

Goldstein, J. (1994). *The Unshackled Organization*. Productivity Press, Portland, OR.

Gouldner, A. (1964). *Patterns of Industrial Bureaucracy*. Free Press, New York.

Granovetter, M. S. (1973). 'The strength of weak ties', *American Journal of Sociology*, **78**, pp. 1360–1380.

Hall, R. I. (1976). 'A system pathology of an organization: The rise and fall of the *Saturday Evening Post*', *Administrative Science Quarterly*, **21**, pp. 185–211.

Hampden-Turner, C. (1990). *Charting the Corporate Mind*. Free Press/Macmillan, New York.

Hannan, M. and J. Freeman (1977). 'The population ecology of organizations', *American Journal of Sociology*, **82**, pp. 929–964.

Hayek, F. A. (1948) *Individualism and Economic Order*. University of Chicago Press, Chicago, IL.

Hirschhorn, L. (1990). *The Workplace Within: Psychodynamics of Organizational Life*. MIT Press, Cambridge, MA.

Hyman, R. (1987). 'Strategy or structure? Capital, labour and control', *Work, Employment and Society*, **1** (1), pp. 25–55.

Jacques, E. (1955). 'Social systems as a defence against persecutory and defensive anxiety'. In M. Klein, P. Heimann and P. Money-Kyrle (eds.), *New Directions in Psychoanalysis*. Tavistock Publications, London, pp. 25–44.

Johnson, G. (1987). *Strategic Change and the Management Process*. Blackwell, Oxford.

Kauffman, S. A. (August 1991). 'Antichaos and adaptation', *Scientific American*, pp. 78–84.

Kauffman, S. A. (1992). *Origins of Order: Self Organization and Selection in Evolution*. Oxford University Press, Oxford.

Kets de Vries, M. F. R. (1980). *Organizational Paradoxes: Clinical Approaches to Management*. Tavistock Publications, London.

Kets de Vries, M. F. R. and D. Miller (1984). *The Neurotic Organization*. Jossey-Bass, San Francisco, CA.

Krackhardt, D. (1992). 'The strength of strong ties: The importance of philos in organizations'. In N. Nohria and R. G. Eccles (eds.), *Networks and Organizations*. Harvard University Press, Boston, MA, pp. 216–239.

Lawrence, P. R. and J. W. Lorsch (1967). *Organization and Environment*. Harvard University Press, Cambridge, MA.

Menzies, I. (1975). 'A case study in the functioning of social systems as a defense against anxiety'. In A. Coleman and W. H. Bexton (eds.), *Group Relations Reader*, A.K. Rice Institute, Washington, DC, pp. 281–312.

Merton, R. K. (1957). *Bureaucratic Structure and Personality in Social Theory and Social Structure*. Free Press, New York.

Miller, D. (1990). *The Icarus Paradox: How Excellent Organizations Can Bring about Their Own Downfall*. Harper Business, New York.

Mintzberg, H. and J. A. Waters (1985). 'Of strategies deliberate and emergent', *Strategic Management Journal*, **6** (3), pp. 257–272.

Mueller, R. K. (1986). *Corporate Networking: Building Channels for Information and Influence*. Free Press, New York.

Nicolis, G. and L. Prigogine (1989). *Exploring Complexity: An Introduction*. W. H. Freeman, New York.

Nohria, N. and R. G. Eccles (1992). *Networks and Organizations*. Harvard Business University Press, Boston, MA.

Nonaka, I. (1988). 'Creating organizational order out of chaos: Self renewal in Japanese firms', *California Management Review*, Spring, pp. 57–73.

Nonaka, I. (November–December 1991). 'The knowledge-creating company', *Harvard Business Review*, pp. 96–104.

Parker, D. and R. D. Stacey (1994). 'Chaos management and economics', IEA Hobart Paper 125, Institute of Economic Affairs, London.

Pascale, R. T. (1990). *Managing on the Edge: How Successful Companies use Conflict to Stay Ahead*. Viking Penguin, London.

Peters, E. E. (1991). *Chaos and Order in the Capital Markets: A New View of Cycles, Prices and Market Volatility*. Wiley, New York.

Pettigrew, A. (1973). *The Politics of Organizational Decision Making*. Tavistock Publications, London.

Pettigrew, A. (1977). 'Strategy formation as a political process', *International Studies of Management and Organisation*, **7** (2), pp. 78–87.

Pettigrew, A. (1985). *The Awakening Giant*. Blackwell, Oxford.

Pfeffer, J. (1981). *Power in Organizations*. Ballinger, Cambridge, MA.

Prigogine, I. and I. Stengers (1984). *Order Out of Chaos: Man's New Dialogue with Nature*. Bantam, New York.

Quinn, R. E. and K. S. Cameron (1988). *Paradox and Transformation*. Ballinger/Harper & Row, New York.

Schein, E. H. (1985). *Organizational Change and Leadership*, Jossey-Bass, San Francisco, CA.

Schumpeter, J. A. (1934). *The Theory of Economic Development*. Harvard University Press, Cambridge, MA.

Senge, P. M. (1990). *The Fifth Discipline: The Art and Practice of the Learning Organization*. Doubleday Currency, New York.

Stacey, R. D. (1991). *The Chaos Frontier: Creative Strategic Control for Business*. Butterworth-Heinemann, Oxford.

Stacey, R. D. (1992). *Managing the Unknowable: The Strategic Boundaries Between Order and Chaos*. Jossey-Bass, San Francisco, CA. (Also published in the U.K. as *Managing Chaos*, Kogan Page, London.)

Stacey, R. D. (1993). *Strategic Management and Organisational Dynamics*. Pitman, London.

Thompson, J. D. and A. Tuden (1959). 'Strategies, structures and processes of organizational decisions'. In J. D. Thompson and J. Woodward (eds.), *Comparative Studies in Administration*, University of Pittsburgh Press, Pittsburgh, PA.

Waldrop, M. M. (1992). *Complexity: The Emerging Science at the Edge of Order and Chaos*. Viking, London.

Weick, K. (1969/1979). *The Social Psychology of Organizing*. Addison-Wesley, Reading, MA.

Wheatley, M. J. (1992). *Leadership and the New Science: Learning about Organisation from an Orderly Universe*. Berrett-Koehler Publishers, San Francisco, CA.

Wolfram, S. (September 1986). 'Computer software in science and mathematics', *Scientific American*, pp. 19–26.

Zajac, E. J. and M. S. Kraatz (1993). 'A diametric forces model of strategic change: Assessing the antecedents and consequences of restructuring in the higher education industry', *Strategic Management Journal*, Summer Special Issue, **14**, pp. 83–103.

Zajac, E. J. and S. M. Shortell (1989). 'Changing generic strategies: Likelihood, direction and performance', *Strategic Management Journal*, **10** (5), pp. 413–431.

Zimmerman, B. J. (1992). 'The inherent drive towards chaos'. In P. Lorange, B. Chakravarthy, A. Van de Ven and J. Roos (eds.), *Implementing Strategic Processes: Change, Learning and Cooperation*. Blackwell, London, pp. 35–51.

Margaret J. Wheatley

CHAOS AND THE STRANGE ATTRACTOR OF MEANING

Thus before all else, there came into being the Gaping Chasm, Chaos, but there followed the broad-chested Earth, Gaia, the forever-secure seat of the immortals . . . and also Love, Eros, the most beautiful of the immortal gods, he who breaks limbs

(Hesiod)

Several thousand years ago, when primal forces haunted human imagination, great gods arose in myths to explain the creation of the world. At the beginning was Chaos, the endless, yawning chasm devoid of form or fullness. And there also was Gaia, mother of the earth, she who brought forth form and stability. In Greek story, Chaos and Gaia were partners, two primordial powers engaged in a duet of opposition and resonance, creating everything we know.

These two mythic figures again inhabit our imagination and our science. They have taken on new life as scientists explore more deeply the workings of our universe. For me, this return to mythic wisdom is both intriguing and comforting. It signifies that even as we live in the midst of increasing turbulence, a new relationship with Chaos is possible. Like ancient Gaia, we are being asked to partner with Chaos, understanding it as the life process that releases our creative power. From Chaos' great chasm comes both support and opposition, creating the "light without which no form would be visible" (Bonnefoy 1991, 369–70). We, the generative force, give birth to form and meaning, organizing Chaos through our creativity. We fill the void with worlds of our own making and turn our backs on him. But we must remember that deep within our Gaian centers, so the Greeks and our science tell us, is the necessary heart of Chaos.

The heart of chaos has been revealed with modern computers. Watching the behavior of a chaotic system as it is tracked on a computer screen is a mesmerizing experience. The computer records the evolution of the system, displaying each moment of the system's chaotic behavior as a point of light on the screen. Because of the computer's speed, we can soon observe how the system is evolving. The system careens back and forth with raucous unpredictability, never showing up in the same spot twice. But as we watch, this chaotic behavior weaves into a pattern, and before our eyes order emerges on the screen. The chaotic movements of the system have formed themselves into a shape. The shape is a "strange attractor," and what has appeared on the screen is the order inherent in chaos (see illustration) [. . .].

Strange attractors evoke feelings of awe in most who observe them. Poetic language frequently creeps into the descriptions offered by scientists. Other types of attractors are well-known, but these newly discovered ones were named *strange* by two scientists, David Ruelle and Floris Takens, because they wanted a name that was deeply suggestive (Gleick 1987, 131). As Ruelle says, "The name is beautiful and well-suited to these astonishing objects, of which we understand so little" (in Coveney and Highfield 1990, 204).

To describe this dance between turbulence and order, Ruelle reaches for several metaphors: "These systems of curves, these clouds of points, suggest sometimes

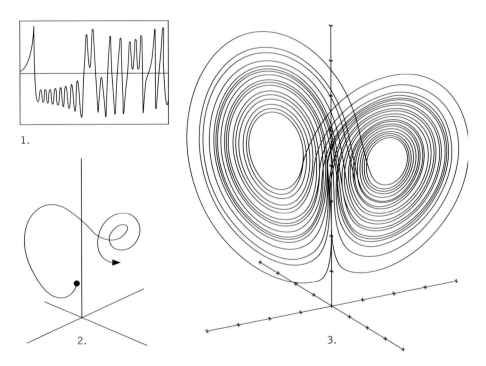

Strange attractor. 1. Traditional plots of one variable show a system in chaos. 2. If the system is plotted in multiple dimensions in phase space, the shape of chaos, the strange attractor, gradually becomes visible. 3. As the system's chaotic wanderings are plotted over time (the system never repeats its behavior exactly), the attractor reveals itself. This butterfly or owl-shaped strange attractor reveals the order inherent in a chaotic system. Order always is displayed as a shape or pattern. *From Gleick, 1987. Used with permission.*

fireworks or galaxies, sometimes strange and disquieting vegetal proliferations. A realm lies there of forms to explore, of harmonies to discover" (in Coveney and Highfield 1990, 206). Briggs and Peat paint a similarly compelling picture of the drama and beauty of strange attractors forming:

> Wandering into certain bands, a system is . . . dragged toward dis-integration, transformation, and chaos. Inside other bands, systems cycle dynamically, maintaining their shapes for long periods of time. But eventually all orderly systems will feel the wild, seductive pull of the strange chaotic attractor. (1989, 76–77)

Chaos has always partnered with order – a concept that contradicts our common definition of chaos – but until we could see it with computers, we saw only turbulence, energy without predictable form. Chaos is the last state before a system plunges into random behavior where no order exists. Not all systems move into chaos, but if a system becomes unstable, it will move first into a period of oscillation, swinging back and forth between two different states. After this oscillating stage, the next state is chaos, and it is then that the wild gyrations begin. However, in the realm of chaos, where everything should fall apart, the strange attractor emerges, and we observe order, not chaos.

A strange attractor becomes visible on a computer screen because scientists have developed new ways of observing the system's wild and rich behavior. Its behavior is displayed in an abstract mathematical space called phase space. In phase space, scientists can track a system's movement in many more dimensions than was previously possible. Shapes that could not be seen in only two dimensions now appear, dancing on the screen, luminous and enticing.

In phase space, the system operates within a basin of attraction. This figurative basin is where the system explores millions of possibilities, wandering to different places, sampling new configurations of itself. But its wandering and experimentation respect a hidden boundary which is gradually revealed as the shape of its strange attractor. The system does not wander off into infinity. It is important to note that this boundary is not defined *for* the system; scientists do not create it. The boundary *lives within the system*, becoming visible as it explores its space of possibilities. The order is already present; it has now become discernible.

To see how chaotic processes reveal the order inherent in a system requires that we shift our vision from the parts to the whole. Briggs and Peat, in their exploration of the mirror world of chaos and order, suggest that wholeness is "what rushes in under the guise of chaos whenever scientists try to separate and measure dynamical systems as if they were composed of parts . . ." (1989, 74–75). The strange attractors that form on our screens, Briggs and Peat suggest, are not the shape of chaos. They are the shape of wholeness. When we concentrate on individual moments or fragments of experience, we see only chaos. But if we stand back and look at what is taking shape, we see order. Order always displays itself as patterns that develop over time.

In much of new science, we are challenged by paradoxical concepts – matter that is immaterial, disequilibrium that leads to stability, and now chaos that is ordered. Yet the paradox of chaos and order is not new. As ancient myths and new science both teach, every system that seeks to stay alive must hold within it the potential for chaos, "a creature slumbering deep inside the perfectly ordered system" (Briggs and Peat 1989, 62). It is chaos' great destructive energy that dissolves the past and gives us the gift of a new future. It releases us from the imprisoning patterns of the past by offering us its wild ride into newness. Only chaos creates the abyss in which we can recreate ourselves.

Most of us have experienced this ride of chaos in our own lives. At the personal level, chaos has gone by many names, including "dark night of the soul" or "depression." Always, the experience is a profound loss of meaning – nothing makes sense in the way it did before; nothing seems to hold the same value as it once did. These dark nights have been well-documented in many spiritual traditions and cultures. They are part of the human experience, how we participate in the spiral dance of form, formlessness, and new form. As we reflect on the times when we personally have descended into chaos, we can notice that as it ends, we emerge changed, stronger in some ways, new. We have held in us the dance of creation and learned that growth always requires passage through the fearful realms of disintegration.

Chaos' role in the emergence of new order is so well-known that it seems strange that Western culture has denied its part so vehemently. In the dream of dominion over all nature, we believed we could eliminate chaos from life. We believed there were straight lines to the top. If we set a goal or claimed a vision, we *would* get there, never looking back, never forced to descend into confusion or despair. These beliefs led us far from life, far from the processes by which newness is created. And it is only now, as modern life grows ever more turbulent and control slips away, that we are willing again to contemplate chaos (see Hayles 1990). Whether we explore its dynamics through new science or ancient myths, the lesson is important. The destruction created by chaos is necessary for the creation of anything new.

Chaos theory studies a particular variety of chaos, known as deterministic chaos. In an interesting way, this branch of science became involved in a debate that had been going on in philosophy and spiritual thought for many centuries. Is this a deterministic world where our lives are predetermined? But if this is true, what about free will? It was this unresolved tension between predictability and freedom that attracted some early scientists of chaos. The science seemed to resolve this argument; it provided an explanation for how freedom functions in an orderly universe. The shape of the entire system is predictable or predetermined. But how this shape takes form is through individual acts of free agency: "The system is deterministic, but you can't say what it's going to do next" (Gleick 1987, 251). Or as organizational planner T.J. Cartwright puts it, "Chaos is order without predictability" (1991, 44).

The shape of chaos materializes from information feeding back on itself and changing in the process. This is the familiar process of iteration and feedback described in much of new science. It is the same process that results in self-organization, and also the creation of fractals [. . .]. This process succeeds in creating newness because it takes place in a system that is nonlinear. Nonlinearity has been described by Coveney and Highfield as "getting more than you bargained for" (1990, 184). In the past, science tended to ignore nonlinearity because it was just too hard to deal with. Science was focused on prediction, and nonlinear systems refuse prediction. To avoid the messiness and pursue the dream of determinism, nonlinear equations were "linearized." Once they were warped in this way, they could be handled by simpler mathematics. But this process of linearizing nature's non-linear character blinded scientists to life's processes. Life, in the words of scientist Ian Stewart, is "relentlessly non linear." The recognition of nonlinearity and the newer mathematical tools of chaos theory have made it possible once again to see more clearly how life works (Capra 1996, Ch. 6).

In a nonlinear world, very slight variances, things so small as to be indiscernible, can amplify into completely unexpected results. When a system is nonlinear and webbed with feedback loops, repetition feeds the change back on itself, causing it to amplify and grow. After several iterations, a variance that was too small to notice can cause enormous impact, far beyond anything predicted. The system suddenly takes off in unexpected directions or responds in surprising ways. One familiar example of this is the proverbial straw that broke the camel's back. No one knew that such a small difference would cause collapse because no one could see what else had been going on inside the camel. In a nonlinear world, there is no relation between the strength of the cause and the consequence of the effect.

From classical science, our culture has come to believe that small differences average out, that slight variances converge toward a point, and that approximations can give a fairly accurate picture of what might happen. But chaos theory exposes the world's nonlinear dynamics, which in no way resemble the neat charts and figures we have drawn so skillfully. In a nonlinear system, the *slightest* variation can lead to catastrophic results. Hypothetically, were we to create a difference in two values as small as rounding them off to the thirty-first decimal place (calculating numbers this large requires astronomical computing power), after only one hundred iterations the whole calculation would go askew. The two systems would have diverged from each other in unpredictable ways. This behavior demonstrates that even infinitesimal differences can be far from inconsequential. "Chaos takes them," physicist James Crutchfield says, "and blows them up in your face" (in Briggs and Peat 1989, 73).

Edward Lorenz, a meteorologist, first drew public attention to this with his now famous "butterfly effect." Does the flap of a butterfly wing in Tokyo, Lorenz queried, affect a tornado in Texas (or a thunderstorm in New York)? Though unfortunate for the future of accurate weather prediction, his answer was "yes." And in organizations, we frequently experience these "flaps." A casual comment at a meeting flies through the organization, growing and mutating into a huge misunderstanding that requires enormous time and energy to resolve. And many organizations have learned that events occurring in a relatively minor part of their business suddenly grow to threaten their overall viability. Before disaster struck in Union Carbide's plant in Bhopal, India, the plant contributed a mere 4% to corporate profits. However, this horrific tragedy led to a major restructuring of the entire company and a serious decrease in its overall valuation. And in Alaska, how much ecological and cultural devastation on a grand scale was created from the actions of one oil tanker, the *Exxon Valdez*?

Science has been profoundly affected by this new relationship with the nonlinear nature of our world. Many of the prevailing assumptions of scientific thought have had to be recanted. As scientist Arthur Winfree expresses it, the old dream of science was of a universe that was unaffected by slight changes:

> The basic idea of Western science is that you don't have to take into account the falling of a leaf on some planet in another galaxy when you're trying to account for the motion of a billiard ball on a pool table on earth. Very small influences can be neglected. There's a convergence in the way things work, and arbitrarily small influences don't blow up to have arbitrarily large effects. (in Gleick 1987, 15)

But chaos theory has proved these assumptions false. The world is far more sensitive than we had ever dreamed. We may harbor the hope that we will regain predictability as soon as we can learn how to account for all variables. (Titles of conferences and books reveal this dream; two recent ones to cross my desk are "Conquering Uncertainty" and "Mastering Complexity.") But in fact these desires for mastery and prediction can never be satisfied in this nonlinear world. We would do better to abandon that search entirely. In nonlinear systems, iteration helps small differences grow into powerful and unpredictable effects. In complex ways that no model will ever capture, the system feeds back on itself, magnifying slight variances, communicating throughout its networks, becoming disturbed and unstable – and prohibiting prediction, ever.

Iteration launches a system on a journey that visits both chaos and order. The most beautiful consequences of iteration are found in the artistry of fractals. There is a difference between fractals and strange attractors. Strange attractors are self-portraits drawn by a chaotic system. They are always fractal in nature, being deeply patterned, but they are a special category of mathematical object. Estimates are that there are only about two dozen different strange attractors. In contrast, fractals describe any object or form created from repeating patterns evident at many levels of scale. There are an infinite number of fractals, both natural and human-made.

Fractals can be generated with computers by taking a few nonlinear equations and continuously feeding back into the system the results of those equations [. . .]. It is not any one solution that matters, but the composite picture of those behaviors that emerges after countless iterations. As individual solutions are plotted, the whole of the system emerges in the form of detailed, repetitive shapes.

Everywhere in this intricate fractal landscape, there is self-similarity. The shape we see at one magnification will be similar to what we'll find at all others. No matter how deeply we look, peering down through magnifications of more than a billion, the same forms are evident. There is pattern within pattern within pattern. There is no end to them, no scale small enough that these intricate shapes cease to form. We could follow the creation of these shapes forever, and at ever finer levels, there would always be something more to see [. . .].

Fractals entered our world through the research of Benoit Mandelbrot, then at IBM. (Infinite patterns had been described in the early twentieth century by a few mathematicians, but their work lay dormant until quite recently.) In naming them,

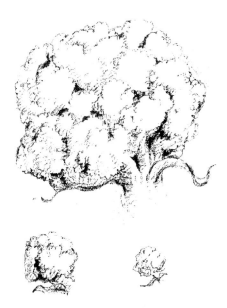

Broccoli's fractal qualities are easy to notice: the same shape appears at many different levels, from full head to tiny floret.

Mandelbrot gave us a language, a form of geometry, that allows us to comprehend nature in new ways. Fractals are everywhere around us, in the patterns by which nature organizes clouds, rivers, mountains, many plants, tribal villages, our brains, lungs, and circulatory systems. All of these (and millions more) are fractal, replicating a dominant pattern at several smaller levels of scale [. . .]. We live in a universe of fractal forms, but until recently, we lacked a means for seeing them. Now that we can see them, there are some wonderful lessons to be learned.

One primary lesson I have learned from fractals is that a world ordered by patterns does not explain itself through traditional measures. The infinite intricacy of fractals defies precise measurement. Mandelbrot's seminal fractal exercise was a simple question posed to colleagues and students: "How long is the coast of Britain?" As his colleagues soon learned, there is no answer to this question. As we zoom in, there are more and more details to measure. Creeping along the coastline, even if we chose to measure every rock on every outcrop, there would always be more to measure at ever smaller levels of scale.

Since fractals resist definitive assessment by familiar tools, they require a new approach to observation and measurement. What is important in a fractal landscape is to note not quantity but *quality*. How complex is the system? What are its distinguishing shapes? How do its patterns differ from those of other systems? In a fractal world, if we ignore qualitative factors and focus on quantitative measures, we doom ourselves only to frustration. Instead of gaining clarity, our search for quantification leads us into infinite fogginess. The information never ends, it is never complete, we accumulate more and more but understand less and less. When we study the individual parts or try to understand the system through discrete quantities, we get lost. Deep inside the details, we cannot see the whole. Yet to understand and work with the system, we need to be able to observe it *as a system*, in its wholeness. Wholeness is revealed only as shapes, not facts. Systems reveal themselves as patterns, not as isolated incidents or data points (see Capra 1996, Ch. 3).

In organizations, we are very good at measuring activity. In fact, that is primarily what we do. Fractals suggest the futility of searching for ever finer measures that concentrate on separate parts of the system. There is never a satisfying end to this reductionist search, never an end point where we finally know everything about even that one small part of the system. Scientists of chaos study shapes in motion. If we were to understand organizations in a similar way, what would constitute the shapes in motion of an organization?

Different answers to this question are emerging from studies of organizations as whole systems. Learning to look for wholeness is a new skill for us, and it has been difficult not to rely on old measures, even when we know they don't give us the information we need. But seeing patterns is not a foreign skill for us; we are, after all, a pattern-recognizing species, and even as infants we are very adept at noticing them. But after so many years of data analysis that has left us drowning in increasing minutiae, we need to help one another to reconnect with this innate ability. Together we must discipline ourselves to lift our heads from the pages and screens where charts dance hypnotically before us and enter into the world of form and shape.

The first step is to realize what we are looking for. A pattern has been defined rather succinctly as any behavior that occurs more than once. This seems elementary, but it is important to note what we are trying to see. So first we need to encourage each other to look for recurring behaviors and themes, to stay away from the seduction of examining isolated factors or individual players. Often patterns become discernible if we ask simple questions: "Have we seen this before?" "What feels familiar here?" To see patterns, we have to step back from the problem and gain perspective. Shapes are not discerned from close range. They require distance and time to show themselves. Pattern recognition requires that we sit together reflectively and patiently. I say patiently not only because patterns take time to form, but because we are trying to see the world differently and there are many years of blindness to overcome.

Fractals are extraordinarily complex objects. Their complex structure – such as the folds of human brains or the dense structure of lungs – provides increased capacity to process information and resources. But this complexity is created through processes that are quite different from human-created complexity. Fractal complexity originates in simplicity. Chaos scientist Michael Barnsley was intrigued to see if he could recreate the shapes of natural objects by deducing the simple equations that would describe their forms. He calls this the "Chaos Game." The game begins by ascertaining the essential information about the basic shape of the fractal (his first attempt was with a fern). These equations are surprisingly simple, devoid of the levels of precise prescriptive information we might think was necessary. He then sets the equations in motion to feed back on themselves. They are free to follow their own iterative wanderings, working at many different levels of scale, showing up in different sizes. With this approach, he can successfully reproduce an entire garden of plants on his computer [. . .].

His work with fractals and the Chaos Game is surprising and instructive. First, Barnsley shows us that determinism still operates in this universe. The shapes that he creates are predictable, determined by the initial formula. But indeterminism also

The Chaos Game

What is the essential shape of a complex, curvy fern? It's a pattern of four straight lines.

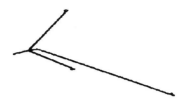

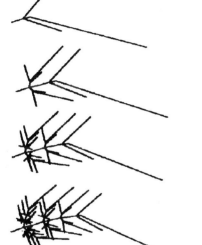

When this pattern repeats and repeats, free to change size but not shape, the complexity and beauty of the fern emerges. The pattern must always connect with what is already on the page, and in this example, it must appear in an upright position.

All fractal patterns are created as individuals exercise both freedom and responsibility to a few simple rules. Complex structures emerge over time from simple elements and rules, and autonomous interactions.

Drawing used with permission, Linda Garcia, 1991 (in *The Fractal Explorer*, Dynamic Press, Santa Cruz, CA).

plays a key role. He cannot predict how the formula will next solve itself, or where the pattern will show up on the screen. It seems that with a few simple principles or formulas, combined with the freedom to develop and move about, nature creates the complexity and intricacy of form we see everywhere.

Many disciplines have seized upon fractals, testing whether self-similar phenomena occur at different levels of scale in both natural and human-made systems. From business forecasters and stock analysts who have observed a fractal quality to stock market behaviors, to physiologists who describe how the fractal quality of brain and lung tissue gives it far greater capacity, to architects who explain the beauty of buildings and towns as the repetition of harmonious patterns, fractals have entered the imagination and research of many disciplines. They have provided a very different lens for comprehending the workings of the natural world. They have revealed the partnering of chaos and order that gives birth to beauty.

And I believe that fractals have direct application for how we understand organizations. All organizations are fractal in nature. I can't think of any organization that isn't deeply patterned with self-similar behaviors evident everywhere. I am often struck by eerily similar behaviors exhibited by people in an organization, whether I'm meeting with a factory floor employee or a senior executive. I might detect a recurring penchant for secrecy, or for openness, for name-calling, or for thoughtfulness. These recurring patterns of behavior are what many call the culture of the organization. I believe we all experience this fractal nature of organizations in any of our encounters with them. As customers, we can learn how employees are treated by their bosses by noticing how the employees treat us. As a consultant, I was taught that I would be able to spot the dominant issues of the client system by noticing how the client interacted with me.

Fractal order originates when a simple formula is fed back on itself in a complex network. Except for the shape that is contained within this simple formula, there are no other constraints on behavior. Organizations that display a strong commitment to their values make good use of this fractal creation process. In these organizations, it doesn't matter where you go, whom you talk with, or what that person's role is. By observing the behavior of a production floor employee or a senior executive, you can tell what the organization values and how it chooses to do its work. You hear the values referred to even in casual conversation. You feel the values are real and alive. And in true fractal fashion, these vital agreements do not prevent individuals from embodying them in diverse and unique ways. Self-similarity is achieved not through compliance to an exhausting set of standards and rules, but from a few simple principles that everyone is accountable for, operating in a condition of individual freedom.

The potent force that shapes behavior in these organizations and in all natural systems is the combination of simply expressed expectations of purpose, intent, and values, and the freedom for responsible individuals to make sense of these in their own way. Organizations with integrity have truly learned that there is no choice but to walk their talk. Their values are truthful representations of how they want to conduct themselves, and everyone feels deeply accountable to them. Just as in the Chaos Game, the organization's principles contain sufficient information about the intended "shape" of the organization, what it hopes to accomplish and how it hopes to behave. When each person is trusted to work freely with those principles, to interpret them, learn from them, talk about them, then through many iterations a pattern of ethical behavior emerges. It is recognizable in everyone, no matter where they sit or what they do.

It is the nature of life to organize into patterns. This recognition welcomes us into a different approach to organizational change. We can see that it is important to look for and identify the patterns that reveal themselves through behavior. Together we can decide whether we would prefer different behaviors. If we do, we need to figure out the values and agreements that we think will support these new behaviors. Then we work together to see what it means to live into these new agreements. This work requires awareness, patience, and generosity. Behaviors don't change just by announcing new values. We move only gradually into being able to act congruently with those values. To do this, we have to develop much greater awareness of how we're acting; we have to become far more self-reflective than normal. And we have to help one another notice when we fall back into old behaviors. We will all slip back into the past – that is unavoidable – but when this happens, we agree to counsel one another with a generous spirit. Little by little, tested by events and crises, we learn how to enact these new values. We develop different patterns of behavior. We slowly become who we said we wanted to be.

These ideas speak with a simple clarity to issues of effective leadership. They recall us to the power of simple governing principles: guiding visions, sincere values, organizational beliefs – the few self-referential ideas individuals can use to shape their own behavior. The leader's task is first to embody these principles, and then to help the organization become the standard it has declared for itself. This work of leaders cannot be reversed, or either step ignored. In organizations where leaders do not practice what they preach, there are terrible disabling consequences. Barbara Ley Toffler, a consultant specializing in ethics, reports that employees respond with "less commitment to the institution, less commitment to the institution's goals, customers, and clients." She comments that senior executives "have got to really, genuinely, walk the talk, practice what they preach, live out what they say" (in McLenahen, 1999).

Leaders are also obligated to help the whole organization look at itself, to be reflective and learningful about its activities and decisions. Mort Meyerson, a retired CEO, says that one of the primary tasks of a leader is to make sure the organization knows itself (in "Everything I [Thought I] Knew About Leadership Is Wrong" 1996). The leader's role is not to make sure that people know exactly what to do and when to do it. Instead, leaders need to ensure that there is strong and evolving clarity about who the organization is. When this clear identity is available, it serves every member of the organization. Even in chaotic circumstances, individuals can make congruent decisions. Turbulence will not cause the organization to dissolve into incoherence.

When chaos has banged down the door and is tossing us around the room, it is difficult to believe that clear principles are sufficient. Anytime we experience chaos, our training urges us to interfere immediately, to rush in, to stabilize, to prevent further dissolution. Certainly one of the strongest critiques we make of each other is to say, "You're out of control." But if we can trust the workings of the world, we will see that the strength of our organizations is maintained if we retain clarity about the purpose and direction of the organization. When things become chaotic, this clarity keeps us on course. We are still able to make sense, even if the world grows mad.

In this chaotic world, we need leaders. But we don't need bosses. We need leaders to help us develop the clear identity that lights the dark moments of confusion. We need leaders to support us as we learn how to live by our values. We need leaders to understand that we are best controlled by concepts that invite our participation, not policies and procedures that curtail our contribution. During the past several years, there has been enough research to demonstrate the enduring strength and resiliency of companies that have strong values (Collins and Porras 1993). But to this research we can now add the voice of chaos theory. Seemingly chaotic processes work with simple formulas to create astonishing complexity and capacity.

In chaos theory it is true that you can never tell where the system is headed until you've observed it over time. Order emerges, but it doesn't materialize instantly. This is also true for organizations, and this is a great challenge in our speed-crazed world. It takes time to see that a well-centered organization really has enough invisible structure to work well. Many of these organizations are already out there, beckoning to us from the future. But if they have not been part of our own experience, we are back to acts of faith. As the universe keeps revealing more of its ordering processes, hopefully we will understand that systems achieve order from clear centers rather than imposed restraints.

One of the mysteries of chaos theory is that no one knows where order comes from. Scientists don't design order into the initial equations. Ever since my imagination was captured by the phrase "strange attractor," I have contemplated whether such an organizing mystery exists in organizations. What is it that would be so attractive that it would hold our behavior within a boundary and keep us from wandering into formlessness? It seems clear to me now that values create such attractors. But by far the most powerful force of attraction in organizations and in our individual lives is *meaning*. Our greatest motivation in life, writes Viktor Frankl in his stunning presentation of logotherapy, "is not to gain pleasure or to avoid pain but rather to see a meaning . . ." (1959, 115).

In all types of organizations, too many filled with people exhausted, cynical, and burned-out, I have witnessed the incredible levels of energy and passion that can be evoked when leaders or colleagues take the time to recall people to the meaning of their work. It only takes a simple but powerful question: "What called you here? What were you dreaming you might accomplish when you first came to work here?" This question always elicits a deep response because so few of us work for trivial purposes. Most people come to their organizations with a desire to do something meaningful, to contribute and serve. Everybody needs, as philosopher and management scholar Charles Handy says, "an inner belief that you are in some sense meant to be here, that you can leave the world a little different in a small way" (in Hesselbein and Cohen 1999, 130). If we are asked to recall that inner belief, and if we hear our colleagues speak about their own yearnings to make a small difference, we feel new energy for the work and for each other. The call of meaning is unlike any other, and we would do well to spend more time together listening for the deep wells of purpose that nourish all of us.

One quality particular to human beings is the need to know "Why?" We need to understand and ascribe meaning to things. When we are able to reflect on our experience and develop our interpretation, we can endure even the most horrendous events. Even horrific accidents do not appear then as random assaults; we make sense of them from a grander logic. As organizations continue to experience so many momentous challenges, we do a great disservice to one another if we try to get through these times by staying at a superficial level or believing we are motivated only by self-interest. We have a great need to understand from a larger perspective why we are confronted with dislocation and loss. We have to be willing to speak about events from this deeper level of meaning.

We also need to acknowledge the shadow side of life – the sorrow and suffering that has come into our experience. We surface these dark shadows not to mend them or make them disappear, but simply to acknowledge they are part of the reality of life. When leaders honor us with opportunities to know the truth of what is occurring and support us to explore the deeper meaning of events, we instinctively reach out to them. Those who help us center our work in a deeper purpose are leaders we cherish, and to whom we return love, gift for gift. It is only meaning that enables us to summon our Gaian energy from Chaos' depths. With meaning as our centering place, we can journey through the realms of chaos and make sense of the world. With meaning as our attractor, we can recreate ourselves to carry forward what we value most.

Spirals etched into a temple stone around 3000 B.C. in Malta. These spirals sprout leaves, depicting how chaos gives birth to new life.

We can use our own lives as evidence for this human thirst for meaning. As we mature in life, we search to see a deeper and more coherent purpose behind the events and crises that compose our lives. What shape has my life taken? What is my purpose? Can I now see that seemingly random events were part of a greater plan? Do "chance" meetings now seem to have been not at all accidental? Each of us seeks to discover a meaning to our life that is wholly and uniquely our own. We experience a deepening confidence that purpose has shaped our lives, even as it moved invisibly in us. Whether we believe that we create this meaning for ourselves in a senseless world, or that it is offered to us by a purposeful universe, it is, after all, only meaning that we seek. Nothing else is attractive; nothing else has the power to cohere an entire lifetime of activity. We become like ancient Gaia, boldly embracing the void, knowing that out of Chaos' dark depths we have the strength to give birth to order.

References

Bonnefoy, Y. (1991) *Mythologies*, University of Chicago Press, Chicago.

Briggs, J. and Peat, F. D. (1989) *Turbulent Mirror: an illustrated guide to chaos theory and the science of wholeness*, Harper and Row, New York.

Capra, F. (1996) *The Web of Life: a new scientific understanding of living systems*, Anchor, New York.

Cartwright, T. J. (1991) Planning and Chaos Theory, *Journal of the American Planning Association*, 57: 44–56.

Collins, J. C. and Porras, J. I. (1993) *Built to Last: successful habits of visionary companies*, HarperBusiness, New York.

Coveney, P. and Highfield, R. (1990) *The Arrow of Time: a voyage through science to solve time's greatest mystery*, Fawcett Columbine, New York.

Frankl, V. (1959) *Man's Search for Meaning*, Beacon, Boston, MA.

Garcia, L. (1991) *The Fractal Explorer*, Dynamic Press, Santa Cruz, CA.

Gleick, J. (1987) *Chaos: making a new science*, Viking, New York.

Hayles, N. K. (1990) *Chaos Bound: orderly disorder in contemporary literature and science*, Cornell University Press, Ithaca, NY.

Hesselbein, F. and Cohen, P. M. (eds) (1999) *Leader to Leader*, Drucker Foundation, New York.

McLenahen, J. (1999) Your Employees Know Better: companies can't get away with bad ethics programs, *Industry Week*, 1 March: 12–13.

Meyerson, M. (1996) Everything I Thought I Knew About Leadership Is Wrong, *Fast Company*, 2(April–May): 71ff.

- Levy, D. (1994) Chaos Theory and Strategy: theory, application and managerial implications, *Strategic Management Journal*, 15: 167–178.
- MacIntosh, R. and MacLean, D. (1999) Conditioned Emergence: a dissipative structures approach to transformation, *Strategic Management Journal*, 20: 297–316.
- Pascale, R. T. (1999) Surfing the Edge of Chaos, *Sloan Management Review*, Spring: 83–94.
- Stacey, R. (1995) The Science of Complexity: an alternative perspective for strategic change processes, *Strategic Management Journal*, 16: 477–495.
- Wheatley, M. (1992/1999) Chaos and the Strange Attractor of Meaning, in *Leadership and the New Science: Discovering Order in a Chaotic World*, 2nd edition, Chapter 7: 114–134. Berrett-Koehler, San Francisco, CA.

We met on a wet October day in 2004 at Ross Priory on the banks of Loch Lomond in Scotland to talk about the selection of articles included in this part. After much discussion about the overall structure of this Reader we turned on the tape recorder and started to talk about what we were trying to point to in bringing these articles together. What follows is an edited transcript of the tape-recorded discussion. Themes in the conversation are highlighted in bold periodically.

Donald: So I suppose we should start with why these five articles are included in Part One?

Direct application of natural science concepts to social phenomena

Ralph: Well, for me they've all got the same kind of underlying approach in that they take ideas, insights, notions or concepts from the natural sciences of complexity and apply them directly to organizations without questioning or exploring the validity of doing so.

Doug: What do you mean by the natural sciences of complexity?

Ralph: Well, the theories of mathematical chaos, complex adaptive systems and dissipative structures, some or all of which form the basis of the readings in this part. What they are all doing, and my own article in this part is an example, is saying that organizational theorists should pay attention to the science of complexity because organizations *are* non-linear networked feedback systems. It therefore follows logically, I wrote at the time, that the fundamental properties of such systems should apply to organizations. That's what I mean by directly applying, just taking it for granted that organizations are systems. That is what all these readings share in common – they just continue with the idea that an organization is system without any questioning of that idea.

Donald: Do they assume that the elements of this system are the human members of the organization?

Ralph: That normally is what people would say.

The challenge of complexity: to Newton or systems thinking?

Donald: I think all the readings convey two things. One is that they all appear to attack orthodoxy. As one reads them they seem to imply that everything you thought you knew about organizations is just about to be proved wrong. There's an enthusiasm for this apparently new body of theory that appears to give an alternative and more realistic view of what organizations are and how they behave. In some articles, I think particularly ours and Pascale's, there's a notion that this new theory is much more fitted to the current era because it's an era of change and competition. There's a massive generalization of what the environment currently is as well.

Robert: There's the presentation of a contrast between Newtonian ways of thinking and complex ways of thinking. The unspoken part of that is an assumption that if you were running a business in the 1920s, or 1930s, or 1940s you would have been able to survive with Newtonian thinking but that the world is now too fast, too complex, too diverse to allow that to happen. The readings are presented as responding to some need for a new way of understanding organization and management.

Doug: Well, the sense of urgency in Wheatley's chapter is that in order to remain or become leaders, people will have to know about the new sciences, which take on the feel of secrets that some people have discovered. Having access to these secrets gives them competitive advantage over others who don't.

Ralph: But in all of this frequent comparison with Newton's thought, what doesn't get noticed is that all the writers doing this are all talking about organizations in terms of systems just as most of the orthodoxy they are attacking does. What the new science approach and the orthodoxy have in common is seeing an organization as a system. Orthodoxy had already largely moved on from Newtonian thinking to systems thinking but the complexity writers kept making comparisons with a Newtonian paradigm. What we did not see is that the real challenge, the comparison that should be made, the question that should be asked is whether an organization really is a system or not. But this wasn't being expressed in any of these readings. It was taken for granted that an organization is a system and that you could therefore directly apply the findings of the natural scientists about the properties of non-linear systems to an organization because it is also a system.

Donald: And by apply, you mean adopt the vantage point of an external observer.

The external, objective observer

Ralph: Yes, that's the other very other common feature of the readings in Part One and, inevitably in taking that vantage point, there is immediately the implication that this thing, this system called an organization can be moved about by the objective observer. For example in my article, I compare three different dynamics, arguing that non-linear interaction may lead to stable outcomes or to unstable outcomes or to indeterminate outcomes in bounded instability. I wrote that the difficulty lies in sustaining an organization that is bounded instability and the implication there is that someone outside the interaction is going to be able to do this. In other parts of the article I'm sort of arguing a different perspective. What I'm trying to get at is to try to understand the functioning of an organization from within one's participation with others, but I never manage to express it like that.

Doug: But I think other writers in Part One are trying to argue the same thing. They are not simply taking the perspective of the detached observer. For example, Wheatley immediately has the idea of participation and coming from Senge's thought,[1] it was obviously participation understood from a systems perspective. So you both end up oscillating between the position of the external observer of the system, on the one hand, and talking as if you were a participant in the system, on the other hand.

Donald: Well, I think we certainly did that in our article. We're quite explicit about the fact that deep structure is something that you can collectively identify through participation in the system, but you can then nevertheless stand back from that and treat it as though it is an object that you can manipulate and change, giving rise to new emergent detail.

Dealing with paradox

Doug: This becomes a key distinction to do with how people deal with paradox. People began to identify paradox in a naive sort of way as meaning that you could simply be an external observer at one time and be a participant another time, whereas another much more radical way of looking at paradox would be that you are both at the same time.

Robert: And I think that the paradox theme doesn't particularly jump out from this first set of readings. Although, in rereading your article, Ralph, there's a section about paradox but just as a passing reference. Your argument is that when paradox becomes the central focus then organizations are viewed as non-equilibrium systems. So, at that point your article seems to be arguing that you can treat organizations as complex adaptive systems because of the existence of paradox. I think that's a very important point but it is made almost en route to other points, whereas in later writing you do see paradox as much more important.

Ralph: Well, the emphasis on paradox is there in Pascale's earlier book, *Managing on the Edge*, although it is much less evident in the later book, *Surfing the Edge of Chaos*, from which his reading in Part One is drawn. Pascale briefly refers to paradox, so it is not easy to see what he means by it. In the earlier work, *Managing on the Edge*, he definitely looks at paradox in the 'both . . . and' sort of way that Doug has just described, you do one and then you do the other but not in any paradoxical sense of 'at the same time'.

Donald: I think that the other issue common to the readings in Part One is that as an external observer there's something that you can do to these systems to bring them so to speak into a fluid state 'at the edge of chaos'. If I were to place them in order of their commitment to the notion that you can manipulate systems, then probably the most overt is Pascale, who provides rather macho prescriptions, talking about action which is tough and tense but can be done and when you can do it, everything is going to happen for you and it'll be great. In our article, Robert and I say that if you can create far from equilibrium conditions and you can reframe deep structure and manage positive feedback, then you won't know exactly what you're going to get on the other side of it, but you'll get something and probably it will be good. We were kind of optimistic as well. I then think that even in your article, Ralph, although less explicit, there is a similar mentality. You say that to be an innovative, creative type of organization you need to be in the zone between order and disorder, the realm of bounded instability. You don't go as far as us in saying 'here's some tips on how to get there' but you imply that it's a good place to be if you can get there and managers ought to somehow be ready for that challenge. Then Levy, I think, takes chaos theory as a metaphor and is much less explicit about what people ought to do, but that's partly because he's taking an industrial perspective. And then, I think, Wheatley talks about participation but almost goes to the other extreme and says we can't do anything. The only thing you can really do is surrender and give in to these cosmic patterns that are absolutely good.

Ralph: I think that what I'm saying in my article is much more that you can't know what will happen. I stress unpredictability and paradox. You're right in saying that I don't make much of paradox but what attracted me to this idea of 'the edge of chaos' or 'bounded instability' was its paradoxical nature. I do say in the article that bounded instability is paradoxical in that it is both stable and unstable at the same time. But despite saying that, I found it very hard to hold onto and it gets very confusing when I say that a system could be in the stable zone, or the unstable zone, or the paradoxical one in between, because that implies what we have just been talking about, the possibility of moving the system from one zone to another. Whereas now I would understand that our interactions are always paradoxically stable and unstable at the same time.

Doug: Well, I think the type of thinking we have just been talking about comes from Cartesian mathematics, which abstracts from time and locates a phenomenon in a geometric space according to coordinates. Then by operating on the coordinates you, the objective observer, can move the phenomenon around in the geometric space. To me, there's a fundamentally naive take in the initial surge of enthusiasm for chaos and complexity theories which takes over the metaphysics of the natural sciences that underpins the idea of the independent observer. So what happens in the readings in Part One is that an intention to achieve something for an organization is taken as unproblematic. That intention is not regarded as an emergent phenomenon, but simply naively taken as given. But the intention is, as a matter of fact, itself an emergent phenomenon. It emerged from interaction.

Donald: I think that's a fair comment. In our article, we talk about two categories of phenomena. When we wrote that article, we thought that you could have naturally emergent phenomena and you could have artificially designed and intentionally constructed phenomena. We were very clear that to some extent an organization is an artificial achievement in the face of natural phenomena and natural processes. In some way or another, we wanted to release the stranglehold of inappropriate managerial interventions to let the natural phenomena flourish because with this may come great things, if you are lucky. And, frankly, I think this kind of idea comes through in all the readings in Part One. I've actually got a quote in Ralph's article too. He says that 'sustaining organizations at the edge of instability is far more difficult than giving in to the pull of either stability or instability'. So there's an intention there which is almost above and beyond the naturally emergent phenomenon.

Robert: And I think there is a contradiction in many of the earlier articles on complexity and organizations, not just these readings that we've selected for this part. Systems are presented as natural phenomena and it is implied that they naturally tend to evolve to the zone between stability and instability, whether you call it bounded instability or the edge of chaos. Yet, many writers then present some managerial prescriptions, the Pascale article is a notable example, for how one would go about intentionally making sure your organization gets to the edge of chaos and then stays there, accruing all the benefits of being there.

Causality and control

Doug: But there's something very important to notice in thinking about intention in the way you are mentioning now and this is the implied notion of causality. This is a simple link between cause and effect of the if–then kind, which predates systems thinking. In other words, it ignores the 'insides' of systems thinking which takes us beyond thinking in extremely reductive simple cause–effect links.

Donald: I agree, we were reflecting a kind of black box mindset in which the inside of an organization doesn't matter – the organization is a monolith that can be moved around, and I think this is another important distinction, moved around in accordance with the dictates of the intellect. I think that running through all the readings in Part One, there's a notion that emergent dynamics . . .

Doug: . . . are actually subject to a designing intellect. This is what I think is exceptional about Ralph's work, in a way that other people didn't do: he kept insisting on unpredictability and not knowing while other people put them away into the background. I think your article, Robert and Donald, challenged the naive assumption of cause–effect in a way that many other people weren't really into.

Robert: It's interesting for me, with the benefit of rereading these articles after several years, that I think most of the articles are on the surface positioning the manager as an intellectual deity as it were, who decides that his organization should be on the edge of chaos and so he will do the following in order to make sure that this happens. And yet, they all have their own way, I think, of hinting at a more sophisticated understanding. So, in Ralph's article, there's the first mention for me of this shadowy, invisible, informal system recognizing that what you say and do as manager in certain situations is not all that goes on in organizations. In our article, I think there's some discussion about the nature of the rules of deep structure and how they emerge. There's also some discussion in our article of first and second order rules. In the Levy article there's a really interesting piece where he talks about rules and he uses the analogy of chess. It is important to distinguish between the patterns of behaviour which constitute strategy from the underlying rules of the games, and I think that's Levy's way of trying to surface something about objectivity and rationality of the system and yet something else that goes on, something that is more creative, more about relating between actors in the situation.

Doug: I think that many people saw the limitations we are talking about now. This was the immense attraction of autopoiesis when it came on the scene. A number of people thought that this theory solved the problem of agency located in the objective observer and agency located in the system. In this theory, the components of a system are living human beings, agents, but the system is also seen as a living system so that the agency then moves to the system. The system itself, quite literally for these people, takes on a life of its own. What the theory of autopoiesis says is a tremendous advance in terms of thinking about theories of life but the question is whether you can use it in terms of organizations of human beings.

Donald: Thinking about the set of readings together, I think they have all got a fundamental irony, regardless of their content or the theory they use. They all draw their theoretical framework from the natural sciences, say complex adaptive systems. In the natural sciences such systems are self-organizing and emergent, which means that there is no one choosing the path of the whole system. Nevertheless, all the readings in Part One suggest that, when it comes to human organizations, we can choose to be in a complex adaptive system or we can choose not to be. There are things you can do that will get you there and things that you can do that will not. We talk about a different way of looking at the world, management and organizations, but then we've all kind of said, there is a choice here, whether you want to be like this or not.

Ralph: I don't think that in my article I was saying there is a choice because I was claiming that organizations are complex adaptive systems and as such have no choice.

Donald: But you also talk in the article, Ralph, about organizations which are in stable equilibrium.

Ralph: But that's because these are possibilities for complex adaptive and chaotic systems. At certain parameter values, or certain levels of connection, they produce stable equilibrium when connectivity is low, while at high levels of interconnection they produce randomness and in between they produce bounded instability.

Donald: But wouldn't you acknowledge that in the way you wrote it at the time there's a normative flavour to the way in which you say that?

Ralph: Because I'm being very definite about innovative organizations having to be operating at the edge . . .

Donald: Absolutely, I've got that . . .

Ralph: It's the only way they could operate.

Donald: But in order for a system to be creative it must be driven far from equilibrium.

Ralph: Well, that implies that there would be some choice of which dynamic you experience but there couldn't be any choice, you couldn't choose not to be a complex adaptive system in the way that I was . . .

Donald: No, I understand, and to be fair, although it is open to interpretation, you're not saying that it must be driven by managers to far from equilibrium. It might be driven by natural forces to far from equilibrium.

Doug: But other people did say that managers must drive their organization far from equilibrium. For instance Pascale says this in his article.

Donald: And we said in our article that you have to take specific actions to reach disequilibrium.

Robert: I think, possibly at the time we wrote our piece, Ralph, we projected onto your writing a more prescriptive sense, that you must choose to be at the edge of chaos. We did not think of organizations potentially existing in any one of these three states, that they are all categories of complex systems.

The debate about emergence

Ralph: You remember, Donald and Robert, the first time we met some ten years ago, our rather intense argument then was about whether you could in some sense condition, unleash or get hold of, of emergence. I was always of the view that the very definition of emergence means that you can't do any of those things. So you couldn't really choose to be at the edge of chaos and no one would be able to get hold of an organization and move it there.

Doug: The reason that this whole thing about choice came up was because the dominant way of thinking held that the edge of chaos was 'good' and being in it was 'good', euphoric even. Of course you would want to be in this wonderful generative state if you could be. How did that come about?

Ralph: Well, it's about creativity. If you are going to argue that to survive you have to be innovative and creative . . .

Robert: . . . in today's competitive environment . . .

Ralph: . . . then the implication would be that the survivors, and of course this is in the natural science version of this as well, the survivors are those who are poised at the edge of chaos and therefore it has to be good. But in my article, I don't think I argued that the edge of chaos was inevitably good. I wrote about it being very anxiety arousing.

Robert: The Pascale article overtly says that the economic benefits of being at the edge would be good in that the performance of the organization would be substantially improved. It is clear in some of the things that he says about the fishbowl experience at Shell. He talks about being at the edge in terms of high stress, high pressure, in fact, about working long hours under high stress.

Doug: Managers were told to get people out of the comfort zone, to let them know that their job is not so secure . . .

Donald: I think there has also been sensitizing to the notion of 'emergence' in the strategic management literature. Mintzberg's critique of the rational planning school of strategy resonated with many people.[2] He said that strategy could be an emergent phenomenon but, rather frustratingly for a lot of people, he didn't tell them how to do it. In our article we started using the word emergence from the complexity sciences, thinking it meant much the same as Mintzberg's emergence. We thought complexity would help us to understand emergent strategy.

Robert: I think my view, at the time, was that Mintzberg gave a post hoc way of observing what had been whereas the contribution we were offering, in our article, was looking forward in time with a view to managing or stewarding emergence as it unfolds, rather than just observing that's what we've been doing over the last ten years . . .

Donald: . . . and, at the same time, Porter's positioning approach to strategy was under attack from the resource-based view of the firm.[3] The latter were saying that things aren't as knowable as we first thought, so that managers needed what they were calling learning skills and knowledge to unleash the dynamic capabilities of the organization. I think, when writing our article, we thought that this might be a nice way of explaining how we can have all the energy of emergent strategy but with just enough mechanical underpinning to make it useful for managers, in effect having your cake and eating it too. So, although we mentioned the unpredictability of the emergent detail, we stressed will power, purpose, politics and human agency as giving the ability to manipulate the bigger emerging picture. We felt we were not simply lifting ideas from the natural sciences but were bringing in human agency. In your work, Ralph, I see that in taking up ideas from the natural sciences, you were also saying that human intention was also an emergent phenomenon, making the bigger emergent picture unpredictable.

Doug: Your expression 'having your cake and eating it too' is not a facile one. It is exactly what I mean by the 'both . . . and' position. In the 1990s, a whole management literature was developed proclaiming that managers could do this 'both . . . and'. You could choose to be a revolutionary manager, once you had identified the right situation, and then in another situation you could be an evolutionary manager. This view goes through management literature, cultural theory, leadership theory . . .

Donald: I think it would be very helpful for this discussion if you could explain a bit further the distinction between 'both . . . and' thinking and paradox.

'Both . . . and' thinking and paradox

Doug: Well, the first position would be an 'either . . . or' position, where it is either this or that and you have to make a choice. For instance, some people argue that Napoleon was a brilliant revolutionary who brought Europe a giant step forward but other people argue that Napoleon was a complete despot who destroyed the social institutions of Europe. So, in the 'either . . . or' position you would argue that he is either a brilliant revolutionary or a despot. To move to the 'both . . . and' position you would say he was *both* a revolutionary saviour of other European countries *and* a despot in France.

Donald: So the options are spatially spread out . . .

Doug: Yes, or over time and this is what people like Hampden-Turner mean by dilemma or paradox.[4] On this view you work out the paradox of an organization and resolve it. But, what I would consider the genuine paradoxical would be to say that Napoleon as a complex individual, in each and every action, was both at the same time . . .

Donald: So they're not spatially or temporally separated?

Doug: And that becomes a very irritating position to try to hold. As soon as you reduce it to a 'both . . . and' there is always this feeling of relief from the tension of trying to hold together Napoleon as this complex despotic revolutionary personality, which is what he was. This leads to reductionist thinking, where the manager says he is a revolutionary in this situation and a routine manager in another and all he has to do is make the right choice. This then puts all the pressure on the individual to get it right instead of seeing that the individual in the social setting is the full complexity of reality.

Donald: Then we can say that another feature common to the readings in Part One is that, at a meta-theoretical level, they take a 'both . . . and' position. Most of the readings start by saying that organizations can be understood in terms of mechanisms in a basically stable work universe but that, in an ever changeful universe, they have to be understood as complex dynamic phenomena.

Robert: And a lot of them position this by pointing out that a lot of our management models come from straightforward economics, which comes from Newtonian thinking. Then they say that, over the past ten or fifteen years, natural scientists have been discovering wonderful things, making mechanistic thinking inappropriate. The implication is that we have been slow to realize that our subject area should be revolutionizing itself. I think we all have that as an opening gambit, saying we're stuck with this old model and everybody else has moved on but us. What would it mean for us if we were to adopt these ways of thinking?

Doug: But in terms of management theories, system thinking had already made a tremendous advance beyond mechanistic, behavioural thinking. And that's the scene, if you will, that complexity ideas entered into. The real question was whether complexity ideas went beyond systems thinking or not, particularly whether they went beyond the 'both . . . and' reduction. People had reduced the strengths of systems thinking to a simple cause–effect instead of seeing that systems theory could take organizations beyond cause–effect and behavioural thinking, which someone like Senge sees very clearly. That's what is exciting about systems thinking. But does complexity go beyond this? The comparison with Newtonian thinking is a kind of straw argument, simply the easy one. It is the comparison with systems thinking that is the difficult one.

Donald: But that's the point, Doug. In a way, all of these readings set up, to some extent, an 'either . . . or' logic. They each have their own view of the world which they then compare with a fairly mechanistic view of the world and then say the way forward is with their view.

Ralph: I agree that all the readings are making the wrong comparison . . .

Doug: But to express what I think is a strength of Pascale's position, Pascale is someone who actually goes out and talks a lot to people in organizations. He knows their language, and when you talk to these people you realize that the basis of their thinking is actually cause–effect. Managers are mostly thinking in behaviouralistic terms and Pascale is then able to write about these things in a way that appeals to them because he knows his audience.

Ralph: So in practitioner terms it wasn't a straw man comparing complexity with Newtonian thinking, because this is the way actual practising managers tend to think.

Robert: And that's partly because they have been through the MBA Programme as well. They have been fed formulae and straightforward views of how to adopt a position in a particular marketplace or maximize the . . .

Ralph: That's right, a lot of the literature and the education of managers certainly isn't informed by second-order systems thinking but a more reductionist form of first-order systems thinking.

More on control, gap analysis and feedback

Donald: But the cause–effect thinking is closely linked to the desire to be in control. There is another theme in the readings in Part One which has to do with the dominant form of thinking and behaviour in organizations to do with control, particularly in terms of negative feedback, closing gaps and doing what you said you were going to do. In different ways, the readings point to the limits of this form of control. I think Ralph is very explicit in saying that you can't predict or determine in advance what's going to happen. Wheatley also says it but in a different way, involving surrender to the whole.

Doug: But I would try to look at it in another way. I would say these ways of thinking are ways of trying to talk about controlling power.

Donald: But isn't that an interesting omission from all of these readings? None of them really talk about power at all . . . in theoretical terms.

Ralph: Well, in my article I'm very explicit about the links between cause and effect disappearing and therefore the implication is that you can't be, that no one can be, in control. But I was doing this by taking some quite challenging ideas from the natural sciences and, in order to make sense of them in terms of organizations, was using the notions of systems and feedback already familiar in organizational literature. I now think the explanation I was giving was completely inappropriate in that I was trying to explain the non-linear dynamics as a flipping between negative and positive feedback, which is a cybernetic concept. This is not appropriate when you are talking about iterative, temporal non-linear process.

Doug: But it is a move away from simple cause–effect, as Senge very clearly shows in his book. So systems dynamics clearly moves away from simple cause–effect, as does . . .

Robert: And in the Pascale article, he talks about a precise tension between amplifying and damping feedback, in relation to your . . .

Ralph: Well, you see then, that he is using the same explanation that I'm using, which is that there is this pull in two different directions between damping and amplifying feedback. But that's a cybernetic way of thinking about a system or a process which isn't actually a cybernetic system. Feedback implies an externally set reference point against which the behaviour of the system is to be measured to identify a gap and then a decision is triggered to dampen or amplify the gap. But what the models of complex adaptive systems are trying to get at is the internal, spontaneous capacity of the system to evolve, without any reference to an externally set reference point.

Robert: And I suppose, in our article, our argument was that groups of individuals who were managers in organizations could negotiate these reference points and have some prior view of reference points in the form of rules, or something of that sort, against which the unfolding dynamic could be connected.

Ralph: Then, if you would try to understand that as a complex process, the rules or the reference points would not be being externally set, they would be being negotiated and there would be a process of negotiation.

Robert: When Donald and I came down for that tense conversation with you and Patricia [Shaw], I think I certainly entered that conversation with the view that we were, in an archaeological sense, unearthing these rules and left the conversation with a more helpful view that we were co-creating them but that they nonetheless served a purpose. The rules weren't somewhere in the foundations of the building as things that concretely existed but nonetheless a group of people, at a given point of time, could hold a very useful and meaningful conversation about what they had been in the past and what they might aspire to in the future.

Doug: But if you move to that position you wouldn't be able to call it a reference point.

Donald: Well, but I think you could still talk about an origin, so to speak. The notion of reference point comes in, I think, when you have got a gap to close with reference to an imagined, forecast or predetermined state. You close the gap through negative feedback which then returns you to some equilibrium or designed stable state. Whereas, with positive feedback, the feedback propels the system away from the equilibrium concept of a reference point. This is vaguer and has more to do with origins.

Ralph: But you're still multiplying a gap in relation to a reference point, so it's still a gap and amplifying is amplifying . . .

Doug: But as I understand it, the reference point is a basis for a whole theory of leadership in which the leader discovers the reference point and uses positive and negative feedback to manipulate the gap . . .

Ralph: That's right.

Donald: I think that's fair. I think that the readings in Part One were trying to point out that if you're talking about feedback in organizations, which many people were, then there's another kind. It is not just about negative feedback. There are also positive feedback processes that destabilized organizations rather than stabilized them.

Ralph: Which systems dynamics had already identified . . .

Donald: But the other things from systems dynamics, which we certainly relied on in our article, was the notion of archetypes. So instead of the idea of reference points, we had a notion of organizations moving from one archetype to another. We said you couldn't predict emergent details, but you could nevertheless have some feel for the archetypal pattern that was likely to bound emergent variety. Some of the other readings have this notion of some kind of archetypal pattern likely to unfold.

Back to emergence again

Ralph: And one of the things that we also want to try and get our minds clearer about is how each of these readings is using the concept of emergence because a lot of the desire to at least condition emergence, or try to design it a little bit, I think arises from a view of emergence as something that just happens. It feels totally unacceptable in social organizational terms to say that what's happening is just happening without any reason or . . .

Doug: I think what underpins that type of thinking is the influence of Jantsch's book, *The Self-Organizing Universe*, which Wheatley is very much influenced by.[5] You get a picture of a self-organizing universe that we can only tune ourselves to. That's where you get this kind of passive idea that it is just happening out there and then when things go wrong it is because you're not getting it right, you're not in tune . . .

Ralph: You're not participating.

Doug: Yeah, you're not participating in that sense . . .

Donald: I think that, in a way, it was that idea that we took most exception to. We thought it doesn't just happen, and if we accept that it doesn't just happen then maybe we can influence what actually happens . . .

Ralph: Which certainly we do, because we are creating the patterns that are emerging
. . .

Donald: But we thought . . .

Ralph: But they don't just happen, precisely because of what we are doing.

Donald: Because of our creative action. I think, at the time, we thought that a small group of one or two people in the organization could determine what happens by intervention in what we call deep structure.

Ralph: But if what is emerging is emerging precisely because of what we are all doing in interaction with each other, that immediately precludes the possibility that any one of us, or small group of us, can influence the widespread pattern of inter-action between other people by doing something like alter the deep structure or set a vision. The key point is not being able to step outside of our own local interactions and influence a much wider global . . .

Doug: This is linked to the problem around cause–effect. Ideas like deep structure and archetype are ways of expressing a simple cause–effect link. They are causes you can then influence.

Ralph: The important point is that the readings in Part One argue for a move away from cause–effect implications for control but then come back to just that. We want to move away from the mechanistic cause–effect but then can't and have to come back to archetypes and deep structures.

Robert: And I suppose that this links to my earlier observation about this inherent contradiction of observing that organizations naturally find themselves at the edge of chaos and then asking what you have to do to get there. In our own paper there are prescriptions: you should try to introduce instability; you should manage feedback; you should be managing and altering deep structures. In Pascale's article there are prescriptions about what one should do and what one should manage and so on.

Ralph: I can't remember if I do that in this article but if I haven't then I was certainly
     giving some prescriptions in books . . .

Donald: Yeah, you do that in the *Long Range Planning* article,[6] where you've got six
     or seven steps . . .

Ralph: I know, prescriptions like 'Pay attention to the quality of this or that'.

Doug: But in a sense, what I think we are getting at, in a lot of different ways, is that
     these initial enthusiastic reactions produced these contradictions which then
     moved thought on. People saw that this doesn't work, you go in this direction and
     it's a dead end, so what do you do? How do you think further? It's extremely
     productive.

Robert: I think we should acknowledge Ralph's pioneering role, in that he published
     his first piece in 1911, according to his article, on page 486 [of the original publi-
     cation, and page 87 of this text], to be internally and spontaneously changeable
     and innovative, a non-linear feedback system has to operate in chaos at the edge
     of instability . . . then it says in brackets . . . Stacey 1911.

Donald: He was more pioneering than I thought.

Doug: He's also a hell of a lot older than I thought.

The meaning of chaos, the edge of chaos and dissipative structures

Donald: I would quite like to spend some time talking about the term chaos because
     it was an important term in most of the readings. They all say that chaos in
     mathematical terms means something quite different to chaos in lay terms but then
     they do not use it consistently in a mathematical sense. It is used in different ways
     at different times. The same goes for the notion of 'the edge of chaos'. At the time
     of writing our article, Robert and I took exception to this notion and actually set
     up dissipative structures as an alternative view. We brought together the notions
     of dissipative structures and punctuated equilibrium. The question the four of us
     have explored before is whether the two notions are consistent or inconsistent with
     each other. We took the punctuated equilibrium model and argued that dissipative
     structure theory explains the movement from one equilibrium state to another.
     Dissipative structures go through phase transitions in which they go from one state
     through dissipative processes into another state. This is one issue. Another issue
     that is presented in all the readings in Part One, but not in ours, is the notion that
     there is a golden zone somewhere between order and disorder, or between order
     and chaos, called the edge of chaos, where things spontaneously manifest them-
     selves. The implication is that if you can hover in that zone, avoiding the tidal
     destruction of chaos and the rigidity of mechanisms, you will get some benefits.
     I think that was where Robert and I took a different position. In our article we use
     Prigogine's terms and talk about descending into chaos and it is out of that chaos
     that order emerges.[7] For the spontaneous development of novelty, you have to go
     through chaos in much the same way that water flowing down a river passes
     through whirlpools and rapids and on the other side . . .

Robert: That is in stark contrast to the Pascale article. He says that equilibrium is a
     precursor to death and there is a zone in which one can reside that is neither too

orderly nor too chaotic. Our view was that you don't reside in this but pass through it periodically; you can move between relatively stable states through some process of upheaval out of which some new order will emerge but that order will crystallize into some stable state.

Doug: But Prigogine was not thinking in this way. As I understand it, all the readings in Part One, including yours, use very Cartesian ways of trying to think about change. It was Langton who came up with the metaphor the edge of chaos.[8] Prigogine talked about phase transitions at the bifurcation point.

Donald: That's why we said that it was the bifurcation that was chaotic and that this chaos is a state between order and disorder. So where does the idea of an 'edge' come in?

Ralph: But you see these terms are used in different ways. Prigogine uses the terms disorder, chaos and fluctuations interchangeably. What he's talking about there is what Peter Allen, whose chapter is in Part Two, refers to as micro diversity of events. Micro diversity is different to mathematical, low dimensional mathematical chaos, which is this paradoxically stable–unstable pattern we talked about earlier. So chaos, mathematical chaos is this particular dynamic which occurs at particular parameter values for iterated deterministic non-linear equations. Now when you move to complex adaptive systems, we're not talking about the deterministic equations, we're talking about the interacting rule sets called agents. Here the word chaos means high dimensional chaos, that is, random behaviour. The term 'edge of chaos' refers to a paradoxical dynamic which is stable and unstable at the same time but which is being generated by agent interaction rather than deterministic equations. When you introduce micro diversity into this interaction, in the senses of the agents being different to each other, then you get spontaneous novelty or evolution, which in human terms could be understood as learning. Whereas, in mathematical chaos and dissipative structures, there is no equivalent of learning.

Donald: This has confused us. So what you're saying is that in the term edge of chaos, the word 'chaos' is not the same as the mathematical chaos of dynamical systems theory.

Ralph: I found that terribly confusing as well. When Prigogine uses the word fluctuation, which seems to be interchangeable with the word chaos, he does so with reference to phenomena which are held far from the equilibrium by some constraint. The effect of this is to amplify the fluctuations to the point were symmetry is broken and it is this symmetry breaking which is the bifurcation point.

Donald: I thought that symmetry breaking was in the fluctuation or oscillations which were chaos in the mathematical sense. So, we took the title of Prigogine's book *Order out of Chaos* to mean that you have to immerse in the chaos, descend into it, and come out of it again. That is why the idea of dwelling always at the edge of chaos seemed strange to us.

Doug: But it was revolutionary for Prigogine to introduce this word paradox which had long been banned from the natural sciences. He introduces the word paradox and says because they are not separate.

Donald: But what's not separate Doug?

Doug: The order and disorder.

Donald: No, because chaos is the simultaneous presence of both.

Ralph: In which case, it is not equilibrium, and you see . . .

Donald: But you can move in and out of it, Ralph. Our point was that you can have different states and could cycle through them, whereas, your 'edge of chaos theorists' thought that you could just hang about there. We didn't think that was possible and that's what the prescriptions in the article by Pascale, and in Eisenhardt's work,[9] implied, as did your article.

Ralph: But the dissipative structure dwells, if you like, far from equilibrium. It was telling that in an email exchange after our last discussion, Peter Allen said that when he worked with Prigogine he wouldn't allow anyone to use the word equilibrium . . .

Donald: That's right, yeah.

Ralph: Because his whole point is about paradoxical patterns. A dissipative structure is a paradox in that it is a structure which is continually dissipating. My under-standing of this is that, in a state of equilibrium, any perturbation is quickly corrected to pull you back to the equilibrium, but in a far-from-equilibrium dissipative structure, the perturbation may be very easily amplified. So, near equi-librium change is extremely difficult and stability is easy, while for a dissipative structure far-from-equilibrium change is very easy and stability is very difficult. At equilibrium, time is irrelevant but far from equilibrium time is essential – dissipative structures are history dependent. Prigogine makes a big thing about the irreversibility of time, the arrow of time.

Donald: But I suppose our concern was not whether dissipative structures are far from equilibrium, which we would accept obviously, but the systems are far-from-equilibrium dissipative structures for a time but then move back to equilibrium so giving the pattern of punctuated equilibrium. We didn't think of organizations as dissipative structures perpetually residing at the edge of chaos.

Robert: Because in the natural science original work, where they talk about the need for a perpetual feed of energy, the parameters of the far-from-equilibrium zone have to do with temperature, or pressure, or some sort of chemical reaction. You could artificially maintain a continuous supply of energy that allows the system to dissipate enough for an infinite time, whereas in organizational settings, I just had great difficulty in buying this wonderful infinite source of energy that would keep the organization poised, on the edge of chaos.

Donald: But it is even more extreme than that. The whole point of organization is to do just the opposite. The organization is a defence against dissipative structure type behaviour, with its anxiety and stress. People naturally organize towards stable systems, therefore . . .

Ralph: You see this is part of what, in a sense, is present in all of the readings in Part One. What I mean is that they do not explore the really radical insight that complexity type thinking might bring. Instead they stay with the idea that an organization has to be stable. But what the argument pointed to by dissipative structures and complex adaptive systems that evolve, continually evolve to the edge of chaos, is that all living systems are at the edge of chaos and that's how they stay alive and evolve. Therefore, Prigogine's argument is that all living systems and more than that, others too, are dissipative structures far from equilibrium. But it's very different from the little experiments in the laboratory where a fluid is held far from equilibrium by an inflow of heat controlled by the experimenter. This experiment is a laboratory simulation of the whole climate system of an internally spontaneous system which sustains itself at the very precarious boundary in which life is possible.

Donald: But that, in a way, is our point. Prigogine was not talking about human organization and these organizations are not necessarily living systems. So we were objecting, if you like, to what we saw as the lifting of that idea and imposing it on human organizations. For us, to some extent, organizations were possibly the precise opposite; they were artificial constructions instead of living systems. It gave us this kind of combination I suppose of dissipative structures between equilibrium states.

Doug: But we need to be very sensitive to using the word equilibrium. You are talking in the 'both . . . and' way, having both dissipative structures and punctuated equilibrium at different times.

Donald: I think this what you said earlier on and at that time we were very clearly into that kind of thinking.

Ralph: I would like to suggest that we have lunch, as it is one o'clock.

NOTES

1   See for example Senge, P. (1990) *The Fifth Discipline: the art and practice of the learning organization*, Currency/Doubleday, New York.

2   See for example Mintzberg, H. (1978) Patterns in Strategy Formulation, *Management Science*, 24(9): 934–948.

3   Porter, M. (1980) *Competitive Strategy*, The Free Press, New York.

4   Hampden-Turner, C. (1990) *Charting the Corporate Mind: from dilemma to strategy*, Basil Blackwell, Oxford.

5   Jantsch, E. (1980) *The Self-Organizing Universe*, George Braziller, New York.

6   Stacey, R. (1996) Emerging Strategies for a Chaotic Environment, *Long Range Planning*, 29(2): 182–190.

7   See, for example, Prigogine, I. and Stengers, I. (1984) *Order out of Chaos: man's new dialogue with nature*, Bantam, New York.

8   See, for example, Langton, C (ed.) (1997) *Artificial Life: an overview (complex adaptive systems)*, The MIT Press, Cambridge, MA.

9   Brown, S. and Eisenhardt, K. (1998) *Competing on the Edge: strategy as structured chaos*, Harvard Business School Press, Boston, MA.

PART TWO

Categorizing complexity

EDITORS' INTRODUCTION AND COMMENTARY

In Part One, we considered a range of articles that drew on concepts such as chaos theory and dissipative structures from the natural sciences and attempted to translate concepts directly from the natural to the social sciences and, in particular, to the realms of organization and management. The readings presented in this second part can perhaps best be viewed as symptomatic of a period of pause as regards the enthusiastic application of ideas from the complexity sciences and the adoption of a somewhat more introspective, reflective and questioning stance on the part of some researchers.

In different ways, all the readings in Part Two seek to identify the different ways in which ideas from the complexity sciences were being used in relation to organizations and, in some cases, how these differences are related to each other. In so doing the readings reveal tensions between emerging schools of thought and relate these tensions to different assumptions being employed by researchers in the conduct of their enquiries. On the one hand, assumptions relate to the implicit choices that researchers make in defining and specifying system parameters such as boundaries, members and interactions; on the other, they reveal more fundamental choices such as views on the applicability of systems concepts to human processes and related ontological and epistemological considerations.

In particular, attention centres on how, if one defines organizations as complex systems, one deals with issues which have been absent in natural science treatments: issues such as agency, uncertainty as to what constitutes a system element; how one deals with membership of multiple systems and how one specifies a system's boundary. Specifically and perhaps unsurprisingly given the importance attached in the complexity sciences to concepts such as emergence, the readings share a concern for the implications of the 'human dimension' for our understanding of organizations as complex adaptive systems; i.e. what the consequences of human agency (and how we think about it) are for self-organization (and how we think about it).

As such, the readings in Part Two draw attention to two responses to the above issues. One, which might be called the scientific response, lays out key modelling assumptions and points towards an approach based on building more thoughtful and sensitive models of human systems which are taken to be ontologically real. The other, which might be termed a more philosophical response, highlights some of the ontological and epistemological difficulties involved in the application of systems thinking to complex human organizations, in turn pointing towards a rethink of how we might fruitfully combine ideas from the complexity sciences with constructivist traditions in social psychology and philosophy.

Peter M. Allen

EVOLVING COMPLEXITY IN SOCIAL SCIENCE

From Gabriel Altmann and Walter A. Koch (eds) *Systems: New Paradigms for the Human Sciences* 1998, pp. 3–38. Copyright © 1998 by Walter de Gruyter GMBH & Co., Berlin. Reprinted with permission of the publisher.

1 Introduction

The new paradigm of "evolving complexity" is of fundamental importance for the human sciences, and in this chapter we shall attempt to present a clear description of the conceptual framework that it provides, as well as a real example which illustrates all of the levels/styles of description that can be created. In particular, it will be shown that the new paradigm of evolving complexity is not a "biological" metaphor, but simply concerns the basic principles of mathematical modelling and the assumptions that are made in obtaining a reduced description of reality. In other words, the models that will be discussed here are all "correct" within the stated assumptions, since they are simply based on "balance equations" (accounting) of the variables. The fundamental feature of any mathematical model of course is that it concerns aspects of the system which can be "counted", and this is perhaps an important limitation on their overzealous use in decision making, since we may "buy" success in the countable aspects of our system at the expense of the uncountable.

In order to make sensible and effective decisions, however, it is necessary to be able to imagine appropriate options for action, and to have at least some knowledge of the probable consequences of each possible choice. Clearly, this concerns something related to "prediction", but which would more correctly be called the ability to "explore possible futures". Unfortunately, until recently, the conceptual and mathematical basis for such a vision in the human sciences has not existed. This is because there has been no *science* of change for human systems. Instead, in politics there have been ideologies concerning the benefits of free markets, or of central planning, and in business and commerce people have simply relied on using a mixture of experience and intuition, with, in both cases, the rather mixed success that we see around us. The conceptual framework of traditional science, that of mechanical and equilibrium systems, simply was not appropriate for human systems, and underlay the emergence of the "two cultures" of western civilization, where the artistic and cultural matters were considered to be quite separate from the scientific. Indeed, the former were thought of as "local and particular", subject to fashion and whim, while science was thought of as universal and objective, above any particular cultural view.

In this paper we shall show a hierarchy of models which correspond to different degrees of aggregation over the classification scheme as well as of spatial and temporal detail. The simplest of these provide a deterministic model of fixed structure, where the behaviours of the subsystem cannot change, while the more ambitious of these models lead naturally to an evolutionary dialogue between the individual and collective levels and generate an evolving taxonomy of interdependent, changing behaviours, leading to an "ecological" structure. These represent a new domain of organization beyond the "mechanical", where the identities and behaviours of the actors are mutually interdependent, the system has many possible responses to perturbations, and where success is related to the capacity to change, adapt and to maintain diverse and varied strategies. This view of suboptimal behaviours, imperfect information, mistaken inferences and the power of creativity is contrasted with the traditional mechanical representations of human systems.

2 System dynamics, self-organization and evolution

If we examine any region, domain or organization and consider the actors, artifacts and activities that have been present in the landscape, then after dating and classifying them, an evolutionary tree of some kind emerges, possibly with discontinuities suggesting disaster and invasion, but nevertheless suggesting a changing "cast of characters" and of behaviours, over time. On the left, we have "reality". It is drawn as a cloud, since we can say little about it other than that it includes all detail of everything, everywhere, as well as all perceptions and all points of view. However, if we simply list what we see then it includes a landscape with people of many kinds performing a variety of tasks, businesses, factories, homes, vehicles, and also fossils, disused mines and factories, closed railways, buried cities and evidence of much that has disappeared.

By constructing a series of taxonomic rules concerning the differences and similarities of the objects, activities and actors present at different times then we will find an "evolutionary tree", showing that behaviours, forms, artifacts and types of actor have emerged and evolved over time.

This is really subjective however, since the differences that we choose to recognize reflect already our particular vision of what is "important" in a social and economic system. The rules of classification that we use are seldom explicitly justified however, and often result from previous experience of such systems. Are there socioeconomic "types" and if so, what are they? Do demographic

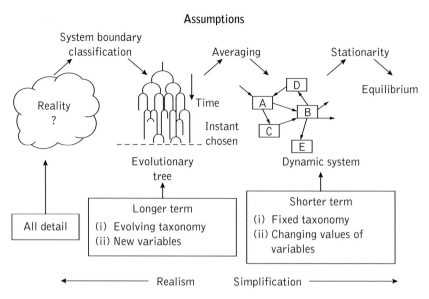

Figure 1 Data and classification of populations and artifacts leads to the picture of an evolutionary tree of some kind, while mathematical models have been of fixed taxonomy

characteristics reflect economic categories? Do firms of the same sector and size behave similarly? What is a sector? Is there as much variation within a group as between groups? Whatever the precise arguments advanced, in order to "understand" a situation, and its possible outcomes, we do classify the system into components, and attempt to build mathematical models that capture the processes that are increasing or decreasing these different components.

At any particular moment therefore, we identify the different objects or organisms that are present, and attempt to write down some "process dynamics" describing the increase and decrease of each type. We apply the traditional approach of physics, which is to identify the *components* of a system, and the *interactions* operating on these, both to and from the outside world and between the different populations of the system.

The non-equilibrium "Systems Dynamics" model shown on the right of Figure 1 appears to capture the behaviour or functioning of the system as a result of the causal relationships that are present. This gives a mechanical representation of the system which looks as though it can be run on a computer, to give predictions. However, as we see clearly from our broader picture of Figure 1 which shows the "evolutionary tree", the predictions that such a model can give can only be correct for *as long as the taxonomy of the system remains unchanged*. The mechanical model of deterministic equations that we can construct at any given time has no way of producing "new" types of objects, new variables, and so the "predictions" that it generates will only be true until some moment, unpredictable within the model, when there is an adaptation or innovation, and new behaviour emerges.

Let us consider carefully the assumptions that have to be made in order to arrive at a description in terms of system dynamic equations. Such systems are characterized by dynamical equations of the type:

$$\frac{dx}{dt} = G(x, y, z, \ldots)$$

$$\frac{dy}{dt} = H(x, y, z, \ldots) \tag{1}$$

$$\frac{dz}{dt} = J(x, y, z, \ldots)$$

where G, H, and J are functions which have nonlinear terms in them, leaping to changes in x, y and z which are not simply proportional to their size. In this example we have chosen three coupled equations, but obviously, according to the problem being modelled this could be any number. The functions such as G, H, J express the effects on x, y and z of the different mechanisms present, and as well as being possibly a function of the state of the system, they also involve parameters expressing the functional dependencies. These parameters reflect three fundamentally different factors in the working of the system:

- the values of *external* factors, which are not modelled as variables in the system. These reflect the "environment" of the system, and of course may be dependent on spatial coordinates. Temperature, climate, soils, world prices, interest rates are possible examples of such factors.
- the effects of *spatial interaction*, of juxtaposition, of the entities underlying the system. Often these will express nonlinear effects of density for example.
- the values corresponding to the "performance" of the entities underlying x, y or z, due to their *internal* characteristics like technology, level of knowledge or particular strategies.

These three entirely different aspects have not been separated out in much of the previous work concerning nonlinear systems, and this has led to much confusion. Nonlinear dynamical equations display a rich spectrum of possible behaviours in different regions of both parameter space and initial conditions. They range from a simple approach to a homogeneous steady state, characterized by a *point* attractor, through that of sustained oscillation of a *cyclic* attractor, to the well known *chaotic* behaviour characteristic of a strange attractor. These can be homogeneous, but, much more importantly, they can involve spatial structure as well, and the phenomenon of *self-organization* can be seen as the adaptive response of a system to changing external conditions, even if it is viewed as having fixed attributes for its microscopic entities, that is to say, fixed values for the parameters describing the internal characteristics of the microscopic entities. In other words, we shall see that self-organization is a collective, spatial response to changing conditions rather than an evolutionary response on the part of its constituent individuals.

In order to see this let us first consider the assumptions that are made in deriving System Dynamics equation such as in (1). In the complex systems that underlie something like the "economy", there is a fundamental level which involves individuals and discrete events, like making a widget, buying a washing machine, driving to work etc. However, instead of attempting to "model" all this detail, these are treated in an average way, as has been shown elsewhere (Allen, 1990). In order to reduce the probabilistic dynamics governing the discrete microscopic events and individuals underlying the system and to derive deterministic, mechanical equations to describe the dynamics of a system, two assumptions are required:

Assumption 1:
- microscopic events occur at their average rate, average densities are correct.

Assumption 2:
- individuals of a given type, say x, are identical, or have a normal distribution of diversity around the average type.

Making or not making these assumptions leads to different types of models, but it should always be underlined that the less assumptions are made, the more general a model is, since it contains the others as special cases.

(I) Equilibrium models

In addition to making the two assumptions above, the simplest description can be obtained by assuming in addition that the system will move rapidly to a stationary state. In neoclassical economics, much of spatial geography, and many models of transportation and land-use, the models that are used operationally today are still based on equilibrium assumptions. Locations of jobs and residences, land values, traffic flows etc. are all assumed to reach their equilibrium configurations "sufficiently rapidly" following some policy or planning action, so that an apparent output sequence can be shown. Really though, these methods simply do not consider time realistically. Some more extreme practitioners even justify the use of such equilibrium assumptions through the theory of "rational expectations" based on the claim that people can perfectly anticipate what everyone will do, thus taking the system to equilibrium even faster.

The attraction of the assumption of "equilibrium" is the simplicity that results from having only to consider simultaneous and not dynamical equations, and also that it seems to offer the possibility of looking at a decision or policy in terms of a stationary state "before" and "after" the decision, with an "evaluation" of "costs" and "benefits" made on these.

(II) Non-linear dynamical systems

However, nonlinear dynamics, System Dynamics, are what results from a modelling exercise when *both* assumptions are made but equilibrium is not assumed. This is clearly more general than an equilibrium model since the latter is contained as a special case when certain conditions can be shown to hold. What is important to note however, is that nonlinear dynamics is interesting precisely because the system does not necessarily run to a single equilibrium state, but can exhibit a rich spectrum of possible behaviours. They can:

(a) have different possible stationary states. So, instead of a single, "optimal" equilibrium, there may exist several possible equilibria, possibly with different spatial configurations, and the initial condition of the system will decide which it adopts;

(b) have different possible cyclic solutions. These might be found to correspond to the business cycle, for example, or to long waves;

(c) it may exhibit chaotic motion of various kinds.

A given set of nonlinear equations may, for different parameter values, have several different attractor basins, corresponding to different possible stable solutions of type (a), (b), or (c), but such systems cannot *of themselves* cross a separatrix to a new basin of attraction, and therefore can only continue along trajectories that are within the attractor of their initial condition. Compared to reality then, such systems lack the "vitality" to spontaneously jump to the regime of a different attractor basin.

(III) Self-organizing systems

This "self-organizing" behaviour is obtained for a system if the *first assumption is not made*. That is to say that the non-average fluctuations of the variables are retained in the description, and in the original work, Nicolis and Prigogine (1977) called the phenomenon "Order by Fluctuation". Mathematically this corresponds to using a deeper, probabilistic dynamics of Markov processes (Bharucha-Reid, 1960) and leads to the "Master Equation" which while retaining assumption 2, assumes that events of different probabilities can and do occur. So, sequences of events which correspond to successive runs of good or bad "luck" are included, with their relevant probabilities. As has been shown elsewhere (Allen, 1988) for systems with nonlinear interactions between individuals, what this does is to destroy the idea of a *trajectory*, and gives to the system a collective adaptive capacity corresponding to the spontaneous spatial reorganization of its structure. That is to say that the presence of "noise" can allow the system itself to cross separatrices and adopt new regimes of collective behaviour, corresponding to spatial or hierarchical organization, and this can be imitated to some degree by simply adding "noise" to the variables of the system. The "noise" probes the stability of any existing configuration and when instability occurs, leads to the emergence of new structures. In other words, self-organization can be seen as a *collective adaptive response* to changing external conditions, and results from the addition of noise to the deterministic equations of system dynamics.

The fact is that in the real system unpredictable runs of good and bad luck, represented by "noise", can and do occur, and these deviations from the average rate of events mean that a real system can "tunnel" through apparently impassable potential barriers, the separatrices in state space. As a result it can switch between attractor basins and explore the global space of the dynamical system in a way that the dynamical system cannot.

(IV) Evolutionary complex systems

Let us now make the distinction between self-organization and evolution. Here, it is the assumption 2 that matters, namely that all individuals either are identical and equal to the average type, or have a diversity that remains normally distributed around the average type. Here we show that the distribution of micro diversity is the result of the local dynamics occurring in the system, and hence that it is governed by, and in the long term governs the dynamical system. The real world is of course characterized by *microscopic diversity* which underlies any classification scheme of variables chosen as representative at any particular time. The effects of this have been described elsewhere (Allen and McGlade, 1987a, 1987; Allen, 1988, 1990 . . .) and so we shall only review them briefly below.

We can summarize the different levels of model from deterministic equations to full evolutionary models as shown in Figure 2.

Obviously, all macroscopic systems are "complex" systems, since they are composed of a hierarchy of subsystems, leading ultimately to atoms and molecules. However, if there exist macroscopic components, whose internal structure can be assumed to be fixed during the system run, then the hierarchy can be "cut" and the model will correctly describe the course of events, providing that the integrity of the components is not compromised, and indeed that they do not adapt and change in the light of their experience. For systems made up of micro components with fixed internal structure, their interactions can lead to *self-organization*. However, if the micro components have diverse internal structures, then *evolution* can take place as the emergent macrostructure affects the local circumstances experienced by individuals, and this affects the relative performance of different kinds of individuals which in turn changes the macrostructure generated.

Complex systems modelling, when micro diversity is considered explicitly, leads naturally to a hierarchy of linked levels of description. Rapid changes will occur when the behaviour and strategies of individuals do not provide them with a satisfactory payoff in the macrostructure that exists, and so eccentric and deviant behaviour will be amplified and will lead to a structural reorganisation of the system. *Stability, or at least quasi-stability will occur when the microstructures are compatible with the macrostructures they both create and inhabit.*

In order to understand and model a system, we must derive a reduced description, which creates simplicity at the cost of making increasingly strong assumptions. The simplifications arise by taking averages, and writing in terms of *typical* elements of the system according to the classification scheme that has been chosen. Underneath the "model" there will always be the greater particularity and diversity of reality. In the mechanical view (II), predictions can be made by simply running the equations forward in time, and studying where they lead. Is there a unique "attractor", into which all initial states eventually fall, or are there many possible final

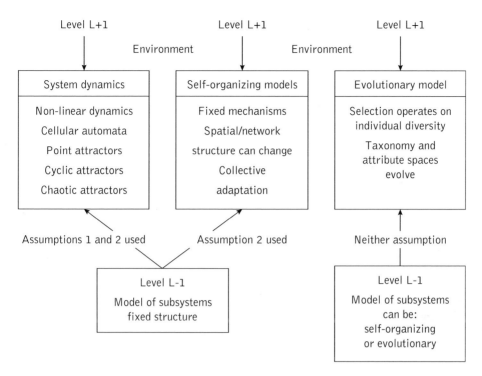

Figure 2 The hierarchy of modelling in which level L sits within L+1, and is constituted of elements at level L-1: deterministic and self-organizing models link L-1 to L, but the evolutionary model relates the full, nested hierarchy, L-n, …L-1, L, L+1, …L+n

end points? Does the system continue in a series of eternal cycles? Or, does it display chaotic behaviour, as the trajectory wraps itself around a "strange attractor"? With self-organizing systems (III) we may find that the system can spontaneously move from one type of behaviour to another as the "noise" explores different attractor basins. The aim of the model then becomes to explore the different possible regimes of operation of the system, and the probabilities of moving towards these different attractors. However, we should remember that models (II) and (III) are only of any significance if the *equations and the fixed mechanisms* within them *remain a good description* of the system. But, from the picture of the evolutionary tree in Figure 1 that we know really characterizes complex systems, the taxonomy of the system, the variables present and the mechanisms which link them, actually *change over time*. Because of this, any dynamical system that we are running as a model of the system will only be a good description for as long as there is no evolutionary change, and no new variables or mechanisms appear.

In order to explore the behaviour of systems without assumptions 1 or 2, with endogenously generated innovations and selection we define a "possibility space", a space representing the range of different techniques and behaviours that could potentially arise. In practice, of course, this is a multidimensional space of which we would only be able to anticipate a few of the principal dimensions. This "possibility space" will be inhabited by diverse individuals and groups whose performance will reveal the payoff of specific kinds of non-average behaviour [see Figure 3]. In biology,

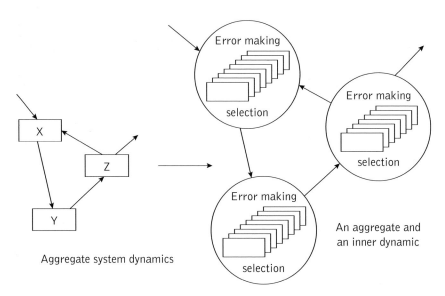

Figure 3 In reality we have an "inner" dynamic within the macroscopic system dynamics: micro diversity, in various possible dimensions, is differentially selected, leading to adaptation and emergence of new behaviours

genetic mechanisms ensure that different possibilities are explored, a population spread from any pure condition. In human systems the imperfections and subjectivity of existence mean that techniques and behaviours are never passed on exactly, and therefore that exploration is always present as a result of the individuality and contextual nature of experience. Physical constraints mean that some behaviours do better than others, and so imitation and growth lead to the increase of some behaviours and the decline of others.

By considering dynamic equations in which there is a "diffusion" outwards in character space from any behaviour that is present, we can see how such a system would evolve. If there are types of behaviour with higher and lower payoffs, then the diffusion "uphill" is gradually amplified, that "downhill" is suppressed, and the "average" for the whole population moves higher up the slope. This is the mechanism by which adaptation takes place. This demonstrates the vital part played by exploratory, non-average behaviour, and showed that, in the long term, evolution selects for populations with the ability to learn, rather than for populations with optimal, but fixed, behaviour (Allen and McGlade, [1989]).

Let us consider a "possibility" or "character" space in which the "payoffs", the adaptive landscapes, are really generated by the interactions of a population with the other populations in the system. In the space of "possibilities" closely similar behaviours are considered to be most in competition with each other, since they require similar resources, and must find a similar niche in the system. However, we assume that in this particular dimension there is some "distance" in character space, some level of dissimilarity, at which two behaviours do not compete. In Figure 4 we start off an experiment with a single population in an "empty" resource space, resources are plentiful, the average at the centre of the distribution grows better than the

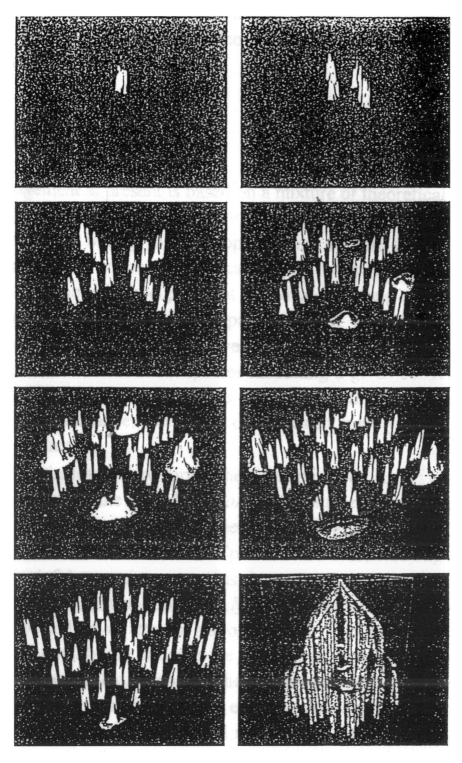

Figure 4 In this case the landscape explored by the emergent behaviours is shaped by them: despite a constant level of error making, periods of structural stability are separated by periods of change; the final frame shows the evolutionary tree generated by the system

eccentrics at the edge. The population forms a sharp spike, with the diffusing eccentrics suppressed by their unsuccessful competition with the average type. However, any single behaviour can only grow until it reaches the limits set either by its input requirements, or for an economic activity, by the market limit for any particular product. After this, it is the "error-makers" that grow more successfully than the "average type", as they are less in competition with the others, and the population *identity* becomes unstable. The sharply spiked distribution spreads, and splits into new behaviours that climb the evolutionary landscape that has been created, leading away from the ancestral type. The new behaviours move away from each other, and grow until in their turn they reach the limits of their new normality, whereupon they also split into new behaviours, gradually filling the resource spectrum.

In Figure 4 we see the changing qualitative structure of the system over time, in some two-dimensional possibility space. In this way, instead of simply evolving towards the peaks of a fixed evolutionary landscape, through their interactions populations really create the landscape upon which they move, and by moving across it change it. So the different behaviours present grow, split off, and gradually fill the possibility space with an "ecology" of activities, each identity and role being formed by the mutual interaction and identities of the others. The limit of such a process would be given by the amount of energy that is available for useful work that can be accessed by the "technological" possibilities potentially open to the system.

While the "error-making" and inventive capacity of the system in our simulation are a constant fraction of the activity present at any time, the system evolves in discontinuous steps of instability, separated by periods of taxonomic stability. So, there are times when the system structure can suppress the incipient instabilities caused by the innovative exploration of its inhabitants, and there are other times when it cannot suppress them, and a new population emerges. Although competition helps to "drive" the selection process, what is observed is that a system with "error making" explorations of behaviour evolves towards structures which express synergetic complementarities. In other words, evolution evolves towards cooperative structures, involving pairs, triplets, and so on. This corresponds to the emergence of "hyper cycles" in physical and chemical systems (Eigen and Schuster, 1979).

Several important points can now be made. Firstly, a successful and sustainable evolutionary system will clearly be one in which there is *freedom* for imagination and creativity to explore at the individual level, leading to micro diversity which can be differentially selected. Secondly, the evolution of our system leads to a highly cooperative system, where the competition per individual is low, but where loops of positive feedback and synergy are high. In other words, the *free evolution of the different populations, each seeking its own growth, leads to a system which is more cooperative than competitive.* From this work we find that the discovery of cooperativities, and the formation of communities of players with a shared interest in each other's success, is the outcome of the evolutionary process.

The third important point, particularly for modellers, is that from observing the population data it would be impossible to infer the "correct" model equations. Because any single behaviour could be playing a positive, or negative role in a self, or pair or triplet etc. interaction, it would be impossible to "untangle" its interactions and infer the equations simply by noting the population's growth or decline. The system itself, through the error-making search process, can find stable arrangements of multiple actors, and can self-organize a balance between the actors in play, and the interactions that they bring with them, but this does not mean that we can deduce what the web of interactions really is. This certainly poses problems for the rational analysis of complex human situations.

3 Fishery management: a model of complexity

In this section let us illustrate all these different points with a particular case for which models corresponding to (I) Neo-Classical, Equilibrium Approach, (II) System Dynamics, (III) Self-Organizing Systems, (IV) Evolutionary, Learning Systems. The system is the Scotian Shelf Groundfish fishery off the Canadian Atlantic coast.

(I) Equilibrium approach

Fishery management at present is based on a mixture of theoretical concepts and practical considerations. The theoretical approaches have two fundamental aspects: the biology of fish populations and the theories of economics. The former is concerned with calculating the growth characteristics of fish, assessing how fast weight is put on, when spawning occurs etc. and also with establishing the relevant parameters of a particular species' population dynamics. In practice, however, instead of modelling the interactive processes of the different species inhabiting a given ecosystem, the equations discussed are for each species separately, with the effects of other species, of food abundance, and indeed of fishermen, merely represented by exogenous parameters.

In addition, instead of exploring the "dynamics" of such systems, the emphasis has been on the *equilibrium or static* solutions of such equations. Initially, this sprang from the laudable desire to look at the "long term yield" of a fishery, rather than the immediate "profit". However, studying the equilibrium solution of deterministic equations immediately rules out the possibility that the long term situation may be *dynamic* – that a fish population may always change and never attain a stationary state. These notions of determinism and of equilibrium underlie the concept of "maximum sustainable yield" that has dominated much of fishery management thinking for many years. In reality, fish populations, fishing effort, technology and even markets all change over such a time scale, and in addition, if the model is used to make management decisions, then clearly these must also disturb the system and invalidate the model on which they are based.

The underlying model of the traditional approach to Fisheries Science was that of the logistic equation for a single species,

$$\frac{dx}{dt} = bx(1 - \frac{x}{N}) - mx - Fx$$

x is the population of fish, b a "birth" or "recruitment" rate, N is some limiting factor for maximum density, m is the natural mortality and F is the fishing mortality.

The equilibrium solution of this is:

$$x° = N\left(1 - \frac{(m+F)}{b}\right)$$

which leads to the equation for the total yield of the fishery as a function of effort, F,

$$Yield = Fx° = FN\left(1 - \frac{m}{b}\right) - F^2\frac{N}{b}$$

which is a parabola describing how the equilibrium yield from fishing with an effort F rises from zero, passes through a maximum (the famous "maximum sustainable yield", MSY) and then falls off to zero.

By adding to this curve the linear costs of fishing effort, including a "normal profit", then the economic equilibrium point could be shown to be quite possibly beyond the point of maximum sustainable yield [see Figure 5].

Originally then, fisheries management was based on the idea of reducing fishing effort to such a level that it was either at, or just below, the maximum sustainable fishing effort. These ideas have been pursued and complicated over the years, but the fundamental principles have remained unchanged. The point is that the fishery has to be "at equilibrium" for these equations to apply, and this turns out to be simply not true. In order for Figure 5 to apply, equilibrium must hold, and for this the fishing effort must not change, the fish stock must have a constant recruitment, b, and natural mortality, m, and in addition the price of fish must not change. These shortcomings, and the fact that prices do in fact change so that economic equilibrium is also incorrect, have been highlighted by various authors (Beddington, 1979; Beddington and May, 1977; May et al., 1979), and by Allen and McGlade (1987[b]). We shall not go into detail here.

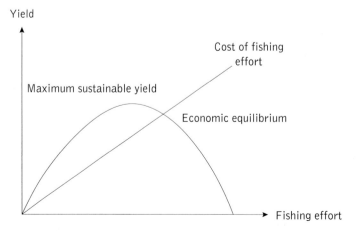

Figure 5 A schematic view of the "equilibrium" model for fisheries management

(II) Non-linear systems dynamics

Moving from the oversimplification of the right-hand side of Figure 1 we come to the possibility of developing a System Dynamics model of the fishery, in which the factors like fish stocks, fishing effort, prices and so on will be allowed to vary over time. The data for the model comes from the Nova Scotia Groundfish fisheries, which are mainly concerned with the catch of three species: Haddock, Cod and Pollock. This catch data is extremely variable, and certainly does not suggest "equilibrium". If we smooth out the yearly cycles of seasonal fishing then we perceive very large underlying trends, and the most obvious mechanism is that of the inter-action between fishermen and fish, an interaction which essentially is that of a predator and its prey. It corresponds to a mechanism that relates an increase in fishing effort (number of vessels and time spent fishing) and a high "catch rate" to a large fish stock, and inversely relates a decrease in fleet size to low catches.

Our equations describe the changes in five variables (x_1, x_2, x_3, y and p). The first three are the populations of young fish (1 and 2 year olds), of medium fish (3 and 4 year olds) and of old fish (5 and over). The fourth equation describes how fishing effort responds to the revenue and profit obtainable by fishing haddock, and the fifth equation takes into account the change in price of fish as supply, demand and price change.

$$\frac{dx_1}{dt} = bx_3\left(1 - \frac{Tx}{N}\right) - m_1 x_1 - s_1 x_1 y - \frac{x_1}{T_1}$$

$$\frac{dx_2}{dt} = \frac{x_1}{T_1} - m_2 x_2 - s_2 x_2 y - \frac{x_2}{T_2}$$

$$\frac{dx_3}{dt} = \frac{x_2}{T_2} - m_3 x_3 - s_3 x_3 y$$

For the boats:

$$\frac{dy}{dt} = ry\left(\frac{p(w_1 s_1 x_1 + w_2 s_2 x_2 + w_3 s_3 x_3)}{c + pr} - 1\right)$$

For the price of fish:

$$\frac{dp}{dt} = rrp\left(\frac{MA}{(p + \in p_3^4)^e (w_1 s_1 x_1 + w_2 s_2 x_2 + w_3 s_3 x_3)} - 1\right)$$

where

w_i	=	weight at age I
b	=	rate of production of x_1 per adult
Tx	=	total fish biomass

m = natural mortality
T_i = time span of group I, $I = 1.2$
y = number of boat/effort units
c = cost of fishing for each boat
pr = profit desired in order to maintain effort
r = rate of response of effort
rr = rate of response of price
MA = market per unit time at unit price
p = price
e = elasticity of demand
ε = demand cut-off parameter

If we study the behaviour of these equations for the simplest possible situation where there is no price mechanism, then we find that there is a single stationary state, and that the factor $(1 - Tx/N)$ ensures that it is stable. Figure 6 shows a typical deterministic trajectory of the system in a damped oscillatory motion towards the stable stationary state. However, it should be noted that the characteristic time in which the system goes to equilibrium is greater than 40 years for any reasonable values of the parameters.

If our model behaves like the real fishery, then it may be very useful to examine the effects of different management strategies, or of a growth or decline in demand for fish. However, when we compare the trajectories of the system with the real data then we see that while the model runs to equilibrium, reality does not seem to. Also, observations concerning the recruitment (b) of young fish into the fishery do not correspond to the smooth assumption we have made. In fact, there are very large *fluctuations in the recruitment rate* of young fish, and these may correspond to

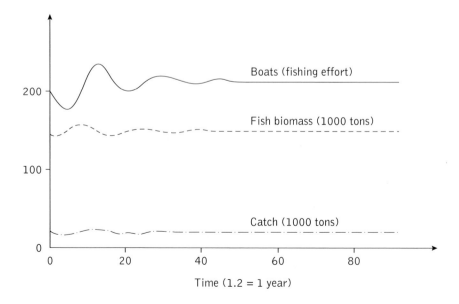

Figure 6 The model of equations (1) run deterministically

unpredictable movements of warm water up the coast, from the Gulf Stream flowing across the Atlantic. This is where we now move towards a Self-Organizing model of the fisheries, because we now can put into our model the non-average rate of recruitment that is really the case.

(III) A self-organizing model of the fishery

The important point here is that we are simply going to relax the assumption (1) that the rates of the different processes represented in the model are not in fact always average but in fact fluctuate around an average. In particular, it is known that for Haddock recruitment (b) there are good years, average years and bad years, and we have data concerning the distribution of these. If we add random terms (add noise) into the value of b, then our model will be a more accurate representation of the mechanisms involved. We ensure that on average, over a long period, the average value of b is maintained, but that in each particular year we may find either high, medium or very low rates.

The result is dramatic. In Figure 7 we see how the system *amplifies* these random fluctuations in b and sets itself into relatively violent, irregular oscillations. Turning off the fluctuations would lead to a stationary state after some 30 or 40 years, but clearly, to the question "Are cyclic crises in fisheries of natural or man made origin?" we may suggest a new answer – both. The human responses can amplify relatively rapid fluctuations and generate large Volterra-Lotka type oscillations with a period of around 15–20 years. However, without this natural "background" noise, there would be nothing to amplify, and the fishery would be stable (Nisbet and Gurney, 1982). So, our improved model tells us that the large changes in landings that are observed in reality are indeed predicted by the model. Instead of a system that moves to equilibrium and a state that could be discussed in terms of the MSY etc.

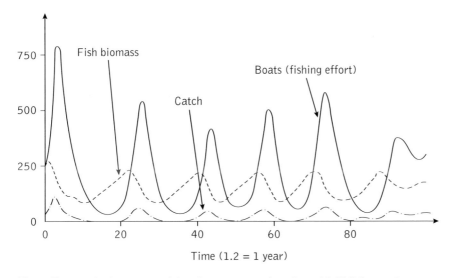

Figure 7 Exactly the same model and parameter values, but with "b" fluctuating

we find irregular oscillations of "boom and bust" for the fleets. Management should really concern itself with the problem of overcoming this cyclical behaviour, rather than discussing which equilibrium state should be the target.

We can study the evolution of the system in terms of the "probability" of finding it with a particular value of fish and boat population. In order to do this, we therefore plot each time step on the phase space (the space of the possible boat and fish populations) of the system, and then accumulate the number of phase points in each small region, giving rise to a "mountain" in the third dimension that shows us the regions of phase space in which the system spent most time.

For example, if we run our system for 1000 years of fishing, with different values of r, the rate of response of the fishermen, we find the Figures 8 and 9. These show us that increasing r makes the system less and less stable, and leads to more violent oscillations in the size of the fishing fleet and the fish stocks.

However, if we ask "What kind of *behaviour* can *invade* the system?", then we find that fleets with larger values of r will always replace those with smaller values. Similarly, higher values of s, corresponding to better technology, will also "invade", as will lower values of c. All of these are "economically rational" in the short term, and yet all of them lead, in the long term, to lower yields and to a much more unstable system.

Now we shall study our model with the parameter rr, of price response, not equal to 0, then our model will simulate the situation where fish stocks, fishing

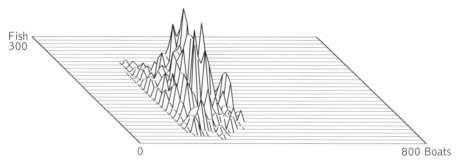

Figure 8 The probability of finding values of x and y if the model is run for 1000 years: here $r = 0.02$, a slow rate of response; fish are in units of 1000 tons

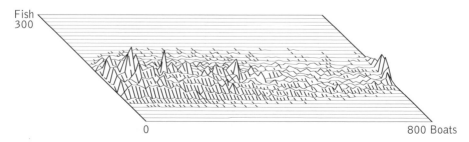

Figure 9 For a fast rate of response, $r = 2$, corresponding to the ability to double effort in 6 months, we see a very flat distribution. The deterministic solution will almost never be observed, and enormous oscillations will occur

effort, profits, demand and price are all determined dynamically within the system. While many simulations resemble the previous ones, with a simple, noisy cycle of "boom and bust" dynamic for the fishery, for low "elasticity of demand" an entirely new situation can emerge.

This is shown in Figure 10 where we see that the system has "discovered" a second "basin" of attraction. It corresponds to a regime of very low fish stocks, very large oscillations of fishing effort, and to very high-priced fish. Depending on the parameter values, the two basins of attraction can vary in their depth, and in their nearness to one another. However, the important point of principle remains that a system can oscillate in years, giving no indication of the existence of "other" regimes. It can also flip-flop in and out of the basins in an unpredictable manner and over a relatively short time. What it shows us then is that for the same fish, the same fishermen, the same price mechanism and the same demand for fish, the *system* can operate in two qualitatively different modes, which offer quite different satisfactions to the different actors of the system.

In fact, we can use our model to run through the "evolution" of a typical fishery. It will start with low technology, subsistence fishing for just the local community. At some point a price mechanism or an equivalent will appear in order to adjust the demand and supply. Once this appears, then in a "young" fishery that is hardly exploited the "price" of fish is very low. This leads naturally to an expansion of the "market", and to greater demand for fish. Competition then leads to higher technology, lower costs, faster reactions and more powerful boats. Although at first these tend to hold down cost increases, as fish become more difficult to catch, so price increases. At some point, if free competition persists, the system will suffer collapse either of the entire industry, or into the "high price" basin where fish are a rare "luxury", supporting perhaps a thriving industry. This kind of *strategic insight* is given by the model, together with a much better picture of how the fisheries may evolve, and of the real effects of different policy options.

An important point resulting from this discussion is that our model, which is giving such complex behaviour, is in fact only a non-spatial model for a single species of fish. In the next section, therefore, we shall describe a multi-species spatial model where fishing behaviour can be modelled much more correctly, and where the fisherman's knowledge and his information play a vital role.

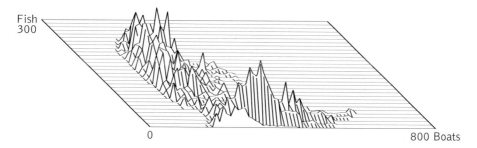

Figure 10 For an elasticity of demand of 0.5, a second basin of oscillation can appear corresponding to very low catches of very high-priced fish

(IIIa) A self-organizing spatial, multispecies, multifleet model

In this section we take the modelling to the next step in disaggregation. Here instead of adding all the figures for different zones together, we shall consider a spatial model with 40 zones. The model will take into account the information which fishermen have concerning fish abundances, and the "expected revenue" that could be obtained from fishing a particular zone, and our model will capture the knowledge that exists concerning fish stocks. This is by no means a trivial matter because essentially this information comes from the fishing activity of other boats, and therefore there is a tendency for the pattern of fishing to structure spatially because high catches result in a concentration of effort and, in consequence, high catches in that zone. Areas where fishing boats are absent send no information about potential catch and revenue. This provides a spatial positive feedback mechanism that structures fishing patterns.

We have used a very simple "logistic" equation for each fish species, and we have assumed that there is competition between them. In our equations, however, we must add a subscript for the zone I, and a superscript for the species k.

The second equation is that governing the spatial distribution of fishing boats, or effort. It has two essential terms. The first takes into account the increase or decrease of fishing effort in zone I, by fleet L, according to how profitable it is. If the catch rate is high for a species of high value, then revenue greatly exceeds the costs incurred in fishing there, provided that the zone is not too distant from the port. Then effort will increase. If the opposite is true then effort will decrease. The second term takes into account the fact that due to information flows in the system (radio communication, conversations in port bars, spying etc.) to a certain extent each fleet is aware of the catches being made by others. Of course, boats within the same fleet may communicate freely the best locations, and even between fleets there is always some "leakage" of information. This results in the spatial migration of boats according to the "expected profit" that may be made at the different locations. Let us first write down the equations.

Our equations are:

$$\frac{dx_i^k}{dt} = b^k x_i (1 - tx_i / N_i) - m^k x_i - \sum_L \frac{s^L x^k y^L}{1 + \sum_k s^L x^k \tau}$$

$$\frac{dy_i^L}{dt} = ry_i^L \left(\frac{\sum_k \dfrac{s^L x_i^k y^L}{1 + \sum_k s^L x^k \tau}}{c_i + pr} - 1 \right) + \xi \sum_{j \neq i} \frac{y_j^i A_{ij}^L}{\sum_{i'} A_{i'j}^L} - \xi y_i \frac{\sum_{j \neq i} A_{ji}^L}{\sum_L A \neq L_{ji}} \tag{2}$$

b^k	=	the birth rate of fish type k
tx_i	=	the total fish biomass of each zone
N_i	=	the total carrying capacity of each zone
m^k	=	the natural mortality rate
s^L	=	the encounter rate of fish and boats

$1/\tau$ = the maximum catch rate
r = the rate of response of effort
p^k = price per kg of fish k
c_i = cost per unit time of fishing at I
pr = desired profit level
A_{ij}^L = the attractivity of I viewed from j, by L
ξ_{ij}^L = the mobility of the spatial migration

Now, the really new feature in this equation, as compared to our previous model (III), is the spatial dimension, and the way that the pattern of fishing shifts according to the "attractivity" of the different zones. What factors are taken into account in the "attractivity"?

For these terms we use the idea of "boundedly rational" decision makers, who do not have "perfect" information or absolutely "rational" decision making capacity. In other words, each individual has a *probability* of being attracted to zone I, say, given by

$$P(i) = \frac{A_i}{\sum_j A_j}$$

where A_i is the attractivity of zone I. Since probability must vary between 0 and 1, we see that A must always be defined as positive, and a convenient form is:

$$A_i = e^{lU_i} \tag{3}$$

where U_i is a "utility function". U_i constitutes the "expected profit" of the zone I, taking into account the revenue from the "expected catch" and the costs of crew, boat and fuel etc. that must be expended to get it.

The particular form used for U_i is:

$$U_{ij} = \alpha_1 \sum_{L'} \in (L, L') \sum_k \frac{s^{L'} x_i {}^k Y_i^{L'}}{1 + \sigma_k s^k x_i {}^k \tau} \cdot \frac{1}{1 + sy_i^{L'}} - \alpha_2 \phi d_{ij} - \alpha_3 \phi d_{ip,}$$

where
$\in (L, L')$ = the information exchange matrix between fleets L and L'
ϕ = the fuel cost per unit distance
d_{ij} = the distance from I to j
d_{ip} = the distance from I to port

In this way we see that boats are attracted to zones where high catches and catch rates are occurring, but the information only passes if there is communication between the boats in I and in j. This will depend on the "information exchange" matrix, which will express whether there is cooperation, spying or indifference between the different fleets. However, responses in general will be tempered by the distances involved, and the cost of fuel [see Figure 11].

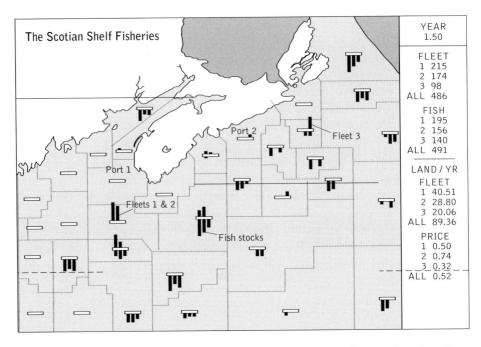

Figure 11 An initial condition of spatial fishing model. Two trawler fleets and one long liner fleet attempt to fish three species (Cod, Haddock and Pollock)

In addition to these effects, however, our equation takes another very important factor into account. That is the factor I in equation (3). This factor expresses how "rationally", how "homogeneously" or with what probability a particular skipper will respond to the information he is receiving. For example, if I is small, then whatever the "real" attraction of a zone I, as expressed in U, the probability of going to any zone is roughly the same. In other words, "information" is largely disregarded, and movement is "random". We have called this type of skipper a *Stochast*. Alternatively if I is large, then it means that even the smallest difference in the attraction of several zones will result in each skipper going, with probability 1, to the most attractive zone. In other words, such deciders put complete faith in the information they have, and do not "risk" moving outside of what they *know*. These "ultra rationalists" we have called *Cartesians*. The movement of the boats around the system is generated by the difference at a given time between the number of boats that would like to be in each zone, compared to the number that actually are there. As the boats congregate in particular locations of high catch, so they fish out the fish population that originally attracted them. They must then move onto the next zone which attracts them, and in this way there is a continuing dynamic evolution of fish populations and of the pattern of fishing effort.

Let us describe briefly some of the preliminary computer runs that we have made for this model. First let us consider the competition between fleets 1 and 2 and the initial condition shown above. Let us run the model for 20 years, and see how the "rationality" I affects the outcome.

In this case fleet 2 beats fleet 1 after 20 years [see Figure 12], so that the rational strategy of $I = 2$ is better than $I = .1$. However, if we repeat the same simulation but with the "Stochast" fleet 1 with a rationality I of .5, and with fleet 2 still at $I = 2$, then we find the result below.

This is a remarkable result. The higher the value of I, the better the fleet optimizes its use of information and in the short term increases profits. But, this does not necessarily succeed in the long term. After leaving the port and locating a first fish aggregate, they "lock on" to this zone and stay fishing there for too long, because it is the only information available. These Cartesians are not "risk-takers" who will go out to zones with no information, and hence they get "locked in" to the existing pattern of fishing. The Stochasts ($I = .5$), providing that they are not totally random ($I < .1$), succeed in both discovering new zones with fish stocks, and also in exploiting those that they have already located [see Figure 13].

This paradoxical situation results from the fact that in order to fish effectively, two distinct phases must be accomplished. First the fish must be "discovered". This requires risk-takers who will go out into the "unknown" and explore, whatever present knowledge is. The second phase, however, requires that when a concentration of fish has been discovered, then the fleet will move in massively to exploit this, the most profitable location. These two facets are both necessary, but call on different qualities.

The simulation system can be used to explore which behavioural strategies work for different fleets and examine how the pattern of fishing results from a process of spatial self-organization, which needs to "fit" the patterns of fish stocks, and of their decline under fishing, and recovery when fishing pressure relaxes. Let us briefly summarize the pattern of behaviours that could evolve in a fishery as the result of experimentation among fishermen.

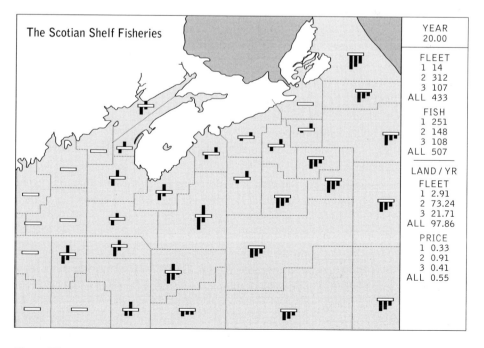

Figure 12 After 20 years fleet 2 (Cartesians $I = 2$) has beaten fleet 1 (Stochasts $I = 0.0$)

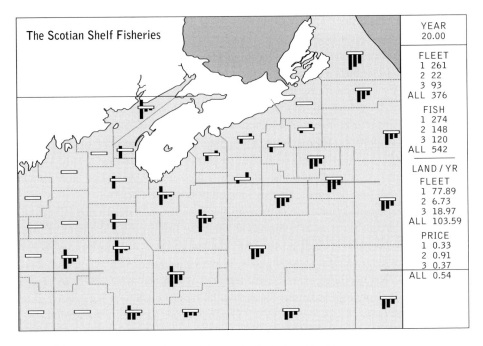

The Scotian Shelf Fisheries

	YEAR 20.00
FLEET	1 261
	2 22
	3 93
	ALL 376
FISH	1 274
	2 148
	3 120
	ALL 542
LAND / YR	
FLEET	1 77.89
	2 6.73
	3 18.97
	ALL 103.59
PRICE	1 0.33
	2 0.91
	3 0.37
	ALL 0.54

Figure 13 Here the Stochast ($I = 0.5$) beats the Cartesian ($I = 2$)

- Fleets find a moderate behaviour with rationality between .5 and 1
- Cartesians try to use the information generated by Stochasts, by following them, and by listening in to their communications.
- Stochasts attempt to conceal their knowledge, by communicating in code, by sailing out at night, and by providing misleading information.
- Stochasts and Cartesians combine to form a cooperative venture with Stochasts as "scouts" and Cartesians as "exploiters". Profits are shared.
- Different combinations of a Stochast/Cartesian behaviour compete.
- In this cooperative situation there is always a short term advantage to a participant who will cheat.
- Different strategies of specialization are adopted, e.g. deep-sea or inshore fishing, or specialization by species.
- A fleet may adopt "variable" rationality, adapting its search effort according to the circumstances.
- In all circumstances, the rapidity of response to profit and loss turns out to be advantageous, and so the instability of the whole system increases over time.

The real point of these results is that they show us that there is no such thing as an Optimal Strategy. As soon as any particular strategy becomes dominant in the system, it will always be vulnerable to the invasion of some other strategy. Complexity and instability are the inevitable consequence of the fishermen's efforts to survive, and of their capacity to explore different possible strategies. The important point is that a strategy does not necessarily need to lead to better global performance of the system in order to invade. Indeed nearly all the innovations that can and will invade the fishing system lead to lower overall performance, and indeed to collapse. Thus, higher technology, more powerful boats, faster reactions etc. all lead to a decrease in output of fish.

In reality, the strategies that invade the system are ones that pay off for a particular actor *in the short term*. Yet globally and over a long period, the effect may be quite negative. For example, fast responses to profit/loss, or improved technology are all things that will invade the system, but they make it more fragile and less stable than before. This illustrates the idea that the evolution of complexity is not necessarily "progress", and the system is not necessarily moving towards some "greater good".

(IV) Evolutionary fishing, learning how to fish

The spatial, self-organizing model developed above did not assume that events proceeded at their average rates, or that fish were distributed evenly throughout the system. As a result the pattern of fishing and the effectiveness of different strategies could be examined and it was found that behaviour that was sub-optimal in the short term was necessary in order to deal with the ongoing problem of responding to the changing pattern of fish. Strategies in reality had not only to harvest known fish stocks successfully, but they also had to find new stocks as the previous ones were fished out, and this entailed a "stochastic" behaviour.

Now we move to the final stage in this example. What happens when we try to develop a model that does not make either assumption 1 or 2 in section 2? So, not only do we have an uneven and changing pattern of fish stocks in the system, but we are also not going to consider that the "taxonomy" of boat types and fleet behaviours is fixed. We can now develop a model that will explore the relative effectiveness of different strategies, and will search for success, not just in geographic space, but also in "strategy space", and will discover robust fishing strategies for us.

To do this, we can run many fleets simultaneously (our current software will run up to 8) from identical initial conditions. The fleets differ, however, in the values of the parameters governing their fishing strategy and whether or not they spy on and copy some other fleets. The more effective strategies will be reinforced and gradually will dominate the less successful strategies. However, when a fleet is losing, then the model stops fishing, and explores the parameter space of the losing fleet, and tries a new value of one of the parameters. If it continues to lose, it will keep searching and changing its behavioural parameters, so that successive fleets will find winning strategies, and our model will gradually evolve sets of compatible behaviours. Each of these will be effective in the context of the others, not objectively optimal. In addition, such a system can adapt to changed external circumstances, and could be used to show us "robust heuristics" for the exploitation of renewable natural resources.

The importance of this model is that it demonstrates how, as we relax the assumptions that we normally make in order to obtain simple, mechanistic representations of reality, we find that our model can really tell us things that we did not know. So, the addition of noise to the non-spatial model allowed us to discover that there were 2 different regimes of operation possible for most fisheries, even though there may have been no hint of this in the observations used to build the model. Secondly, in the spatial model, we found that economically sub-optimal behaviour was necessary in order to fish successfully, and that there was no single "optimal" behaviour or strategy, but there were possible sets of compatible strategies. The pattern of fishing effort at any time cannot be "explained" as being optimal in any way, but instead is just one particular moment in an unending, imperfect learning process involving the ocean, the natural ecosystem and the fishermen.

From this final section, we find that what matters now is even further from the "observed" behaviour of the boats and the fish [see Figure 14]. It concerns the mechanisms, not visible on the screen, by which the parameter spaces of fishing behaviours are explored. Clearly, depending on the mechanisms included in the model, a fleet may respond slowly or rapidly, and with an effective or an ineffective riposte. By running "learning fleets" with different learning mechanisms in competition with each other, our model can begin to show us which mechanisms succeed in successfully accumulating knowledge of how to succeed, and which do not. Our model has moved from the domain of the physical: mesh size, boat power, trawling versus long lining etc. to the nonphysical: how often am I monitoring performance?, what changes could I explore?, how can I change behaviour?, which parameters are effective?, in short – how can I learn?

As a result, we see that by relaxing both assumptions 1 and 2 we move from a mechanical model of physical significance to an evolving model, where behaviour and strategies change as the result of learning, and so the internal nature of the participants changes through time.

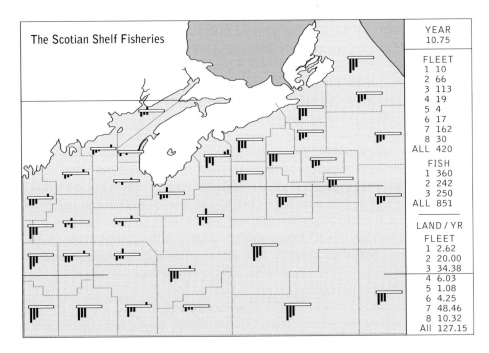

Figure 14 After 30 years fleet 1 has the best strategy, although previously fleet 2 was best and then fleet 3

4 Discussion

We have shown that mathematical modelling is an activity in which "simplicity" is bought at the expense of assumptions. If these are all true, then we have a truly appropriate, and useful model, but if the assumptions do not hold, then our model may be completely misleading. Our reflection considered: equilibrium assumptions where change is assumed exogenous; assumptions of fixed mechanisms leading to nonlinear dynamics, where behaviours change but invariance lies in the preference functions of actors; and finally, evolutionary, learning models in which behaviours and preferences, goals and strategies can change, but the "learning mechanisms" are invariant. These represent successively more general models, each step containing the previous one as a special case, but also of increasing difficulty, and indeed still probably far from "reality". It is small wonder that most people probably have a very poor understanding of the real consequences of their actions or policies.

The discussion of this chapter also brings out much concerning the ideas of "sustainable development" which is in fashion. As we have seen, this idea should not be interpreted as the search for the perfect equilibrium. The world will never stop changing, and what sustainability is really about is the capacity to respond, to adapt and to invent new activities. The power to do this lies not in extreme efficiency, nor can it be had necessarily by allowing free markets to operate unhindered. It lies in *creativity*. And in turn this is rooted in diversity, cultural richness, openness, and the will and ability to experiment and to take risks.

Instead of viewing the changes that occur in a complex system as necessarily reflecting progress up some preexisting (if complex) landscape, we have shown that the landscape of possible advantage itself is produced by the actors in interaction, and that the detailed history of the exploration process itself affects the outcome. Paradoxically, *uncertainty* is therefore *inevitable*, and we must face this. Long term success is not just about improving performance with respect to the external environment of resources and technology, but also is affected by the "internal game" of a complex society. The "payoff" of any action for an individual cannot be stated in absolute terms, because it depends on what other individuals are doing. Strategies are interdependent.

Ecological organization is what results from evolution, and it is composed of self-consistent "sets" of activities or strategies, both posing and solving the problems and opportunities of their mutual existence. Innovation and change occur because of *diversity*, non-average individuals with their bizarre initiatives, and whenever this leads to an exploration into an area where positive feedback outweighs negative, then growth will occur. Value is assigned afterwards. It is through this process of "post-hoc explanation" that we rationalize events by pretending that there was some preexisting "niche" which was *revealed* by events, although in reality there may have been a million possible niches, and one particular one arose.

The future, then, is not contained in the present, since the landscape is fashioned by the explorations of climbers, and adaptability will always be required. This does not necessarily mean that total individual liberty is always best. Our models also show that adaptability is a group or population property. It is the shared experiences of others that can offer much information. Indeed, it pays everyone to help to facilitate exploration, by sharing the risks in some cooperative way, which takes some of the "sting" out of failure. Performance is generated by mutual interactions, and total individual freedom may not be consistent with good social interactions, and hence will make some kinds of strategy impossible. Once again we must differentiate between an "external game", where total freedom allows wide ranging responses to outside changes, and an "internal game", where the division of labour, internal relations and shared experiences play a role in the survival of the system.

Again it is naive to assume that there is any simple "answer". The world is just not made for simple, extreme explanations. Shades of grey, subjective judgements, post-rationalizations, multiple misunderstandings and biological motivations are what characterize the real world. Neither total individual freedom nor its opposite are solutions, since there is no "problem" to be solved. They are possible choices amongst all the others, and each choice gives rise to a different spectrum of possible consequences, different successes and failures, and different strengths and weaknesses. And much of this probably cannot really be known beforehand. We can only do our best to imagine possible futures, and to try to carry on modifying our views about reality, and about what it is that we want.

Mismatches between expectations and real outcome may either cause us to modify our (mis)understanding of the world, or, alternatively, simply leave us perplexed. Evolution in human systems is therefore a continual, imperfect learning process, spurred by the difference between expectation and experience, but rarely providing enough information for a complete understanding.

Instead of the classical view of science eliminating uncertainty, the new scientific paradigm accepts uncertainty as inevitable. Indeed, if it were not the case, then it would mean that things were preordained, which would be a much harder thing to live with. Evolution is not necessarily progress and neither the future nor the past was preordained. Creativity really exists, it is the motor of change, and the hidden dynamic that underlies the rise and fall of civilizations, peoples and regions, and evolution both encourages and feeds on invention. Recognizing this, the first step towards wisdom is the development and use of mathematical models which capture this truth.

References

[. . .]

Allen, P.M. (1988), "Evolution: Why the whole is greater than the sum of its parts". In: Wolff, W., Soedeer, C.-J. & Drepper, F.R. (eds.), *Ecodynamics: 2–30*. Berlin: Springer Verlag.

Allen, P.M. (1990), "Why the Future is not what it was". *Futures, July/August 555–570*.

[. . .]

Allen, P.M. & McGlade, J.M. (1987a), "Evolutionary drive: The effect of microscopic diversity, error making and noise". *Foundations of Physics 17, No. 7, 723–738*.

Allen, P.M. & McGlade, J.M. (1987b), "Modelling complex human systems: A fisheries example". *European Journal of Operations Research 30, 147–167*.

Allen, P.M. & McGlade, J.M. (1989), "Optimality, adequacy and the evolution of complexity". In: Christiansen, P.L. & Parmentier, R.D. (eds.), *Structure, Coherence and Chaos in Dynamical Systems*. Manchester: Manchester University Press.

Beddington, J.R. (1979), "Harvesting and population dynamics". In: Anderson, R.M., Turner, B.D. & Taylor, R.L. (eds), *Population Dynamics: The 20th Symposium of the British Ecological Society, London, 1978: 307–319*. Oxford: Blackwell Scientific Publications.

Beddington, J.R. & May, R.M. (1977), "Harvesting natural populations in a randomly fluctuating environment". *Science 197, 463–465*.

Bharucha-Reid, A.T. (1960), *Elements of the Theory of Markov Processes and their Applications*. New York: McGraw-Hill.

Eigen, M. & Schuster, P. (1979), *The Hypercycle: A Principle of Natural Self-Organization*. Berlin: Springer.

May, R.M., Beddington, J.R., Clark, C.W., Holt, S.J. & Laws, R.M. (1979), "Management of multispecies fisheries". *Science 205, 267–277*.

[. . .]

Nicolis, G. & Prigogine, I. (1977), *Self-organization in Non-equilibrium Systems*. New York: Wiley Interscience.

Nisbet, R.M. & Gurney, W. (1982), *Modelling Fluctuating Populations*. New York: Wiley.

Douglas Griffin, Patricia Shaw and Ralph Stacey

SPEAKING OF COMPLEXITY IN MANAGEMENT THEORY AND PRACTICE

From *Organization* 1998, 5(3): 315–339. Copyright © 1998 by Sage Publications. Reproduced by permission of the authors and publisher.

Abstract

This paper describes a complexity perspective on organizational life by drawing on three distinctive sources. First, we describe the way different natural scientists talk of their work in simulating complex dynamical systems. Second, we listen to the contribution of social scientists in describing the dynamics of human interaction and third, we describe group analytic practice as it illuminates the emotional, pre-linguistic processes at work in the group matrix. We argue that together these insights allow us to speak of the nature of self-organization in human systems in a way that emphasizes intersubjectivity, emergence and de-centred agency in contrast to the dominant voice in much management thinking which emphasizes objectivity, control and individual agency. We then relate how the complexity perspective we describe informs our approach to organizational consulting in which we participate in networks of self-organizing everyday conversation whereby the patterned structure of organizational activity is paradoxically both sustained and changed.

Over the past few years we have been working from what we are calling a complexity perspective in a number of organizations. This is emerging from reflective conversations which explore our experience of working with managers in organizations in the light of our understanding of various sociological, psychological and organizational theories; along with insights arising out of the work of natural scientists, particularly those working at the Santa Fe Institute in the area of complex adaptive systems. It is the last mentioned source which leads us to apply the label 'complexity' to the perspective we are working with.

Although a broad spectrum of writers may be using similar words when talking about complexity they often mean something quite different. In this paper we reflect upon these differences, finding that they are also evident in the work of the Santa Fe scientists themselves. We wish to listen carefully to the voices in the literature speaking of complexity, and in so doing include our own:

- There are *objectifying voices* who speak of systems as pre-given external realities and stand outside them as observers, modelling them in order to identify their dynamics. There are also *intersubjective or relational voices* who speak as subjects interacting with other subjects in the coevolution of a jointly constructed social reality.
- There are *voices of control* who are concerned with the functional aspects of a system, searching for causal links that promise a more sophisticated tool for predicting its behaviour. There are *voices emphasizing emergence* and the radically unpredictable aspects of self-organizing processes and their creative potential.
- There are *voices centred on the individual* positing their ability to act as primary agents in the evolution of the system. There are also *voices of decentred agency* who understand agents and the social world in which they have to live as mutually created and sustained, so that agency lies at both the individual and the collective level.

Authors often argue from assumptions which may not be explicitly stated. This creates a potential for confusion when presenting and trying to speak of complexity in organizations. This paper is an attempt to hear different ways of speaking about complexity in organizations in terms of the distinctions we have made above. First we listen to what we believe to be the dominant management theorizing and argue that it speaks with an objectifying/control/individual voice. When many managers are first presented with notions of complexity they will thus tend, quite naturally, to understand those notions in these terms. We then suggest that some scientists at the Santa Fe Institute also approach their work primarily in the same terms and will, therefore, be fairly easily understood and accepted by managers. Other scientists, however, speak with the intersubjective/emergent/decentred agency voice and are, we find, less easily understood by managers. We believe that life in organizations can only be adequately described in the tension of the conversational field amongst all these voices. We argue that those voices which objectify, focusing on control and individual agency, are more appropriate in articulating contexts close to certainty and agreement, while the others do more to shape contexts far from certainty and agreement. We will explore how notions of human agency to be found in social constructionist theory and group analytic practice bring all these voices we have identified into play. The implications for managing are then drawn together in relation to our practice in organizations.

The dominant voice in management thinking: organizing to realize prior intentions

In our experience most managers perceive themselves as action people who look to theorists to bring them immediate applications. The beliefs about human agency that lie behind these attitudes can be understood in terms of constructivist rationalism, that is, the '. . . doctrine that organizational order is the product of human design . . .' (Tsoukas, 1993: 501). Tsoukas sees the roots of such thinking in creationism, that is, the notion that since:

> . . . both manufactured and biological objects *appear* to have been designed for a purpose . . . they must have had a designer. Our common-sense familiarity with the design of manufactured objects clearly lends credibility to such an analogy. Furthermore, it is not difficult to see how this analogy could be extended to include social institutions as well . . . Since social institutions are obviously human artifacts and they appear to serve certain human purposes, social institutions must have been deliberately designed and, therefore, can be deliberately redesigned. (Tsoukas, 1993: 503)

There is a broad consensus in management theory today which rests on such 'common-sense', rational constructivist arguments. A number of highly popular management theorists speak of changing 'mental models', 'perceptions', 'paradigms' or 'systems of belief' implying that this can be done in an intentional and thus designed way. Some examples are:

- 'The discipline of working with mental models starts with turning the mirror inward; learning to unearth our internal pictures of the world, to bring them to the surface and hold them to rigorous scrutiny' (Senge, 1990: 8).
- 'The change process begins with diagnoses of problems that the participants define as important . . . The experiment, designed by the participants, has clear guideposts to tell them how well they are doing and has clear outcomes to judge results' (Argyris, 1990: 107–8). 'Thus, the individual and the organizational factors must be changed in order for the theories-in-use to be determined early on during the change process' (Argyris, 1990: 117).
- '. . . continuous adaptation and growth in a changing business environment depends on "institutional learning" which is the process whereby management teams change their shared mental models of the company, their markets, and their competitors' (de Geuss, quoted in Senge, 1990: 7).
- '. . . we began to realize that if we wanted to change the situation, we first had to change ourselves. And to change ourselves effectively, we first had to change our perceptions' (Covey, 1992: 18).

What managers are being challenged to do is not only to redesign and reengineer their companies, but also *their selves*.

Many of the writers who imply this ability to intentional design changes in thought structures draw on systems theory and increasingly employ the language of complexity. They point to how small changes in ways of thinking and acting can lead to much larger shifts in the whole system – Senge, for example, refers to this as leverage:

> Tackling a difficult problem is often a matter of seeing where the high leverage lies, a change which – with a minimum of effort – would lead to lasting significant improvement . . . well focused actions can sometimes produce significant, enduring improvements, if they're in the right place. (Senge, 1990: 64)

This is part of what Senge calls 'dynamic complexity'.

We hear the note of constructivist rationalism as these writers talk about complexity in terms of the intention to change, seeing action mainly in terms of achieving goals without exploring the process by which intentions are formed in the first place – usually locating it in the visions and missions of charismatic leaders. We are arguing for a concept of agency which also understands the content of intentions as emerging in action. Later we will also be drawing on a body of experience that indicates to us rather convincingly that human beings simply cannot reengineer themselves in the intentional and intellectual manner suggested by those speaking with the objective/control/individual voice.

But first we turn to a consideration of the complexity theory being developed by the scientists at the Santa Fe Institute.

Scientists speaking of complexity at the Santa Fe Institute: self-organization in networks of interacting agents

We take three writers as our examples of the work being done at the Santa Fe Institute: Holland (1995), Kauffman (1995) and Goodwin (1994). We have selected the three because they seem to us to typify the differences. All are simulating the dynamics of networks of interacting agents. These interact in a nonlinear manner creating wholes which are more than the sum of their parts and are sensitive to small fluctuations. Agents in such networks self-organize to produce emergent order or disorder – unfolding either highly stable patterns of behaviour, or chaotic ones, or paradoxically stable and unstable ones close to the 'edge of chaos'.

Consider first how Holland views complex systems, citing as an example the central nervous systems (CNS):

> Though the activity of an individual neuron can be complex, it is clear that the behavior of the CNS aggregate identity is much more complex than the sum of these individual parts. The behavior of the central nervous system depends on the *interactions* much more than the actions. (Holland, 1995: 3, emphasis his)

He develops his notion of interaction as follows:

> In complex adaptive systems a major part of the environment of any given adaptive agent consists of other adaptive agents, so that a portion

of any agent's efforts at adaptation is spent adapting to other adaptive
agents. This one feature is a major source of the complex temporal
patterns that complex adaptive systems generate. (Holland, 1995: 10)

He then understands this mutual interaction from the perspective of individual
agents: each agent has a 'mechanism for anticipation' that drives its behaviour.
This mechanism is an internal model, or set of rules according to which the agent
acts on the basis of its predictions of the responses of other agents. He speaks
of agents with the capacity for 'lookahead' and 'strategy' (Holland, 1995: 33) and
holds that:

> The use of models for anticipation and prediction is a topic that, in its
> broadest sense, encompasses much of science. It is a difficult topic, but
> not impenetrable. (Holland, 1995: 31)

In presenting his argument in this way Holland is defining the nature of interaction
and the nature of the agents who are interacting in a particular way. He is assuming
that each individual agent has an internal model taking the form of if-then rules, that
is, regularities extracted from previous experience of interaction. He is assuming
that these rules are then used to select a response to other agents on the basis of the
predicted outcome of that response. In other words, each individual agent acts
on the expectation of particular responses to that action on the part of other agents
– the predicted outcome is the criterion for selecting an action. Discovery of
accuracy or inaccuracy of prediction leads to further evolution in the agents' internal
models. In this way the pattern of agent identity emerges and such emergence is
primarily driven by the ordering principle of selection, as accuracy of prediction
makes survival more likely.

Note how these assumptions:

- Treat the field of interaction as discrete rather than continuous – there is a
  discrete sequence in which an agent first predicts, then acts and then achieves,
  or fails to achieve, the expected outcome. We might say that in Holland's
  scheme the agent has a model representing the likely responses of other agents
  and that it then refers to this model in order to act.
- Equate anticipation with prediction. He makes a subtle, taken-for-granted shift
  in his description of emergence, from anticipation identified in the interaction
  to the prediction-based actions of the individual agents.
- Imply that through their interaction individual agents (who make predictions
  and develop individual strategies) reveal an order, a true reality, that was
  merely hidden before the interaction and is revealed by it – the 'Hidden
  Order' referred to in the title to his book.
- Focus on the possibility of predicting that order rather than on the potential
  for the emergence of unique, and thus unpredictable, patterns and forms in
  specific contexts.

With this view of the nature of action and interaction Holland is then able to focus
on the objective, scientific modelling of complex adaptive systems in order to find

the levers that will enable one outside the system to change it in intentional ways. He cites the immune system as an example and sees vaccines as the levers that can restore the efficacy of the immune system in the case of AIDS. The resonance with currently dominant models of agency in the management literature is clear. Again we hear the note of constructivist rationalism. Much as the management theorists mentioned above, he sees individual agents observing, predicting and then changing their internal models and so leveraging the whole:

> Theory supplies landmarks and guideposts, and we begin to know what to observe and where to act . . . One specific piece of understanding that theory could supply is a more principled way of locating 'lever points' in complex adaptive systems. (Holland, 1995: 5)

Kauffman (1995) takes a different position, placing much more emphasis than Holland does on the process of self-organization. He, too, sees a complex system as one consisting of autonomous individual agents who predict as they interact. However, the order that emerges from agent interaction is a *potential* before it emerges as an actual pattern – it is not something *hidden*, waiting to be disclosed but something that is *co-created by the agents*:

> The network within each cell of any contemporary organism is the result of at least one billion years of evolution. Most biologists, heritors of the Darwinian tradition, suppose that the order of ontogeny is due to the grinding away of a molecular Rube Goldberg machine, slapped together piece by piece by evolution. I present a countering thesis: most of the beautiful order seen in ontogeny is spontaneous, a natural expression of the stunning self-organization that abounds in very complex regulatory networks. We appear to have been profoundly wrong. Order, vast and generative, arises naturally. I propose that much of the order in organisms may not be the result of selection at all, but of the spontaneous order of self organized systems . . . If this idea is true, then we must rethink evolutionary theory, for the sources of order in the biosphere will now include both selection *and* self-organization. (Kauffman, 1995: 25, emphasis his)

The individual agents are predicting and then acting, but the overall pattern their interaction produces is emergent in an unpredictable sense. In his view, however, there is still an inevitability about what the system produces – he talks about life as a phenomenon to be expected, not just a chance cobbling together through selection. However, the expectation is not an already existing reality, rather it is a potential unfolded by experience – a movement into the space of the adjacent possible. He is searching for 'the laws of complexity' and identifies the principle of self-organization as a second principle of order which is paradoxically operative simultaneously with the ordering principle of selection.

Goodwin (1994) also focuses on the importance of spontaneous self-organization as generative of order and allies himself closely with Kauffman, but, in considering the wider implications of his own work on the development of biological form, he takes the argument even further, stressing the need for a science of qualities and for participatory engagement as essential for understanding the processes of emergence:

> So we may say that organisms express their natures through the particular qualities of their form in space and in time. The study of biological form now begins to take us in the direction of a science of qualities that is not an alternative to, but complements and extends, the science of quantities. (Goodwin, 1994: 183)

> A science of qualities is necessarily a first-person science that recognises states of participative awareness. (Goodwin, 1994: 220)

> What emerges from such participation is real order that unites properties of the active agent and the context within which the action takes place, experienced as the intrinsic qualities of the emergent form. Quality is not a pattern or a process out there, but a subjective relational experience, which focuses on the paradoxical dynamics of complex wholes while appreciating the perspective of a part. (Goodwin, 1997, public lecture at Schumacher College)

He stresses that the long-term evolution of complex systems is radically unpredictable and uncontrollable but nevertheless intelligible – we can perceive or apprehend the pattern or 'signature' of their evolution. The uncontrollability and the unpredictability do not mean that just anything could happen – there is an immanent rationale to how the system unfolds, a generative process at work that goes beyond the correlation of causes and effects.

We can now see how the three above-mentioned complexity theorists speak in the different voices identified at the beginning of this paper:

- Holland is a theorist who stands outside a complex system and models it, emphasizing its predictable aspects in the interest of finding levers to control it and he implicitly assumes the primacy of the individual as agent in human systems.
- Kauffman too stands outside the complex system and models it but he focuses much more on its spontaneously self-organizing, emergent and hence inevitably unpredictable and uncontrollable aspects. This, however, is counterbalanced by his notions of the autonomous individual agent acting in its own self-interest and surviving if it wins.
- For Goodwin, complexity theory raises questions for the scientific method itself and so he moves to a science of qualities capable of dealing with the nature and creative expression of complex wholes. This emphasizes the processes of self-organization and emergence with their radical unpredictability and uncontrollability, just as Kauffman does, but his participative approach places far more emphasis on the interconnectedness of a complex system so elevating further the relationship between agents as a factor in agency.

We have already seen how Holland's voice resonates with dominant management theory. To hear the voice of emergent and decentred agency in human networks we now turn to the social sciences: Shotter's (1993a, 1993b) view of *social con-structionism* links the self-organizing emergence of *conversational realities* to our practical-moral accountability in the context in which we live and *group analytic practice* gives insight into the *agency of the matrix* which groups form. Then we will move on to describe our approach to our work in organizations.

Social constructionist theory: the self-organization of meaning in human conversation

Shotter argues that the primary human reality is persons in ordinary, everyday conversation. It is in the:

> . . . indeterminacy, undecidability and ambivalence, in which different people meet each other in the socially constructed encounters in everyday life, that political struggles are their most intense. (Shotter, 1993b: 38)

> . . . our daily lives are not rooted in written texts or in contemplative reflection, but in oral encounter and reciprocal speech. In other words we live our daily social lives within an ambience of conversation, discussion, argumentation, negotiation, criticism and justification; much of it to do with intelligibility and the legitimization of claims to truth. (Shotter, 1993a: 29)

He follows Ryle, Austin and Wittgenstein in distinguishing 'knowing that' and 'knowing how' (Ryle, 1949) from a third kind of knowing. He variously refers to this third kind of knowing as 'knowing from within' or 'joint action'. The first two kinds of knowing relate to the description of theories and causal succession, that is, 'words already spoken'. The third kind of knowing has to do with emergence, that is, 'words in their speaking'. This is a performative language (Austin, 1962) which emerges from a context, a 'background' or 'hurly burly' of everyday life, as Wittgenstein (1980) referred to it.

In understanding the 'hurly burly' of ordinary everyday conversation Shotter points to the inadequacy of representational-referential theory. He describes what he calls a rhetorical-responsive social construction of reality in which agents are continuously responding to each others' utterances using rhetorical signs and gestures to persuade each other. In this agents are not acting in the expectation of an outcome; they are not predicting how the others will respond. Instead, agents are continuously calling forth responses in each other in specific contexts. It is out of this continuous background of responses, or anticipation, that meaning emerges spontaneously and this meaning constitutes patterns of co-created agent identity. In ordinary, everyday conversation we do not only *choose* our next words on the basis of *predictions or expectations* of others' next words. It is just as much that our words are *evoked or provoked* by the words others *are speaking* in the continuous, seamless way of conversation. This is clearly an *intersubjective process* rather than one in which the other is seen as an object for prediction. This resonates, we think, with the participative position Goodwin takes on complexity.

Shotter argues that social constructionism is about a 'dialectical emphasis upon both our making of, and being made by, our own social realities' (Shotter, 1993a: 34). In other words human interaction is about both contingency (being made by) and creativity (our making of) and we would argue that this resonates with the two principles of order – selection and self-organization – described above by Kauffman, where novelty emerges into the adjacent possible as self-organizing processes produce the creative possibilities which are available for selection in contingent circumstances.

Shotter (1993a) describes a circular process 'in which people, rooted in a background and making use of the linguistic resources it provides, act back upon those background circumstances (their "world") to give or lend them further form or structure' (see Figure 1).

It is in the iteration around this circle of agency that social interaction produces the emergent patterns that become the properties of the whole which again structure the background.

Shotter distinguishes his understanding of social constructionism from both the modernist scientific perspective and other ways of speaking about social constructionism. He questions how the modernist perspective of privileging theory as prior to action and taking the representational-referential perspective has come to be taken for granted. He finds the answer in the rise of modern science, supported by the Enlightenment philosophers, who established the autonomy of human reason, located in the individual, in order to be freed from the authority of the state and church. He also differentiates his understanding of social constructionist thought from writers such as Rorty (1989), Derrida (1976) and Lyotard (1984). They have been understood by some as advocating a position of 'anything goes'; as having an 'uncritical adherence to a theory of language and representation'; and as having an

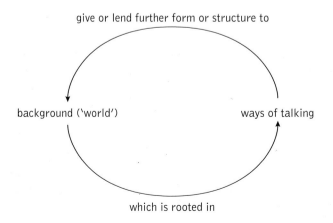

Figure 1 The circle of agency
Source: Shotter (1993a: 36)

'extreme antirealist or sceptical bias' (Norris, 1992: 191). Shotter argues that their approach to social constructionism also remains under the influence of Enlightenment individualism and that their position is essentially 'representational referential' (Shotter, 1993b: 13), that is, constructing individual representations of the world that they then refer to, claiming that none of these individual representations can claim more validity than any other.

Shotter describes how both of the above perspectives have lost the sense of what practical moral identity is really about. His own social constructionist position emphasizes that this cannot be centred in the individual:

> . . . in many of our ordinary, everyday life activities, as we must interlace our actions in with those of others, their actions will determine our conduct just as much as anything within ourselves. The final outcomes of such exchanges cannot strictly be traced back to the intentions of any of the individuals concerned; they must be accounted *as if* 'external' to the participants concerned, *as if* a part of an 'independent reality'. (Shotter, 1993b: 174, his emphases)

He is interested in the kind of knowledge 'one has *only from within a social situation*, a group, or an institution, and which thus takes into account (and is accountable to) the *others* in the social situation within which it is known' (Shotter, 1993b; 7, his emphases).

Exploring how academic or scientific discourse has distanced itself from, and lost a sense of, this primary self-organizing reality, he draws distinctions that we feel can be helpful in differentiating between those speaking of complexity theory in organizations. Several authors differentiate, as does Shotter, between more or less 'radical' forms of social constructionist thought. Chia, for example, draws on Steier (1991) in differentiating 'first order' and 'second order' social constructionists. In the former 'the notion of interpretation or social construction is claimed in the research process, but not "turned back" onto the researchers/theorists themselves' (Chia, 1994: 12), while in the latter it is turned back. Thus, in the first, the researcher describes how social agents construct reality without taking account of the fact that their description is also a construction. Shotter chooses Morgan (1986) as a 'stalking horse' to demonstrate that organizational theory such as his still speaks in terms of 'first order' social constructionism because he describes an organization as a social construction but then implies that managers can operate like scientists using theories as operational tools, as if they were somehow outside of the socially constructed system of which they are a part. Shotter says of Morgan:

> He merely offers improved reading skills. For, as he sees it, theory is still crucial because – even though he has already said that organizations can be many things at one and the same time – he feels that 'practice is never theory-free, for it is always guided by an image of what one is trying to do' (Morgan, 1986; 336). (Shotter, 1993a: 155)

In the additions to the recent second edition of *Images of Organization* Morgan treats chaos and complexity theory, speaking of the 'art of managing and changing "context"' by engaging in 'new actions' which 'help to push the system into a new state more directly' (Morgan, 1997: 268).

> If change is required, how is the transition from one attractor to another to be achieved? (Morgan, 1997: 268)

> . . . it follows that any person wishing to change the context in which they are operating *should search for 'doable' high-leverage initiatives that can trigger a transition from one attractor to another*. (Morgan, 1997: 271, his emphasis)

> In developing mindsets and skills appropriate for the task, they can benefit from understanding the principles of holographic self-organization . . . especially in terms of the role that a focus on the role of 'limits' and 'minimum specs' can play in creating a space in which coherent self-organization can emerge. (Morgan, 1997: 273)

We can hear how Morgan speaks with the objectifying, controlling and individual agency voice about complexity. He takes for granted the objectivity of the scientific observer who, as Shotter points out, speaks 'in terms of forms', 'words already spoken', 'claiming somehow . . . to have floated free of . . . an embedding and to be "based" in certain supposedly undeniable properties of a "subject matter"' (Shotter, 1993b: 139). Shotter describes the subtle shift in temporal focus which makes this 'objectivity' possible, that is, that the 'subject matter' becomes a concrete substrate rather than a continuous unfolding:

> But the fact is, in moving from an ordinary conversational use of lan-guage to the construction of a systematic discourse, there is a transition from a reliance on particular, practical and unique meanings, negotiated 'on the spot' with reference to the immediate context, to a reliance upon links with a certain body of already determined meanings.
> . . . But to be able to talk in this way, as a professional participant in a disciplinary discourse, one must develop methods for warranting in the course of one's talk, one's claims about what 'might be' as being what 'is'. It is by the use of such rhetorical devices – as references to 'special methods of investigation', 'objective evidence', 'special methods of proof', 'independent witnesses', etc. – that those with competence in such procedures can construct their statements as 'factual statements', and claim authority for them as revealing a special 'true' reality behind appearances, without any reference to the everyday context of their claims. (Shotter, 1993b: 25)

Objectifying voices such as those of Holland and Morgan are easily understood by many managers. We would argue that the most important implications of com-plexity theory for organizations lie much more in what Shotter focuses on – the manner in which people's ordinary everyday conversations construct the social reality into which they act. That social reality emerges in a self-organizing way out of the conversational interaction in which they might be trying to construct an image of what they want to do. This enables us to see that when groups of managers in organizations engage in their ordinary everyday conversations about the work, they are doing much more than applying theories, building teams or fostering positive motivational attitudes – they are constructing the nature of their work. Conversations at this ordinary, everyday level do not unfold according to anyone's intention and they cannot be modelled in advance. Each conversation occurs in a unique context to which all of the participants are accountable, and in this sense any model of a previous conversation will have little relevance to any future one as a model. Any attempt to use such a model would destroy the characteristics of ordinary, everyday conversation, turning it instead into a empty ritual. It is also difficult to see how anyone could identify levers in such conversations that they might then use to control their direction.

Group analytic practice: self-organization in the group matrix

We would now like to focus in a different way than Shotter on the unthought pre-linguistic processes that are intertwined in all ordinary everyday conversations. There is a considerable body of theory and practice which deals with such processes and their impact on the social and emotional world people construct in the psychologies of psychoanalysis, analytical psychology, Gestalt and group analysis.

As we saw above, many theorists propose that managers can jointly and individually surface their individual and shared mental models. By this it is meant that managers can identify those assumptions and rules driving their behaviour that exist below the level of awareness and bring them to the level of awareness where they can be discussed and changed before they fall once again below the level of awareness. This is the lever which is supposed to bring about major change in organizations.

Many psychologists are concerned with much the same process – for them one of the aims of analysis and therapy is to bring material people are unaware of into awareness. However, the practice of these psychologists over the past century makes it very clear indeed that this is far from being a simple process. One thing is clear: awareness on its own brings about very little change in thought and feeling structures and this applies not only to those with some form of psychopathology but to everyone. A person may be able to present a very coherent intellectual exposition of his or her behaviour patterns including highly sophisticated explanations of how those patterns came about. That person may also have very powerful desires, intentions and needs to change and yet despite the awareness be quite unable to do so. Change at the intellectual and conversational level is not a sufficient condition for change in thought-feeling structures: intra- and inter-psychic processes at the pre-linguistic level also play a singularly important role in such change.

We will explore what we mean by this from the perspective of one of the depth psychologies, namely, the group analytic method. We use the words 'method' or 'practice' rather than 'theory' because the theory is a loose body of theories drawn from a number of sources while the method or practice is what is distinctive about group analysis. The practice was originally developed by Foulkes (1948, 1964) who drew on a number of sources for his theoretical orientation: psychoanalysis; the critical social theory of the Frankfurt school; notions of network systems from the work of the neurologist Goldstein; theories of processes of culture and civilization from the work of Elias; and the notions of fields of interaction from the early Gestalt psychologists. What is distinctive about Foulkes, however, is his focus on practice, drawing on bodies of theory to illuminate his emergent practice rather than to design it in advance.

The central notion of group analytic practice is that of the matrix, a very similar concept to that of a psychic field put forward by the early Gestalt psychologists. The matrix is the web of communications, both verbal and pre-linguistic, spun by people whenever they come together in a group. It is a web of conversations and feelings, an emotional atmosphere or culture, co-created by the members of a group in their interaction with each other. The matrix emerges out of the interaction, and very importantly the matrix then in a sense creates the individual members of the network that is a group. Winnicott (1965) is often quoted as saying that there is no such thing as an infant, only an infant-mother dyad. By this he meant that the self of the infant emerged out of the early preverbal 'conversation of gestures' between the two and of course the mother is also changed by this experience. They co-create the system in which they are agents and the system creates them. Relational-structure theories of psychic development (Greenberg and Mitchell, 1985) posit that this process of psychic structuring through relationships continues throughout life: each of us changes throughout life as we relate in different ways and as we relate to different others.

This was very much Foulkes' view of the relationship each person has with others in a group. He saw a group as a network in which individuals were the nodes and he saw the agency of change in the matrix of the group. This does not mean that he saw the individual as unimportant – unlike Bion (1967) who thought therapeutic intervention should be at the level of the group alone, Foulkes was clear that the purpose of the group was to treat individuals but the medium of treatment was the group. In practice, then, therapeutic intervention moves back and forth from individual to group levels – a dialectical process. This means that the agency for change is located at both individual and group, or matrix, levels making it necessary to keep shifting attention from one level to another in order to make sense of what is going on.

How does this notion look in practice? A useful starting point is the role of the person who convenes the group. Foulkes was rather careful not to call this person the leader of the group because that would imply prior intention and direction. Instead he suggested the designation of 'conductor' because this captured more the notion of agency for change being located in both the membership (including the conductor) and the matrix of the group. The conductor is a participant in the group, but a participant with a special responsibility for understanding the group as a whole. The conductor resonates during sessions very much with the intersubjective voice we identified earlier on – he or she is a subject amongst other subjects using his or her skills and subjective feelings to empathize with the group and its individual members.

The conductor arrives at the start of a session without any design or intention regarding what will happen during the session. Members may well arrive with some matter on their minds, but whether they get to speak about this issue and how the responses to it will unfold are quite unknown. All in the group, including the conductor, are in a state of not knowing, a state of uncertainty. The conductor almost always waits for someone to speak and then may listen intently, perhaps for a considerable length of time, for emergent patterns not only in the conversation but also in the emotional atmosphere, the matrix, of the group. The conductor might then articulate what he or she sees as an emergent pattern if it seems that this might assist the group to take a further step, or the conductor, more usually, may wait for one of the members to articulate what is happening. The self-organizing nature of the group is evident and the web of pre-linguistic communications is so complex that it could not possibly be entirely, or even mainly, expressed in words. Indeed, one writer, Bollas (1987), uses the concept of the unthought known: much that is pre-linguistic pertains to an existential sense of sensuous lived experience – it is the distinctive idiom of our own existence and our own lived experience of others. Such deep rooted sense of self and other cannot be put into words. This is clear when any of us tries to tell another who we really are – we soon run out of words.

After a group session, a conductor may seek supervision or discuss the evolution of the group both as a way of improving understanding and as a way of containing the feelings stirred up in him or her. It is striking how the language used to understand the processes of the group – the theories brought to bear – differs from that in the group itself. This is because the conductor now moves from the intersubjective voice of participation in the group to the objectifying voice which observes the group in hindsight. In addition to examining verbal communications, the conductor in supervision will use theoretical terms to talk about pre-linguistic processes, terms which are never used in the group meeting proper. The terms include transference to indicate that members have responded to the conductor and each other in terms of early family patterns; counter-transference to describe the conductor's and other members' responses to such; projection to talk about members who saw in others aspects of themselves and then responded as if they were real; projective identification to describe how one unconsciously manipulated others to respond to a projection as if it were really part of them; mirroring to describe how people saw aspects of themselves in each other; resonance to indicate how people responded with similar feelings to others. The conductor may occasionally think in these terms while in the group. So, in carrying out their work, conductors of therapy groups are both allowing and contributing to an intersubjective dynamic field of differing voices.

What does this do for people as they spend session after session conversing and relating to each other in a manner they sometimes experience as frustrating because they cannot see where it is going, a feeling their conductor may well share with them? The experience is that many, but not all, change. Some whose level of mental distress is so high that they cannot function in normal life improve to the point where they can. Others, who are leading useful lives but feel a need to change in some way they are not very clear about, do change. The change we are talking about occurs at a deep level of thinking and feeling, and manifests itself in significant changes in behaviour. However, when such people are asked just how this change came about, they do not know and neither does the conductor of their group. In general it seems that significant change occurs through each person's experience of life in the group, a process in which together they co-create the matrix of the group and changes in each other. The change emerges from the process of self-organization, both slow and fast, orderly and disorderly. But exactly what all this means in specific instances we are not able to say. We maintain that groups in the ordinary, everyday life of organizations function in much the same way in contexts far from certainty and agreement. This is a very different view of change in thought-feeling structures to the one depicted by those who talk about intentional changes in mental models.

It is important to make one other point in relation to this group process. It is not an easy harmonious movement from one thought-feeling structure to another in the manner that talking in terms of mental models implies. The deep thought-feeling processes we are talking about can be labelled 'models' only in the most superficial of senses. They are truly subjective and relational processes which can never be adequately objectified and made conscious. Such subjective senses of self in relation to other are the very 'ground' of each of our existences and when this 'ground' is in any significant way disturbed it raises deep anxiety of which we may be only partially aware. Change always threatens some sense of our being and the anxiety that follows will be defended against very tenaciously. The process of change will be halted unless this deep existential anxiety can be adequately contained. In infancy and childhood it is the good-enough maternal environment and the good-enough family environment of which this is a part which contains in this way. In the group processes we have been describing this good-enough holding environment is the group matrix itself. Such a matrix is characterized by a quality of empathic response and trust which cannot be installed; it emerges in the experience of interaction. Those who talk in terms of intentional changes in mental models pay little attention to the importance of anxiety in the change process. The conductor, then, contributes to the containing matrix both by being there as a participant *and* by managing the 'boundaries' of the group: deciding on the membership of the group, the setting and time of meeting, and a few simple rules governing its conduct.

A complexity perspective on organizational life: self-organization in legitimate/shadow networks

We can now draw together the three disparate perspectives of complexity theory, social constructionism and group analytic practice to illuminate what we have called 'a complexity perspective'.

As we have indicated, complexity theory conceptualizes nature's systems in terms of networks in which agents relate to each other in a nonlinear manner. The powerful insight yielded by this way of conceptualizing is this: agents participate in the network they constitute in a self-organizing manner and in so doing continually produce emergent patterns of relationship across that network. In other words, they co-create the reality into which they are acting and that reality includes themselves.

When such networks evolve in the dynamic context known as 'the edge of chaos' they are capable of producing novel forms. We have pointed to how these insights are being spoken of in objectifying, individual-agent-centred ways which enable complex systems to be modelled in the interest of predictability and control – ways that are quite compatible with dominant ways of thinking about management, but we think are ways primarily appropriate to social conditions close to certainty and agreement. We have also pointed to other ways of talking about complex systems – the intersubjective, decentred agency voices that emphasize the radical unpredictability of novel emergent patterns.

We now want to argue that although the latter voices are much less audible in the literature on managing and organizing processes they do offer important insights into those processes. We are suggesting that the link between complexity theory and organizations can be illuminated by turning to Shotter's form of social constructionism and group analytic practice. The former emphasizes the importance of ordinary everyday conversations in networks of human agents and shows how such conversation self-organizes into coherent patterns of meaning which are the constructed social reality into which human agents act, where that constructed reality includes the human agents themselves. The group analytic perspective is also based on the fundamental importance of conversation but lays great stress on pre-linguistic processes that are just as self-organizing as ordinary everyday conversation. From the group analytic perspective, when human agents in the network that is a group relate with each other in language and in feelings, a matrix, an evolving relational pattern of meaning and feeling, emerges and this is the reality into which human agents act and in so doing change themselves and their context. We have been talking about self-organizing social and psychodynamic networks which give rise to emergent patterns of change that are not predictable.

We now move on to argue that these perspectives of ordinary, everyday conversational life and emotional matrices are the processes people in organizations engage in when they find themselves far from certainty and agreement with each other. We have found it useful to distinguish, conceptually, between two aspects of the network of relationships between people that constitute an organization (Stacey, 1996). On the one hand there is the legitimate system that people join when they become members of an organization – they take up a role in the hierarchy, are asked to adhere to the rules of its bureaucracy and to conform, on the surface at least, to its dominant and officially approved ideology. Note that this legitimate system includes aspects of what is often referred to as the informal system, such as widely recognized 'unwritten rules' and cultural practices that are readily accepted by organizational members as explaining and justifying behaviour. However, as people join the legitimate system, various social contacts from previous experience reconfigure and they begin to form new social contacts. In other words, they enter into group life where they deal with much of the ambiguous, ill-formed, conflictual, emergent sense-making that occurs far from certainty and agreement. We refer to this as the shadow networks of the organization – the matrix, or web, of ordinary everyday conversation and pre-linguistic communications, characterized by great diversity and fluidity and tangential, unexpected relationships to the legitimate aspects of organizational life. In such shadow networks people are affected by and affect each other in very personal ways that may rapidly or gradually change them and the organizing relations between them, as they interact to both support and undermine the legitimate system. The emergence of new patterns of behaviour occurs in this self-organizing process in ways that cannot be controlled in an intentional and directing sense. The notion of a shadow 'system' is easily misunderstood when spoken of objectively. When we talk about shadow interactions and the covert politics and social/psychological processes that constitute them, managers immediately recognize them from their own experience. However, many then seek to objectify the shadow 'systems', seeing them as quite separate from the legitimate. They then want to design them, legitimize and control them. This is impossible to do because of the very nature of the interaction which is not some separate system but rather processes intimately intertwined with the legitimate aspects of the organization.

Speaking of complexity in a participative approach to organizational consulting

We now turn to our own consulting practice (see Shaw, 1997) to describe how we are coming to think and speak of our work with managers and our experience of organizational life. Increasingly we see our consulting assignments as opportunities to work with and in the lively web of human communication in all its guises: structured dialogues, formal meetings and presentations, everyday conversation, gossip and chat, which weaves the living fabric of organizations; attending particularly to the shifting qualities of that conversational field, qualities which form and flow, and which are both prior to and more than that which can be spoken. We do this by exploring what it means to participate in rather than consult to the organizations we work with.

Typically our assignments are based on a perceived need for change by some managers in senior positions who feel responsible and accountable for guiding the development of their organizations. Managers do not ask us to help them with simple puzzles which they can easily isolate from their context and solve. They want assistance when at some level they are aware that they are immersed in a complex of entangled issues whose evolution is indeterminate but which they seek to influence: 'we need to create a more innovative culture'; 'we need to shift our research and manufacturing base into fresh but unspecified territory'; 'we need to reach consensus on a reformulated strategic direction'; 'we want our marketing focus to find the right local/global balance' . . .

In one way or another our early work probes and tries to loosen the language of objectivity, control and individual agency that constricts our clients' ability to talk with one another in terms of the ambiguity and indeterminacy of the intersubjective, co-created, self-organizing experiences that lie unvoiced behind the rhetoric of the management of change. We seek to meet and work with *groups* of managers rather than individuals, always asking the person suggesting a meeting who else is already involved, who else could contribute, who else would be interested, so that we are always joining, and inevitably changing by our participation, an ongoing relational web. We spend time talking about how the goals and intentions we are being asked to pursue with our clients were arrived at, listening carefully for the gaps and discontinuities in what they narrate. Interest in the gaps often evokes further narrative from the same or another person and at best it is possible to reach a situation in which all present glimpse and feel the complex unfolding of events on which the current situation rests.

On one such occasion in the pause and shift in feeling-quality that the conversation had reached at that moment, a senior manager said with a mixture of amusement and awe that it would be necessary to go back to the inauguration of the company, or even before, to fully describe the evolution of a single decision. It seemed obvious to the group conversing that there were a multitude of threads that could be traced, a multiplicity of stories told. How could a decision that they had been explaining with such rational logic and clear objectivity suddenly be revealed as also so tenuous, so unpredictable, so hard to locate anywhere?

It is not difficult from here to touch the equally paradoxical issues of control. What kind of control do these managers believe they have? How do they experience this control? They will say they have control, in a way: they can allocate resources, cut budgets, redesignate roles, set up task forces, authorize acquisitions, but control over the outcomes of each day's complex of activities? Then they will speak of roller coasters and rubber levers, surprises and set-backs, games and miracles. They often express relief and enjoyment at acknowledging together the quixotic, paradoxical experience of being a manager, something both serious and ludicrous. How come so much 'real' business does indeed get done amidst all this playful striving?

It is in the context of having touched or opened with client managers, at least temporarily, this paradox – that the logic of change by design, intention, and control coexists with emergent, unpredictable change that follows a self-organizing logic of its own – that we negotiate the kind of contract we believe we need to be effective. We ask for a well-publicized role in the formal system with due accountabilities in its hierarchy and we agree to work with the existing structures, processes and tasks of the organizations – those management groups, task forces, project teams, site committees, and departmental meetings whose formally authorized conversations hold the forms of current order and seek to create intended change. However, we make it clear that as we do this we will also become active members of the multiple shadow networks that interpenetrate and extend beyond all these existing structures, working with whatever opportunities are generated thereby. There is always some doubt and discomfort about this. How will they know this is worthwhile, whether we are working with the 'right' people, how will they assess the outcomes, how will they monitor this activity, what proportion of the work will be of this kind?

There can only be one answer to this – we do not know because we cannot know, but that doesn't mean that there will be no unfolding sense in what we are doing. We ask them how much of the time they as managers engage in activity in which they only half-know, indeed do not really consciously know at all what they are doing and yet in hindsight can point to the part they played in key events that constitute the official history of the organization. The extent to which we have touched nerves in the organization that resonate to the interplay of all the voices we have identified in this paper is the extent to which we are likely to be employed as consultants.

At this point we usually agree that there will be a group of people who will meet during the assignment to face over and over again the intractable difficulties of measuring 'results', 'success', 'progress', 'value for money'. These meetings are not pre-scheduled but can be initiated by anyone at any time and the membership can change to include others who ask or are asked to join in the discussions. We avoid tidy, finished presentations but seek instead to create a conversational forum. The task is to make emergent collective sense of our work and decide whether to continue. We always ensure that the assignment is financed on the basis of a simple daily rate with termination without financial penalty at any time. In return we ask our clients to accept that we will not be seeking prior approval for any work we do, we will just do it, but can be asked to account for ourselves at any time. At a recent such meeting we asked the CEO of a client company why he was deciding to continue employing us. He paused for a while before answering and then said:

> During this discussion I keep having a sense of recognition. Issues that have been turning up in other conversations with other people suddenly materialize here in a completely different context. Our conversation suddenly makes sense of a number of only half-articulated and apparently unconnected thoughts I've been having. Somehow what you are doing touches a pulse in the organization that I recognize at some level. It's very subtle, but I like that. I realize that the day I start worrying about what you are doing rather than being intrigued, the assignment will already be over.

We understood in his response an attempt to articulate the way members of these 'monitoring groups' are doing something more than checking budgets and outcomes. They are evaluating something intangible and closed to objective measurement. They are feeling for a sense of coherence, of meaningfulness, of self-similar resonance that is recognizable yet makes fresh unpredictable sense of a number of situations. Both past and possible future activity is seen in a new light, as part of another story than the one they were telling. It is conversations like this that live 'on the edge of chaos' as those participating experience the emergence of new patterns of order from apparently disorganized activity.

We very rarely teach 'complexity theory' to assembled groups as in a traditional management development activity in which managers are exposed to various 'tools' and models to 'apply' to their work, although we may be asked to do this as a one-off event in organizations which we would not consider to be clients of our consulting work. Instead, the language of complex networks, self-organization, iteration, non-linearity, self-similarity, creative emergence, life at the edge of chaos, weaves in and out of our conversation as the ideas seem capable of touching or evoking a developing theme.

We will often then leave or send books or articles on various aspects of complexity research and thinking for people to read, following up later to see what kind of response they generate. In this way we try to avoid the sterile jargonizing of every new management fad which sometimes seems like an understandable defence on the part of practising managers to neutralize the subtly disturbing effects of ideas that just might reshape their sense of themselves as managers. Sometimes the material we scatter around creates only small ripples, sometimes it falls on very fertile ground, as for example with a young Italian technical director who devoured a number of articles and books on complexity and told us that reading them had been an enormous pleasure and relief. He felt he had suddenly entered a dialogue in which his private, unshared intuitions were suddenly discussable. He is a highly regarded manager in the company and to go into his office is an extraordinary experience. It is impossible to sit anywhere as every available surface is piled high with papers and documents and messages.

He said that he had realized some time ago, as the demands of his job spiralled ever upwards, that it was misconceived to try to stay on top of all the activities with which he was involved. He arrived each day with certain intentions but held them loosely and let them reorganize with the happenings of the day. He felt that he was becoming more skilful at doing this, but that he had never been able to explain before his sense of being both passive and active in this process, that there was an inner logic to the way things unfolded that was *not* random but which he could not have known in advance. He was inspired by Heraclitus as a young man; his private motto was 'Panta re' – all is flux.

He spoke of his exasperation at the way he felt that he was forced to engage with other managers at the plant in which he worked to render complex situations superficially simple so that they could be put into existing categories. He quoted a number of recent decisions he believed to be grossly misguided that were the outcome of the failure he saw in his colleagues' ability to live with the complex. He wished he could discuss the whole decision-making process in the terms he now saw possible after reading the articles. We asked him who he would want to participate in such a conversation and he named a number of people throughout the company in Europe who had no official existence as a grouping and existed only as a network from his local point of view and he was sure that these people would suggest others. We encouraged him to take his imagined conversational move seriously and worked with him, all of us using the existing relationships and connections we were active in, to see if we could stimulate the organization of such a meeting. The technical manager was astonished at the surprising speed with which people agreed to attend a meeting whose exact purpose was unclear and for which no outcomes were specified. It was as though a signal went out at frequencies other than the purely verbal that caused an aggregating pattern which was self-amplifying. There was no official announcement of this meeting. News of it spread by word of mouth, as people heard others were going or when someone suggested that it would be good to ask x or y. The group which finally convened, in Italy, a few of whom held very senior positions, could not locate themselves or be located by anyone else according to any existing organizational structure or rationale.

The meeting acted as a fluctuation in the existing political and social field of organizational interaction and after the day-and-a-half of open-ended conversation that took place there several people spoke of a shift or change in themselves, or that new patterns of working relationships had developed that extended beyond those who actually participated in the meeting. Like the members of groups in group analytic practice described above, the managers involved found it hard to explain how these personal and organizational changes had come about.

What are some of the pitfalls and difficulties of working in this way? We find a need to be very vigilant about the attempts to objectify and manage the shadow networks rather than participate in them. For example, activity in the shadow system of one organization was evolving a loose network which we had occasionally referred to as the 'next generation'. We were then asked by a senior manager to supply a list of names that he could present to his boss who had asked him to identify a group of 'high potentials' who could be groomed for rapid promotion. We declined to supply such a list, writing to him to explain that our 'list' was carefully kept metaphorical. We had never compiled a literal list; it existed as an evocative idea. To confuse this with a literal list for succession planning purposes which was entirely appropriate in the legitimate system would be to congeal the organizing potential of our symbolic 'list' which referred to a network with shifting membership.

Another difficulty is that to work with the shadow system is to emphasize heterogeneity. It means that the webs of relationship we spin as we work are localized and unevenly distributed. To the legitimate system, with its focus on design, this is anathema – it must favour even-handedness, cross-sections, representative samples, equality, uniformity, controlled flow of information. Yet it is connectivity, difference and fluctuations that sustain a complex system far from equilibrium where self-organizing processes can give rise to emergent patterns of behaviour. It is often uncomfortable and demanding to keep surfacing and finding the nature of ethical behaviour in such situations, where there are no pre-existing guidelines. It is small wonder that managers are tempted to objectify the shadow system as something separate from their legitimate roles. It is much easier than facing the fact that they are participating all the time in both legitimate and shadow systems that are reciprocally conditioning each other and that their actions thereby contribute to both sustaining and subverting the existing order. A complexity perspective that focuses all the time on the essential reciprocity of cooperation and competition, stability and instability, agency at the individual and the collective level encourages managers to explore afresh what it means to act ethically, honourably, and with integrity into the unfolding situations they jointly create.

Finally we would point out that the unfolding dynamics of complex organizing processes have their own rhythms and scales, so that it is important to be able to tolerate the recurring sense of confusion and turbulence as a sense of meaningful pattern at one level of activity dissolves at another, just as it is important to allow the galvanizing effect of suddenly perceiving an emerging pattern to flow into timely and often courageous action that begins to populate what Kauffman calls the 'adjacent possible'. Working with organizational life means working with the process of organizing, its transient finished products and with the characteristic trace or signature of the evolving whole that cannot be grasped from the outside but only experienced in the midst of active and attentive participation.

It is our conviction that one of the major contributions the study of complexity in the natural sciences can offer to management practitioners is a language to give voice and substance to their felt experience of the profoundly creative, dynamic, non-linear, evolving process of organizing which is their daily work, the ground from which decisions, policies and actions eventually produce products and services which characterize the business or institution at any one time.

Conclusion

The nature and consequences of complexity in organizational life are increasingly attracting the attention of management practitioners and thinkers alike. One source of understanding this is from perspectives being developed in the natural sciences and we are concerned in this paper with the work of scientists at the Santa Fe Institute. However, insights from scientific theorizing about nonhuman nature cannot be imported directly – a considerable task of interpretation is required if this importation is to have any validity.

We have argued that the work being done at the Santa Fe is far from monolithic and we have suggested that we can understand different positions taken by those scientists if we listen to their work as distinctive notes struck in a chorus of voices. For some, complex systems are spoken of in objective terms and are modelled in the interest of improving intentional, directing forms of control by individual agents of the system. Here agency is located in individual agents. Others speak of reality as more of an intersubjective construction, a reality co-created by agent interaction, agents who are in turn created by the system of which they are a part and in which behaviour itself is controlled by self-organizing processes that produce emergent patterns.

When the insights of complexity theory are imported in the form put forward by scientists speaking primarily with the objective, controlling, individual voice, they are easily recognizable in terms of dominant management thinking precisely because it is this constructivist rationalist, intentional control and individual agency approach that dominates current management thinking. It is easy for those writers thinking in terms of systems theory, such as Senge, to import these notions of complexity into their already existing frameworks and talk about levering organizational change by accessing and changing mental models.

The voices of other scientists, however, resonate with social constructionist thinking and group analytic practice in that they strike the note of intersubjectivity, emergence and both individual and collective agency. From these perspectives, human agents construct and are constructed by social realities and by pre-linguistic processes that are far too complex to be captured by simplistic notions of mental models that imply an ability to verbalize what it is that drives our behaviour. It seems to be more difficult for many managers to consider the implications of these insights: when they are offered concepts from complexity as theory to be applied, they ask questions and interpret answers, mainly in terms of objectivity, control and individual agency. However, when a complexity perspective such as we have advocated here is used to inform practice and participation in organizational life, rather than offer conceptual tools to be applied, we find it speaks evocatively to the actual lived experience of many managers.

References

Argyris, C. (1990) *Overcoming Organizational Defenses*. Boston: Allyn and Bacon.

Austin, J.L. (1962) *How to Do Things with Words*. London: Oxford University Press.

Bion, W.R. (1967) *Experiences in Groups*. London: Routledge.

Bollas, C. (1987) *The Shadow of the Object*. London: Free Association Books.

Chia, R. (1994) 'Management Research as Speculative Knowledging', in R. Chia (ed.) *In the Realm of Organizations: Essays for Robert Cooper*. London: Routledge.

Covey, S.R. (1992) *The Seven Habits of Highly Effective People*. London, Sydney: Simon and Schuster.

Derrida, J. (1976) *Of Grammatology*. Baltimore, MD: Johns Hopkins University Press.

Foulkes, S.H. (1948) *Introduction to Group Analytic Psychotherapy*. London: Karnac.

Foulkes, S.H. (1964) *Therapeutic Group Analysis*. London: George Allen and Unwin.

Goodwin, B. (1994) *How the Leopard Changed Its Spots: The Evolution of Complexity*. London: Weidenfeld & Nicolson.

Goodwin, B. (1997) 'Complexity, Creativity and Society', LSE Seminar series paper. [. . .] [*Soundings: Media Worlds* 5(Spring): 111–22.]

Greenberg, J.R. and Mitchell, S.A. (1985) *Object Relations in Psychoanalytic Theory*. Cambridge, MA: Harvard University Press.

Holland, J.H. (1995) *Hidden Order: How Adaptation Builds Complexity*. Reading, MA: Helix Books, Addison-Wesley.

Kauffman, S. (1995) *At Home in the Universe: The Search for the Laws of Complexity*. London: Viking.

Lyotard, J.-F. (1984) *The Postmodern Condition: A Report on Knowledge*. Manchester: The University of Manchester Press.

Morgan, G. (1986) *Images of Organization*. Thousand Oaks, CA: Sage.

Morgan, G. (1997) *Images of Organization*, 2nd ed. Thousand Oaks, CA: Sage.

Norris, C. (1992) *Uncritical Theory: Postmodernism, Intellectuals, and the Gulf War*. London: Lawrence and Wishart.

Rorty, R. (1989) *Contingency, Irony and Solidarity*. Cambridge: Cambridge University Press.

Ryle, G. (1949) *The Concept of Mind*. London: Methuen.

Senge, P.M. (1990) *The Fifth Discipline*. New York: Doubleday Currency.

Shaw, P. (1997) 'Intervening in the Shadow Systems of Organizations: Consulting with a Complexity Perspective', *Journal of Organization Change Management* 10(3): 235–50.

Shotter, J. (1993a) *Conversational Realities: Constructing Life through Language*. London: Sage.

Shotter, J. (1993b) *Cultural Politics of Everyday Life*. Buckingham: Open University Press.

Stacey, R. (1996) *Complexity and Creativity in Organizations*. San Francisco: Berrett-Koehler.

Steier, F., ed. (1991) *Research and Reflexivity*. Beverly Hills, CA: Sage.

Tsoukas, H. (1993) 'Organizations as Soap Bubbles: an Evolutionary Perspective on Organization Design', *Systems Practice* 6(5): 501–15.

Winnicott, D.W. (1965) *The Maturational Process and the Facilitating Environment*. London: Karnac.

Wittgenstein, L. (1980) *Remarks on the Philosophy of Psychology*, Vols I and II. Oxford: Basil Blackwell.

Jeffrey Goldstein

EMERGENCE: A CONSTRUCT AMID A THICKET OF CONCEPTUAL SNARES

From *Emergence* 2000, 2 (1): 5–22. Copyright © 2000 by Lawrence Erlbaum Associates, Inc. Reproduced by permission of Jeffrey Goldstein.

> We see that the intellect, so skillful in dealing with the inert, is awkward the moment it touches the living.
>
> (Henri Bergson 1983: 165)

The concept of emergence is playing an increasingly critical role in the quickly expanding field of complexity theory. In a previous article in the inaugural issue of this journal (Goldstein, 1999), I discussed the history and development of the construct of emergence from its origin in the movement called Emergent Evolutionism (see Alexander, 1966; Broad, 1925; Morgan, 1923; and Wheeler, 1926) through its current employment in complexity theory. Although emergence may be an intriguing, even revolutionary, notion, the more one tries to get a clear grasp on the concept, the more it can prove to be elusive and murky. The controversy surrounding the concept did not end with Emergent Evolutionism, but continues to ignite debates concerning the implications of emergence for causality, determinism, predictability, the ontological status of emergent phenomena, and so on.

It appears that emergence is not a concept that comes alone but, rather, tends to carry considerable metaphysical freight. This can be seen in remarks from two leading complexity scientists. First, chaos physicist Doyne Farmer (quoted in Waldrop, 1992: 297) places emergence in a grand evolutionary scheme:

> The key is that there would be a sequence of evolutionary events structuring the matter in the universe in the Spencerian sense, in which each emergence sets the stage and makes it easier for the emergence of the next level.

Second, in similar vein, complexity researcher Stuart Kauffman (Kauffman, 1995: 23) declares:

> A theory of emergence would account for the creation of the stunning order out our window as a natural express of some underlying laws. It would tell us if we are at home in the universe, expected in it, rather than present despite overwhelming odds.

Emergence may indeed go on to reveal matters of cosmic significance, yet this same proclivity for speculation can also set up sundry conceptual snares for the unwary in their appeal to emergence for either descriptive or explanatory purposes. In this article I want to discuss these snares in relation to eight broad issues encountered on the route to adopting the idea of emergence:

- causality
- spontaneity
- predictability
- ontology

- prevalence
- levels
- coherence
- outcome.

Causality

Does emergence violate causality?

The study of complexity is challenging many established assumptions about the dynamics of systems, including the role of causal explanations in complex systems. Some complexity theorists have gone so far as to propose that complex systems may violate the linkage of cause and effect. For example, Ralph Stacey (1996: 187), a pioneer in applying complexity theory to strategic planning and organizational creativity, has charged:

> Causal links between specific actions and specific organisational out-comes over the long term disappear in the complexity of the interaction between people in an organisation, and between them and people in other organisations that constitute the environment.

Stacey, no doubt, is not averring that complex systems are acausal. So, what exactly is he getting at?

There are indeed features of emergence that do seem to make it a good candidate for causality violation, since emergent patterns, structures, and properties are characterized by a radical novelty in comparison to the properties and patterns of the components out of which emergence arises (for more on the role of causality in emergent systems, see Goldstein, 1996). According to chaos/complexity physicist James Crutchfield (1994: 1), emergent structure is:

> not directly described by the defining constraints and instantaneous forces that control a system . . . not directly specified by the equations

of motion . . . [and] cannot be explicitly represented in the initial and boundary conditions.

Consequently the radical novelty of emergent phenomena can appear quite enigmatic.

These recent notions of the implications of emergence for causality were foreshadowed in the philosophical discussions accompanying Emergent Evolutionism, which recognized the novelty of emergents as challenging inherited ideas of causality. For instance, animal behaviorist C. Lloyd Morgan (1923) believed that emergent novelty necessitated a distinction between causality and causation: "causality" would refer to the causal nexus of natural processes; whereas "causation" would allude to a breach in natural processes afforded by emergent novelty – which, in turn, would allow a place for the inclusion of divinity in the natural world. For sure, Morgan's distinction is not particularly enlightening, but this cannot be blamed solely on his theological preoccupations, since they are not all that dissimilar from current-day speculations on the cosmic, evolutionary significance of emergence, as seen in our quotes in the introduction. However murky Morgan's distinction appears, it does point to how emergence pushes us up against traditional notions of causality.

To understand more about the impact of the radical novelty of emergents on the causal nexus of a complex system, it can be helpful to take a look at the phenomenon of chaos, another system dynamic that has been challenging conventional understanding of causality. Philosopher David Newman (1996) has made a case for understanding strange attractors in chaotic systems as instantiations of emergence. Specifically, Newman claims that being in the basin of a strange attractor is an emergent property of a nonlinear dynamical system, since it is a property neither deducible from, predictable from, nor reducible to antecedent conditions or factors. Thus chaos, like emergence, challenges conventional notions of causal connection.

It is crucial to note that chaos is technically termed "deterministic chaos" because, although the outcome is aperiodic and random-like, it can be produced, i.e., "determined," by simple rules. (Here I am leaving out "stochastic chaos," which results not only from deterministic rules but from the admixture of stochastic events in the resulting chaos.) Mathematician Ralph Abraham, a mentor of many of today's leading chaos and complexity scientists, made a very telling observation about chaos that is also pertinent to the causal nexus of emergence:

> An attractor functions as a symbol when it is viewed through an output projection map [map of a system by concentration of some variable into a finite dimension state space] by a *slow observer*. If the dynamic along the attractor is too fast to be recorded by the slow-reading observer, he may then recognize the attractor only by its averaged attributes, fractal dimension, power spectrum, and so on, but fail to recognize the trajectory along the attractor as a deterministic system. (Abraham, 1987: 606; his emphasis)

The failure to discern determinism in such a system is thus not because it is indeterminate, but instead is due to limitations of observers, i.e., their "slowness" compared to the much more rapid unfolding of the system's dynamics. The observer is in an epistemologically deficient position and cannot trace backward from the chaotic attractor the exact sequence of iterations that led to it. But this does not then mean that chaos violates determinism — what it shows, instead, is our incapacity to perceive this determinism. Something like this must be what Stacey means by his remarks that causal links disappear in the complexity of interactions.

Chaos as emergence doesn't violate causality *per se*. Instead, as a macro or global phenomenon, what is violated is our ability to trace all the micro determinates responsible for it. However, in an important sense, this is really just another way of saying that emergence *is* a global or macro phenomenon. One there needs to understand not only how it is determined by micro events (namely the interaction of components), but the terms and constructs that are pertinent to the macro level.

Instead of causality what emergence does indeed tax is the medieval (and still persisting) presumption of *causa aequat effectum*, or, roughly, "causes and effects are equal." This refers to the tendency to think that an effect cannot contain more than what was in the cause alone. Since the radical novelty of emergent phenomena in a complex system is not something contained in the components alone, it would seem that emergence does challenge the notion of an equivalence between effects and causes. The good news, though, is that it is precisely the inequality of cause and effect that makes emergent phenomena so interesting in the first place and worth while for intensive study. Complexity science is finally opening up the "black box" of the radical novelty of emergence, and what is being found inside the box are constructs that themselves are on an emergent level (see Goldstein, 1997a). We shall go into greater detail about the significance of this new qualitative level below.

Spontaneity

Is emergent order for free?

Emergence in complex systems is envisioned to arise from *self-organization*, in contrast to the external or hierarchical imposition of new order on to a system. But another conceptual snare lies in wait here: an overemphasis on the spontaneity associated with the idea of self-organization can lead to a discounting of the conditions that are necessary for these spontaneous processes to occur.

One particularly influential source of this overaccentuation on spontaneity can be found in Stuart Kauffman's (1995: 25) concept of *order for free*:

> Most of the beautiful order seen in ontogeny is spontaneous, a natural expression of the stunning self-organization that abounds in very complex regulatory networks . . . Order, vast and generative, arises naturally.

Kauffman's way of conceptualizing "order for free" is at the basis of his cosmic meditations on emergence of which we saw examples above. "Order for free," in fact, is not that different than the old idea of spontaneous generation or other candidates for spontaneous processes in nature (discussed more fully in Goldstein, forthcoming).

On a more prosaic level, the phrase "order for free" does seem to be a decent way of rendering how emergent patterns and structures arise out of the dynamics of the systems itself and, therefore, don't derive from the intrusion of order represented, for example, in how a cookie cutter makes a shape in dough. However, the phrase also has the unfortunate connotation that there is no cost involved in emergence, which can then lead to neglect of some of the very important determining conditions of emergence.

This kind of "order for free" perspective shows up in allegations on the part of organizational enthusiasts of self-organization that all that is required for self-organization and emergence is simply to interrupt the normal hierarchical command-and-control practices of management. Certainly, there are times when such a strategy can confer tremendous benefits on an organization, but there are other times when this can be a strategy for disaster, a subject to which we will return later. Moreover, this kind of neo-*laissez faire* attitude ignores the fact that one of the sources of the order found in emergent patterns is the containment field or boundaries within which self-organization takes place (see Goldstein, 1999). We can say that emergence is a "qualified" spontaneity but this qualification points to various and sundry "costs" attached to the bringing about of emergence.

Predictability

Is emergence unpredictable?

Along with both of the claims that emergence violates causality and is totally spontaneous is the often-heard insistence that emergence is unpredictable. Indeed, the early emergentists placed unpredictability high on their list of attributes for emergence, along with nondeducibility from and irreducibility to antecedent conditions. Morgan (1923) thought that the same novelty that was supposed to undermine traditional views of causality was at heart unpredictable. As I mentioned in my earlier article (Goldstein, 1999), in complexity theory there is a similar refrain about how the properties, qualities, or patterns of global or macro dynamics are not able to be predicted from knowledge of the components or antecedent conditions alone.

Unpredictability, however, is not the last word on complex systems. First, what is unpredictable in emergent phenomena may not be their most interesting facets. For example, in the famous Benard convection cells studied so exhaustively by Ilya Prigogine and his followers (see Nicolis, 1989), the only thing really unpredictable about the stunning emergent patterns of the hexagonally shaped cells is the direction of their rotation – surely not the main feature of emergence in such systems. What is predictable, however, is that given the right container, and the right liquid, and the right process of heating, the remarkable Benard convection cells will emerge, and their pattern will be quite similar to those observed in previous experiments. This can be seen in the Game of Life (see Poundstone, 1985), where the presence of two emergent patterns called t-tetraminos in close proximity to one another can be used to predict the later emergence of another pattern, the pentadecathelon. At first this relationship was not noticed, so the pentadecathelon was presumed to be an unpredictable emergent; but now that the correlation is established between the t-tetramino and the pentadecathelon, the latter is not nearly as unpredictable. Even in chaotic systems, which are touted as full-blown unpredictability, there is a great deal of predictability due to the attractors of the system that serve to delimit its possible states (Goldstein, 1997b). In the light of such advances in predicting phenomena in complex systems, more and more effort is likely to be put into taxonomies and typologies of emergents. Such classification schemes will be a great help in discovering patterns of sequences and thereby yield even greater predictability.

Moreover, as stated above, much of the order found in emergent phenomena derives from the order inherent in the containers of the self-organizing processes. Knowledge of the order of the containers, therefore, can help in predicting the type of order that will be found in the ensuing emergent processes (see Goldstein, 1999). This, then, adds another measure of predictability to emergence. Furthermore, there is no reason to think that the predictability of emergent patterns in organizations will prove any the less susceptible to increase as careful observation and scrutiny of these patterns deepen over time.

These constraints on the unpredictability of emergence are not meant to suggest that emergent phenomena will yield to total predictability. Instead, my point is that adopting a fatalistic attitude about the supposed total unpredictability of emergence is neither based in fact nor particularly useful in going ahead with studies of emergent phenomena.

Ontology

Is emergence merely provisional?

If the more we learn about complex systems, the more predictable emergence becomes, does this imply that emergent phenomena are merely provisional, epistemological artifacts, lacking an ontological status? Critics of Emergent Evolutionism reached such a conclusion when the theory of quantum bonding came along in the 1930s and demonstrated that the emergent properties of compounds resulting from chemical reactions were deducible from knowledge of the components alone (McLaughlin, 1992). As a result, these commentators argued that the entire construct should be relegated to the status of an epiphenomenon. Does this mean that, as new and more sufficient theories come along, a similar conclusion should be reached about emergent phenomena in complex systems?

It needs to be pointed out that the study of emergent phenomena in complex systems is of a decidedly different nature than the inquiry into the emergent properties of chemical compounds that the theory of quantum bonding provided. The high point of discoveries in complexity science concerns the emergent level itself whereas the searching for micro-determinants as in quantum bonding is basically a side issue. The richness of emergent phenomena requires a set of functional laws congruent with their own level (this requirement was pointed out even in Emergent Evolutionism by, *inter alia*, Samuel Alexander; see Gillett, 1998).

A case in point is the very serviceable construct of an order parameter (Haken, 1981). This, an emergent-level construct, greatly simplifies our understanding of the behavior of the component level; Ockham's razor is at work here. Of course, the use of order parameters doesn't obviate the need for inquiry into the conditions resulting in emergence in complex systems. But discerning such conditions is not the same as tracing the micro events leading to emergence.

Is emergence merely subjective?

Another barrage against the ontological status of emergents concerns the role of subjectivity in the discernment of emergent patterns. Of course, the study of emergence is not unique in the involvement of the experimenter's perceptual perspective in observing the object of study. A particularly egregious case is that of certain interpretations of quantum mechanics, for example where an observer is supposed to affect the collapse of the wave function. The insular ontological status of what is being observed, then, becomes subject to doubt.

Complexity science also has its share in the issue of subjectivity versus onto-logical reality. In my previous article in this journal (Goldstein, 1999), I discussed Crutchfield's (1993) attempts to address the role of subjectivity via his conceptual-ization of emergence as an *intrinsic* capability for computational and, consequently, evolutionary adaptability of the system. Although subjectivity enters into the identification of emergent phenomena, there is nevertheless something inherent, i.e., ontological, about emergents in the computational capacity they confer on complex systems.

Although computational capacity may not be directly relevant to all instances of emergence in complex systems, e.g., emergence in organizations, the core of what Crutchfield is alluding to still seems to be pertinent in general. This has to do with how emergent patterns, structures, and properties add some kind of potency in the form of greater adaptability than such systems would otherwise contain. If emergence can indeed bequeath this potency, then, from a purely pragmatic per-spective, emergent phenomena must have considerable ontological status. Certainly, as the sciences of complex systems advance, better theories will be developed explaining more about how emergent phenomena are constituted out of lower-level components and processes. Crutchfield's own "particle" theory of emergence is an example. Yet enough is being discovered about emergent levels with constructs commensurate with those levels, and micro explanations will not completely supplant their usefulness.

Moreover, one need not go as far as Crutchfield's response, since the issue of subjective bias in studying emergence is not substantially different than that in any other scientifically informed discipline. That is why psychological researchers, for example, spend so much time worrying about inter-rater reliability. Identifying emergent phenomena demands a similar conscientiousness and a similar community of practice. Starting with subjectivity doesn't entail us necessarily ending up there.

Otherwise, we would all be condemned to a solipsistic existence. Hence, in my opinion, subjective bias does not ring the death knell for emergence any more than it does for other attempts to find patterns in our environments.

Prevalence

How ubiquitous is emergence?

Emergent Evolutionist C.L. Morgan (quoted in Tully, 1981: 35) once exclaimed, "it is beyond the wit of man to number the instances of emergence." The reference was to all living creatures as instantiations of emergence. This pleroma of emergents has grown even larger with the recent additions of neo-emergentists. Thus, in the study of cellular automata, there are parameter values in which emergence is abundantly prevalent. Of course, it is precisely because of the fascinating systems behavior at these values that so much of the study of complex systems takes place at them. But, we must remember that these values are set by experimenters. So why should we expect the same prevalence outside the laboratory?

Computer scientist and pioneer of complexity theory John Holland (1998) warns about confusing authentically emergent phenomena with instances of "serendipitous novelty" that ubiquitously surround us, for example the play of light on waves. For Holland, if emergence is to be a meaningful construct, it must be more rare than all the multifarious combinations of patterns that we perceive in our environment. Holland's criterion to distinguish emergence from other such concatenations of patterns is one often heard in complexity circles: "Emergence . . . occurs only when the activities of the parts do not simply sum to give activity of the whole" (1998: 14). In another article (Goldstein, 1999), I have described a certain arbitrariness incumbent in defining emergence as "more than the sum of the parts."

What I want to call attention to here, in contrast to Holland, is how it may indeed be valid to refer to the play of light on waves as an authentic example of emergence, at least from the point of view of novelty, irreducibility and so on. Emergence, after all, does include novelty and it is serendipitous in the way that it takes advantage of the confluence of many factors, including random ones. So, operationally, it may be impossible to distinguish emergence from "serendipitous novelty." However, I don't think that this amounts to a significant issue, since the crux of the matter is not so much what counts or doesn't count for emergence as how important the instance of emergence is to the agenda or intention on the part of observers of or participators in emergent phenomena. The play of light on waves may be unimportant for certain purposes or intentions of observers, but I can imagine where it could be quite important for others, such as for Claude Monet.

In terms of organizations, can it not be said that emergence is going on all over the place, since people are continually interacting? Working entirely alone is unquestionably rare. But interaction itself is not enough to lead to emergence. It must be interaction that ushers forth some novel pattern, structure, process, or pattern; moreover, a pattern that exhibits a type of coherence not found among the interactional agents alone. However, even such emergent patterns may be of negligible importance for organizational dynamics. An example might be several employees spontaneously meeting in a restaurant at lunchtime, sitting together, and as a result regularly meeting for Tuesday lunch. How important is such an emergent lunch pattern? It could be an authentically emergent pattern, but it is not immediately obvious how important it would be for organizational functioning (of course, it might prove to be extremely significant if these lunch meetings ended up generating creative ideas that were used back in the workplace).

It seems to me that for emergence to be a useful construct it must be neither rare nor everywhere. If it is too unusual it will have little to do with everyday organizational dynamics. If it is everywhere, then it loses any explanatory power. But once recognized, the more important issue is what it adds to or detracts from the organization.

Levels

The conflation of levels

Inherent in the very definition of emergence is the notion of a level distinction between the preliminary components (the micro level) and the emergent patterns (the macro level). Thus, the early emergentists conceived of evolution as a series of discontinuous emergences of new qualitative levels of reality (see Blitz, 1992). A parallelling level distinction is made by contemporary complexity theorists. For example, Chris Langton (Lewin, 1992), when referring to a graphic illustration of emergence, points upward to a global, emergent level "up here" and downward to a component, interaction level "down here." And Bedau (1997) points to the level distinction when he characterizes emergent phenomena as being "autonomous" in respect to the underlying processes.

Some sort of hierarchical stratification seems a necessary component of any doctrine of emergence. In this vein, the dynamicist Diner (Diner, Fargue, and Lochak, 1986: 276) underscored that in the evolution of a dynamical system there is a required "explicit passage from one level to the other . . . to disclose the appearance of these [emergent] properties."

This level distinction can be overlooked by organizational theorists in their fervor about the role that attractors may play in organizational dynamics. Thus, we are hearing about the leaders' visions as attractors or incentive and other reward systems as attractors. But attractors are a construct whose proper level is the emergent level, not the local interaction level, whereas leadership vision and corporate rewards are more appropriately understood as local, component-level phenomena.

Again, turning to dynamical systems theory can shed some light on what I am getting at concerning the emergent level of attractors. In the period-doubling route to chaos found in the logistic map (to calculate populations at discrete time intervals with a simple nonlinear difference equation), different attractors emerge as the control parameter increases (see Feigenbaum, 1983). When the dynamics become trapped at a fixed point attractor, the population gets stuck at a particular amount and does not change after that. If the parameter is raised, a period 2 attractor emerges, and this sequence of period doublings occurs all the way to chaos.

At what level are these attractors? Imagine that you are a little being traveling along the parabola. You come to a fixed-point attractor and it is like a wall you can't get beyond. This wall seems to be of the same nature as the parabolic road you are on, so it seems like the attractor is on the same ontological level as the road. But that is only because you are a one-dimensional being. Actually the attractor is a phenomenon that arises out of the dynamics of the system represented by the logistic equation. As such, attractors "deform" the possibility space of movement along the parabola from their higher-level vantage point: they come from above, so to speak, and constrain the behavior below. This, of course, doesn't make them miraculous – they arise out of the particular dynamics of these nonlinear inter- actions when certain parameter values become critical, i.e., at bifurcation. But they are a higher-level emergent construct.

Similarly, organizational attractors need to be understood as phenomena on the global or emergent level. How this emergent level emerges from organizational dynamics nevertheless needs to be further clarified. The question, then, is what are the underlying dynamics of complex systems that serve to shape the specific emergent phenomena that occur in organizations, and not how lower-level activities function as attractors.

The interaction of levels

Although the level distinction between emergents and components needs to be kept in mind to utilize the insights of complexity theory more adequately in organ- izational research, an opposite snare also lurks: believing that there is some inseparable barrier between the level of the components and the level of emergent patterns. These levels are both distinct and interactive at the same time. As Diner (Diner, Fargue, and Lochak, 1986: 277) pointed out, researchers will try to see not only how the whole is generated by the parts, but also how the parts are generated by the whole: "The local properties get a real meaning only through their relation to the global properties." This is one of the aspects of emergence highlighted by Chris Langton: a bottom-up, top-down feedback going on among the levels. Similarly, Ralph Abraham (1987) has described self-organization in terms of the output of the system influencing the control parameters.

Here, we see what can be termed a *transgression of levels*. This transgression, however, is not a conflation but a maintenance of the level distinction while at the same time trespassing it. This makes the study of emergence in complex systems a much more messy affair, and in organizational applications there will be a great deal of opportunity to get confused about what is happening on what level. But this kind of confusion can be taken as a good sign that one is getting close to the real essence of emergence.

Coherence

One of the defining characteristics of emergent phenomena in complex systems is a coordination, correlation, or coherence that is not present in the antecedent conditions of the components alone. An example of this coherence can be seen in the various emergent structures of the Game of Life that travel across the cells of the array, enduring through time. The property of coherence is one of the meanings of the typification of emergents as supposedly being "more than the sum of the parts."

Applied to organizations, it is often supposed that the coherence of emergent phenomena is a good thing because of its facilitative role, say, in high-performance teams. Certainly, coherence can be an important asset in organizational dynamics, as borne out by numerous studies of team functioning. Very recently, Michael Lissack and Johann Roos (1999: 16) have pointed out the crucial role that coherence must play in effective leadership: "Finding coherence, enabling coherence, and communicating coherence are the critical tasks of leadership."

A question arises in this context, however, as to whether the type of coherence manifested in emergence in complex system research is necessarily the kind of coherence from which organizations might benefit. This doubt becomes especially troublesome in the light of emergent coherence's conceptualization by certain pioneers of complexity theory. A particularly strident example can be found in the Synergetics school founded by one of the trailblazers of complexity theory, German physicist Hermann Haken (1981). According to Haken, emergence – for example laser light – represents collective processes that reinforce themselves and eventually gain:

> the upper hand over the other forms of motion and, in the technical jargon of synergetics, *enslave* them. These new processes of motion, also called modes, thus imprint a macrostructure on the system . . . If several of these collective motions, which we also call order parameters, have the same rates of growth, they may in certain circumstances cooperate with each other and thus produce an entirely new structure . . . a new order will occur. (1981: 236; my emphasis)

The obviously poor choice of word in "enslave" points to more than a semantic issue – is this the kind of picture of coherence that is needed in organizations? In fact, I think these connotations of overly rigid coherence also show up in the buzzword "consensus." In my experience, what most people mean by consensus is premature conformity to some group norm – in which case we could honestly say that it "enslaves" them.

Of course, coherence need not denote such rigid conformity. For example, coherence in the sense of boundaries or containment does seem a good idea, at least some of the time, at least when containment doesn't simply reinforce nonadaptive organizational "silos." What is needed is a paradoxically sounding nonconsensus coherence. This points to how much more work is needed in organizational applications of complexity to begin even to recognize and adequately describe the kinds of organizational phenomena on which complexity theory can shed some light.

Outcome

How beneficial is emergence?

Amid all the hoopla surrounding self-organization and emergence, it is often assumed that they are necessarily a good thing, that systems exhibiting them are significantly better off, or, at least, that something problematic in these systems is markedly ameliorated. To be sure, the tendency to emphasize the beneficial nature of emergence seems to be a taken-for-granted attitude in complexity science. This can be seen in complexity theorist Luc Steels' (1994) distinction between first- and second-order emergence: first order is a property not explicitly programmed in; whereas second order is emergent behavior that confers additional functionality generating an "upward spiral of continuing evolution." A similar bias toward the advantageous status of emergence can be seen in James Crutchfield's point about intrinsic emergence being an additional computational capacity coming about from emergent patterns in a complex system.

However, this emphasis on the positive value of emergence derives mostly from the computational framework of much of complexity research. Within such a framework, the enhancement of computational capacity does seem to be a good thing and therefore the enthusiasm over it is warranted. What happens next, though, is that complexity theorists jump beyond the immediate computer simulations and speculate further about how such an increase in computational capacity would aid in the evolution of all complex systems. A similar bias for believing that self-organization and emergence are nothing but advantageous for a complex system can also be seen in organizational applications. I myself have given in to this enthusiasm for the salving effect of self-organizational processes for evoking organizational creativity and motivation (see for example Goldstein, 1994, 1997a).

Strong caveats nevertheless seem to be in order here. First, consider the case of the former Yugoslavia. The central hierarchical control mechanism was dismantled and, consequently, the society self-organized, and became fraught with emergent political structures. Unfortunately, a great deal of these emergent structures were formed around pre-existing fault lines of ethnic differentiation and hatred. Dismantling control mechanisms and thereby encouraging self-organization and emergence, therefore, doesn't necessarily mean that you're going to have a better state of affairs than existed before.

Self-organization and emergence are powerful forces that must be channeled appropriately. One of the challenges is how we can constructively create conditions so that they do indeed tend toward a better state of affairs. Here, there is a need for work on the "boundaries" that will contain anxiety and anarchic impulses (see Goldstein, 1994). These "boundaries" are akin to the earlier mentioned "containers" that shape the structure of emergent phenomena taking place within them. These boundaries can be psychological (e.g., a sense of safety), social (e.g., rules of inter-action), cultural (e.g., rituals and stories), technological (e.g., computer networks), even physical (e.g., the actual physical attributes of the workplace). Working on the boundary dimension influences the turns that processes of emergence take. Experimenting with changing the boundaries, therefore, is a crucial step in learning how to guide emergence in constructive dimensions. Emergence can certainly be a very powerful advantage to a complex, human system, but much continuing ground work needs to be done to insure that it takes a constructive direction.

Conclusion

Charles Sanders Peirce (Taylor, [1998]) once wrote that in science and mathematics metaphysics leaks in at every joint. I have tried to point to where conceptual snares exhibiting a metaphysical tinge can leak in when it comes to using the construct of emergence. In the face of these snares, I am suggesting that those applying the idea of emergence tread cautiously and try to be aware of the assumptions underlying its application. Are these assumptions getting in the way of or aiding in the pragmatics of application?

Good physics doesn't ensure good metaphysics. And at least one of the first steps toward constructive metaphysics is to recognize where it exists in hidden form, then to surface it, and then to consider if the particular flavor of metaphysics is in congruence with the aims of the applier of emergence. Emergence is a charged concept and as such can obfuscate as much as enlighten. It would be unfortunate if carelessness in using the construct of emergence contaminated future directions before they were even taken.

Note

This article is an elaboration and expansion of a presentation at the *Complexity and Organization Conference*, Toronto, Ontario, April 4, 1998.

References

Abraham, R. (1987) "Dynamics and self-organization," in F. E. Yates, A. Garfinkel, D. Walter, and G. Yates (eds) *Self-organizing Systems: The Emergence of Order* (Life Science Monographs), NY: Plenum, 599–613.

Alexander, S. (1966) *Space, Time, and Deity: The Gifford Lectures at Glasgow: 1916–1918*, 2 vols, NY: Dover Publications.

Bedau, M. (1997) "Weak emergence," *Philosophical Perspectives*, 11 (Mind, Causation, and World): 375–99.

Berge, P., Pomeau, V., and Vidal, C. (1984) *Order Within Chaos: Towards a Deterministic Approach to Turbulence*, L. Tuckerman (trans.), NY: Wiley.

Bergson, H. (1983) *Creative Evolution*, A. Mitchell (trans.) Latham, MA: University Press of America.

Blitz, D. (1992) *Emergent Evolution: Qualitative Novelty and the Levels of Reality*, Dordrecht: Kluwer Academic.

Broad, C. D. (1925) *The Mind and its Place in Nature*, London: Routledge and Kegan Paul.

Clark, A. (1996) "Happy couplings: emergence and explanatory interlock," in M. Boden (ed.) *The Philosophy of Artificial Life*, Oxford: Oxford University Press, 262–81.

Crutchfield, J. (1993) "The calculi of emergence: computation, dynamics, and induction," Santa Fe Institute Working Paper # 94–03–016, electronically published. Also in *Physica D*, 1994 – Special issue on the Proceedings of the Oji International Seminar: Complex Systems – From Complex Dynamics to Artificial Reality, held April 5–9, Numazai, Japan.

Crutchfield, J. (1994) "Is anything ever new? Considering emergence," Santa Fe Institute Working Paper #94–03–011, electronically published. Also in G. Cowan, D. Pines, and D. Meltzer (eds) *Integrative Themes*, Santa Fe Institute Studies in the Sciences of Complexity XIX, Reading, MA: Addison-Wesley.

Diner, S., Fargue, D., and Lochak, G. (eds) (1986) *Dynamical Systems: A Renewal of Mechanism*, Singapore: World Scientific.

Feigenbaum, M. (1983) "Universal behavior in nonlinear systems," in D. Campbell and H. Rose (eds) *Order in Chaos*, Amsterdam: North Holland, 16–39.

Gillett, C. (1998) "Chaos, cosmology, and three concepts of emergence," paper presented at the Eighth Annual International Conference, Society for Chaos Theory in Psychology and the Life Sciences, Boston, MA, August 2.

Goldstein, J. (1994) *The Unshackled Organization: Facing the Challenge of Unpredictability through Spontaneous Reorganization*, Portland, OR: Productivity Press.

Goldstein, J. (1996) "Causality and emergence in chaos and complexity theories," in W. Sulis (ed.) *Nonlinear Dynamics and Human Behavior*, Singapore: World Scientific Publishing, 161–90.

Goldstein, J. (1997a) "Riding the waves of emergence: leadership innovations in complex systems," in C. Lindberg, P. Plsek, and B. Zimmerman (eds) *Edgeware: Complexity Resources for Health Care Leaders*, Cranbury, NJ: VHA, IX17–IX36.

Goldstein, J. (1997b) "Map-makers, explorers, and tricksters: new roles for planning and prediction in nonlinear, complex systems," in C. Lindberg, P. Plsek, and B. Zimmerman (eds), *Edgeware: Complexity Resources for Health Care Leaders*, Cranbury, NJ: VHA, V3–V31.

Goldstein, J. (1998) "Emergence: history, directions, and creative cognition," paper presented at the Winter Conference 1998, Society for Chaos Theory in Psychology and the Life Sciences, Northampton, MA, February 14.

Goldstein, J. (1999) "Emergence as a construct: history and issues," *Emergence*, 1(1): 49–72.

Goldstein, J. (forthcoming) "Emergence in complex systems: creative transgressions and radical novelty," manuscript in preparation.

Haken, H. (1981) *The Science of Structure: Synergetics*, New York, NY: Van Nostrand Reinhold.

Holland, J. (1998) *Emergence: From Chaos to Order*, Reading, MA: Addison-Wesley.

Kauffman, S. (1993) *The Origins of Order: Self-organization and Selection in Evolution*, New York, NY: Oxford University Press.

Kauffman, S. (1995) *At Home in the Universe: the Search for Laws of Self-organization and Complexity*, New York, NY: Oxford University Press.

Kellert, S. (1993) *In the Wake of Chaos*, Chicago: University of Chicago Press.

Kelly, K. (1996) *The Logic of Reliable Inquiry*, New York, NY: Oxford University Press.

Langton, C. (1986) "Studying artificial life with cellular automata," in D. Farmer, A. Lapedes, N. Packard, and B. Wendroff (eds) *Evolution, Games, and Learning: Models for Adaptation in Machines and Nature*, Proceedings of the Fifth Annual Conference of the Center for Nonlinear Studies, Los Alamos, NM, May 20–24, Amsterdam: North-Holland, 120–49.

Lewin, H. (1992) *Complexity: Life at the Edge of Chaos*, New York, NY: Macmillan.

Lissack, M. and Roos, J. (1999) *The Next Common Sense*, London: Nicholas Brealey.

McLaughlin, B. (1992) "The rise and fall of British emergentism," in A. Beckermann, H. Flohr, and J. Kim (eds) *Emergence or Reduction: Essays on the Prospects of Nonreductive Physicalism*, Berlin: Walter de Gruyter, 49–94.

Morgan, C. Lloyd (1923) *Emergent Evolution: the Gifford Lectures Delivered in the University of St. Andrews in the Year 1922*, New York, NY: Henry Holt.

Newman, D. (1996) "Emergence and strange attractors," *Philosophy of Science*, 63: 245–61.

Nicolis, G. (1989) "Physics of far-from-equilibrium systems and self-organization," in P. Davies (ed.) *The New Physics*, Cambridge: Cambridge University Press.

Pepper, S. (1926) "Emergence," *Journal of Philosophy*, 23: 241–5.

Poundstone, W. (1985) *The Recursive Universe: Cosmic Complexity and the Limits of Scientific Knowledge*, Chicago, IL: Contemporary Books.

Stacey, R. D. (1996) *Complexity and Creativity in Organizations*, San Francisco, CA: Berrett-Koehler.

Steels, L. (1994) "The artificial life roots of artificial intelligence," *Artificial Life I*, 1/2 (Fall/Winter): 75–110.

Taylor, E. I. (1998) "William James' prophecy on the demise of positivism in American psychology," in Robert Rieber and Kurt Salzinger (eds) *Psychology: Historical and Theoretical Perspective*, Washington, DC: APA Press.

Tully, R. E. (1981) "Emergence revisited," in L. Sumner, J. Slater, and P. Wilson (eds) *Pragmatism and Purpose: Essays Presented to T. Goudge*, Toronto: University of Toronto Press, 261–77.

Waldrop, M. (1992) *Complexity: The Emerging Science at the Edge of Chaos and Order*, New York, NY: Simon and Schuster.

Weiss, N. (1987) "Dynamics of convection," in M. Berry, I. Percival, and N. Weiss (eds) *Dynamical Chaos: Proceedings of the Royal Society of London*, Princeton: Princeton University Press: 71–85.

Wheeler, W. (1926) "Emergent evolution of the social," in E. Brightman (ed.) *Proceedings of the Sixth International Congress of Philosophy*, New York, 33–46.

EDITORS' DISCUSSION OF THE READINGS IN PART TWO

- Allen, P. (1998) Evolving Complexity in Social Science, in G. Altmann and W. A. Koch (eds) *Systems: new paradigms for the human sciences*, Walter de Gruyter, New York.
- Griffin, D., Shaw, P. and Stacey, R. (1998) Speaking of Complexity in Management Theory and Practice, *Organization*, 5(3): 315–339.
- Goldstein, J. (2000) Emergence: a construct amid a thicket of conceptual snares, *Emergence*, 2(1): 5–22.

After lunch and a short walk, between rain showers, along the banks of Loch Lomond, we returned to Ross Priory to talk about the readings we had decided to include in Part Two. While the readings in Part One exemplify enthusiastic attempts to apply the natural sciences of complexity to organizations, the readings in Part Two are examples of writing which seeks to identify the different ways in which ideas from the complexity sciences were being used in relation to organizations. What we are pointing to here is the more discriminating approach that more or less followed the first attempts to take up the complexity sciences. We started our discussion with the chapter by Peter Allen.

Ralph: Peter distinguishes between four types of models of reality. These are equilibrium models, dynamical systems models including mathematical chaos, self-organizing models, by which he means dissipative structures, and the fourth type is complex evolutionary systems. The move from one to the next has to do with dropping assumptions that are made in the previous one. So, the first one, the equilibrium model, is based upon the assumption that the entities comprising the model are homogeneous and that events impinging on the system are average events. This means that all of the micro dynamics, the micro diversity, is assumed away. And then you get equilibrium and any small change is rapidly dampened away so that the system rapidly and predictably returns to its stable state. The model has no internal capacity to change. It can only be changed from the outside. The next model, systems dynamics and chaotic systems, drops the assumption that the system will move to equilibrium. Now you can get unpredictability but the system does not have the internal capacity to move spontaneously to another pattern or attractor. The third model, self-organizing systems or dissipative structures, does not assume a move to equilibrium either and in addition drops the assumption about average events. This model introduces non-average events in the form of fluctuations, modelled as a random variable or noise. Now some element of the micro dynamics has been introduced and the model displays the internal capacity to move spontaneously from one pattern or attractor to another, but only to another pattern that is already there, rather like an archetype. The final model drops the assumptions dropped by the models mentioned so far and in addition drops the assumption of homogeneous entities or agents. It introduces agents that are different from one another and you therefore get much richer micro diversity and the consequence of this is that the model now has the internal capacity to produce novel attractors spontaneously. This is a model that can evolve and so is much closer to the reality we experience than any of the other models. I think the Allen chapter provides us with a very useful way of distinguishing between different ways of using the complexity sciences in relation to organizations. For example, my article in Part One does not differentiate between a deterministic mathematically chaotic system, which is Allen's second model, and a complex adaptive system consisting of heterogeneous agents, which is Allen's model four. I just lumped them together without seeing the important difference.

Robert: At a generic level, although he's not talking about organizational examples, this reading makes you see the combination of assumptions that are at play in any of the pieces of writing.

Donald: Peter's chapter links the models to one another by means of the underlying assumptions. Whereas other readings introduce focus on the tensions between various schools of thought, he shows where these tensions come from and how they are all related to assumptions. The other readings in Part Two open up a lot of the problems, and while Peter doesn't close them down, he does say a bit about where these issues come from. I think he begins to talk about the role of theory in all of this.

Ralph: When you see models in this way you can then ask which one is likely to be more useful for thinking about human interaction and I think it is what Peter Allen calls the complex evolutionary model, which is really the same kind of model in terms of properties as heterogeneous complex adaptive systems. So I think that the important distinction has to do with whether agents are assumed to be homogeneous or heterogeneous. In the former case the model displays only one pattern, one attractor, and does not have the spontaneous capacity to move to another pattern. As soon as you get to the heterogeneous complex adaptive systems you have models which can evolve.

Donald: This helps us to reflect on the work that was done in the readings in Part One which we discussed this morning. They were a bit variable and ambiguous on the degree of heterogeneity or homogeneity within these systems. Many of the authors didn't mention these assumptions and we kind of assumed, if anything, homogeneity. Ralph, I think you probably assumed, or explicitly stated, heterogeneity . . .

Ralph: No, it wasn't very explicit.

Donald: Right. So that might be one of the themes that Peter's framework of assumptions is usefully pointing to, but another thing that the reading drew our attention to, in research terms, was how you deal with, or what are the consequences of, the heterogeneity of organizations . . .

Ralph: . . . of the people in organizations . . .

Donald: Of people in organizations, yes . . .

Doug: Another issue is the issue of human freedom and how we could fit that into the models which are being suggested. This leads to a different idea of process which, although not yet in our article, we were moving towards and later developed.

Donald: I suppose an interesting question to ask, Doug, is what it was that moved you off in this direction? You know, where did this departure come from? Can you recall?

Doug: I think it was around the difference of views around the idea of self-organization. We saw real contradictions in what we were trying to say and what other people were trying to say.

Ralph: I remember the big thing that really got us thinking was those very intense conversations we had about agency. In all of these models, the agents are actually rule-following programmes as in agent-based models or a set of equations if the modelling is at a macro level. Agency then has simply to do with rules. So the debate we began to have was around the relationship between the individual and the social. I remember one of those PhD group meetings [on the Hertfordshire Doctoral Programme] where I was being really insistent that, if we were going to use the ideas of complex adaptive systems, then we had to identify what or who were the agents in these complex adaptive systems in organizational terms. That is when we started having this long-running debate about whether the individual was an agent or not and then . . .

Robert: As opposed to what?

Ralph: As opposed to, well this is what we had great difficulty with, though it seemed like individual agency was opposed to the system or the group or something else as agent.

Doug: Closely connected to this is the question of what is self-organizing, organizing itself. I can remember the first time I suggested it was communicative acts that were self-organizing, in effect were agents, which is what Luhmann suggests.[1] In that Lake District meeting you hit the roof and said 'Communicative acts! What is that?'

Ralph: And this was also tied up with our discussion of the theory of autopoiesis, which Luhmann also uses. I reacted very strongly against this notion of auto-poietic communicative acts because from what I was hearing it sounded completely disembodied and ignored the individual. Neither of us was very clear at that time but you were arguing against the idea of an individual as an autonomous agent and I was saying that the agent has to be the individual and could not be an abstract communicative act.

Doug: It was this debate that motivated me to return to reading Mead.[2]

Ralph: And then, of course, at the same time I was doing the group analytic training and starting to come across the work of Elias.[3] So then, I was sort of moving to saying that if the individual isn't the agent, then the group might be in some sense. But then gradually we moved to the position you took in your thesis, Doug.[4] Individuals form the social while being formed by it at the same time. So we left behind the notion of the autonomous individual and moved to Elias's kind of idea of interdependent people, giving a paradoxical theory of agency. In your thesis, Doug, you also introduced Mead's social act of gesture and response, where the agent is an individual human body, but you can never understand that individual human body as autonomous. So you then get this paradoxical idea of agency where the agent is forming the social while, at the same time, being formed by it, so . . .

Doug: Mead introduces the word 'gesture' instead of 'intention' because 'intention' is always understood as a simple act. He says it's never a simple act because the gesture and response are the social act, it is one act.

Donald: So, after your first round of work you started to challenge and tackle some of the assumptions that you had been making and some of the definitions that had been used. Robert and I also began to see that other people were using similar terms in different ways and so we started asking questions about what these terms actually meant. More importantly in some senses, we started asking what we meant by them. So after that meeting with you, for example, we went back and concluded that we were not very clear about what a social system is. If the human is the element of the social system, then we have to recognize that humans are members of many systems. What are the implications of this multiple membership of systems? How do you get around this problem of a person being a member of many systems at once? That's when we, through a colleague of ours, started looking at Luhmann and the possibility that social systems were actually systems of communication. At the time we had some difficulty with this but we started asking the question and we also, I think, had this question about the consequences of self-organization for agency. What does it mean that human beings are intentional actors if we are to think in terms of systems in the natural sciences where the agents don't have these attributes?

Doug: We're talking about a theory of action where the element is not simply the individual.

Donald: But in a way, the interesting thing is that, although at that time we didn't have that much interaction with one another, many writers seem to have taken some serious steps to reflect on what they had been doing and what they were actually talking about. I think this comes through in Goldstein's article in this part.

Doug: I felt uncomfortable with the notion of system from the beginning because I knew, for instance, that in 1951 Talcott Parsons had moved away from thinking of the individual as the element in a system.[5] He saw that it could not be the individual because the individual brings too much into it and contaminates the model of the system completely. This is what Luhmann then built on and the individual disappears.

Ralph: That is what I reacted against so very much.

Doug: Instead we need the notion of an emergent person.

Donald: When we were looking at Luhmann's ideas, to be honest, we didn't focus on theoretical conversations much but tried to talk these ideas through with practitioners and engage in experimental action with organizations. We were thinking about alternative explanations from evolutionary economics or learning theory, where the element of the system can be thought of as the routine.

Robert: We assumed that rules, whether found or socially created, were important but become more problematic if you think about them in a social setting where there is some degree of choice about whether to engage in the process of their creation and whether or not to adhere to them. You see this every day in organizational life where someone at a meeting agrees to a proposal and then goes off and does something completely contradictory in a different setting. This introduces the notion of membership of multiple systems. You may be part of a formal management team where you have to be saying that some activity is the right thing to do but a member of some informal grouping in the organization where clearly that is not what you want to happen and so you want to lobby against it. I think the use of these research networks of organizational partners talking about these things, based on their real experiences, was very helpful. I found it very helpful to take a story about some incident in an organization and try to bring it to life around conceptual thinking about what the element of the system is. I think we flirted with Luhmann's notion that the element is the communication or the communicative act, but didn't feel that this progressed us very far in terms of being able to work through examples.

Doug: But this is why usually discussions get very emotional and aggressive. People feel very strongly about the issues and the thing is they see the question but they don't have the answer. They can see that the answer the other person is offering can't possibly be right but then can't propose an acceptable alternative. At one of our PhD meetings, we just started going around and around this question about the individual and agency. We couldn't get out of it and literally exhausted ourselves. This is what Goldstein does again and again in his article in this part. He raises the questions and identifies what he calls snares. He does not reach any solutions but the issues he raises are the right issues.

Doug: Well, I think it is unsatisfying, the way he then just stops and says we'll have to see.

Ralph: So the readings in Part Two are trying to explore, in a way those in Part One were not, key concepts such as the meaning of self-organization in human interaction, the meaning of emergence for humans, and what all of this saying about human agency. What does agency mean when you move from a simulation on a computer to actual human beings interacting?

Donald: I think Goldstein's article asks these questions and to some extent leaves them hanging. Your article, Doug and Ralph, takes it a stage further in that you begin to say that different groups mean different things by these terms and have got different assumptions underpinning their approach to the subject. You mention three basic orientations that can be found in organizational management theory and in the natural complexity sciences. Could you say a bit about the distinctions between different groups of researchers?

Ralph: One perspective was taken by Murray Gell-Mann[6] and John Holland.[7]

Doug: Another perspective on self-organization was taken by Brian Goodwin.[8] We then moved on to the distinction I came up with in writing my book about leadership. This was the differences between those taking the Kantian perspective and those taking a more Hegelian idea of process. That is what I've been doing since as a way of trying to differentiate perspectives. As soon as you see people talking about ontology and epistemology you know you are in a Kantian discussion because those have to be the issues if, with Kant, you believe that reality is hidden and we can't know it directly. This is the position of Holland and Gell-Mann.

Donald: Tying that back to your article, Doug, you identified, on the one hand, a rational, objectifying voice of control concerned with functionality and outcome.

Doug: Yes, that's what the readings in Part One were doing in directly applying complexity ideas to organizations.

Donald: There was another group who were more relational voices, more inter-subjective in their orientation, and you talked about decentred agency.

Doug: We were using this term at that time.

Donald: Goldstein's article, although it asks a lot of interesting and pertinent questions, does so from a fairly functional point of view. For example, he sees emergence and self-organization as powerful forces which must be channelled appropriately. Emergence is a force that we can choose to unleash. I think that he's saying that if we want to understand how to do that effectively then we really have to understand the concept in a lot more detail. When I read your review, Doug and Ralph, you seem to be saying that we can't talk about self-organization and emergence in this way. I think your article is closer to Peter's chapter – you and Peter have a lot more in common in that respect. You're trying to develop your conceptual understanding of complexity, based on your own experience. The readings in Part One simply take ideas across from the natural sciences to the social but your reading in this part is saying that as soon as you begin this translation you find it has actually been done already.

Ralph: Well, not entirely. Goldstein's article goes back in history and looks at how emergence was talked about long before complexity. He points out that Wheeler was talking about emergence in the social sciences in 1926.

Doug: And Russ Marion also goes back to Kant, who uses the term self-organizing systems.[9]

Robert: After the initial burst of enthusiasm for the new natural sciences, the readings in Part Two are pointing to much earlier work in the social sciences about the nature of being in organizational settings.

Donald: But also it began for some of us the process of gradually withdrawing from the systems idea. You see this particularly in your work, Ralph and Doug, where you explicitly consider prior work in social sciences disciplines like psychology, psychoanalysis, philosophy and sociology, whereas there is a different stream of complexity theory which has gone more into the natural sciences' rigour side of things.

Robert: In moving more and more into the social sciences' treatment of self-organization and emergence are we moving away from complexity theory altogether?

Ralph: No, I think what remains important is insights about how global patterns emerge in local interaction and there's nothing mysterious about it. Elias did say this before the natural scientists and he used the language of self-organizing and emergence to talk about the interplay of human intentions in what he called a civilizing trend. On the other hand, Mead was talking about detailed micro inter-action. I think what the models and the computer simulation in the complexity science do is show that there's nothing mysterious about this link between micro interaction and widespread pattern.

NOTES

1 Luhmann, N. (1984) *Soziale Systeme*, Suhrkamp, Frankfurt am Main.
2 Mead, G. H. (1934) *Mind, Self and Society*, University of Chicago Press, Chicago, IL.
3 Elias, N. and Scotson, J. L. (1994) *The Established and the Outsiders*, Sage, London.
4 Griffin, D. (1998) *Dealing with the Paradox of Culture in Management Theory*, doctoral thesis, University of Hertfordshire.
5 Parsons, T. (1951) *The Social System*, Free Press, New York.
6 Gell-Mann, M. (1995) *The Quark and the Jaguar: adventures in the simple and the complex*, Abacus, New York.
7 Holland, J. (2000) *Emergence: from chaos to order*, Oxford University Press, Oxford.
8 Goodwin, B. C. (1994) *How the Leopard Changed its Spots: the evolution of complexity*, Weidenfeld & Nicolson, London.
9 Marion, R. (1999) *The Edge of Organization: chaos and complexity theories of formal social systems*, Sage, Thousand Oaks, CA.

Complexity in social settings

EDITORS' INTRODUCTION AND COMMENTARY

In Part Two, we saw evidence of a somewhat introspective turn, in which authors sought to identify the different ways in which ideas from the complexity sciences were being used in relation to organizations, revealing some tensions between emerging schools of thought. To some extent this theme continues in the readings in Part Three, though it is clearly focused on work in which researchers are primarily concerned with the social as opposed to the natural sciences.

The readings in Part Three cohere around questions of applicability and development of 'complexity thinking' in human settings. Eschewing the direct transfer of models and theories from the natural sciences, each reading takes some ideas from complexity theory and explores how, if at all, such ideas may be built upon in the context of established lines of thinking in social theory and philosophy in order to enrich our understanding of human action in organizations.

The readings therefore collectively depart from the problem-solving, performance-improving or experience-enhancing mentality of Part One. They move away from the implicit search for a manageable relation between emergent properties and processes of interaction towards an engagement with the somewhat messy and often unintelligible and unpredictable nature of everyday life in organizations.

However, they do so in different ways: Stacey retains the ideas of emergence and self-organization and asks the question of what these might mean for human action. Chia, and Tsoukas and Hatch, by contrast, seem to start with concepts such as non-linearity and incompressibility and question the extent to which such ideas can enrich our understanding of human organization. This distinction – between a focus on human action or on human organization – may perhaps be key to determining the stance that each reading ultimately adopts on important issues (often dichotomies) which emerge from the readings issues such as reification, epistemology–ontology, subject–object, inside–outside, first order, second order, paradox and their roles in our theorizing about organization.

For example, concern with human organization seems to accompany a clear separation between the human world and the natural world – and a view of human experience as a subjective interpretation of, or response to, ontologically real nature; this leads Chia to reject complexity thinking as an extension of reductionism and simply not up to the job of understanding real organizational experience, whilst for Tsoukas and Hatch it highlights the requirement for acknowledging a subjective counterpart to the complexity of nature and developing sensitivity to inter-subjective 'narrative' complexity. Stacey, on the other hand – focusing on human action – denies the deconvolution of experience into separable subjective and objective components and draws attention to the inherently paradoxical and transformative nature of everyday experience.

Robert Chia

FROM COMPLEXITY SCIENCE TO COMPLEX THINKING: ORGANIZATION AS SIMPLE LOCATION

From *Organization* 1998, 5(3): 341–369. Copyright © 1998 by Sage Publications. Reproduced by permission of the author and publisher.

Abstract

Recent developments in the sciences of complexity have led to a rise in interest in the application of such insights to the understanding of social phenomena such as organization. This essay seeks to examine the fundamental differences between social and natural systems and to thereby render more transparent the possible limitations of a science of complexity for the analysis of organization. Against this science of complexity, it counterposes the kind of *complex thinking* inspired by philosophy, literature, art and the humanities to show how such forms of linking may be more adequate to the task of revealing to us the whole spectrum of human lived experiences; something which we argue here that the complexity sciences, in the current form they take, remain unable to access.

> All our belief in objects, all our operations on the systems that science
> isolates, rest in fact on the idea that time does not bite into them.
> (Bergson, 1911: 9)

Introduction

In her introduction to *Philosophy in a New Key*, the Whiteheadian philosopher Susanne K. Langer (1942) observed that every age in the history of thought is marked by the tenacity with which it clings on to its own peculiar sets of preoccupations. Its concerns are peculiar to its epoch not just for obvious practical reasons, but also for deeper reasons of intellectual growth and formation. If we examine more carefully the oftentimes slow formation and accumulation of doctrines which collectively mark that history, we may discover that it is a particular mode of handling problems rather than their substantive content which assigns them to a particular epoch. As such, the task of any critical inquiry into the formation of new ideas must begin with a systematic excavation of the deeply entrenched presuppositions informing the thinking of a particular age. Such a prudent attitude must necessarily be adopted for what has come to be called the *sciences of complexity*.

In a number of intellectual quarters now, the fundamental ideas of complexity science have been used to throw new light on fields as diverse as meteorology, irreversible thermodynamics, epidemiology, non-linear dynamics and even socio-biology and genetics. Within the field of organization studies, there have been several recent attempts to 'apply' concepts such as 'self-organizing systems' (Senge, 1993), 'non-linearity' (Stacey, 1993), and the notions of 'self-similarity' and 'strange attrac-tors' (von Krogh and Roos, 1995) to social phenomena in general and organizational systems in particular. Whilst the straightforward translation and application of these notions, inspired by the physical sciences, can oftentimes throw fresh light on social phenomena, the qualitative differences between the inert material world and the living social worlds are often downplayed in the process. Issues of subjec-tivity, meaning, the limitations of language, and the essentially interpenetrative and transformative character of human experiences mean that the strict conceptual categories deployed so effectively in the explication of natural phenomena cannot be so easily transposed to the social realm. This essay seeks to examine the fundamental differences between human social systems and natural systems, and to thereby render more transparent the possible limitations of a *science* of complexity for social analyses. Against this science of complexity, it counterposes the kind of *complex thinking* inspired by philosophy, literature, art and the humanities to show how such a complex form of thinking may be more adequate to the task of revealing to us the whole spectrum of human lived experiences; something which the complexity sciences remain unable to access.

A science of complexity

The last 20 years, in particular, have seen a radical re-evaluation of the nature of 'chaos' and 'complexity', and more fundamentally of the relationship between order and disorder (see, for example, Serres, 1982; Gleick, 1987; Hayles, 1990, 1991; Waldrop, 1992). Traditionally, order and disorder have been regarded as natural opposites. Order is that which is classifiable, analysable and fully accountable within a discourse of rationality. Disorder, on the other hand, was what could not be expressed through the conceptual grids of modern science except as a limited form of statistical generalization. Recent developments in the science of complexity, however, have initiated a radical reconceptualization of the nature of 'chaos' and of the relationship between order and disorder. In contemporary science, chaos is now conceptualized as extremely complex information rather than as an absence of order and these insights have been successfully applied to phenomena as diverse as dripping water faucets (Shaw, 1984), measles epidemics (Schaffer and Kot, 1985), schizophrenic eye movements (Huberman, 1987) and fluctuations in fish population (May, 1976) as well as the analysis of the stock market (Brock, 1989). All these impressive path-breaking attempts at explicating seemingly randomized phenomena point to the potency and attractiveness of the complexity sciences for helping us deal with the highly complex and multifaceted character of modern life. It was, therefore, almost inevitable that the principles of a science of complexity would eventually be deployed to the understanding of complex social phenomena such as society and organization without a critical examination of its possible limitations.

To begin with, what exactly do we mean when we say that something is 'complex'? The Nobel laureate physicist Murray Gell-Mann offers an intriguing and perceptive way of appreciating the meaning of complexity. For him, the degree of complexity refers to:

> . . . the length of the shortest message that will describe a system, at a given level of coarse graining, to someone at a distance, employing language, knowledge, and understanding that both parties share (and know they share) beforehand. (Gell-Mann, 1994: 34)

There are two significant implications of this way of defining complexity. One is that the experience of complexity, for Gell-Mann, is related to the difficulty, or otherwise, of transmitting information that would suitably and adequately account for the phenomena encountered. This definition implies that complexity is not necessarily an external state of affairs but rather intrinsically related to the observing system that is experiencing the phenomena. The length of the description is inherently dependent upon who or what is doing the describing thereby making the experience of complexity subject-dependent. Thus any definition of complexity 'is necessarily context-dependent, even subjective . . . In actuality, then, we are discussing one or more definitions of complexity that depend on a description of one system by another, presumably a complex adaptive system, which could be a human observer' (Gell-Mann 1994: 33). A second implication is that complexity is linked to the compressibility or otherwise of information. The more such information can be compacted into a crisp, precise expression, the less 'complex' it is deemed to be.

What Gell-Mann's definition draws our attention to is the fact that complexity is more about the *experiencing* of seemingly complex phenomena and the amount of *effort required* to articulate this experience into transmissible form rather than about objective complex states of affairs existing independent of the observer-system. Contrary to the populist notion of a science of complexity with established immutable principles designed to deal with ever-more complex configurations of relations in both the natural and social world, it transpires that the basic premise of a science of complexity is the *systematic and deliberate descriptive reduction of the complexes of human experiences into a transmittable and understandable form*. In other words, the science of complexity is principally a deliberate programme of *simpli-*

fication in which the vague complexes of sense-experience are systematically compressed and converted into a conventionally recognizable and accepted form of discourse. Complexity science is thus ultimately reductionistic in its intent.

Gell-Mann's approach to understanding complexity helps to throw light on what Tsoukas (1998) following Barrow (1991) calls 'algorithmic compressibility'. Tsoukas begins by making a basic distinction between what he calls 'propositional knowledge' and 'narrative knowledge'. Propositional knowledge is knowledge involving the formulation of conditional 'if, then' statements relating to an observed set of empirical conditions. Narrative knowledge, on the other hand, is knowledge organized and expressed through stories, anecdotes and examples. For Tsoukas, propositional statements are 'predicated on the assumption that the phenomenon they refer to is patterned and composed of objectively available elements which can be re-presented via an abbreviated formula' (Tsoukas, 1998: 97). However, in cases where no pattern is discernible, there is no available abbreviated formula to capture the informational content and hence the whole sequence has to be tediously described in full detail thereby rendering the description 'complex' in Gell-Mann's definitional terms. Algorithmic compressibility, on the other hand, denotes the ability to compress a large mass of 'observational statements into a few clearly stated propositional statements thereby enabling economy of effort, transferability, and remote control' (Tsoukas, 1998: 97). This means that propositional knowledge operates on the principle of algorithmic compressibility and is a kind of knowledge-compacting process in which the maximum informational content is communicated through the shortest possible description. A mathematical theorem or equation is the archetypal exemplar of this propositional form of knowledge. Transposed into Gell-Mann's terms, what this means is that phenomenal experiences are considered 'simple' or 'complex' depending on how easily they lend themselves to comprehensive description and formulaic analyses (i.e. the extent of the algorithmic compressibility attainable). Since propositional knowledge is that which is algorithmically compressible, it, as a form of knowledge, is not predisposed to deal with non-propositional (i.e. truly complex) forms of understanding. All forms of propositional knowledge are thus reductionistic and hence intrinsically unable to deal with complex phenomenal experiences at their own level of articulation.

The prestige, privilege and instrumentalized value given to propositional forms of knowledge is, thus, closely linked to its capacity to economically compress and reduce what would otherwise be deemed to be vague and unwieldy forms of understanding into a compacted frame of presentation in order to facilitate ease of comprehension, transferability and appropriate deployment. It is, in reality, another way of understanding how the still-dominant priorities and method of science continue to dictate our contemporary modes of thought including especially the sciences of complexity. Indeed, the whole of modern science continues to be underpinned by the related principle of *operationalism* as an imperative in the knowledge-building process. Operationalism involves the deliberate and exhaustive translation of concepts and ideas into explicit measurable forms in order to render them more amenable to cognitive manipulation. Thus, as the physicist P.W. Bridgeman (1928) claimed in *The Logic of Modern Physics*, from the point of view of operationalism, any concept is nothing more than the set of operations which define it. Thus, the concept is synonymous with its corresponding set of operations. He writes:

> To adopt the operational point of view involves much more than a mere restriction of the sense in which we understand 'concept', but means a far-reaching change in all our habits of thought, in that we shall no longer permit ourselves to use as tools in our thinking concepts of which we cannot give an adequate account in terms of operations. (Bridgeman, 1928: 31)

Bridgeman's injunction implies that there cannot be any surplus or excess of meaning to any of the operationalized concepts. Any intimations of a field of knowing beyond that which is explicable is rendered illegitimate by the logic of scientific operationalism. In effect this rejection of an inarticulate or inarticulatable form of knowing which does not easily lend itself to algorithmic compressibility means that science in general and complexity science in particular is authorized to deal with phenomena *only if they lend themselves to the principles of operationalism*. Phenomena, or aspects of phenomena, which do not lend themselves to operationalization must be deemed to be non-existent. In this way it becomes possible for complexity science to generate its own vocabulary of terms which encapsulate what are deemed to be the unique features associated with it. Terms such as 'self-organizing', 'butterfly-effect', 'the edge of chaos', 'non-linearity', 'self-similarity' and 'strange attractors' become rich and powerful as well as economical forms of expression. They, therefore, provide the explanatory axes for a science of complexity. Thus, the very idea of a 'science' of complexity paradoxically entails the systematic reduction or simplification of otherwise vague and indefinable complexes of sensations into a taxonomic language that lends itself to quantifiable measures and to purposeful action. Such is the nature of modern analysis in general and scientific analysis in particular.

It thus becomes clear to us that the function of scientific analysis is not so much about attaining an understanding of nature, but about the development of an instrumentalized form of thinking primarily concerned with the construction of tools for aiding our adaptive actions. However, because of this orientation, human intelligence treats the real as comprising solid inert objects rather than as living organisms because that is the only form of knowledge it is capable of generating. As the French philosopher Henri Bergson writes:

> Let us start, then, from action, and lay down that the intellect aims, first of all, at constructing. This fabrication is exercised exclusively on inert matter, in this sense, that even if it makes use of organized material, it treats it as inert, without troubling about the life that animates it. And of inert matter itself, fabrication deals only with the solid; the rest escapes by its very fluidity. If, therefore, the tendency of the intellect is to fabricate, we may expect to find that whatever is fluid in the real will escape it in part, and whatever is life in the living will escape it altogether. *Our intelligence, as it leaves the hands of nature, has for its chief object the unorganized solid*. (Bergson, 1911: 161–2, emphasis original)

In other words, the intellect is incapable of establishing a sympathy with fluid living nature. It awkwardly brutalizes the moment it touches the fluid and the living and thus is characterized by a natural inability to comprehend the dynamic complexities of life.

Taxonomic and dynamic complexities

Much of the literature on complexity, because it treats the latter as a stable and external condition rather than a consequence of our phenomenal engagement, does not discriminate between the various ways in which our experiences of complexity differ. However, it is possible to differentiate between two different forms of complexity that we may encounter. For the purposes of this discussion, we shall call them *taxonomic* and *dynamic* complexities. It is argued here that this distinction is central to an understanding of the limitations of the complexity sciences which, despite their apparent distancing from the classical sciences, nevertheless continue to rely on related metaphysical presuppositions.

Taxonomic complexity

One of the perennial key issues of any scientific inquiry is the problem of 'essences' – of how to adequately account for the nature and status of types of species, things, situations and other similar modes of differentiation within a general scheme of things. The classical Platonic view of such essences is that they constitute a fixed and unchanging realm of reality, which can be faithfully located, classified and represented through adequate systems of ordering. This 'taxonomic' orientation, first inspired by Aristotle and subsequently pursued by Linnaeus and Darwin amongst others, has become the definitive feature of modern Western thought. Through this method of ordering, the world is presented to us as naturally differentiated and hence isolatable and locatable into pre-existing systems of classification. As greater and greater varieties of experiences are encountered, they are inserted into this 'master' taxonomic register for the purpose of future recall and conceptual synthesis. The creation of classificatory categories and taxonomies as systems of differentiations is, therefore, always also accompanied by such integrative attempts to relate the various elements together. From this preoccupation, complexity is said to be high when the number of 'combinatorial' relationships rise (often exponentially) with an ever-increasing number of elements inserted in a system of classification since each new addition must now be in some way made to relate to the pre-existing ones. Thus a proliferation of possible combinations marks the path from the simple to the complex in this static ordering of things. Taxonomic complexity thus is intrinsically related to the initial programme of differentiation associated with the creation of stabilized self-identities, and the subsequent attempt to reassemble these previously differentiated elements back into a coherent conceptual system. Understood thus, complexity in the social world arose from what we now understand as the deliberate and even obsessive preoccupation with the systematic rationalization of society in all its myriad forms: 'professionalization', 'disciplines', 'division of labour', 'administration', 'bureaucracy', etc. This widespread rationalization of virtually every aspect of modern life in (particularly) Western societies has been explored and analysed in great detail by influential thinkers such as Weber (1948), Foucault (1970, 1979), Schoenwald (1973), Elias (1979–82) and Miller (1987) amongst others.

For example, Miller (1987) in his penetrating discussion of Jeremy Bentham's programme for social reform explores in some detail Bentham's proposed 'methodization' for the regulation and control of society. Methodization entailed the spatial and temporal division of all categories of individuals: workers at their bench, pupils at school, prisoners in their cells, and so on. This process of classification and counting enabled rational representation to become a key practice in the administration of society. Thus: 'Books must be kept . . . Chronological entries will be made daily, methodological entries, products, population tables, stock inventories, health records, moral conduct records, requests . . .' (Miller, 1987) – all these were to be religiously adhered to for the purpose of aiding social administration. It is the cumulative aggregation of such rationalizing practices over time which has produced the kind of complex and oftentimes dysfunctional social systems that become so highly dependent on the superior information processing capabilities of computers.

In an unpublished paper (but available on the World Wide Web) that explores this almost inexorable 'technologizing' of the world, Cooper (1995) similarly notes that a pervasive feature of the modern world is its '"program" of *differentiation*' in which the world is first *broken up* into clear-cut, definite things occupying clear-cut, definite places in space and time, and in so doing creating a freely available pool of infinitely usable resources which can be combined and recombined in an infinitude of ways. These differentiated elements can then be reconstituted as a temporary 'assemblage' to meet immediate functional needs. For Cooper, this is the basic driving force behind the idea of *mass-production* and the automobile is one good example of such a reassembled object involving the creation of a whole complex of new relationship configurations. However, it is the paradigm of the alphabet which best exemplifies the possibilities and potentialities, as well as infinite complexities, created by this initial process of linear differentiation. Rescher (1996) observes that, even if the number of constituents of a system were small, 'the ways in which they can be combined to yield products in space-time might yet be infinite' (p. 79). In the case of the alphabetic system, we are able to produce, from the initial 26 characters, impressive combinations of syllables, words, sentences, paragraphs, books, genres and so on. The seemingly inexhaustible libraries of books produced in the last few centuries is a testimony to the potency of the alphabetic system as a form of human expression. Indeed, the whole sinew of Western thought is built up upon the ever-increasingly complex variations rendered possible by it.

Likewise, even a nature made up of finite and unchangeable elements can yield an endless steady stream of new phenomena: '"new" not necessarily in kind but in their functional interrelations and thus in their theoretical implications' (Rescher, 1996: 79). This kind of operational or functional complexity generated by the 'taxonomic urge' (McArthur, 1986) to fix the flux and flow of the world in spatial terms for the purpose of regulation and control must, however, be distinguished from the idea of a *dynamic complexity*. In this latter instance, a heightened awareness of the indivisibility of movement and change marks the entry into a radically different mode of thought in which temporality and duration involving 'the continuous progress of the past which gnaws into the future and which swells it as it advances' (Bergson, 1911: 5) are accentuated. It is the unique ability to achieve an 'intellectual sympathy' with our phenomenal experiences which marks the transition from reliance on a static representationalist paradigm of thought to thinking in terms of the complex dynamics of evolving systems.

Dynamic complexity

In addition to the common, modern experience of taxonomic complexity, we also have an intuition that accounting for human experiences can be much more complex than it is often made out to be because of the inherent fluidity of life situations, and the acute sense of transience and temporality accompanying the profusion of events encountered in the moment-to-moment heterogeneous becoming of our lives. This awareness leads us to realize that our linguistic forms of expression, which are dominated by descriptive states rather than by an awareness of the primacy of movement and transformation, are oftentimes inadequate to the task at hand. Thus, the American philosopher William James, as well as Bergson and Alfred North Whitehead amongst others, have found it necessary to more creatively express their understanding of the inherent complexity of the human condition in distinctly different terms from that familiar to the sciences of complexity. For James the complex novelty issuing from each new moment of living experience cannot be discretely differentiated. Reality, as we experience it, does not 'issue by jumps and jolts'. Instead it 'leaks in insensibly . . . All the old identities at last give out, for the fatally continuous infiltration of otherness warps things out of every original rut' (James, 1910: 350). Likewise, Bergson (1946/92) points out that 'Reality is global and undivided growth, progressive invention, duration: it resembles a gradually expanding rubber balloon assuming at each moment unexpected forms' (p. 95). This highly evocative 'ballooning' image of reality implies that our experience of temporality and duration is that which prolongs the before into the after and prevents them from being pure, isolatable, instantaneous moments. Each moment of our experiencing absorbs the preceding ones, transforming them and in that very process transforming itself into a new and novel experience.

The *dynamic complexity* associated with living systems is qualitatively different from the assumed discrete and unchangeable (or at least relatively stabilized) states which encourage the creation of taxonomic systems of classification and their attendant version of complexity. In the former case, complexity arises not from the increasingly bewildering array of possible combinations, but from the immanent *in-one-another-ness* of moments of experience and hence their intrinsic non-locatable interpenetrative nature. Unlike the natural sciences which are able to deal only with isolatable and instantaneous presents, where the past is not assumed to be inextricably bound up with the present, thinking in terms of dynamic complexity 'implies a real persistence of the past in the present, a duration which is, as it were, a hyphen, a connecting link . . . Continuity of change, preservation of the past in the present, real duration – the living being seems, then to share these attributes with consciousness' (Bergson, 1911: 24). This view is entirely foreign to the world of the physicist or mathematician who is condemned to deal with 'a world that dies and is reborn at every instant' (Bergson, 1911: 23). In other words a world that has no history.

Contrary to commonly held notions of time, our experience of temporality and change is one of *absolutely indivisible movement* and it is this indivisibility which renders conventional analytical approaches adopted by mathematics and the physical sciences impotent in helping us fully understand the nature of such experience of change. This is, once again, convincingly argued by Bergson (1911) in *Creative Evolution* where he maintains that the intellect is an *effect* of living nature predisposed to stabilizing and spatializing our experiences, to entifying such experiences into discrete elements, and to creating rigid conceptual boundaries for dealing with them (Bergson, 1911: x). The intellect feels at home with inanimate objects, especially among solid objects, where our action finds its fulcrum and our industry its tools. Such an attitude works with inert objects, but not with living systems which are by nature fluid, transient and perpetually changing, hence unlocatable in space. This is especially the case when we begin to examine the realms of human consciousness.

In *Time and Free Will*, Bergson (1913a) begins by noting that the intensities of states of consciousness are often misleadingly compared in quantifiable terms. Thus we talk about a sensation being twice, thrice, or even four times more intense than another. Although this is commonly accepted as unproblematic, Bergson points out that, whilst this manner of speaking may be helpful for comparing different entities in spatial terms (i.e. in terms of size, etc.), thereby relying on the notion of extensive magnitude, it should not be used for psychic states where the intensity of experience is what really counts. Intensity here relates, not so much to the magnitude with which an emotional response is felt, but to the *pervasiveness* of the sensational experience within the conscious system. Bergson writes:

> For example, an obscure desire gradually becomes a deep passion. Now you will see that the feeble intensity of this desire consisted at first in its appearing to be isolated and, as it were, foreign to the remainder of your inner life. But little by little it permeates a larger number of psychic elements, tinging them, so to speak, with its own colour: and lo! your outlook on the whole of your surroundings seems now to have changed radically. How do you become aware of a deep passion, once it has taken hold of you, if not by perceiving that the same objects no longer impress you in the same manner? . . . The fact is that, the further we penetrate into the depths of consciousness, the less right we have to treat psychic phenomena as things which are set side by side. When it is said that an object occupies a large space in the soul or even that it fills it entirely, we ought to understand by this simply that its image has altered the shade of a thousand perceptions or memories, and that in this sense it pervades them . . . But this wholly dynamic way of looking at things is

repugnant to the reflective consciousness, because the latter delights in clean cut distinctions, which are easily expressed in words, and in things with well-defined outlines, like those which are perceived in space. (Bergson, 1913a: 9)

For Bergson, therefore, the intensities of conscious experience are marked by *qualitative* rather than *quantitative* change and this qualitative change exhibits an indivisibility which only an intuition can adequately grasp.

Dynamic complexity is thus associated with a living reality that is perpetually becoming, renewing itself and perishing. It recognizes that the primary units of analyses are not discrete, isolatable and stabilized entities, but perpetually changing configurations of relations which are continuously transforming themselves. This implies that the current established system of symbolic expressions cannot adequately capture the sense of fluent indeterminacy and temporality intrinsic to life. Our dominant images of time, movement and change must be radically overhauled if we are to begin to meaningfully re-engage at the level of conscious experience.

Temporal complexification: a Bergsonian reconstrual of time, movement and change

Our common-sense conceptions of time inevitably rely on spatial expressions. Time appears to us as linear, discrete and quantifiable and therefore lending itself to cognitive manipulation. However, this notion of time is far removed from the experience of our consciousness. Here the sense of duration, continuity and associated emotional responses arising therefrom is acutely felt to be intimately woven into our subjective apprehension of time. Take the simple everyday act of putting a lump of sugar into a cup of coffee or tea. In this simple act, Bergson (1911) observes, 'I must, willy-nilly, wait until the sugar melts' (p. 10). This little fact is, however, big with meaning because it implies that my sense of the time taken is associated with my own impatience. The point being made is that this experience of time which is associated with my impatience is not that of mathematical time. Rather: 'It coincides with my impatience, that is to say with a certain portion of my own duration, which I cannot protract or contract as I like. It is no longer something *thought*, it is something lived. It is no longer a relation, it is an absolute' (Bergson, 1911: 10). Our sense of time is irretrievably linked to our own sense of becoming and perishing. Time, in this sense, is relative to our conscious awareness. Moreover this real lived time is indivisible because it contains a whole compressed succession of memories which are meaningful to us only in their collective composition.

This view of time is vastly contrary to our commonly-held views. When we speak of time, we generally think of it as a homogeneous medium, an external independent dimension like space which provides one of the organizing axes for charting our life experiences. But for Bergson (1913a), this is an entirely mistaken way of construing time because 'Time, in so far as it is a homogeneous medium, and not concrete duration, is reducible to space' (Bergson, 1913a: 98). It is in reality a spurious concept brought about by the 'trespassing of the idea of space upon the field of pure consciousness' (Bergson, 1913a: 98). It is this smuggling of spatial metaphors onto the plane of consciousness which has led us to construe time in the way mathematicians and physicists take it to be. On the other hand our concrete experience of time as pure *duration* is 'nothing but a succession of qualitative changes, which melt into and permeate one another, without precise outlines, without any tendency to externalize themselves in relation to one another, without any affiliation with number' (Bergson, 1913a: 104). Once we attribute a homogeneity to duration, we surreptitiously introduce space as the sole dimension of experience. On the other hand, inner duration is the continuous life of a memory 'which prolongs the past into the present, the present either containing within it in a distinct form the ceaselessly growing image of the past, or, more probably, showing by its continual change of quality the heavier and still heavier load we drag behind us as we grow older' (Bergson 1913b: 38). For Bergson, without this survival of the past in the present, there would be no duration, but only instantaneous moments.

Much the same critique that Bergson applies to our reconstructed and spatialized view of time carries over into his analysis of our construal of movement and motion. If we analyse the concept of motion we find that we are bound to say that motion is effectively movement taking place in space. And, when we claim that this motion is divisible into discrete moments, we discover that it is really the space travelled that we are thinking of, as if this space is interchangeable with the movement itself. If we reflect further, says Bergson (1911), we find that:

> . . . the successive positions of the moving body really do occupy space, but that the process by which it passes from one position to the other, a process which occupies duration and which has no reality except for a conscious spectator, eludes space. We have to do here not with an *object* but with a *progress*: motion, in so far as it is a passage from one point to another, is a mental synthesis, a psychic and therefore unextended process . . . We are thus compelled to admit that we have here to do with a synthesis which is, so to speak, qualitative, a gradual organization of our successive sensations, a unity resembling that of a phrase in a melody. (Bergson, 1911: 111)

Therefore, there are two aspects of motion that we need to distinguish from one another: the *space traversed* and the *act* by which we traverse it. The latter is not reducible to the former. Yet this is precisely what science and mathematics do since they cannot deal with the qualitative element of time: the notion of *duration*. Thus science and mathematical formulae may, in their analyses, indeed increase the number of simultaneous instants and positions which they take into consideration by making the intervals very small. They may even use differentials to show that it is possible to increase without limit the number of these intervals of duration. Nonetheless, they will never be able to represent the essential duration experienced in the interval itself. This is because 'although the moving body occupies, one after the other, points on a line, motion itself has nothing to do with a line' (Bergson, 1911: 120). It is this confusion between *motion* and *space traversed* which has led to the famous logical paradoxes postulated by Zeno of Elea, a follower of Parmenides in ancient Greece.

The problem of how enduring substances can *act* to destabilize their world so as to bring about new states of affairs has bedevilled numerous Greek metaphysicians from the very outset. It was Zeno who was perhaps the first to draw attention to what appeared to be a logical absurdity in the Heraclitean-inspired claim that movement and change were natural aspects of reality. Zeno is said to have formulated some 40 paradoxes of which only four seem to have survived. These four, the Dichotomy, the Achilles, the Arrow and the Stadium, all point to the patent absurdity of movement and change. For instance, in the Arrow, the problem is formulated thus: 'At each moment of an arrow's flight it is at a certain place, exactly equal to its own length so that at no moment can it occupy a place greater than its own length. Therefore, logically, there are no moments left when it could move from one place to another, so that it, in fact, never moves at all'. Presented thus, there clearly appears to be a valid reason for doubting the possibility of change.

Likewise, in the case of Achilles and the Tortoise, Achilles races against the tortoise whom he generously but fatally, so it seems, allowed a head start. For, according to Zeno, Achilles must first reach the tortoise's starting point in order to catch up with the tortoise. However, while he does so, the tortoise has moved on to a new position so that Achilles must now reach this new position. When he does this the tortoise has, yet again, moved on to a third position so that Achilles is never able, according to this logic, to catch up with the tortoise. In effect Achilles has to do infinitely many things before ever overtaking the tortoise. Like the previous example, Zeno again concludes that movement and change in position are impossible and therefore false. Both these examples appear to vindicate the belief in the existence of an objective, unchangeable reality which can, therefore, be subjected to scientific scrutiny and taxonomic classification.

However, Bergson (1991) in *Matter and Memory* uses his distinction between *movement* and *trajectory* to resolve Zeno's paradoxes which he (Bergson) maintains is a 'false problem'. For Bergson, the trajectory is indeed infinitely divisible but real movement is not. Movement is the only thing that happens in time. It occurs as a single unity. Thus the Arrow simply flies through the air and never *is* at any one point at an instant, because there are no instants in real processual time. Zeno, thus, is guilty of mistaking movement and duration for the infinite number of possible points on a line of trajectory; an error we all too commonly make when we mistake clock-time for our durational *experience* of time. Or, to put it in more familiar terms, Zeno is guilty of mistaking the 'map for the territory'.[1]

Likewise, Achilles simply moves until he catches up with his tortoise, no matter what we say about the *ground* over which he moves. It, therefore, becomes more evident through these two examples that what process theorists like Bergson are attacking about the dominant attitude of science is the uncritical adoption of a view which analyses movement into a set of rests; a kind of 'counterfeit movement' which underpins virtually every modern conceptualization of time and movement. He writes:

> We argue about movement as though it were made of immobilities and, when we look at it, it is with immobilities that we reconstitute it. Movement for us is a position, then another position, and so on

indefinitely. We say, it is true, that there must be something else, and that from one position to another there is the *passage* by which the interval is cleared. But as soon as we fix our attention on this passage, we immediately make of it a series of positions, even though we still admit that between two successive positions one must indeed assume a passage. We put this passage off indefinitely the moment we have to consider it. We admit that it exists, we give it a name; that is enough for us: once that point has been satisfactorily settled we turn to the positions preferring to deal with them alone. We have an instinctive fear of those difficulties which the vision of movement as movement would arouse in our thought. (Bergson 1946/92: 145)

For Bergson, all real movement is indivisible and cannot be treated as a series of distinct states which form, as it were, a line in time. Bergson's main claim is that the temporal structure of our experience does not consist of putting together pre-given discrete items. On the contrary, so-called discrete elements are only apparent when we find it necessary to pluck them from our *continuing* experience in order to represent them in spatial terms. This overpowering tendency to *spatialize* time provides the dominant mode of thought governing our contemporary comprehension of reality. One of Bergson's crucial contributions, therefore, is to alert us to the important distinction between the time of consciousness, *temps vécu*, and the time of the physicist or the clock-time of everyday use. Whereas the latter consists of discrete points juxtaposed in a homogeneous medium, which has all the characteristics of space, the former is a *duration*, a fusion of heterogeneous instants, an indivisible flux and becoming. Time, as we normally understand it, is not, it turns out, an absolute dimension of the real, but a figment of our imagination as Eoyang (1989: 280) perceptively argues.

Corresponding to this reconstrual of time and movement, in terms of duration and mobility, our perception of change requires similar conceptual revision. The idea of change, however, is more confidently asserted by those who use it to analyse contemporary society. We say that change exists, that everything is changing; that change is the very law of things. In effect, we have never stopped saying that everything changes yet when we are confronted with the practical application of this proposition we act as if we believed that at the bottom of things there are stability and invariability. Hence, although we speak of change ever so easily, we do not sufficiently contemplate the nature of change and its true implications. Bergson (1946/92) maintains that 'In order to think change and see it, there is a whole veil of prejudices to brush aside, some of them artificially created by philosophical speculation, the others natural to common sense' (p. 131). For Bergson, movement and change are reality itself. We are easily misled by language which is biased to static description. For instance, we talk about the 'state of things'. But what we call a state is in effect the appearance which a change assumes in the eyes of an observing being who him/herself is changing according to an identical or analogous rhythm. Take, for example, a sunny summer day and we are stretched out on the grass. We look around us – everything is at rest; there is absolute immobility – no change. But the grass is growing, the leaves of the trees are developing or decaying – we ourselves are growing older all the time. That which seems at rest, simplicity itself, is but a composite of our ageing with the changes which take place in the grass, in the leaves, in all that is around us.

What we identify as 'things' or enduring 'states' are secondary effects produced in a situation analogous to that which occurs when two trains move at the same speed, in the same direction, and on parallel tracks. For passengers in each of the two trains, the other train is effectively stationary. But this clearly *exceptional* situation is what allows the travellers in the two trains to hold out their hands to one another or talk to each other since they are 'immobile' in this special sense. *Every apparently stable situation is, thus, the result of the coincidence between the degree of change in the object of attention and the change of the person who perceives it.* This immobility is what, then, enables us to act upon things and to allow things to act upon us. Immobility is, thus, the prerequisite for all action, and being such, 'we make of it an absolute, and . . . see in movement something which is superimposed' (Bergson, 1946/92: 144).

However, whilst the breaking up of change into static states enables us to act upon them and whilst it is practically useful to focus on the end-states rather than on change itself, we deliberately create insoluble problems by failing to recognize the true changeable nature of reality. It is a mistake to construe reality as a sea of stability with scattered islands of change. Instead, the opposite is true. Stability is the exception, not the rule, especially in lived reality. For Bergson, once we imbibe this truth, many of the great philosophical enigmas, such as the great debates between realism and idealism, and the relationship between substance and change, will no longer arise. All these difficulties arose from shutting our eyes to the evident indivisibility of the process of change.

Reconstruing time in terms of experienced *duration*, disentangling the confusion between *movement* and trajectory and recovering the mobile, changeable character of reality leads us to a different comprehension of the complexities of the human condition. It impels us to consider an alternative set of intellectual priorities and the postulating of a radically different form of thinking and knowing from that which has shaped modern science. Here the Bergsonian method of 'intuition' and the art theorist Norman Bryson's (1982) idea of a *logic of the glance* provides an alternative *decentred*, and temporally-sensitive investigative stance for dealing with the complexities of lived experience.

Towards complex 'decentred' thinking

The Bergsonian critique of the overpowering tendency to spatialize time, movement and change, and to reconstruct these key concepts in spatial terms, has led us to reconsider what a truly complex form of thinking might entail in contrast to the kind of 'counterfeit' version underpinning the complexity sciences. In the case of the latter, we start from the immobile and conceive and express movement only as a function of this immobility, endeavouring to catch it with our static 'net' of ready-made concepts. Hence, we only 'obtain in this way a clumsy imitation, a counterfeit of real movement' (Bergson, 1913b: 45). Whilst, admittedly, this spatialized and static version of time, motion and change is a necessary prerequisite for constructing a relatively stabilized and liveable world, something which the intellect is eminently suited to do, it has also led to a falsely held view of reality in which the prevailing assumption remains that movement and change are epiphenomenal aspects of an essentially stable reality that can be systematically investigated and unproblem-atically represented through the established symbolic codes of modern science. Such a deeply-entrenched attitude is attributable to what the mathematician-turned-philosopher A.N. Whitehead has called the widespread belief in 'simple location'. By simple location he meant 'the concept of an *ideally isolated system*' (Whitehead, 1926/85: 58) which embodies the unquestioned assumption of a fundamental character of things in which entities are believed to exist as discrete isolated systems in space-time. Without this enormous assumption 'science, or indeed any know-ledge on the part of finite intellects would be impossible' (Whitehead, 1926/85: 58). This assumed property of simple location provides the underlying rationale for the entire epistemology of *representationalism* since it serves as the foundational basis for 'anchoring' thought and hence centring our phenomenal experiences for the purposes of rational analysis. For, if phenomena are simply locatable and iden-tifiable, they immediately become more amenable to systematic classification and causal analysis.

Thus, the entire attitude of modern science, including the sciences of com-plexity, revolves around the axis of centred thinking which itself is predicated upon the prior spatializing and quantification of natural and social phenomena. As we have shown in our discussion of Bergson's inquiry into the status of conscious states, whilst it may be less problematic to treat the former in such terms, the latter involves intensive magnitudes rather than extensive magnitudes and hence does not lend itself to analysis through the terms of simple location. Instead, a form of complex, *decentred thinking* is required for understanding such phenomenal experiences.

The thoroughly compelling Bergsonian reconstrual of our concrete appre-hension of time, movement and change, as we have seen, leads us to recognize the interpenetrative and indivisible character of such experiences and hence their intrinsic non-locatability. Thus, duration is above all that which 'prolongs the before into the after and prevents them from being pure instantaneous moments' (Bergson, in Alexander, 1957: 22). Whilst material objects, according to the principle of simple location, are frequently marked out as occupying space side-by-side and external to one another, this method of simplification will not work for conscious 'states' since, strictly speaking, consciousness is dynamic and not static. The experi-ence of pure duration takes a form in which both the past and the present states are fused 'into an organic whole, as happens when we recall the notes of a tune, melting, so to speak into one another' (Bergson, 1911: 100). For Bergson, as well as other process philosophers such as Whitehead, the past, present and future must not be construed as discrete instantaneous moments unproblematically separable from one another. Instead, real time is a living reality, not discrete, not spatial in character. Each moment of experience 'confesses itself to be a transition between two worlds, the immediate past and the immediate future' (Whitehead, 1948: 224). The future necessarily lives actively in its antecedent world of the present which, in turn, is itself immanent in the immediate past. This lived experience of time is reminiscent of the 'in-one-anotherness' which Heidegger (1962) alluded to in his discussion of the Other in *Being and Time*.

The upshot, then, of this penetrating critique of centred thinking, launched by Bergson and sustained by Whitehead, is that the still-dominant belief that things and events are unproblematically given to us as fully constituted and self-identical cognitive experiences has been rendered unsupportable. Yet this seductive belief in the possibility of attaining full instantaneous presence in our conceptual schema has spawned the *logocentric* attitude in social analysis. Logocentrism as *the* defining mode of Western thought rests on a 'metaphysics of presence' which privileges the immediacy and obviousness of observed phenomena. These are deemed to be 'simple, intact, normal, pure, standard, [and] self-identical' (Derrida, 1977: 236). As Cooper (1989) emphasizes: 'logocentric presence is thus a form of covertly willed prior knowledge . . . by claiming to be a kind of "perfect" foundation or origin' (Cooper, 1989: 490) for validating the status of formal knowledge. Cooper and Derrida's deconstructive reading of logocentrism, therefore, follows in the vein of Bergson and Whitehead's dismantling of the unsupportable presuppositions of modern science.

To think complexly, therefore, is to avoid the seductive appeal of the metaphysics of presence, to resist the overwhelming tendency to think in terms of simple location, and to recognize the immanent, enfolded and implicate character of phenomena. Things are never straightforwardly what they appear to be since, in the cumulative multiplicity of acts required in bringing them 'present' to our senses, they are always already loaded with traces of the past and are thus the constructed effects of differences and deferrals in meaning and perception. Immanence, otherness and in-one-anotherness are, thus, different ways of alluding to what the poet William Blake meant when he wrote those immortal lines:

> To see a World in a Grain of Sand
> And a Heaven in a Wild Flower
> Hold Infinity in the Palm of your Hand
> And Eternity in an Hour.
>
> (William Blake, *Auguries of Innocence 1*)

The method of intuition and the logic of the glance

The notion of intuition as a means of achieving insights into reality has received much attention amongst modern philosophers. Spinoza (1985), for example, saw intuition as a deep feeling of a resonance or coincidence between the act by which our mind comes to know truth perfectly, and the operation by which God engenders it. Similarly, Schopenhauer (1968) regarded all great scientific discoveries as a result of a sudden intuition, a flash of insight which is not simply the result of a systematic process of abstract reasoning whilst Schelling (1988) also maintained a doctrine of intuition as supra-rational. For Kant (1963), on the other hand, all our intuitions are essentially infra-intellectual. Whatever their differences, the prevailing view of intuition, therefore, has tended to emphasize the almost mysterious nature of this alternative form of knowing. This is a view which is radically at odds with that of Bergson.

The intuitive method

For Bergson, intuition is a rigorous philosophical method intended to reconnect us with our concrete and mobile reality. Intuitive philosophy involves the deliberate reversing of our habitual direction of the work of thought and of thereby attaining a level of 'intellectual sympathy' with this concrete, living reality. This can come about only through gradually weaning our thought processes away from our obsessive reliance on the crutches provided by symbolic representation. For Bergson, intelligence and intuition are two different but complementary ways of knowing reality. This is because scientific inquiry tends to become less and less objective and more and more symbolic in proportion as it proceeds from the physical to the vital. The intellect is, thus, most at home dealing with inert matter whilst intuition is particularly suited for understanding human lived experience. This means that the intuition achieved through a rigorous deconstruction of symbolic systems is eminently suited to grasping the fluid and mobile character of reality. Metaphysical inquiry, then, 'is the science which claims to dispense with symbols' (Bergson, 1913b: 8). This act of internal knowing, attained through such a process of rigorous deconstruction, unlike that achieved through analysis, is *absolute*. The infinite plurality and apparent complexity of views we have about reality are really a consequence of the intellect's inability to grasp the latter from the 'inside' and to thereby feel the pulsation of its soul. Thus:

> What is relative is the symbolic knowledge (generated) by pre-existing concepts, which proceed from the fixed to the moving, and not the intuitive knowledge which installs itself in that which is moving and adopts the very life of things. This intuition attains the absolute. (Bergson, 1913b: 63)

For Bergson, intellectual analysis reduces the object of our inquiry to conceptual elements already established a priori and hence to analyse is to fundamentally express an object of interest as a function of something other than itself thereby alienating it from itself. All analysis is thus a translation into the pre-defined symbols of representation and the organizing codes associated with them. In this way, analysis 'multiplies without end the number of its point of view in order to complete its always incomplete representation, and ceaselessly varies its symbols that it may perfect the always imperfect translation' (Bergson, 1913b: 7). Intuition, however, through the systematic destructuring of the predominant habit of thought and the system of symbolic representation associated with it, brings us in contact with the reality of duration, movement and change. It leads us to recognize that the apparently stable and immobile character of our social world is only an artificial effect of the forceful *slowing down* of an essentially mobile reality, in order to accommodate our practical need for order and stability. This is not to denigrate intellectual analysis, only to remind ourselves that the intellect is associated with the need for practical action rather than with a reflective contemplation on the nature of reality. It carves out and renders significant only that which is of practical interest while the penumbra or vague fringes of perception which have no direct bearing on action are neglected.

Intuition, on the other hand, is a method of *thinking in duration*; of thereby *temporally* synthesizing the multiplicity of fleeting images into a coherent whole. An illustration may serve to make this point clearer. A visitor to Paris, of an artistic temperament, makes some sketches of the city, writing underneath them, by way of memento, the word 'Paris'. As he has actually seen Paris he is able, with the help of the original intuition he has of that unique whole which is Paris as he has experienced it, to place his sketches therein and synthesize them. But there is no way of performing the inverse operation. It would be impossible, even with thousands of sketches, to achieve the intuition necessary to give oneself the impression of what Paris is like if one has never been there. Intuition is thus something which we grasp, albeit in small handfuls, but with the sureness of discipline.

In introducing the possibility of achieving such an intuition, Bergson's main point is to show that humans are capable of attaining a knowledge deeper than that which the intellect can possibly give. But such an intuition cannot be easily attained. Much mental and emotional effort has to be invested in the manner akin to what is commonly held to be exemplary scholarly research. Thus, it is impossible to have an intuition of reality, that is, an intellectual sympathy with its innermost nature, unless its confidence has been won by a long comradeship with its external manifestations. Through such scholarly reflections we are able to go beyond ready-made concepts. We become able to develop 'supple, mobile, and almost fluid representations, always ready to mould themselves on the fleeting forms of Intuition' (Bergson, 1913b: 18). Bergsonian intuition, therefore, is in no way a mysterious thing. It is something which we all possess to a greater or lesser degree. We cannot attain intuition without some degree of intellectual labour. Yet, however valuable the intellect may be practically, it is not the ultimate form of knowing. On the other hand, the clearest form of penetrating intuition comes to us from the works of great artists. What we call 'genius' is simply the power possessed by great painters, musicians and poets to see more than we see and of enabling us, by their expressions, to penetrate further into reality ourselves.

Humankind has found intellect the more valuable faculty for practical use and has thus denied the equivalent status to intuition. Yet:

> Intuition is there, but vague and, above all, discontinuous. It is a lamp almost extinguished which only glimmers now and then for a few moments at most. But it glimmers whenever a vital interest is at stake. On our personality, on our liberty, on the place we occupy in the whole of nature, on our origin, and perhaps also on our destiny, it throws a light, feeble and vacillating, but which none the less, pierces the darkness of the night in which the Intellect leaves us. (Bergson, 1911: 282)

The Bergsonian method of intuition, thus, marks that tentative and hesitating venture into a more dynamically complex method of inquiry. What are subliminal about Bergsonian intuition are its fleeting characteristics, the sense of transience it conveys, and the inherent temporal instability of its form of knowing – one which finds sympathetic resonance with what the art theorist Norman Bryson (1982) calls the *logic of the glance*.

The logic of the glance

Whilst Bergson's intuitive approach to addressing the complexity of phenomenal experiences may be rather unique, he is by no means alone in the search for an alternative approach to understanding the concrete and durational character of the human condition. For the contemporary art theorist Norman Bryson, the dominant factor in shaping our current forms of knowing is that of ocular vision and in particular in the 'method' of the *Gaze*.

In a fascinating study of the methods of Western painting and Chinese painting, Bryson observes that Western painting is predicated on the '*disavowal of deictic reference*' whilst painting in China is predicated on the 'acknowledgement and indeed the cultivation of deictic markers' (Bryson, 1982: 89). What Bryson means by the term 'deictic' is a certain feature of paintings in which 'The work of production is constantly displayed in the wake of its traces; in this tradition the body of labour is on constant display, just as it is judged in terms which, in the West, would apply only to a *performing* art' (Bryson, 1982: 92, emphasis original). For Bryson, this is in stark contrast to most Western paintings in which the individual history of a painting, in the course of its transformation into a completed piece of work, is largely irretrievable. This is because, although it is evident that the visible surface has been worked over and over again:

> . . . the viewer cannot ascertain the degree to which other surfaces lie concealed beneath the planar display. The image that suppresses deixis has no interest in its own genesis or past, except to bury it in a palimpsest of which only the final version shows through, above an interminable debris of revisions. (Bryson, 1982: 92)

In Picasso's paintings, for instance, the work of erasure stops only when the first image is totally obliterated and the viewer cannot ever work out how the final image has come to be what it is:

> Like the stylus in the mystic writing pad, the brush traces *obliteratively*, as indelible effacement; and whatever may have been the improvisional logic of the painting's construction, this existence of the image in its own time, of duration, of practice, of the body, is negated by never referring the marks on canvas to their place in the vanished sequence of local inspiration. (Bryson, 1982: 93)

Chinese painting, on the other hand, has always selected a form which:

> . . . permits a maximum of integrity and visibility to the constitutive strokes of the brush: foliage, bamboo, the ridges of boulder and

> mountain formations, the patterns of fur, feathers, reeds, branches, in
> the 'boned' styles of the image; and forms whose lack of outline (mist,
> aerial distance, the themes of still and moving water, of the pool and the
> waterfall) allows the brush to express to the full the liquidity and
> immediate flow of the ink. (Bryson, 1982: 89)

In the art of Chinese painting, the mastery of the stroke lies in the subliminal ability
to paint out the traces that have brought the strokes into being whilst the easel
paintings of the West are 'autochthonous, self-created, parthenogeneses, virgin-
births' (Bryson, 1982: 95). In one case the process of becoming is incorporated into
the painting whilst in the other process has been eliminated. The painting is placed
outside duration.

Bryson uses this distinction to reflect on two logics of presentation: the Gaze
which is fixing, prolonged and contemplative, and the Glance which is 'a furtive
or sideways look whose attention is always elsewhere' (Bryson, 1982: 94). Painting
of the Gaze attempts to arrest and extract form from fleeting process. It is a vision
disembodied, a vision decarnalized. Thus, in the Gaze, the painter: 'arrests the flux
of the phenomena, contemplates the visual field from a vantage-point outside the
mobility of duration, in an eternal moment of disclosed presence' (Bryson, 1982:
94). The Gaze is penetrating, piercing, fixing, objectifying. It is a violent act of
forcibly and permanently 'present-ing' that which otherwise would be a fluxing,
moving reality. Painting of the Glance, on the other hand, addresses 'vision in the
durational temporality of the viewing subject; it does not seek to bracket out
the process of viewing, nor in its own techniques does it exclude the traces of the
body of labour . . . calligraphic work cannot be taken in all at once . . . since it has
itself unfolded within the *durée* of process' (Bryson, 1982: 94).

It is not difficult to see that what Bryson (1982) is getting at in this penetrating
analysis is the fundamental difference between two vastly contrasting attitudes
towards understanding our lived experience. Although he used a comparison of
Western and Chinese paintings to illustrate his point, this by no means meant that
one attitude was found to the exclusion of the other. Rather, it is the pervasiveness
of each of these contrasting perspectives which differentiates East from West. We
can now begin to see that Bergson's attempt to deconstruct the symbolic systems
of representation in order to achieve an Intuition with mobile reality is a form of
thinking in duration not unlike that exemplified by Bryson's logic of the Glance.
Thus, both these intellectual attitudes presuppose reality to be mobile, fluxing and
flowing. They also recognize that in order to more faithfully represent this
understanding we require an attitude which privileges temporal duration and which
thereby undermines the intellect's ability to dictate the visuality of vision. Intuition
and the Glance

> strike at the very roots of rationalism, for what it can never apprehend
> is the geometric order which is rationalism's true ensign . . . the Glance
> finds in itself no counterpart to the enduring, motionless and august
> logic of architectural form, since all it can take in is the fragment, the
> collage . . . all it knows is dispersal – the disjointed rhythm of the retinal
> field. (Bryson, 1982: 122)

It is this peripheral vision, the corner-of-the-eye form of knowing, which we unconsciously subject ourselves to in our everyday apprehension of reality.

Organization as simple location

What then can we make of this new decentred attitude towards movement and change in terms of the study of complexity and organization? For one thing, we are led to realize that the ontological act of organization is an act of arresting, stabilizing and simplifying what would otherwise be the irreducibly dynamic and complex character of lived-experience. Organization is an inherently simplifying mechanism and the idea of 'complex' organization(s) is in effect an oxymoron. It is none other than a 'counterfeit' version of real dynamic complexity rendered static by applying the pre-cast symbols of representation in order to produce the kind of taxonomic complexity previously discussed. For another thing, we are led to realize that all of the social reality that we find so immediately necessary and familiar and to which we oftentimes attribute an independent existence is real only to the extent that it comprises the collective aggregation of habituated social norms and behavioural codes such that there is a regular coincidence between a representation and that which a particular society takes to be its reality. Such a coincidence must be understood as analogous to the situation of the two trains previously discussed. We are able to reach out to one another, communicate through language and act on things only because our relative speeds of transformation have been artificially arrested through acts of simple location. Each visual act of Gazing facilitates simple location and produces a representation which locates it outside the durational experience.

Through such proliferation of representations and their storing up in a collective repository, an increasingly large number of coincidences are established thereby creating a sufficient density of interactional events which, in turn, precipitate the social habits that, collectively, make society possible. Thus a socially constructed reality, *alienated* from our raw experiences, is achieved in which all those practical norms that govern the stance of human beings towards one another and towards their particular historical environment become more and more established. The slow and complex evolutionary formation of modes of thought, codes of behaviour, social manners, dress, gestures, postures, the rules of law, ethical codes, disciplines of knowledge and so on serve to orient us towards our environment and towards others in our social interactions. It is this 'meta' approach to the understanding of social organization as a complexity-reducing and reality-constituting activity which marks complex thinking from the preoccupation of the complexity sciences. Organization, in this wider sense, is an ontological activity involving the historical aggregation of simple-locating micro-efforts to produce recognizable social objects which are collectively sanctioned by a particular community. Organization, in this sense, is about 'world-making'. In this regard, the various historico-social analyses undertaken by Weber (1948), Foucault (1979) and Elias (1979–82), amongst others, point us towards the wider societal impact of organization as a generic reality-structuring feature of modernity.

Thus, as Weber observed, the modern preoccupation – even obsession – with such myriad forms of ordering as taxonomic classification, professionalization, the creation of 'disciplines', administration and bureaucracy, reflects the general drift towards the kind of secular rationalization which took place in Europe during and after the Enlightenment. For Weber, the extent and direction of this process of rationalization could be measured by the degree with which even such an apparently subjective area of experience as that of music was assimilated into the codified language of modernity. Thus: 'The fixation of clang patterns, by a more concise notation and the establishment of the well-tempered scale; "harmonious" tonal music and the standardization of the quartet of wood winds and string instruments as the core of the symphony orchestra' (Weber, 1948: 51) were all seen by Weber as telling instances of the seemingly inexorable process of organization and ratio-nalization occurring all around him and in every sphere of human activity. Likewise, as Richard Schoenwald (1973), in a fascinating unravelling of the great social reforms which took place in Victorian England during the 19th century reveals, the task of such organizational initiatives was to teach men that they had to change their personal habits fundamentally in order to become more acceptable to the new rationalized norms of urban life. Thus:

> Learning that some smells are good and others are bad, re-enacts the great scene in man's developmental history when he began to walk erect. He could not maintain erect posture and still yield to the array of tempting aromas at ground level which drew his less highly developed forebears . . . Stand up straight and act like a human being! You have to learn to live with other people, with lots of them in big cities, and you have to learn that they can't find your smells as beguiling as you do, or everyone will be down on all fours and riot and rampage will run in the streets! Turn your nose away from the smell of your lower parts, turn your eyes and your mind to higher things. (Schoenwald, 1973: 672)

To maintain itself, modern society must proclaim that things have their rightful and wrongful places, whether within the biological organism or in the social field. The concept of the orderly body in an orderly society gradually became a fundamental but largely unconscious presupposition of an increasingly industrialized world. This logic of social organization propagates a familiar form of reasoning which holds even today.

> Industrial society rests on order;
> order means everything in its place;
> dirt is whatever is not where it should be; . . .
> then a society bent on order should put the body into order by putting
>   order into the body;
> society gains order by 'training'.
>   (Schoenwald, 1973: 674)

Nowhere is this ordering of the body more evident than in the process of excretory regulation that a child has to undergo in learning to grow up. In its first efforts towards learning to control bodily outputs – how pressing the need, how suitable the time and place – the child also gains basic conceptions of the disciplinary norms of work. Thus, even the rationalization of excretory behaviour was a crucial feature of the systematic organization of modern Western reality. Society must arrange both for the disciplined retention and scheduled letting-go in conformity with the axioms of orderliness. Hence, crucially, 'the water closet and the sewers as bringers of order . . . underscore and reinforce the restraints and controls necessary to keep an industrialized society producing and consuming' (Schoenwald, 1973: 683). Pragmatically, because of the scale of social changes required, the Victorian sanitary movement provided one of the most effective means for inculcating habits of orderliness for the otherwise unwieldy masses. A new and previously unimagined social reality was brought into being through the cumulative aggregation of these micro-organizational initiatives.

It is in relation to this socially constructed body of codes, and not in relation to some immutable, universal and transcendent reality with pre-defined causal structures, that the realism of a social system of representation should be understood. In other words, a representation is considered real precisely because it coincides with a community's social codes, traditions and practices, and not because it relates to some timeless and universal Platonic forms.

All such evolutionary formations of complex social codes and behavioural patterns are a consequence of the deliberate and cumulative efforts of civilization in *conceptually slowing down* an otherwise interminable fluxing and changing physical reality. Such efforts have been necessary to facilitate the establishment and co-ordination of an increasingly large number of interlocking and complex human exchanges. Understood as such, organization must be viewed as an instrument for enabling purposeful action. To organize is to supply with 'organs'; to provide the necessary instruments by which things can be *done*, by focusing and concentrating a set of nascent tendencies in a manner which produces economy of action.

The overwhelmingly organizational character of modernity is, thus, the cumulative precipitate of a multiplicity of historical acts which served to carve out, arrest and simply locate what would otherwise have been a vague, unwieldy and shapeless mass of human experiences. At its most fundamental level, the act of organizing entails a whole complex of optic operations in which the logic of the Gaze is systematically applied to the visual field of experience. In this way, subjective phenomenal experiences are simply located, fixed, externalized, and objectified into isolatable elements ready for reconstitution by the intellect. These are the rudiments of the organization of visuality and consequently of organized worlds.

Understood thus, organization becomes an interminable ontological quest of carving out and retaining a version of reality from what would otherwise be an amorphous and indistinguishable mass through the initial seemingly innocuous act of looking. As we have tried to show, when we look, what we see is not simply light but intelligible form. For human beings, to collectively orchestrate their visual experiences, it is necessary that each submit his or her retinal experience to the socially established body of codes. Between the seeing subject and the world is inserted the entire sum of social discourse which makes up the culturally constructed visuality that makes it different from the pristine unmediated visual experience that the logic of the Glance attempts to reveal. In this way the social organization of vision, brought about by the logic of the Gaze, is a fundamental form of centring activity which directs us to see things in the discrete and isolatable manner more socially acceptable in the West. What we see and how we see are necessarily determined by the pervasiveness of this form of visual organization.

The Glance, on the other hand, is the attempt to accentuate the primacy of an unfocused, de-differentiated visual field of experience which precedes visual objectification. In a Glance, there is always visual 'contamination' in that the past carries over into the present and refuses to be blocked off by the imperative of formal organization. The Gaze, on the other hand, achieves a far more successful severing of its historical trace through the act of simple location. Greater focus is achieved at the expense of the exclusion of its context. Through the widespread reliance on this latter form of visual organization, we are able to produce self-identical social objects with a stable location in a singular position, in space-time, and as possessing an enduring form with clearly bounded outlines.

Organization is what makes possible the dominant world-view in which entities appear as self-evidently separate and isolatable, and hence representable in unproblematic terms. It is, however, important to remember that: 'The concept of the entity can be preserved only by an optic that casts around each entity a perceptual frame that makes a *cut* from the field and immobilizes the cut within the static framework' (Bryson, 1988: 97). As soon as the frame is weakened or withdrawn (through the contaminating effect of the Glance), the object becomes temporally entwined with its past and future as part of a mobile continuum that refuses logical differentiation in any simple manner. Take, for instance, a flower. Its existence is only a phase of the evolving transformation between seed and dust 'in a continuous exfoliation or perturbation of matter' (Bryson, 1988: 97). It cannot be said to occupy a single location since it is always implicated in the universal field of transformation of which it forms a part. The form of the seed is always already turning itself into a flower and the flower becoming dust so much so that 'The present state of the object appearing as the flower is inhabited by its past as seed and its future as dust, in a continuous motion of postponement, whose effect is that the flower is never presently *there*, any more than seed or dust are there' (Bryson, 1988: 99). Individual objects as they appear to us in their apparently pristine and constituted form are, therefore, already temporally-abstracted and simply located for our conceptual convenience through this organization of vision.

In more direct terms, the process of organizing social worlds comprises a complex and dynamic web of interlocking visual acts of arresting, punctuating, isolating and classifying of the essentially undivided flow of human experiences for the purpose of rendering more controllable and manipulable such phenomenal experiences of the world. Human organizing, therefore, through the conscious ordering of our day-to-day phenomenal experiences, operates as a necessary and fundamental uncertainty-reducing process.[2] Organization, therefore, is an ongoing reality-constituting and reality-maintaining activity which enables us to act purposefully in response to a deluge of competing and attention-seeking external stimuli. Simplification of the complex and the consequent economizing of effort in action is thus the ultimate aim of the impulse to organize. Through organization, the various facets of our experiences, including our experience of self, acquire immediate and unproblematical self-identity.

What complexity science needs to contend with in order to begin to think more complexly is the *natural attitude* (Bryson, 1982) which treats objects of knowledge as existing unproblematically 'out there' before our cognitive intervention. This essay has attempted to show that, even before phenomena can be understood in all their complexity, they must be made first to 'appear' cognitively. Social objects, in particular, have to be 'brought forth' through visual acts of individuation and representation. In this process, a whole complex of discursive and visual operations have already been co-ordinated and deployed. This co-ordination and deployment of visual techniques and strategies to bring about the appearance of phenomena and to therefrom construct a stable and liveable world is what we mean by organization as simple location.

Notes

1   This tendency of mistaking the map for the territory is discussed extensively in A.N. Whitehead's (1926/85) *Science and the Modern World* where he talks about the 'fallacy of misplaced concreteness' in which we inadvertently mistake our concepts of reality. It is also discussed in the work of Bateson (1979) and elaborated upon in Weick's (1994) seminal discussion on the use of cartographic myths in organizations.

2   Weick (1979), in his classic text *The Social Psychology of Organizing*, emphasizes this very point that organization is essentially about the reduction of equivocality and the rendering coherent of an otherwise uncertain and ambiguous state of affairs. However, despite Weick's important insights, his intellectual preoccupations remain circumscribed by the problematic of 'sense-making in organizations': a concern which prevents him from realizing that organization, in its more fundamental ontological sense, is what lies behind the processes of individuation that produce apparently autonomous units like 'individuals', 'organizations' and 'society'. Our concern, on the other hand, is the formulation of a *social theory of organization* in which the reality-constituting processes of modernity are rendered more transparent and accessible.

References

Alexander, I.W. (1957) *Bergson: Philosopher of Reflection*. London: Bowes and Bowes.

Barrow, J. (1991) *Theories of Everything*. London: Vintage.

Bateson, G. (1979) *Mind and Nature*. New York: Dutton.

Bergson, H. (1911) *Creative Evolution*. London: Macmillan.

Bergson, H. (1913a) *Time and Free Will*. London: George Allen.

Bergson, H. (1913b) *An Introduction to Metaphysics*. London: Macmillan.

Bergson, H. (1946/92) *The Creative Mind*. New York: Citadel Press.

Bergson, H. (1991) *Matter and Memory*. New York: Zone Books.

Bridgeman, P.W. (1928) *The Logic of Modern Physics*. New York: Macmillan.

Brock, W. (1989) 'Chaos and Complexity in Economic and Financial Science', in G.M. von Furstenberg (ed.) *Acting Under Uncertainty: Multidisciplinary Conceptions*. Boston: Kluwer Academic Publishers.

Bryson, N. (1982) *Vision and Painting: The Logic of the Gaze*. London: Methuen.

Bryson, N. (1988) 'The Gaze in the Expanded Field', in H. Foster (ed.) *Vision and Visuality*. Seattle: Bay Press.

Cooper, R. (1989) 'Modernism, Postmodernism and Organizational Analysis 3: The Contribution of Jacques Derrida', *Organization Studies* 10(4): 479–502.

Cooper, R. (1995) '"Assemblage" Notes', unpublished manuscript, Centre for Social Theory and Technology, Keele University (available on World Wide Web http://WWW.keele.ac.uk/depts/stt/home.htm).

Derrida, J. (1977) 'Limited Inc.', in S. Weber and H. Susman (eds) *Glyph 2*. Baltimore: Johns Hopkins University Press.

Elias, N. (1979–82) *The Civilising Process* (2 volumes). Oxford: Blackwell.

Eoyang, E. (1989) 'Chaos Misread: Or, There's Wonton in My Soup!', *Comparative Literature Studies* 26: 271–84.

Foucault, M. (1970) *The Order of Things*. London: Tavistock.

Foucault, M. (1979) *Discipline and Punish*. London: Penguin.

Gell-Mann, M. (1994) *The Quark and the Jaguar: Adventures in the Simple and the Complex*. London: Little, Brown.

Gleick, J. (1987) *Chaos: The Making of a New Science*. New York: Viking Penguin.

Goodman, N. (1984) *Of Mind and Other Matters*. Cambridge, MA: Harvard University Press.

Hayles, N.K. (1990) *Chaos Bound*. Ithaca, NY: Cornell University Press.

Hayles, N.K. (1991) *Chaos and Order: Complex Dynamics in Literature and Science*. Chicago: University of Chicago Press.

Heidegger, M. (1962) *Being and Time*. New York: Harper and Row.

Huberman, B. (1987) 'A Model for Dysfunctions in Smooth Pursuit Eye Movement', working paper, Palo Alto Research Centre, Palo Alto, CA.

James, W. (1910) *A Pluralistic Universe*. New York: Longmans, Green.

Kant, I. (1963) *Critique of Pure Reason*. Translated by N. Kemp-Smith. London: Macmillan.

Langer, S.K. (1942) *Philosophy in a New Key: A Study in the Symbolism of Reason, Rite, and Art*. Cambridge, MA: Harvard University Press.

McArthur, T. (1986) *Worlds of Reference: Lexicography, Learning and Language from the Clay Tablet to the Computer*. Cambridge: Cambridge University Press.

May, R. (1976) 'Simple Mathematical Models with Very Complicated Dynamics', *Nature* 261: 459–67.

Miller, J.-A. (1987) 'Jeremy Bentham's Panoptic Device', *October* 41: 3–29.

Rescher, N. (1996) *Process Metaphysics: An Introduction to Process Philosophy*. New York: State University of New York Press.

Schaffer, W.M. and Kot, M. (1985) 'Nearly One-Dimensional Dynamics in an Epidemic', *Journal of Theoretical Biology* 112: 403–7.

Schelling, F.W.J. (1988) *Ideas for a Philosophy of Nature*. Cambridge: Cambridge University Press.

Schoenwald, R. (1973) 'Training Urban Man', in H. Dyos and M. Wolff (eds) *The Victorian City: Images and Realities*, Vol. 2. London: Routledge and Kegan Paul.

Schopenhauer, A. (1966) *The World as Will and Representation*, Vol. 1. New York: Dover.

Senge, P. (1993) *The Fifth Dimension: The Art and Practice of the Learning Organization*. London: Century Business.

Serres, M. (1982) *Hermes: Literature, Science, Philosophy*. Baltimore: Johns Hopkins University Press.

Shaw, R.S. (1984) *The Dripping Faucet as a Model Chaotic System*. Santa Cruz: Aerial.

Spinoza, B. (1985) *The Collected Works of Spinoza*. Translated by E. Curley. Princeton: Princeton University Press.

Stacey, R. (1993) *Strategic Management and Organizational Dynamics*. London: Pitman Publishing.

Tsoukas, H. (1998) 'Forms of Knowledge and Forms of Life in Organized Contexts', in R. Chia (ed.) *In the Realm of Organization: Essays for Robert Cooper*. London: Routledge.

von Krogh, G. and Roos, J. (1995) *Organizational Epistemology*. New York: St Martin's Press.

Waldrop, M.M. (1992) *Complexity: Life at the Edge of Chaos*. New York: Simon and Schuster.

Weber, M. (1948) *From Max Weber*. Edited by H.H. Gerth and C.W. Mills. London: Routledge.

Weick, K.E. (1979) *The Social Psychology of Organizing* (2nd edition). Reading, MA: Addison-Wesley.

Weick, K.E. (1994) 'Cartographic Myths in Organizations', in H. Tsoukas (ed.) *New Thinking in Organizational Behaviour*. Oxford: Butterworth Heinemann.

Whitehead, A.N. (1926/85) *Science and the Modern World*. London: Free Association Books.

Whitehead, A.N. (1948) *Adventures of Ideas*. London: Penguin.

Ralph Stacey

LEARNING AS AN ACTIVITY OF INTERDEPENDENT PEOPLE

From *The Learning Organization* 2003, 10(6): 325–331. Copyright © 2003 by Emerald Group Publishing Ltd. Republished with permission of the publisher. www.emeraldinsight.com/tol.htm

[. . .]

Abstract

This paper argues that to talk about organisations learning is to reify and anthropomorphise organisations. Instead of thinking of an organisation as if it were a thing or a person it is closer to experience to think of an organisation as the patterning of people's interactions with each other. This paper explores the assumptions that are being made when we talk about organisations or groups that learn, or about individuals learning in groups or organisations. It suggests an alternative to thinking in these ways, namely, that learning is an activity of interdependent people. If one takes the view an organisation is the organising activities of interdependent people, it leads to a particular perspective on learning. Much of the communicative and power relating activities of interdependent people takes the form of continually iterated patterns of repetition in which meaning and power figurations have the quality of stability which we call identity. But because of the nonlinear iterative nature of human interaction there is always the potential for small differences to be amplified into transformative shifts in identity. Learning is then understood as the emerging shifts in the patterning of human communicative interaction and power relating. Learning is the activity of interdependent people and can only be understood in terms of self-organising communicative interaction and power relating in which identities are potentially transformed. Individuals cannot learn in isolation and organisations can never learn.
[. . .]

This paper is one of a number in a special issue titled "The implications of complexity and chaos theories for organisations that learn". That title immediately points to an important question, which one might pose in the following terms: do organisations learn or is it individuals and groups in organisations who learn? If one thinks that it is individuals and groups inside an organisation that learn then one focuses attention on individual and collective learning processes. If it is thought that it is organisations that learn then attention is focused on what it is about an organisation that makes learning possible.

A distinction along these lines is used by Easterby-Smith and Araujo (1999) to identify two strands in the literature to do with organisations and learning. They distinguish between the literature on organisational learning and that on the learning organisation. They say that the former "has concentrated on the detached observation and analysis of the processes involved in individual and collective learning inside organizations" (Easterby-Smith and Araujo, 1999, p. 2). The literature on the learning organisation, on the other hand, is concerned with "methodological tools which can help to identify, promote and evaluate the quality of learning processes inside organizations" (Easterby-Smith and Araujo, 1999, p. 2) and in so doing this literature identifies "templates, or ideal forms, which real organizations could attempt to emulate" (Easterby-Smith and Araujo, 1999, p. 2). Easterby-Smith and Araujo (1999) argue that there is a growing divide between the two strands. Those writing in the organisational learning tradition are interested in "understanding the nature and processes of learning" (Easterby-Smith and Araujo, 1999, p. 8). Those writing in the tradition of the learning organisation are more interested in "the development of normative models and methodologies for creating change in the direction of improved learning processes" (Easterby-Smith and Araujo, 1999, p. 8).

Easterby-Smith and Araujo (1999) distinguish between a technical and a social strand in the organisational learning literature. The technical strand takes the view that organisational learning is a matter of processing, interpreting and responding to quantitative and qualitative information, which is generally explicit and in the public domain. Key writers in this tradition are Argyris and Schon (1978) with their notions of single and double loop learning. The social strand focuses attention on how people make sense of their work practices (Weick, 1995). This strand utilises Polanyi's distinction between tacit and explicit knowledge (Polanyi and Prosch, 1975). It focuses attention on the socially constructed nature of knowledge (Brown and Duguid, 1991), the political processes involved (Coopey, 1995), and the importance of cultural and socialisation processes (Lave and Wenger, 1991). The literature on the learning organisation also displays technical and social interests. The former tends to focus on interventions based on measurement and information systems, while the latter focuses on individual and group learning processes in a normative manner (Senge, 1990; Isaacs, 1999; Nonaka and Takeuchi, 1995).

For me, the claim that organisations learn amounts to both reification and anthropomorphism. I argue that organisations are not things because no one can point to where an organisation is – all one can point to is the artefacts used by members of organisations in their work together. In our experience, the organisation qua organisation arises as the patterning of our interactions with each other. I also argue that we depart from our direct experience when we think of the organisation as organism. To sustain the claim that an organisation is in any sense a living organism, we would need to point to where this living body is. Since an organisation is neither inanimate thing nor living body, in anything other than rather fanciful metaphorical terms, it follows that an organisation can neither think nor learn. But the alternative is not all that satisfactory either. To claim that it is only individuals who learn is to continue with the major Western preoccupation with the autonomous individual and to ignore the importance of social processes. One might try to deal with this objection by saying that it is both individuals and groups who learn. But that runs into the same objection as saying that organisations learn. The claim that groups learn is also both reification and anthropomorphism. A group, like any organisation or any other social institution for that matter, is the patterning of people's interactions with each other and patterns can neither think nor learn. Furthermore, to talk about individuals who learn in organisations or in groups is also problematic because, once again, this implies that the group and the organisation exist somewhere as a different "place" or "level" to people. If this were not so, how could people be in a group or organisation? This paper explores the assumptions that are being made when we talk about organisations or groups that learn, or about individuals learning in groups or organisations. The paper will also suggest an alternative to thinking in these ways, namely, that learning is an activity of interdependent people.

I will be distinguishing, then, between two different ways of thinking about the individual and the group. The first separates individuals and groups as different levels of existence. This splitting of individual and organisation is central to the systems thinking that dominates the literature on learning and organisations. This is essentially a way of thinking in terms of dualisms or dualities. I want to contrast this with a way of thinking in terms of paradox in which individual and group/organisation are aspects of the same processes of interaction between people (Stacey, 2001). This way of thinking is built on the work of Mead (1934) and Elias (1939). For Mead, mind, self and society arise simultaneously and for Elias, the individual is the singular and the social is the plural of interdependent people. There are then no separate levels, only paradoxical processes of individuals forming the social while at the same time being formed by it. Learning is then to be thought of as the activity of interdependent people.

My colleagues and I (Stacey et al., 2000) have combined the work of Mead, Elias and others with insights from complexity theories to suggest what we have called a complex responsive processes theory of organisations. This paper will review how one might think of learning and organisations from this perspective. We have used some of the work in the complexity sciences as a source domain for analogies with human action, understood from the psychological/sociological theories of Mead and Elias. I will not be referring to chaos theory in this paper for the following reason. In chaos theory the term "chaos" has a precise mathematical meaning. It defines a particular dynamic, the strange attractor, which is a feature of deterministic nonlinear equations operating at certain parameter values. Since chaos is a property of deterministic rather than evolving relationships it cannot have anything to do with learning. Human action is not deterministic – it evolves. By definition that which is deterministic cannot learn. Chaos theory can, therefore, only ever be used as a loose metaphor for anything in the human domain. Some types of complex system simulation do, however, demonstrate the capacity to evolve and it is, therefore, to these that we might turn for analogies with human action.

Dichotomies, dualisms/dualities and paradox

Consider first the difference between thinking in terms of dualism/dualities as in systems thinking and thinking in terms of paradox as in temporal process thinking (Stacey, 2003).

In thinking about the individual and the group/organisational/social, one immediately encounters the distinction between the one and the many. One could regard this distinction as a dichotomy, which is a polarised opposition requiring an "either . . . or" choice. Methodological individualism chooses the "one" side of the polarity, the individual, and from this perspective, learning is the activity of autonomous individuals. Methodological collectivism chooses the "many" side of the polarity and from this perspective, learning is a social phenomenon. There has been a long and unresolved debate between these two positions, the upshot of which is the conclusion that it is unsatisfactory to regard the problem of the one and the many, the individual and the social, as a dichotomy.

Another approach, then, is to think in terms of a dualism or a duality. This mode of thinking has a "both . . . and" structure. Instead of choosing between the "one" and the "many", one keeps both but locates them in different spaces or times. It is this dualistic approach that dominates thinking about learning and organisations. On the one hand, the individual (the "one") is thought of as an autonomous individual, where mind is "inside" that person. Mind is then thought of as an "internal world" consisting of representations, maps and models of what is "outside" the person. In other words, mind is thought of as a whole or system of interacting parts contained within a boundary. The actions of a person are selected by this system, part of which the individual is aware of (explicit) and part of which the individual is not aware of (tacit). On this basis, individual learning is thought of as changes in mental models, both tacit and explicit. A particular form of causality, usually not stated explicitly, is implied in this way of thinking. It is assumed that individual human action is caused by the objectives and plans the individual chooses on the basis of his or her mental model and learning is the rational action of choosing to change the mental model and so the action. Causality here takes a rationalist form (Stacey et al., 2000).

When the "one" is thought of in these terms, there is no option but to think of the "many" (group, organisation and society) as a system existing "outside" the individual. This system is then thought of as a bounded entity consisting of individuals who are its parts. The system is formed by the interaction of the individuals and exists at a higher level than the individuals, following laws of its own, which might be thought of as emergent properties. Process has a particular meaning here – it is the interaction of individuals to create an entity outside of themselves. It is then easy to think of such an entity as a thing, a kind of super-individual with its own mind and intentions, even a living entity with a life of its own. From this perspective it is not problematic to think of an organisation as able to learn, where learning is understood as changes in organisational routines and strategies. Organisational learning becomes a form of cultural development and the task becomes one of identifying the organisational features that enable or obstruct such cultural development or organisational learning. It becomes the province of leaders to identify the vision or mission according to which the organisation and its culture should develop. The powerful design the system according to which they and other members of the organisation should interact. The powerful are supposed to make the choices according to which the organisation, an objective reality outside of them, is to develop. They are to enfold what is to be unfolded by the development of the organisation. This immediately implies a particular form of causality, which is again not usually made explicit. That causality is formative in the sense that it is the process of development which is forming the organisation in the sense of unfolding what is already enfolded into it.

The difference between dichotomies and dualisms/dualities is immediately apparent. Unlike the thinking in dochotomies, the way of thinking outlined in the last two paragraphs does not choose between individual and social. It locates them in different "spaces" and then posits a connection between them. Individuals form the social system through their choices of its objectives and the design of interactions between individuals and then the social system affects the actions of those individuals who are parts of the organisational system. The result is a dual causality. There is both the rationalist causality of the choosing individuals and the formative causality of the system that they are parts of. Thinking in this way naturally leads people to look for the features of an organisation, such as teamwork, that enable or block the learning of individuals. However, while thinking in terms of dualisms/dualities is different to thinking in terms of dichotomies in the way just described, they are similar in another respect. The "either . . . or" thinking of dichotomies and the "both . . . and" thinking of dualisms/dualities both satisfy a precept of Aristotelian logic, which requires the elimination of contradictions, such as the one and the many, forming and being formed by at the same time, because they are a sign of faulty thinking.

As an alternative to thinking in terms of dichotomies and in terms of dualisms/dualities, one could think of the problem of the one and the many as a paradox. There are a number of different definitions of a paradox. First, it may mean an apparent contradiction, a state in which two apparently conflicting elements appear to be operating at the same time. Paradox in this sense can be removed or resolved by choosing one element above the other all the time or by reframing the problem to remove the apparent contradiction. There is little difference between paradox in this sense and dualism/dualities and this is the meaning of paradox that is usually taken up in the literature on systemic views of organisations. However, paradox may mean a state in which two diametrically opposing forces/ideas are simultaneously present, neither of which can ever be resolved or eliminated. There is, therefore, no possibility of a choice between the opposing poles or of locating them in different spheres. Instead, what is required is a different kind of logic, such as the dialectical logic of Hegel. In this kind of logic, the word paradox means the presence together at the same time of contradictory, essentially conflicting ideas, none of which can be eliminated or resolved. Indeed it is this conflict that gives rise to the transformation that is central to Hegel's dialectical logic. A technical example of this is the concept of mathematical chaos. Here chaos is a dynamic, a pattern, that is stable and unstable at the same time. In this dynamic, stability and instability are inseparable – what we have is the paradox of stable instability or unstable stability. The contradiction between stable and unstable has not been resolved but rather transformed into a different dynamic in which the meanings of stability and instability have been transformed. The causality implied in this kind of dialectical logic is transformative. However, this is only a rather dry technical example of the dialectical logic. Essential to Hegel's dialectical logic is its social dimension.

Hegel held that one cannot begin, as Kant had done, with an isolated individual subject experiencing the world and then ask how a world of experience gets built up out of the inner world of purely subjective experience. Rather, one must begin with an already shared world of subjects making judgements in the light of possible judgements by others. Hegel accorded central importance to recognition, linking it to desire, particularly the desire for desire of the other. It is through mutual recognition that individuals sustain patterns of entitlements and commitments, the social, and it is in the social that the knowing subject, mind, emerges. Hegel emphasised the historical specificity of human self-conceptions upon which society is founded. Person and subject are given content only by the social institutions in which each individual achieves social identity through interdependence and mutual recognition. So, for Hegel, mind or consciousness is manifested in social institutions, that is, ways of life, which give identities, self concepts, to individuals. Here, then, the "one" and the "many" are neither dichotomies nor dualisms/dualities, but poles of a paradox which are transformed into both individual identity/consciousness and social relations at the same time. It is in this tradition that Mead argues that mind, self and society arise together at the same time and Elias argues that the individual is the singular and the social is the plural of interdependent people.

What is an organisation?

If one takes this paradoxical, dialectical perspective, then how does one think about the nature of a group, organisation or society? Mead (1934) explains the simultaneous emergence of mind and society in terms of the social act in which one gestures to another and in so doing calls forth a response from that other. Gesture and response are inseparable phases in one act which constitutes meaning. Here meaning does not lie in the gesture alone because the meaning of the gesture cannot be known until there is a response. If one person shouts this means aggression if the other responds with an angry shout, but it could mean a warning if the other takes evading action. Consciousness arises when the one making a gesture calls forth in him/herself a similar response to that called forth in the one to whom he/she is gesturing. He/she can then know what he/she is doing. Mead calls this social act a significant symbol. A conversation of gestures in significant symbols make possible far more sophisticated forms of cooperation, of society, because those interacting can know what they are doing and signal to others what they intend. Mead points to the particular importance of the vocal form of significant symbol, namely language, in human interaction. Mind is arising at the same time as human social interaction is arising on the conversation of significant symbols. Mind takes the form of a private role play/silent conversation of the gesturer and of the responder. Mind is the process of an individual body gesturing and responding to itself at the same time as it is gesturing and responding to others, the social. Mind and society are therefore simply different aspects of the same processes of communicative interaction in which meaning is arising. Interdependent individuals are interacting with each other in a way in which they are taking the attitudes of others, of the group and of society as a whole, to their gestures. They are also interacting in a way in which they are taking the attitude of the group or society to themselves. As subjects (the "I") they are taking themselves as objects (the "me" or attitude of the society to the "I") and it is in this process that self-consciousness arises.

What Mead is explaining here are processes of communicative interaction that constitute both mind and society at the same time. They are simultaneously forming and being formed by each other at the same time. One is not at a different level to another and it makes no sense to think of one inside the other. Instead of thinking in terms of spatial metaphors, of levels and inside–outside, Mead's explanation focuses our attention on how the actions of human bodies are creating patterns of meaning in their iterated interaction with each other. As people interact, coherent patterns of meaning, of knowledge, are perpetually iterated. These continually emerging patterns take thematic forms, both narrative and propositional, both conscious and unconscious, and they organise the experience of being together. Such themes are iterated in the repetitive form of habit but always with the potential for transformation. Such patterns are patterning themselves in the local interaction between people, a point to be explained later in relation to complexity theory. The result is a way of thinking about human action that moves away from the dual rationalist-formative causality referred to above to a transformative causality (Stacey *et al.*, 2000).

This is a key aspect of what colleagues and I have called complex responsive processes. Organisations are patterns of communicative interaction between interdependent individuals. Another key aspect of complex responsive processes of human relating is to be found in the work of Elias (1939).

For Elias, all human relating imposes constraints on those relating, while at the same time enabling those relating to do what they could not otherwise have done. This is, of course, what power means – power is enabling constraints between people. Instead of thinking of power as the possession of some and not of others, Elias understands power as a characteristic of, a pattern in, all human relating. In human relating some are more constrained than others so establishing a figuration of power relations in which the distribution of power is not equal. As they interact, the power relations, the pattern of enabling constraints, emerges, shifts and evolves. Elias describes in some detail how ideologies unconsciously sustain figurations of power relations. He also connects emerging and iterated patterns of power relations with identity. Power figurations operate to include some people in a group and exclude others in the interest of sustaining power relations and in the course of doing this, powerful group identities are created. Elias calls these "we" identities and shows how inextricably linked such "we" identities are to each individual's "I" identity.

These closely connected aspects of power relations, ideology and identity are also key aspects of complex responsive processes of relating between human bodies. Organisations are patterns of power relations sustained by ideological themes of communicative interaction and patterns of inclusion and exclusion in which human identities emerge. There is yet another key element in the theory of complex responsive processes. This is provided by analogies drawn from particular kinds of computer simulation to be found in what has come to be called the sciences of complexity. The simulations model the dynamics of iterated, nonlinear interaction between entities. These simulations reveal some abstract properties of interaction between digital symbols. An agent in the simulations is an algorithm, that is, a string of digital symbols. When these agents are sufficiently different to each other and when they are sufficiently connected to each other, then the simulations display the capacity to evolve in novel, unpredictable ways (see, for example, Allen, 1998a, b; Ray, 1992; Kauffman, 1995). What the simulations are demonstrating is that it is quite possible that widespread, coherent pattern will emerge from the local inter-action between agents. Widespread coherent, evolving patterns emerge from local interaction in the complete absence of an overall blueprint plan or programme. This process is termed self-organisation, which can be understood as interaction patterning itself from within, as it were. When the interacting agents are different enough from each other, then nonlinear iteration can amplify these differences into novel widespread pattern. The pattern of interaction here is transforming itself from within. These properties provide an abstract analogy for human interaction if translated into the human domain using suitable theories of psychology and sociology to provide the attributes of being human.

A key aspect of complex responsive processes of human relating is their self-organising emergent nature in which communicative interaction and power relating patterns itself. The causality is transformative and there is nothing above or below interaction itself that is causing the coherent patterning. Organisations are then self-organising patterns of communicative interacting and power relating between human bodies in the living present. In the living present, individuals are interacting with each other in their own local situations. The basis of their action is their current expectations of the future, conditioned by their accounts of the past, where those accounts of the past are influencing expectations for the future and expectations of the future are influencing the current accounts of the past. This view of organisation focuses attention on the way in which ordinary everyday conversations between people are perpetually creating the future, in the present, in the form of shifting patterns of communication and power relations. What is being perpetually created is nothing other than inseparable individual and collective identities. Organisations are then self-organising patterns of conversation, of meaning, in which human identities emerge.

To summarise, the argument presented in this section leads to the conclusion that an organisation is the thematically patterned activities of interdependent people, which constitute their closely interconnected individual and collective identities.

Complex responsive processes of learning

If one takes the view presented above on the nature of an organisation as the organising activities of interdependent people, it leads to a particular perspective on learning. Much of the communicative and power relating activities of interdependent people take the form of continually iterated patterns of repetition in which meaning and power figurations have the quality of stability which we call identity. But because of the nonlinear iterative nature of human interaction there is always the potential for small differences to be amplified into transformative shifts in identity. Learning is then understood as the emerging shifts in the patterning of human communicative interaction and power relating. Learning is emerging shifts in the thematic patterning of human action. Another way of saying this is to say that learning is the emerging transformation of inseparable individual and collective identities. Learning occurs as shifts in meaning and it is simultaneously individual and social. Learning is the activity of interdependent people and can only be understood in terms of self-organising communicative interaction and power relating in which identities are potentially transformed. Individuals cannot learn in isolation and organisations can never learn.

The immediate implication of such a view of the nature of learning is that it will inevitably give rise to anxiety. This is because the experience of challenges to, and shifts in one's individual–collective identities are existentially threatening. It becomes important then to pay particular attention to how people respond to anxiety because defensive ways of dealing with anxiety inevitably close down learning processes. Also of great importance is that transformative learning involves moving into the unknown. People cannot know in advance what patterns of identity they are moving to and moving into the unknown in this way can easily be seen by others to be incompetence. In a social order that greatly prizes competence, understood as knowing, it is deeply shaming not to know. The social process of shame (Aram, 2001) is thus inextricably involved in learning processes and it becomes important to understand how people respond to the potential for shame.

References

Allen, P.M. (1998a), "Evolving complexity in social science", in Altman, G. and Koch, W.A. (Eds), *Systems: New Paradigms for the Human Sciences*, Walter de Gruyter, New York, NY.

Allen, P.M. (1998b), "Modeling complex economic evolution", in Schweitzer, F. and Silverberg, G. (Eds), *Selbstorganisation*, Dunker and Humblot, Berlin.

Aram, E. (2001), "The experience of complexity: learning as the potential transformation of identity", unpublished thesis, University of Hertfordshire, Hertford.

Argyris, C. and Schon, D. (1978), *Organizational Learning: A Theory of Action Perspective*, Addison-Wesley, Reading, MA.

Brown, J.S. and Duguid, P. (1991), "Organizational learning and communities-of-practice: toward a unified view of working, learning and innovation", *Organization Science*, Vol. 2 No. 1, pp. 40–56.

Coopey, J. (1995), "The learning organization: power, politics and ideology", *Management Learning*, Vol. 29 No. 3. pp. 193–214.

Easterby-Smith, M. and Araujo, L. (1999), "Organizational learning: current debates and opportunities", in Easterby-Smith, M., Burgoyne, J. and Araujo, L. (Eds), *Organizational Learning and the Learning Organization*, Sage, London.

Elias, N. (1939), *The Civilizing Process*, Blackwell, Oxford.

Isaacs, W. (1999), *Dialogue and the Art of Thinking*, Doubleday, New York, NY.

Kauffman, S.A. (1995), *At Home in the Universe*, Oxford University Press, New York, NY.

Lave, J. and Wenger, E. (1991), *Situated Learning: Legitimate Peripheral Participation*, Cambridge University Press, New York, NY.

Mead, G.H. (1934), *Mind, Self, and Society: From the Standpoint of a Social Behaviorist*, University of Chicago Press, Chicago, IL.

Nonaka, I. and Takeuchi, H. (1995), *The Knowledge-Creating Company: How Japanese Companies Create the Dynamics of Innovation*, Oxford University Press, Oxford.

Polanyi, M. and Prosch, H. (1975), *Meaning*, University of Chicago Press, Chicago, IL.

Ray, T.S. (1992), "An approach to the synthesis of life", in Langton, G.C., Taylor, C., Doyne Farmer, J. and Rasmussen, S. (Eds), *Artificial Life II*, Santa Fe Institute, Studies in the Sciences of Complexity, Vol. 10, Addison-Wesley, Reading, MA.

Senge, P.M. (1990), *The Fifth Discipline: The Art and Practice of the Learning Organization*, Doubleday, New York, NY.

Stacey, R.D. (2001), *Complex Responsive Processes in Organizations: Learning and Knowledge Creation*, Routledge, London.

Stacey, R.D. (2003), *Strategic Management and Organisational Dynamics: The Challenge of Complexity*, 4th ed., Pearson Education, London.

Stacey, R.D., Griffin, D. and Shaw, P. (2000), *Complexity and Management: Fad or Radical Challenge to Systems Thinking*, Routledge, London.

Weick, K. (1995), *Sensemaking in Organizations*, Sage, Thousand Oaks, CA.

Haridimos Tsoukas and Mary Jo Hatch

COMPLEX THINKING, COMPLEX PRACTICE: THE CASE FOR A NARRATIVE APPROACH TO ORGANIZATIONAL COMPLEXITY

From *Human Relations* 2001, 54(8): 879–1013. Copyright © 2001 by The Tavistock Institute. Reproduced by permission of the authors and Sage Publications.

Abstract

Complexity is not only a feature of the systems we study, it is also a matter of the way in which we organize our thinking about those systems. This second-order complexity invites consideration of the modes of thinking we use to theorize about complexity, and in this article we develop the idea of second-order complexity using Jerome Bruner's contrast between logico-scientific and narrative modes of thinking. Using Bruner's framework, we examine and critique dominant forms of thinking about organizational complexity that are rooted in the logico-scientific mode, and suggest alternatives based in the narrative mode. Our evidence for the value of doing this comes from the logic of complexity theory itself, which we claim indicates and supports the use of the narrative mode. The potential contribution of the narrative approach to developing second-order thinking about organizational complexity is demonstrated by taking a narrative approach to the matter of recursiveness. By extension, similar insights are indicated for other features that logico-scientific thinkers commonly attribute to complex systems, including non-linearity, indeterminacy, unpredictability and emergence.

[. . .]

Introduction

A central assumption in organization science has been that organization is an intrinsic feature of the social world. Social systems in general, and business organizations in particular, are thought to be organized in one way or another, and it is the task of organization scientists to find out how and why. To this end, two schools of thought can be broadly distinguished. One is sociological-historical-anthropological in orientation; it seeks to produce accounts explaining the specific features of organization(s), either employing what Mohr (1982) called 'the variance model' of explanation, or through tracing back the lineage of organizational features to historical-cum-institutional or cultural factors (e.g. Geertz, 1973: Granovetter, 1992). There is a great deal of methodological and theoretical diversity within this school, but there is also a common theme: the *social* sciences can offer an account of social organization.

The second school is the cybernetic-systemic one. Here organization is conceived much more broadly: it is thought to be a feature of the cosmos at large, not just of social collectivities (Capra, 1996). Both living forms and non-living matter are taken as being organized, and the suggestion is that there is a great deal to be learned about social organization by looking at the organization of the non-social world. Indeed, organizational cybernetics and systems theory have been built upon this premise (Beer, 1981; Miller, 1978). The recent surge of interest in exploring social organization(s) through the science of complexity falls firmly within this category. Proponents of this school argue that we can enhance our understanding of social organization(s), in particular of business organizations operating within a market economy, through modeling them on, that is, by finding analogies with, natural and biological systems (Holland, 1995; Stacey, 1996).

Both schools of thought have been heuristically useful; they have helped generate a great deal of research and have significantly advanced our understanding of organization(s). However, less often has the question been asked whether organization might be a feature not only of the world (social and/or natural), but also of our thinking about the world. In other words, in order for cognitive beings to be able to act effectively in the world we must organize our thinking. As Piaget so aptly remarked, 'intelligence organizes the world by organizing itself' (quoted in von Glaserfeld, 1984: 24). Following this reasoning, one way of viewing organizations as complex systems is to explore complex ways of thinking about organizations-as-complex-systems; in this article we explicate this view, which we call second-order complexity. We further note that entering the domain of second-order complexity – the domain of the thinker thinking about complexity – raises issues of interpretation (and, we argue, narration) that have heretofore been ignored by complexity theorists.

In shifting the focus from first- to second-order complexity, we expose epistemological and methodological issues that have important implications for how we position ourselves and our approach to organizational complexity. Put most simply, is it better to explore complex thought processes (second-order complexity) in relation to an assumed objective world (first-order complexity), in which case the variance model-based methods of natural science appear to be indicated? Or should we, instead, explore along the lines of sociological-historical-anthropological approaches that employ interpretive methods and are more likely to view the objectivity of the world as a social construction? Although few within the cybernetic school may have considered the second option, our thesis is that, not only does interpretive research within the social science school suggest the value of doing so, but also the developing logic of complexity theory itself is entirely compatible with an interpretive, and in our case a narrative, approach.

Indeed, similarities between complexity theory and literary studies have been explored by a number of authors (Argyros, 1992; Dyke, 1990; Hayles, 1990, 1991; Reisch, 1991; Stonum, 1989), although these have tended to focus on poststructural analysis rather than the narrative aspects of second-order complexity, which is our focus here. Although there are important connections between poststructuralism and the narrative approaches we explore, our ambition is not to compare traditions or analyze developments within literary theory, but rather to suggest ways to apply narrative literary theory to the study of organizational complexity. There is, however, one sense in which our approach to complexity is similar to that of post-structural literary theorists who have addressed this topic. Like them, we take the view that the key concepts of complexity science do not so much constitute a theory with predictive validity as a guide for interpretation (Hayles, 1990).

From the interpretive perspective, chaos and complexity are metaphors that posit new connections, draw our attention to new phenomena and help us see what we could not see before (Rorty, 1989). This is the contribution they make to our understanding of organizational complexity. Such a perspective departs radically from the established orthodoxy, which is derived mainly from the Santa Fe Institute (Waldrop, 1992). Whereas most Santa Fe scientists tend to conceive of complexity in the classic reductionist manner of searching for the common principles under-lying a variety of utterly different systems (see for example Holland, 1995), the perspective adopted here seeks to generate new insights, and thus contribute to expanding the possibilities for thought and action, through the use of the narrative perspective and of the metaphor of complexity (Morgan, 1997; Rorty, 1989).

To frame our thesis we employ a distinction between logico-scientific and narrative modes of thought developed by Bruner (1986, 1996). We use this frame-work to make a comparison of cybernetic and interpretive social science approaches and use this comparison to suggest the value of developing a narrative approach to complexity theory. We then explicate and critique the logico-scientific mode of thinking within the context of complexity theory itself and point out the multiple ways in which the narrative mode compensates for the inherent limitations of logico-scientific thinking. We conclude with a peek at what we believe developing a narrative approach to understanding organizational complexity would offer.

Complexity and its interpreters: logico-scientific and narrative modes of thought

In *Actual minds, possible worlds*, Bruner (1986) claimed that:

> There are two modes of cognitive functioning, two modes of thought, each providing distinctive ways of ordering experience, of constructing reality. The two (though complementary) are irreducible to one another. Efforts to reduce one mode to the other or to ignore one at the expense of the other inevitably fail to capture the rich diversity of thought.
>
> (p. 11)

Bruner called the two modes of thought 'logico-scientific' (or paradigmatic) and 'narrative', arguing that:

> the types of causality implied in the two modes are palpably different. The term *then* functions differently in the logical proposition 'if x, then y' and in the narrative *recit* 'The king died, and then the queen died.' One leads to a search for universal truth conditions, the other for likely particular connections between two events – mortal grief, suicide, foul play.
>
> (pp. 11–12)

To compare the two modes, Bruner claimed, is to understand the difference between a sound argument and a good story. He contrasts the logico-scientific and narrative modes on a variety of dimensions, which we have summarized in Table 1 and expand upon in later sections of this article.

Viewed from a higher logical level, it could be said that the logico-scientific mode itself constitutes a particular type of narrative – and, indeed, a narrative it is. However, following Bruner, it is analytically useful to keep the two modes distinct, as they are characterized by a different logical organization and, as shown later, are connected to different types of actions. Moreover, the usefulness of this distinction for the study of second-order complexity comes in recognizing that the two modes capture much of the difference between the understanding we glean from variance models and from interpretive accounts in the fields of organization science mentioned earlier. Of course, when social organization is described using such different modes of thought, it is not surprising that different views should emerge. What is intriguing about structuring the comparison between social science and cybernetic approaches in this way is that it points to the absence of the narrative mode within complexity theory (see Figure 1). If Bruner is correct in arguing that narrative mode thinking is important, then this absence in the discussion of complexity deserves discussion. It is this absence that we intend to address in this article. In this part of the article we briefly review narrative approaches within interpretive organization studies, then make the case for considering complexity to be a matter for interpretive study, and finally specify what we mean by a narrative approach to complexity.

Table 1 Comparison of Bruner's two modes of thought

	Logico-scientific mode	Narrative mode
Objective	Truth	Verisimilitude
Central problem	To know truth	To endow experience with meaning
Strategy	Empirical discovery guided by reasoned hypothesis	Universal understanding grounded in personal experience
Method	Sound argument Tight analysis Reason Aristotelian logic Proof	Good story Inspiring account Association Aesthetics Intuition
Key characteristics	Top-down Theory driven Categorical General Abstract De-contextualized Ahistorical Non-contradictory Consistent	Bottom-up Meaning centered Experiential Particular Concrete Context sensitive Historical Contradictory Paradoxical, ironic

Source: Bruner (1986: 11–43)

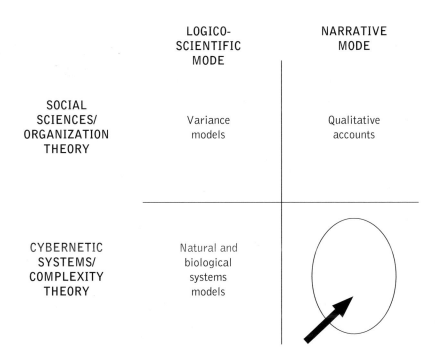

	LOGICO-SCIENTIFIC MODE	NARRATIVE MODE
SOCIAL SCIENCES/ ORGANIZATION THEORY	Variance models	Qualitative accounts
CYBERNETIC SYSTEMS/ COMPLEXITY THEORY	Natural and biological systems models	

Figure 1 Framing the interpretive approach to complexity theory

Narrative approaches to interpretive organization studies

One of the foremost proponents of narrative in the study of organizations, Czarniawska (1997a, 1997b, 1998), defines three narrative approaches offered to organization studies thus far: narrating organizations, collecting stories, and organizing as narration. Narrating organizations consists of telling about organizations using a narrative structure (e.g. a sequence of events or plot, in literary terminology). This approach most often produces case studies, though Czarniawska also includes in this category fictional stories and novels relating organizational life (e.g. Joseph Heller's *Something happened*). Czarniawska says that the second category, collecting stories, was initially focused on documenting cultural artifacts (e.g. Martin, 1982; Martin et al., 1983; Smircich & Morgan, 1982; Wilkins, 1983), but has recently turned to storytelling within organizations as an approach to capturing the narrative mode of meaning construction (e.g. Boje, 1991; Boyce, 1995; Gabriel, 1995; Shaw et al., 1998).

Czarniawska's final category of organizing as narration is where she places interpretive organizational research, to which she sees her work contributing (Czarniawska, 1997a, 1997b, 1998). This grouping applies the interpretive devices of literary theory to the narratively structured data of interpretive research (e.g. Barry, 1997; Corvellec, 1997; O'Connor, 1995). However, because not all interpretive organizational research derives from literary theory (e.g. much was developed on the basis of anthropological or sociological traditions), we feel that, to a large extent, the narrative approach falls within interpretive studies rather than the other way around. In any case, we are in full agreement with Czarniawska (1997a: 29) when she claims that the interpretive approach 'further[s] our understanding of the complex and unpredictable – the major concern and interest of current organization studies'.

Why complexity is a matter of interpretation

What is complexity? It is our contention that the puzzle of defining the complexity of a system leads directly to concern with description and interpretation and therefore to the issue of second-order complexity. There is apparently no consensus around when a system should be regarded as complex. As Waddington (1977: 30) remarks: 'no one has yet succeeded in giving a definition of "complexity" which is meaningful enough to enable one to measure exactly how complex a system is'. Casti (1994: 10) concurs and admits that 'the line of demarcation between the simple and the complicated is a fuzzy one'. Waddington notes that complexity has something to do with the number of components of a system as well as with the number of ways in which they can be related. But is it indisputably clear what the components of a system are or how they are related?

Echoing mathematical information theory (Hayles, 1990; Shannon & Weaver, 1949), Casti (1994: 9) defines complexity as being 'directly proportional to the length of the shortest possible description of [a system]' (see also Gell-Mann, 1994: 30–41). If, for example, in a series of numbers there is a clear pattern, whereas in another series the numbers are placed randomly, the latter is more complex than the former, because no shorter description of it can be given other than repeating the series itself (Barrow, 1995). However, the length of a description cannot be determined objectively; it depends on the chosen language of description, as well as on the two parts of the communication process. A stone, says Casti (1994), is a very simple object to most of us (that is according to a commonsense description of it), but to a geologist it is rather more complicated. The conclusion Casti draws from this is that complexity is, in effect, in the eye of the beholder: 'system complexity is a contingent property arising out of the interaction *I* between a system *S* and an observer/decision-maker *O*' (Casti, 1986: 149). To put it more formally, the complexity of a system, as seen by an observer, is directly proportional to the number of inequivalent descriptions of the system that the observer can generate (Casti, 1986, 1994). The more inequivalent descriptions an observer can produce, the more complex the system will be taken to be.

Casti's definition of complexity is an interesting one for it admits that the complexity of a system is not an intrinsic property of that system; it is observer-dependent, that is, it depends upon how the system is described and interpreted. Consequently, if an observer's language is complex enough (namely, the more inequivalent descriptions it can contain) the system at hand will be described in a complex way and thus will be interpreted as a complex system. What complexity science has done is to draw our attention to certain features of systems' behaviors which were hitherto unremarked, such as non-linearity, scale-dependence, recursiveness, sensitivity to initial conditions, emergence. It is not that those features could not have been described before, but that they now have been brought into focus and given meaning (Hayles, 1991; Prigogine, 1989; Shackley et al., 1996).

To put it another way, physics has discovered complexity by complicating its own language of description. We argue that a similar refocusing occurred in organization science when interpretive approaches were developed drawing attention to issues such as reflexivity (e.g. Chia, 1996; Cooper & Burrell, 1988; Giddens, 1991; Woolgar, 1988), narrativity (e.g. Czarniawska, 1997b; Czarniawska-Joerges, 1994; Hatch, 1996; Van Maanen, 1988; Weick & Browning, 1986), and paradox, ambiguity and contradiction (e.g. Feldman, 1991; Filby & Willmott, 1988; Hatch & Ehrlich, 1993; March & Olsen, 1976; Meyerson, 1991; Poole & Van de Ven, 1989; Putnam, 1985; Quinn & Cameron, 1988; Weick, 1979; Westenholtz, 1993).

Weick (1979) was one of the first to argue for an observer-dependent definition of organization. His notion of organizing made us realize that what we experience as organization is the outcome of an interactive sense-making process. Moreover, a constant theme of Weick's thought, like Bateson's, has been an appreciation of the paradoxical nature of organizational behavior (see also Brunsson, 1989; Hatch, 1997; Pascale, 1990; Perrow, 1977; Quinn & Cameron, 1988; The Price Waterhouse Change Integration Team, 1996). For instance, Weick (1979: 222) gives the example of a bank whose very functioning is inherently paradoxical. A bank's motto is 'To make money you have to lend it rather than store it'. But the bank acts as if this statement is both true and false. Says Weick (1979: 222):

> [The bank] acts as if the statement is true by continuing to select from
> enacted inputs those occasions where there is an opportunity to lend

money at a profit. It acts as if this statement is false by urging customers to be thrifty and use the bank as a repository for the results of that thrift. It is good to save and bad to borrow, it's good to borrow and bad to save. That complicated definition is something a bank must manage as a routine matter.

Notice how appreciating the paradox of the bank demands appreciation of second-order complexity (i.e. statements describing a bank's behavior). The bank is pursuing two contradictory policies simultaneously. Because more than one (in this case, two) inequivalent descriptions of the bank's behavior can be generated, it is seen as being more complex than it would otherwise be.

How could one, practitioner-cum-observer, hope to make sense of such behavior? What might be an appropriate mode of thought able to accommodate contradictions? If practitioners are to increase their effectiveness in managing paradoxical social systems, they should, as Weick (1979: 261) recommends, 'complicate' themselves (see also Bateson, 1979; Beer, 1973; Weick, 1995). But complicate themselves in what way? By generating and accommodating multiple inequivalent descriptions, practitioners will increase the complexity of their understanding and, therefore, will be more likely, in logico-scientific terms, to match the complexity of the situation they attempt to manage (Bartunek et al., 1983; Bolman & Deal, 1991; Bruner, 1996; Morgan, 1997), or, in narrative terms, to enact it (Weick, 1979).

Hatch and Ehrlich (1993) provide an example of managers complicating themselves via narrative activities. In their study of the humor of a management team, these researchers found that managing security issues (i.e. finding effective means of securing the assets of the corporation against pilfering and theft) placed managers in the role of guarding their own employees. However, the guard role contradicted their attempts to encourage trust and teamwork in their unit, another important item on the corporate agenda. Reflection on their status as guards in a system demanding a collaborative form of organization was a recurrent theme in their joke making. As Koestler (1964) has shown, humor is built upon bisociation – the ability to mentally and emotionally traverse both paths of a bifurcating line of thought, the recognition of which provokes laughter (see also Mulkay, 1988). Thus any potential choice point can become a point of bisociation by shifting from one level of complexity (serious, rational, linear) to another (humorous, playful, paradoxical). Bisociation through humor permitted the managers of Hatch and Ehrlich's study a more complex view of their organization, complex in the sense that it offered a both/and, rather than an either/or, orientation to the contradictions of managing and organizing. What is more, in taking the form of a joke, the bisociation becomes linked to narrative because joking is one way for managers to narrate their experiences (and their organizations).

We argue that the features of complex systems described by complexity theory (non-linearity, scale dependence, recursiveness, sensitivity to initial conditions, and emergence) can only be appreciated and acted upon from the position of second-order complexity. This claim is based on our assumption that the features of complexity are descriptions and interpretations assigned by complex observers to systems whose existence itself is a matter of definitional agreement. Expanding the focus from the system itself (first-order complexity) to also include those who describe the system as complex (second-order complexity) exposes the interpretive-cum-narrative dimensions of complexity.

The interpretive dimensions of complexity

Complexity science highlights at least five properties that are proposed to be held in common by natural, biological, and social systems (see Casti, 1994; Crutchfield et al., 1986; Davis, 1990; Hayles, 1989, 1990, 1991; Kamminga, 1990; Kellert, 1993; Stewart, 1993):

1   Complex systems are non-linear: there is no proportionality between causes and effects. Small causes may give rise to large effects. Non-linearity is the rule, linearity is the exception.
2   Complex systems are fractal: irregular forms are scale dependent. There is no single measurement that will give a true answer; it depends on the measuring device. For example, to the question 'how long is the coast-line of Britain?' there is no single answer, for it hinges on the scale chosen to measure it. The smaller the scale, the larger the measurement obtained.
3   Complex systems exhibit recursive symmetries between scale levels: they tend to repeat a basic structure at several levels. For example, turbulent flow can be modeled as small swirls nested within swirls, nested, in turn, within yet larger swirls.
4   Complex systems are sensitive to initial conditions; even infinitesimal per-turbations can send a system off in a wildly different direction. Given that initial conditions cannot be adequately specified with infinite accuracy, complex systems have the tendency to become unpredictable.
5   Complex systems are replete with feedback loops. Systemic behavior is the emergent outcome of multiple chains of interaction. As the level of organiza-tion increases, complex systems have the tendency to shift to a new mode of behavior, the description of which is not reducible to the previous descrip-tion of the system's behavior. These emergent novelties represent points of bifurcation.

Positioning the narrator as the interpreter of these five properties moves us from the logico-scientific to the narrative mode and presents complexity as a second-order phenomenon. To see this, imagine yourself in the position of the person describing a system in the terms listed above. Although you may call non-linearity, scale dependence, recursiveness, sensitivity to initial conditions and emergence properties of the system, they are actually your descriptive terms – they are part of a vocabulary, a way of talking about a system. Why use such a vocabulary? Is it because it corresponds to how the system really is? Not quite. Because the system cannot speak for itself, you do not know what the system really is (Rorty, 1989). Rather, you use such a vocabulary because of its suspected utility – it may enable you to do certain things with it. A new vocabulary, notes Rorty (1989: 13), 'is a tool for doing something which could not have been envisaged prior to the development of a particular set of descriptions, those which it itself helps to provide'. Our language cannot be separated from our goals and beliefs (Taylor, 1985). Switching to the narrative mode of thinking makes this obvious because, in narrative mode, the researcher making claims about systems is in full view – his/her goals and desires are reflected in his/her language. It is thus that second-order complexity is engaged – the complexity (subjectivity) of the researcher (i.e. narrator) attempting to understand complexity is revealed and made available for analysis.

To see the transformation of properties into descriptors by the means of bringing the researcher-narrator into our frame of reference, take the case of non-linearity. The lack of proportionality between causes and effects captures our attention precisely because we expect linearity. We interpret the non-linearity of complex systems as counterintuitive or surprising, but the surprise rests on our perspective and in our violated expectations, not in the system we describe in this way. Similarly, scale dependence is not a property of systems, but of our interpretation of them; it is our concepts that are indeterminate, not the system we describe using these concepts. From a position of second-order complexity, recursiveness, sensitivity to initial conditions and emergence are likewise revealed as interpretations. To shift perspective from one level to another, to define where an event begins and ends, and even to consider some congregation of occurrences to be a system, are all interpretive moves, not properties of systems (Checkland, 1981). In other words, the complexity we discover when we apply the methods of complexity science is a function of the second-order complexity we introduce by our involvement.

We claim that the narrative approach gives us access to second-order complexity, which we demonstrate later by taking a narrative approach to recursiveness. However, this is not the only case we can make for the narrative approach to organizational complexity; a strong case can be made from within complexity science itself. To develop this case, we critique the logico-scientific mode of thinking and examine its limitations, for it is in relation to the limits of logico-scientific thought that the contribution of the narrative approach is perhaps most easily understood by those who have never before considered taking a narrative approach.

The logico-scientific mode of thinking and its limitations

As historians of science and philosophers have shown, the rise of scientific rationalism in post-17th century Europe involved a radical shift in how humans thought about the world (see Feyerabend, 1987; Foucault, 1966; Macintyre, 1985; Shapin, 1996; Toulmin, 1990). Toulmin (1990: 200) sums up the shift as a search for a 'rational method' motivated by a 'decontextualized ideal' – the ideal of universal, general, and timeless knowledge (Toulmin, 1990: 30–6). Nowhere have the principles of the 'rational method' been manifested more clearly than in Newton's work, whose influence on the social and economic sciences has been profound (Cohen, 1994; Mirowski, 1989; Smith, 1997).

The 'Newtonian style' (Cohen, 1994: 77), or what other researchers call the 'Galilean style' (Varela et al., 1991: 17), involves a particular approach towards the world, the main features of which are as follows. First, the scientific method deals with the '*primary qualities*' (Goodwin, 1994; Pepper, 1942) of the phenomena under investigation (e.g. mass, velocity, position, etc.), which can be quantified and measured. Second, science constructs idealized models of the phenomena it studies, either with the help of mathematics or through the creation of controlled conditions in a laboratory, or both (Latour, 1987). A consequence of the Newtonian style is that it is both acontextual and ahistorical. It is acontextual insofar as it involves 'switching off' all contextual influences upon the phenomenon under study so that its intrinsic properties may be revealed to the scientist (Ackoff, 1981; Kallinikos, 1996). It is ahistorical because it is marked by synchrony (Kellert, 1993): the state of a system is thought to be known solely in terms of the way the system is at a particular moment. As Kellert (1993: 93) remarks: 'Physics considers that we know everything relevant about a system if we know everything about it at one point in time'.

There are several examples of the Newtonian style of thinking in the social sciences. Cohen (1994) relevantly discussed the case of Malthus' theory of population, and Mirowski (1984, 1989) showed that neo-classical price theory was developed in the late 19th century as an imitation of energy physics. In psychology, the study of cognition has long been conducted in the laboratory (Lave, 1988; Salomon, 1993; Varela et al., 1991). For example, commenting on memory research, Banaji and Crowder (1989: 1192) are only slightly able to conceal their distaste for complexity. 'The more complex a phenomenon,' they note, 'the greater the need to study it under controlled conditions, and the less it ought to be studied in its natural complexity.' Finally, in organization science, Barnard (1976: xl–vi) remarked that 'abstract principles of structure may be discerned in organizations of great variety, and that ultimately it may be possible to state principles of general organization'. Notice how easily Barnard moves from talking about organizations to talking about organization. Behind the awesome variety of organizations there is an underlying set of universal principles of organization. How does one discover those principles? Through the study of aggregates of the phenomenon at hand under statistically controlled conditions (Ansoff, 1991). In other words, as soon as one dispenses with the contingent, as well as deceptive, experience of diversity, one comes upon a small set of generally applicable principles. Experiential contingency gives way to theoretically contrived necessity (Reed, 1996).

From the above it follows that social scientists should search for regularities obtained under well-specified conditions, establish their validity and, ideally, codify them in the form of rules to be followed by practitioners (Tsoukas, 1994, 1998). Notice how well scientific rationalism fits within Bruner's logico-scientific mode of thought (Table 1), and how equally well Bruner's narrative mode represents the Other against which logico-scientific thinkers have defined themselves.

What form does logico-scientific knowledge take? How is it organized? Ideally, it consists of propositional statements: 'if, then' statements relating a set of empirical conditions, called the factual predicate ('If X . . .'), to the consequent, that is to a set of consequences that follow when the conditions specified in the factual predicate obtain ('. . . then Y'; see Holland, 1995; Johnson, 1992; Schauer, 1991). As Bruner (1986: 12–13) notes, propositional knowledge:

> employs categorization or conceptualization and the operations by which categories are established, instantiated, idealized, and related one to the other to form a system. . . . It deals in general causes, and in their establishment, and makes use of procedures to assure verifiable reference and to test for empirical truth. Its language is regulated by requirements of consistency and noncontradiction.

What might be examples of propositional knowledge in organization studies? There are plenty: 'if size is large then formalization is high'; 'if technological complexity is high (or low), then work is non-routine'; 'if the organization uses a prospector strategy, then centralization is low'; 'if environmental uncertainty is low then centralization is high', and so on (see Baligh et al., 1990; Glorie et al., 1990; see also Mintzberg, 1979, 1989; Webster & Starbuck, 1988). These conditional statements serve as explanations of certain recurring organizational phenomena and purport to be the basis for formulating rules for guiding human action in the future.

Propositional knowledge is recursively employed: organizational scientists explain and predict organizational phenomena by means of propositional statements such as those mentioned above; and practitioners are guided in their work by rules, namely by statements prescribing that 'in circumstances X, behavior of type Y ought, or ought not to be, or may be, indulged in by persons of class Z' (Twining & Miers, 1991: 131). The factual predicate of rules is derived from events that occurred in the past and is meant to guide action in the future. Thus any novel situation is described by decomposing it into familiar parts, the behavior of which can be described by tested rules (Holland, 1995). In that sense, the future is understandable in (i.e. reducible to) the terms of the past; time does not really matter because the new is comprehensible in terms of the old.

Thinking propositionally and managing by rules has certain advantages which stem mainly from the fact that propositional statements are abstract and defined exclusively in terms of their syntax. Thus they are applicable across a variety of contexts after a particular interpretation (i.e. semantics) has been attached to them in each particular case (Casti, 1989; Kallinikos, 1996; Tsoukas, 1998). However, an excessive reliance on the propositional mode of thinking has certain limitations. What are they? First, propositional statements are generalizations that, by themselves, cannot deal with particular circumstances or singular experiences. Second, propositional statements incorporate purposes and motives that cannot be formulated propositionally. And third, propositional statements do not include time, thus leading to paradoxes. It is each of these limitations of propositional knowledge to which the narrative mode of thinking offers a complementary strength (Table 2). Later we expand on each of the limitations and point out how a narrative approach offers an important 'corrective' to knowledge about organizational complexity. Each 'corrective' is developed more fully in the following section in which we suggest how a narrative approach to complexity might look.

Table 2 The limits to logico-scientific thinking and some narrative 'correctives'

Logico-scientific limits	Narrative 'correctives'
Imperfect generalizations	Contextuality and reflexivity
Tacit justification	Expression of purposes and motives
Requires consistency and non-contradiction	Temporal sensitivity

Imperfect generalizations

Rules are generalizations connecting types of behavior by types of actors to types of situations. To assert the existence of a rule is necessarily to generalize (and categorize, label), just as to institutionalize human interaction is, of necessity, to imply the existence of rules (Berger & Luckmann, 1967). Rules, however, are implemented locally, namely within contexts in which idiosyncratic configurations of events may occur in a manner that has not been specified by a rule's factual predicate (Shackley et al., 1996; Tsoukas, 1996). The circumstances confronting a practitioner always have an element of uniqueness that is not, and cannot be, specified by a rule. In other words, the indeterminacy of local implementation cannot be eliminated (Brown & Duguid, 1991; Orr, 1990). In commonsense terms, what can go wrong, will go wrong. Only the practitioner possessing 'the knowledge of the particular circumstances of time and place' (Hayek, 1945: 521) can undertake effective action in the moment. The 'tyranny' of the local, the particular, and the timely cannot be escaped in the context of practical reasoning (MacIntyre, 1985; Taylor, 1993).

Notice that the rules the practitioner applies are derived from what has been known about previous failures or successes, thus the practitioner comes ready equipped with historical understanding of sorts. But this aggregate, codified, past-derived knowledge is not very useful when it comes to examining a particular problem (Orr, 1996). To comprehend a particular problem the practitioner needs to follow a bifurcation path (Kellert, 1993). As Prigogine (1980: 106) observes with reference to natural systems, 'interpretation of state C implies a knowledge of the history of the system, which has to go through bifurcation points A and B'. Put very simply, one cannot understand why a system is at point C without understanding *how* it came to be there. That historical 'knowhow' cannot be provided by propositionally organized renderings of human experience in organizational settings; instead it requires a contextually sensitive narrative understanding – in short, it needs a story with a plot (see Bruner, 1996; Dyke, 1990; MacIntyre, 1985; Reisch, 1991). The question is, what mode of thinking might take the features of practical reasoning and historically based knowhow into account? As is shown later, narratively organized knowledge provides such a mode.

Tacit justification

Underlying the implementation of rules is the achievement of a certain goal or the fulfillment of what Schauer (1991: 26) calls 'justification'. For example, the manual issued by a photocopier company to service technicians includes rules such as: 'If this error code is displayed then check this or do that.' The justification for this rule is obviously the company's desire to satisfy the customer in the most efficient manner. A rule's factual predicate ('If this error occurs . . .') is causally related to the rule's justification – the satisfaction of the customer will be brought about by following the rule.

Why does one need justifications?'Justifications exist', says Schauer (1991: 53), 'because normative generalizations are ordinarily instrumental and not ultimate, and justifications are what they are instrumental to'. A justification lies behind the rule, it is the reason for having a rule. As such, justifications are implied; they are not explicitly contained in the rule. This is important, for in order to fulfil the justification, one may occasionally need to break the rules (e.g. when the machine displays a misleading error code)! However, within a purely propositional framework of knowledge, such a paradoxical requirement cannot be accommodated. As Bruner (1986: 13) noted, the 'requirements of consistency and noncontradiction' are constitutive of this mode of thinking. The conclusion should deductively flow from the premises (Hayek, 1982).

Moreover, given that a justification is implicit, it cannot be conveyed to practitioners in a propositional form. Just like Polanyi's (1975: 39) tacit knowledge, a justification is 'essentially unspecifiable': the moment one focuses on it, one ceases to see its meaning. If a justification were to be propositionally articulated it would inevitably be based upon a further implicit justification, and this implicit–explicit polarity would be reproduced ad infinitum. Justification is to a rule what a shadow is to an object. It follows, therefore, that in the propositional mode of thinking, why practitioners should follow a particular rule, cannot be conveyed; what a rule is for cannot be stated. A rule provides the method but not the purpose. As we show later, the exploration of purposes (and motives) is in the domain of narrative mode thinking.

Consistency and non-contradiction

In an organized context, managing by rules alone leads inescapably to paradoxes that cannot be accommodated by logico-scientific thinking. The reason is that time is not included in the logic of propositional statements. As Bateson (1979: 63) insightfully noted, 'the *if* . . . *then* of causality contains time, but the *if* . . . *then* of logic is timeless'. For example, the if . . . then in 'If the temperature falls below 0°C, then the water begins to freeze' is different from the if . . . then in 'If Euclid's axioms are accepted, then the sum of all angles in a triangle is 180 degrees'. The first statement makes reference to causes and effects, whereas the second is part of a syllogism; the first includes time, the second is timeless (Prigogine, 1992). When causal sequences become circular (van Foerster, 1981), their description in terms of logic becomes self-contradictory – it generates paradoxes (Bateson, 1979; Beer, 1973; Capra, 1988; Clemson, 1984). However, as we show below, narrative, because of its sensitivity to the temporal dimension of experience, is well suited to avoid (or reveal) such conflations of logic and causality.

To sum up, the key features of the propositional mode of thinking are as follows: it deals in generalizations, its justification of rules is tacit, it is regulated by the requirements of consistency and non-contradiction, and it ignores time. If, as argued above, second-order complexity is seen as a property of the interaction between an observer O and a system S, and considering that a propositionally thinking observer is led to neglect the particular, the local, and the timely, all of which are important features of the life-world (the world-as-experienced) (Varela et al., 1991), it follows that the quality of interaction between O and S for such an observer will tend to be poor. This is because an observer guided by propositional thinking alone will be unable to handle paradoxical requirements or contradictions such as those illustrated above with examples provided by Weick (1979) and Hatch and Ehrlich (1993). Such paradoxes and contradictions, by definition, cannot be handled by propositional logic according to which one should aim for consistency and non-contradiction in (as well as between) one's thinking and one's acting.

Finally, it is interesting to note that although propositional thinking requires that paradoxes be formally avoided, action that is guided exclusively by propositional thinking tends to generate paradoxes. Ironically, what is avoided in logic turns up in practice! Thus a propositionally thinking observer will find it difficult to manage a system that is characterized by non-linearity, feedback loops, and sensitivity to initial conditions – the very features used to define a system as complex. It is precisely these features, however, that favor the narrative mode and argue for the narrative approach, to which we now turn.

The narrative approach

More important than the novelty of its knowledge claims in mathematics and physics, the wider appeal of complexity science stems from its contribution to the emergence of a new imagery in terms of which the world may be understood (Prigogine, 1997). Such imagery, as has already been mentioned, fosters an awareness of dynamic processes, unpredictability, novelty, and emergence, leading to what Kellert (1993: 114) calls 'dynamic understanding'. The main features of dynamic understanding in the sciences are that it 'is holistic, historical, and qualitative, eschewing deductive systems and causal mechanisms and laws' (Kellert, 1993: 114).

It is interesting to see that notions such as 'holistic', 'historical', and 'qualitative', which have traditionally been the trademark of interpretive social science, are now appearing in the language of physicists. As several researchers have noted (see Capra, 1996; Goodwin, 1994; Hayles, 1990, 1991; Prigogine, 1997; Shotter, 1993; Toulmin, 1990), the appeal of such a vocabulary in scientific discourse signifies the disenchantment with the Newtonian ideal and the attempt to pursue, instead, more meaningful, open-ended, and systemic modes of inquiry. It is precisely the sense of dynamic understanding, as we argued earlier, that the narrative mode of thinking conveys, and we intend to explore what this approach might contribute in the remainder of this article.

In this section we illustrate the narrative approach and second-order complexity via an exploration of the ways in which narrative corrections to logico-scientific thinking produce new insights into complexity issues. However, to adequately illustrate the potential contribution of the narrative approach we feel that we must narrow our ambition to considering just one of the features of complex systems articulated by complexity scientists. Therefore, we concentrate our focus on recursiveness. We do this in order to develop the narrative approach to complexity in a way that reveals its own (i.e. second-order) complexity, as well as illuminating the holistic, historical, and qualitative features of the dynamic understanding in which it deals.

Contextuality and reflexivity

Genette (1980) argues that narrative can refer to three separate things: the written or spoken narrative statement, the events and their relationships that are the subject of the narrative (he calls this the story), or the act of narrating. When the narrative statement and the story are considered together, the issues of interpretation and context become pronounced. This is because the difference between what is told about and what is told gives rise to questions about the meaning of a narrative and the context in which it is interpreted (the act of narrating and the act of listening are both considered to be interpretive acts taking place in specific contexts which inspire and support the development of particular meanings). When the narrative statement and the act of narrating are considered together, the position of the narrator (along with the motives of the narrator, discussed later) becomes an issue for reflection. That is, the difference between the statement and the act of making it causes the narrator to come into view.

Ricoeur (1984) claimed, building on Aristotle's notion of muthos (emplotment) that narrative thinking produces plots. According to Aristotle's *Poetics*, narrative is plot driven. Events, mental states, happenings – in short, the constituents of a narrative (Burke, 1945, described these dramatistically as act, agent, agency, scene, and purpose) – are sequentially placed within the overall configuration that is the plot. To make sense of the particular constituents of a narrative, one needs to grasp its plot. And vice versa; in order for one to understand a plot one needs to grasp the sequence of events that relate its constituent elements (Taylor, 1985). Thus, the parts and the whole are mutually defined and defining, or, in the terms offered by complexity theory, they are recursively ordered. However, the narrative perspective allows us to carry the insight of recursivity further than simply suggesting we look for structural similarity between narratives and plots or between plots and their constitutive elements. Second-order thinking about complexity focuses our attention on how, in making plots, we construct and use narrative thinking. This is what Ricoeur addresses with the concept of emplotment and Bruner with the concept of narrative mode.

Emplotment raises several important issues, the most obvious of which is sequencing. According to Ricoeur (1984) emplotment organizes the continuous flux of experience into describable sequences with beginnings, middles, and ends. We return to the issue of sequencing later in our discussion of temporality. Two others, to be addressed here, concern context and reflexivity.

Contextuality

As Polkinghorne (1988: 36) explained, 'The narrative scheme serves as a lens through which the apparently independent and disconnected elements of existence are seen as related parts of a whole'. Thus, plots give meaning and connection that would otherwise be absent. The connection that plots give is, in part at least, the context provided by the sequence of events and the relationships between them that are highlighted by the sequencing. What happens in a narrative, happens situationally (or situatedly). Providing or invoking a context for meaning making is thus an important part of narrating.

Whereas in logico-scientific thinking, propositions or rules connect categories of behavior to categories of actors and situations, narrative thinking places these elements into a sequenced, contextualized statement with a plot. But once the plot has been constructed, the elements are explicit, local, tangible instances engaged in events with consequences. The narrative mode of thinking enlivens and energizes the emplotted characters and events. In narrating, a narrator communicates and captures nuances of event, relationship, and purpose that are dropped in the abstraction process that permits categorization and correlation in the logico-scientific mode. In narrative we have a more concrete rendering of causality. It is historical and specific, not general and contingent (Table 1). 'This did happen in this way', versus 'this should happen if the following conditions hold'. In terms of addressing organizational complexity, this concreteness is a contribution that narrative approaches make to understanding in that it supplies the specific context within which events occurred. Whereas within logico-scientific thinking context becomes contingency, in narrative mode, context is situation and circumstance. Thus narrative thinking gives us access to and appreciation of context that logico-scientific thinking cannot provide.

Boje (1991) argued that context is essential for interpreting narratives that occur in organizational settings. He claimed that without participating in the organization that contextualizes a narrative, its meaning will be difficult, if not impossible, to grasp. O'Connor shows how context can be revealed using narrative analysis. Hers is a view informed by literary theory in which contextualism refers to the self-containment of a work of literature (i.e. the view that literary works have no reference to things beyond themselves). The literary view supports text analysis (which O'Connor, 1995, illustrates) as a means to reveal the context and embedded assumptions of narrative processes. Boje's work, in contrast, positions the narratives he examines within a broader framework. This broader framework is the organization that provides context for the narrative act (i.e. the telling and interpreting of stories), which is what he means by his phrase 'the storytelling organization'. Thus Boje places narratives within a context of both narrating and organizing, whereas O'Connor looks to texts produced by organizational members for insights into the assumptions, motives and orientations that frame their narrative statements. In either approach, narrative thinking provides sensitivity to the situational particularity missing from the propositional statements favored by the logico-scientific mode of thinking. As can be seen, the narrative mode, in contrast, both demands and engages contextualized understanding and this contextualized understanding contributes to second-order complexity.

Each interpretation invokes a new context producing recursive symmetry of a narrative sort. If complexity is a matter of interpretation, as we have argued, then each 'reading' will produce another layer of context. Thus, taken together, O'Connor and Boje illustrate the connection between complexity theory and narrative. O'Connor's work addresses the fact that narrative statements contain references to the context of the events they tell about, whereas Boje points out that narrative acts also have a context – the context of the teller and their telling which helps to interpret the narrative act. But interpreting the narrative act produces further contextualizing ad infinitum (van Foerster, 1984) – a narrative form of recursive symmetry involving sensitivity to the context of interpretation and the paradox of inescapability from context no matter how many interpretive moves we make. Acknowledgement of this paradox brings narrative consciousness of our embeddedness, which brings us to reflexivity.

Reflexivity

The narrative mode of thinking reminds one that behind every narrative there is a narrator. A story told presupposes a storyteller; it is not an outcome of logical necessity but a product of contingent human construction. As White (1987: 178) argues, echoing Ricoeur, 'narrative discourse does not simply reflect or passively register a world already made; it works up the material in perception and reflection, fashions it, and creates something new, in precisely the same way that human agents by their actions fashion distinctive forms of historical life out of the world they inherit as their past'. In other words, the domain of narrative discourse has verisimilitude. The closest we can come to explaining verisimilitude in logico-scientific terms is to say that narrative discourse is isomorphic with the domain of action: humans reproduce as narrators what they do as agents, and vice versa (MacIntyre, 1985; White, 1987). However, in narrative terms, verisimilitude means more than this; it is the subjective resonance that occurs between the listener's/reader's experience of the world and the narrator's rendition of it. It imparts credibility to the narrative, the narrator and the narrative act (Fisher, 1987), but also provides experience with authenticity (Fisher, 1987).

As we have already argued at some length earlier, appreciating complexity requires a second order of thinking about complexity. That is, not only must we engage with the system under study, we must also confront our own complexity. In narrative terms, complexity theorists are part of the stories they tell about complex systems – they are narrators of complexity (in both senses of that ambiguous phrase, they narrate about complexity and they are complex narrators). Once inside the frame of the story, complexity-theorists-as-narrators are subject to narrative analysis that can be conducted in a variety of ways. One of these ways is suggested by narratology.

Inspired by Genette (1980, 1982, 1988, 1992; see also Hatch, 1996 for an application of narratology to organization theory), narratology concerns the positioning of the narrator in relation to the story told and the narrative act. Genette offered two analytical dimensions to the study of narrative position: narrative perspective (who sees?) and narrative voice (who says?). Genette explained narrative perspective in terms of the relationship between the narrator and the story told which he claimed defines whether the story is seen from an internal or an external point of view. Building on Genette, Hatch (1996) claimed that narrative perspective parallels social scientists' concerns with epistemology (i.e. subjectivism versus objectivism). Genette explained narrative voice in terms of the relationship between the narrator and the narrative act, which he claimed is captured by whether or not the narrator includes him or herself as a character in the story told. Hatch compared this dimension with social scientists' concerns with reflexivity (e.g. Giddens, 1984, 1991; Woolgar, 1988) and pointed out that the question for social scientists is one of deciding whether or not the researcher will be represented in the research story told, which is our interest here.

A step toward appreciating and understanding second-order complexity would be achieved by analyzing the positioning of narrators in writing on complexity theory. We are inclined to argue that narrative positions that are reflexive are more complex than those occupied by the non-reflexive narrators who dominate contemporary social science writing, particularly writing about complexity theory. Because a reflexive narrator does not balk at entering the domain of explicating and commenting upon meaning and interpretation, such narrative positioning should help complexity researchers to reflect critically on the features they attribute to systems (i.e. non-linear, scale dependent, recursive, sensitive to initial conditions, and emergent) and expose the purposes and motivations that link them to the systems they seek to address (e.g. the desire for predictability).

Reflexivity is related to contextuality in the sense that inclusion of the narrator in the narrative involves another layer of context. Narrative thinking reveals a story told by a narrator, occupying a particular position, interpreted by listeners, engaged together in a narrative act. Stories are contextualized by narrators whose positions give context via insight operating inside the context of narrative acts, etc. The recursiveness of context extends to the recursiveness of narrative thinking so that thinker and thought become so intertwined as to render the possibility of disentanglement unimaginable and ourselves more complex.

A deep understanding of second-order complexity has been shown by certain reflexive practitioners who have been aware of their own complexity (subjectivity). For example, Sir Geoffrey Vickers (1983), a senior British civil servant, manifested such awareness in his writings on policy making through his concept of 'appreciative systems' – the value judgments underlying executive decision-making. More recently, the well-known financier George Soros (1994) made 'reflexivity' a central concept of his theory of the operation of financial markets. To the extent that the actor's thinking is part of the situation to which it relates, notes Soros, there is no reality independent of human perceptions. Because an actor's understanding of a situation influences the situation, such an understanding is always imperfect. Being aware of such imperfection (what Soros calls 'participant's bias') makes an actor see social processes as open-ended and brings into focus his/her own role in shaping them.

In other words, for Soros, a reflexive actor – an actor aware of the interplay between his/her thinking and acting – is a more complex actor than a non-reflexive one, because more inequivalent descriptions of a situation can be generated. Whereas for a non-reflexive actor reality has certain definite features which can be captured by a limited number of descriptions, for a reflexive actor, reality is, partly at least, dependent for its description on an observer's vocabulary. In defining a situation, being aware of the role of your own as well as of others' vocabularies enables you to generate more descriptions of it (Tsoukas & Papoulias, 1996).

Purposes and motives

Narrative organization is causal; in narrative accounts it is not only sequence that is important but, crucially, consequence (Randall, 1995). Indeed, causality is what distinguishes a plot from a mere story. As Forster famously remarked '"The king died and then the queen died" is a story. "The king died and then the queen died of grief" is a plot' (Forster quoted in Randall, 1995: 121). In the first instance (in a story) we ask: 'And then?', whereas in the second instance (in a plot) we ask: 'Why?' Whereas, in the logico-scientific mode of thinking an event is explained by showing that it is an instance of a general law, in the narrative mode of thinking an event is explained by relating it to human purpose. Narrative preserves both time (to which we return later) and human agency.

Narrative is infused with motive. Burke (1945, 1954) claimed that motive is a linguistic product because motives are interpretations of our own and others' reasons for acting. As such, they are framed by the discourses in which they and we operate and are couched in terms provided by that discourse. Thus, when we narrate, we give evidence of our motives in a way that is largely (although not completely) absent from our logico-scientific mode of speaking and writing. As a matter of interpretation, motives are presented throughout narratives and may be imputed by the narrators themselves, and/or by their listeners/readers. As interpretations, motives are not fixed entities, they are open to multiple readings framed by the contexts and orientations of the readers caught up in the narrative act (which may include the narrator him or herself).

As a discourse, organization provides the terms in which motives are spoken of. That is, when organizational members are asked to justify their actions, they do so in the terms provided by the organizational discourses in which they participate. For example, downsizing is justified by the necessity of economic circumstance; acquisition in terms of opportunities for revenue creation or profit taking. As discourses change, so justifications change. In the knowledge age, downsizing becomes a matter of reducing redundancies in competence; acquisitions are performed to take advantage of another company's database or to acquire its knowledge resources. As language shifts, so do the terms in which we speak about our motives.

In Part I, 'On interpretation' of *Permanence and change*, Burke (1954) presented his thesis on motives as interpretations and as linguistic products (see also Taylor,

1985). Burke positioned his arguments in contrast to the enterprise of reductionist natural science, claiming that what this orientation excludes from view is 'social motives as such' (Burke, 1954: li). In relating motives to interpretations and positioning both against rationalizing science, Burke (1954: 62) pointed out that:

> Those who look upon science as the final culmination of man's ration-alizing enterprise may be neglecting an important aspect of human response. Even a completely stable condition does not have the same meaning after it has continued for some time as it had when first inaugurated.

In positioning his argument thus, we find Burke's thesis entirely compatible with Bruner's distinction between logico-scientific and narrative modes of thinking. Thus, when Burke discusses motives as absent from rationalizing science but present in ordinary language, we cannot help equating his position with what Bruner called the narrative mode. Moreover, Burke also positions language, and thus the motives that he claimed are constituted by language, within the confines of a particular context or 'orientation' to use his term. A motive, according to Burke (1954: 25), is 'a term of interpretation, and being such it will naturally take its place within the framework of our *Weltanschauung* as a whole'. Motives as interpretations are 'centered in the entire context of judgments as to what people ought to do, how they [prove] themselves worthy, on what grounds they [can] expect good treat-ment, what good treatment [is], etc.'. That is another way of saying that motives, as interpretations, require cultural context to recover or create their meaning. Thus, Burke (1954: 25) concluded, attributions of motive by which people explain their conduct are 'but a fragmentary part of [their] larger orientation,' and 'a terminology of motives . . . is moulded to fit our general orientation as to purposes, instrumentalities, the "good life," etc.'

Burke permits a clear view of what we have called second-order complexity. In describing motivation as a linguistic product situated in a dominant discourse, he suggests a more complicated understanding of motives, an understanding once removed from the psychological level and placed instead at the organizational level where the discourse itself, which defines the terms in which motivation can be spoken of, is located (Harre & Gillett, 1994). By seeing motives in relation to discourse, Burke complicates our understanding and offers a narratological view-point. We say this because to speak about second-order complexity, or the discourse of motives, is to express what is meant by the narrative mode of thinking. That is, the narrative mode, because it instantiates the discourse as well as the story told within it, matches the requirements of addressing second-order complexity.

Organizational complexity, in our view, is well served by a narrative approach precisely because of its relationship to motives. Both being 'linguistic products' in Burke's terms, they have an affinity that we might profit by recognizing. To give just one example, in considering the five features of complex systems presented earlier, acknowledgement of the narrator describing systems in these terms makes us aware of the discourse (i.e. the discourse of complexity theory) that the narrator invokes, and of the positioning of the narrator within that discourse, which gives us our appreciation of his or her motives, in other words, a way to frame the narrator that produces a motivation-rich sense of understanding. Weick, of course, would call this sense-making. But either way, having a device for framing motives leads us to a narrative approach to complexity, and narrative in turn provides a more complex orientation (i.e. both first- and second-order appreciations are accommodated) to the study of organizing. Once again, we engage (enact, employ) recursiveness when we switch to the narrative mode of thinking.

Temporality

Narrative is factually indifferent but temporally sensitive: its power as a story is determined by the sequence of its constituents, rather than the truth or falsity of any of them (Bruner, 1990; Czarniawska, 1998). Temporality, therefore, is a key feature of narrative organization, helping also to preserve particularity. As Hunter (1991: 46) notes with respect to medical narratives:

> By means of the temporal organization of detail, governed by the 'plots' of disease, physicians are able to negotiate between theory and practice, sustaining medicine as an inter-level activity that must account for both scientific principle and the specificity of the human beings who are their patients.

Ricoeur's (1984) treatise on *Time and narrative* supports the claim that a narrative approach to complexity theory uniquely emphasizes the temporal dimension of experience and simultaneously explores the issues of consciousness that are raised by the juxtaposition of narrative and time. As Ricoeur (1984) argued, one cannot engage in narrative as either a narrator or reader/listener without the experience of time. In his study, Ricoeur (1984: 20) demonstrated this with a passage from Augustine's *Confessions*:

> Suppose that I am going to recite a psalm that I know. Before I begin my faculty of expectation is engaged by the whole of it. But once I have begun, as much of the psalm as I have removed from the province of expectation and relegated to the past now engages my memory, and the scope of the action which I am performing is divided between the two faculties of memory and expectation, the one looking back to the part which I have already recited, the other looking forward to the part which I have still to recite. But my faculty of attention is present all the while, and through it passes what was the future in the process of becoming the past. As the process continues, the province of memory is extended in proportion as that of expectation is reduced, until the whole of my expectation is absorbed. This happens when I have finished my recitation and it has all passed into the province of memory.

According to Ricoeur, this passage illustrates how memory (past) and expectation (future) interact to influence attention and thereby produce the threefold present of our experience (the present of the past, the present of the present, and the present of the future). Although this example may seem trivial, Augustine went further, generalizing his point to other levels of experience (Ricoeur, 1984: 22, from Augustine's *Confessions*):

> What is true of the whole psalm is also true of all its parts and each syllable. It is true of any longer action in which I may be engaged and of which the recitation of the psalm may only be a small part. It is true of a man's whole life, of which all his action are parts. It is true of the whole history of mankind, of which each man's life is a part.

These last statements evoke images of fractals and recursive symmetries, but portray them along their temporal rather than their spatial axes. We believe that increasing sensitivity to the ways in which memory and expectation contribute to complexity is a valuable contribution that narrative approaches can make to the study of complexity (in this instance with respect to recursiveness) and organizations.

To carry on a little way exploring what this contribution might look like, we consider another Augustinian idea promoted by Ricoeur – *distensio*. Following Augustine, Ricoeur suggested that, when engaged, memory and expectation extend us across time, allowing us to bridge past and future in the present moment. Things in memory and in imagination are potentially present and *distensio* occurs when we stretch our consciousness across past, present, and future. Furthermore, Ricoeur argued, it is the relationship between expectation, memory and attention forged by *distensio* that gives us the experience of time.

Could it be that through distended experience we construct and make use of the temporal dimension, as Ricoeur suggested? If so, it could likewise be that narrative is part of our distensive capability, both in the sense of invoking memory and expectation, and, as Augustine also showed, via engagement in the process of relegating the future to the past on a moment-by-moment basis. Only that to which we attend can make the journey from expectation to memory, and in this regard, narrative may be an important attention-giving device. If this is the case, then narrative helps us experience time by offering a means of passing expectation into memory. Furthermore, memory and expectation, once engaged, enlarge our consciousness in (and of) the present. Such enlargement increases our complexity.

Ricoeur's '*distensio*' and the way it contributes towards the complexification of the subject can be illustrated nicely by drawing on Weick and Roberts' (1993) study of high reliability organizations. Weick and Roberts developed the notion of 'collective mind', which they take to be, not a given property of a collectivity, but the pattern whereby individuals heedfully interrelate their actions. The more heedfully individuals interrelate their actions, the more likely it is that unexpected events will be handled adequately. The significance of this cannot be overestimated because in high-reliability organizations it is extremely important that interactions between small, unexpected events do not escalate to yield catastrophes.

How might heedful interrelating be increased? Weick and Roberts (1993) suggest three ways, the first of which is directly relevant to our discussion of *distensio*: by making connections across time, activities, and experience. Weick and

Roberts (1993: 366) explain: '[by connecting longer stretches of time] more know-how is brought forward from the past and is elaborated into new contributions and representations that extrapolate farther into the future'. By making connections between the past, the present, and the future, collective mind becomes more complex and, thus, is strengthened, because 'the scope of heedful action reaches more places' (Weick & Roberts, 1993: 366). In this regard, Weick and Roberts (1993: 368) extol the significance of organizational members developing their 'narrative skills', because it is through them that collective mind becomes richer and more complex. 'Stories', argue the authors, 'organize know-how, tacit knowledge, nuance, sequence, multiple causation, means–ends relations, and consequences into a memorable plot' (Weick & Roberts, 1993: 368).

In their study of the use of history by decision makers, Neustadt and May (1986) similarly extolled the virtues of what they call 'thinking in timestreams' – looking at an issue in the present with a sense of the past and an awareness of the future (see also Schon, 1983). Citing examples of several influential USA policy makers, the authors make it clear how the interlacing of past, present, and future complexifies policy makers' thinking, making them potentially more effective. Commenting on George Marshall in particular, Neustadt and May note Marshall's acute sense of history which, while informing his decisions at a point in time, made Marshall focus his eyes 'not only to the coming year but well beyond. . . . By looking back, Marshall looked ahead, identifying what was worthwhile to preserve from the past and carry into the future' (Neustadt & May, 1986: 248). Policy makers' skills in making such connections across time are necessarily of a narrative kind.

As argued earlier, narrative plots can be far more intricate than logico-scientific causal models can, because narrative connections can also be forged through associations that are not causal in the logico-scientific sense. In narrative, for example, things can be connected by co-occurrence, spatial proximity, formal similarity or metaphor, all types of association that logico-scientific modes of thinking try to eliminate as distractions from the discovery of scientific generalizations. Nevertheless, these connections may well help us to understand, in addition to recursiveness (explored above), the non-linearity, indeterminacy, unpredictability, and emergence of complex systems. We leave these explorations for future development of the narrative approach.

Narratives not only allow for multiple connections among events across time, they also preserve multiple temporalities. As well as being linked to clock time, narrative time is primarily humanly relevant time (Ricoeur, 1984): its significance is not derived from the clock or the calendar, but from the meanings assigned to events by actors (Bruner, 1996). In this sense narrative time is not symmetrical. Returning to Forster's and Bruner's example quoted earlier, the moment after the King's death is for the Queen qualitatively different from the moment before his death. Burke (1954: 62) similarly noted that: 'Even a completely stable condition does not have the same meaning after it has continued for some time as it had when first inaugurated.' It is this asymmetry of time (so elegantly argued in the sciences by Prigogine – see Prigogine, 1992, 1997; Prigogine & Stengers, 1984) that gives narrative its dynamic texture. For some researchers narrative time is like a turbulent current 'characterized by an overall vector, the plot, itself composed of areas of local turbulence, eddies where time is reversed, rapids where it speeds ahead, and pools where it effectively stops' (Argyros, 1992: 669). By accommodating multiple temporalities, narratives are far more complex than propositional statements in which, as we saw earlier, time is absent.

Conclusions

To summarize, a narrative approach to complexity theory suggests that our understandings of complex systems and their properties will always be grounded in the narratives we construct about them. When we characterize initial conditions as perturbations of a system, we construct the beginning of a plot (the system is a character or protagonist and the perturbation is a situation or antagonist) that may conclude with the system moving off in a direction that is surprising. As with unpredictable characters in other stories or in life, the complex system is interpreted as volatile or capricious. When the multiple interactions of systemic behavior in complex systems produce emergent (new) modes of behavior, in narrative terms the plot thickens, the characters develop. To put this more reflexively, when we theorize about complexity, we narrate. Being conscious of our narrativity develops the second order of complexity upon which we earlier claimed complexity itself rests. This article has been about developing second-order complexity alongside our appreciation of organizational complexity via a narrative approach.

In presenting arguments in favor of taking a narrative approach to complexity theory, we analyzed the primary mode of thinking typical of complexity theorists and suggested a role that the narrative mode of thinking could play in compensating for the limitations of complexity theory's well-practiced logico-scientific mode of thought. Interpretive organization theory has been used to show how the narrative mode complements and extends the findings of complexity theory and complexifies our thinking about organizational complexity. A few ideas from narrative theory have been presented to give a sense of the contribution that further development of narrative approaches to understanding complexity theory might offer to organization theory. A critique of the logico-scientific mode of thinking indicated absences in complexity theory that narrative theory might fill, and these possibilities have been explored in relation to contextuality, reflexivity, purposes/motives, and temporal sensitivity, all of which were related to recursiveness in order to demonstrate how the narrative approach contributes to understanding organizational complexity.

References

Ackoff, R. *Creating the corporate future*. New York: Wiley, 1981.
Ansoff, I.H. Critique of Henry Mintzberg's 'The design school: Reconsidering the basic premises of strategic management'. *Strategic Management Journal*, 1991, *12*, 136–48.
Argyros, A. Narrative and chaos. *New Literary History*, 1992, *23*, 659–73.
Baligh, H.H., Burton, R.M. & Obel, B. Devising expert systems in organization theory: The organizational consultant. In M. Masuch (Ed.), *Organization, management, and expert systems*. Berlin: de Gruyter, 1990.

Banaji, M. & Crowder, R. The bankruptcy of everyday memory. *American Psychologist*, 1989, *44*, 1185–93.

Barnard, C. Foreword. In H. Simon (Ed.), *Administrative behavior*. New York: The Free Press, 1976.

Barrow, J. Theories of everything. In J. Cornwell (Ed.), *Nature's imagination*. Oxford: Oxford University Press, 1995.

Barry, D. Strategy retold: Toward a narrative view of strategic discourse. *Academy of Management Review*, 1997, *22*, 429–52.

Bartunek, J., Gordon, J. & Weathersby, R. Developing 'complicated' understanding in administrators. *Academy of Management Review*, 1983, *8*, 273–84.

Bateson, G. *Mind and nature*. Toronto: Bantam Books, 1979.

Beer, S. The surrogate world we manage. *Behavioral Science*, 1973, *18*, 198–209.

Beer, S. *Brain of the firm*. Chichester: Wiley, 1981.

Berger. P. & Luckmann, T. *The social construction of reality*. London: Penguin, 1967.

Boje, D. The storytelling organization: A study of story performance in an office-supply firm. *Administrative Science Quarterly*, 1991, *36*, 106–26.

Bolman, L. & Deal, T. *Reframing organizations*. San Francisco, CA: Jossey-Bass, 1991.

Boyce, M. Collective centring and collective sense-making in the stories and storytelling of one organization. *Organization Studies*, 1995, *16*, 107–37.

Brown, J.S. & Duguid, P. Organizational learning and communities of practice. *Organization Science*, 1991, *2*, 40–57.

Bruner, J. *Actual minds, possible worlds*. Cambridge, MA: Harvard University Press, 1986.

Bruner, J. *Acts of meaning*. Cambridge, MA: Harvard University Press, 1990.

Bruner, J. The narrative construal of reality. In J. Bruner (Ed.), *The culture of education*. Cambridge, MA: Harvard University Press, 1996.

Brunsson, N. *The organization of hypocrisy*. Chichester: Wiley, 1989.

Burke, K. *A grammar of motives*. Berkeley: University of California Press, 1945.

Burke, K. *Permanence and change: An anatomy of purpose* (3rd ed.). Berkeley: University of California Press, 1954.

Capra, F. *Uncommon wisdom*. London: Fontana, 1988.

Capra, F. *The web of life*. New York: Anchor Books, 1996.

Casti, J. On system complexity: Identification, measurement, and management. In J. Casti & A. Karlqvist (Eds), *Complexity, language, and life: Mathematical approaches*. Berlin: Springer-Verlag, 1986.

Casti, J. *Paradigms lost*. London: Cardinal, 1989.

Casti, J. *Complexification: Explaining a paradoxical world through the science of surprise*. London: Abacus, 1994.

Checkland, P. *Systems thinking, systems practice*. Chichester: Wiley, 1981.

Chia, R. The problem of reflexivity in organizational research: Towards a postmodern science of organization. *Organization*, 1996, *3*, 31–59.

Clemson, B. *Cybernetics*. Cambridge, MA: Abacus, 1984.

Cohen, B. Newton and the social sciences, with special reference to economics, or, the case of the missing paradigm. In P. Mirowski (Ed.), *Natural images in economic thought*. Cambridge: Cambridge University Press, 1994.

Cooper, R. & Burrell, G. Modernism, postmodernism and organisational analysis: An introduction. *Organization Studies*, 1988, *9*, 91–112.

Corvellec, H. *Stories of achievements: Narrative features of organizational performance*. New Brunswick, NJ: Transaction Publishers, 1997.

Crutchfield, J., Farmer, D., Packard, N. & Shaw, R. Chaos. *Scientific American*, 1986, *255*, 46–57.

Czarniawska, B. *Narrating the organization: Dramas of institutional identity*. Chicago, IL: University of Chicago Press, 1997a.

Czarniawska, B. A four times told tale: Combining narrative and scientific knowledge in organization studies. *Organization*, 1997b, *4*, 7–30.

Czarniawska, B. *A narrative approach to organization studies*. Thousand Oaks, CA: Sage, 1998.

Czarniawska-Joerges, B. Narratives of individual and organizational identities. In S.A. Deetz (Ed.), *Communication Yearbook*, 1994, *17*, 193–221.

Davis, P. Chaos frees the universe. *New Scientist*, 1990, *1737*, 48–51.

Dyke, C. Strange attraction, curious liaison: Clio meets chaos. *The Philosophical Forum*, 1990, *XXI*, 369–92.

Feldman, M. The meanings of ambiguity: Learning from stories and metaphors. In P. Frost, L. Moore, M.R. Louis, C. Lundberg & J. Martin (Eds), *Reframing organizational culture*. Newbury Park, CA: Sage, 1991.

Feyerabend, P. *Farewell to reason*. London: Verso, 1987.

Filby, I. & Willmott, H. Ideologies and contradictions in a public relations department: The seduction and impotence of living myth. *Organization Studies*, 1988, *9*, 335–49.

Fisher, W.R. *Human communication as narration: Toward a philosophy of reason, value and action*. Columbia: University of South Carolina Press, 1987.

Foucault, M. *The order of things*. London: Tavistock/Routledge, 1966.

Gabriel, Y. The unmanaged organization: Stories, fantasies and subjectivity. *Organization Studies*, 1995, *16*, 477–501.

Geertz, C. *The interpretation of cultures*. New York: Basic Books, 1973.

Gell-Mann, M. *The quark and the jaguar*. London: Little, Brown, 1994.

Genette, G. *Narrative discourse: An essay in method* (J.E. Lewin, Trans.). Ithaca, NY: Cornell University Press, 1980.

Genette, G. *Figures of literary discourse* (A. Sheridan, Trans.). New York: Columbia University Press, 1982.

Genette, G. *Narrative discourse revisited* (J.E. Lewin, Trans.). Ithaca, NY: Cornell University Press, 1988.

Genette, G. *The architext* (J.E. Lewin, Trans.). Berkeley: University of California Press, 1992.

Giddens, A. *The constitution of society: Outline of the theory of structuration*. Berkeley: University of California Press, 1984.

Giddens, A. *Modernity and self-identity: Self and society in the late modern age*. Stanford, CA: Stanford University Press, 1991.

Glorie, J.C., Masuch, M. & Marx, M. Formalizing organizational theory: A knowledge-based approach. In M. Masuch (Ed.), *Organization, management, and expert systems*. Berlin: de Gruyter, 1990.

Goodwin, B. *How the leopard changed its spots*. London: Phoenix, 1994.

Granovetter, M. Problems of explanation in economic sociology. In N. Nohria & R.G. Eccles (Eds), *Networks and organizations*. Boston: Harvard Business School Press, 1992.

Harre, R. & Gillett. G. *The discursive mind*. Thousand Oaks, CA: Sage, 1994.

Hatch, M.J. The role of the researcher: An analysis of narrative position in organization theory. *Journal of Management Inquiry*, 1996, *5*(4), 359–74.

Hatch, M.J. Irony and the social construction of contradiction in the humor of a management team. *Organization Science*, 1997, *8*, 275–88.

Hatch, M.J. & Ehrlich, S.B. Spontaneous humor as an indicator of paradox and ambiguity in organizations. *Organization Studies*, 1993, *14*(4), 505–26.

Hayek, F.A. The use of knowledge in society. *The American Economic Review*, 1945, *35*, 519–30.

Hayek, F.A. *Law, legislation and liberty*. London: Routledge & Kegan Paul, 1982.

Hayles, K. Chaos as orderly disorder: Shifting ground in contemporary literature and science. *New Literary History*, 1989, *20*, 305–22.

Hayles, K. *Chaos bound: Orderly disorder in contemporary literature and science*. Ithaca, NY: Cornell University Press, 1990.

Hayles, K. (Ed.) *Chaos and order: Complex dynamics in literature and science*. Chicago, IL: University of Chicago Press, 1991.

Holland, J. *Hidden order: How adaptation builds complexity*. Reading, MA: Addison Wesley, 1995.

Hunter, K.M. *Doctors' stories: The narrative structure of medical knowledge*. Princeton, NJ: Princeton University Press, 1991.

Johnson, P. *Human–computer interaction*. London: McGraw-Hill, 1992.

Kallinikos, J. *Technology and society*. Munich: Accedo, 1996.

Kamminga, H. What is this thing called chaos? *New Left Review*, 1990, *181*, 49–59.

Kellert, S. *In the wake of chaos*. Chicago, IL: University of Chicago Press, 1993.

Koestler, A. *The act of creation*. New York: Macmillan, 1964.

Latour, B. *Science in action*. Milton Keynes: Open University Press, 1987.

Lave, J. *Cognition in practice*. Cambridge: Cambridge University Press, 1988.

MacIntyre, A. *After virtue* (2nd ed.). London: Duckworth, 1985.

March, J.G. & Olsen, J.P. *Ambiguity and choice in organizations*. Bergen, Norway: Universitetsforlaget, 1976.

Martin, J. Stories and scripts in organizational settings. In A.H. Hastorf & A.M. Isen (Eds), *Cognitive social psychology*. New York: Elsevier, 1982.

Martin, J., Feldman, M., Hatch, M.J. & Sitkin, S. The uniqueness paradox in organizational stories. *Administrative Science Quarterly*, 1983, *28*, 438–53.

Meyerson, D. 'Normal' ambiguity? In P. Frost, L. Moore, M.R. Louis, C. Lundberg & J. Martin (Eds), *Reframing organizational culture*. Newbury Park, CA: Sage, 1991.

Miller, J.G. *Living systems*. New York: McGraw-Hill, 1978.

Mintzberg, H. *The structuring of organizations*. Englewood Cliffs, NJ: Prentice Hall, 1979.

Mintzberg, H. *Mintzberg on management*. New York: Free Press, 1989.

Mirowski, P. Physics and the 'marginalist revolution'. *Cambridge Journal of Economics*, 1984, *8*, 361–79.

Mirowski, P. *More heat than light: Economics as social physics, physics as nature's economics*. Cambridge: Cambridge University Press, 1989.

Mohr, L. *Explaining organizational behavior*. San Francisco, CA: Jossey-Bass, 1982.

Morgan, G. *Images of organization* (2nd ed.). Thousand Oaks, CA: Sage, 1997.

Mulkay, M. *On humor*. Oxford: Blackwell, 1988.

Neustadt, R.E. & May, E.R. *Thinking in time*. New York: Free Press, 1986.

O'Connor, E.S. Paradoxes of participation: Textual analysis and organizational change. *Organization Studies*, 1995, *16*(5), 769–803.

Orr, J.E. Sharing knowledge, celebrating identity: Community memory in a service culture. In D. Middleton & D. Edwards (Eds), *Collective remembering*. London: Sage, 1990.

Orr, J. *Talking about machines*. Ithaca, NY: ILR Press/Cornell University Press, 1996.

Pascale, R. *Managing on the edge*, London: Viking, 1990.

Pepper, S. *World hypotheses*. Berkeley: University of California Press, 1942.

Perrow, C. The bureaucratic paradox: The efficient organization centralizes in order to decentralize. *Organizational Dynamics*, 1977, *5*, 3–14.

Polanyi, M. Personal knowledge. In M. Polanyi & H. Prosch (Eds), *Meaning*. Chicago, IL: University of Chicago Press, 1975.

Polkinghorne, D. *Narrative knowing and the human sciences*. Albany: State University of New York Press, 1988.

Poole, S. & Van de Ven, A. Using paradox to build management and organization theories. *The Academy of Management Review*, 1989, *14*, 562–78.

Prigogine, I. *From being to becoming*. San Francisco, CA: W.H. Freeman, 1980.

Prigogine, I. The philosophy of instability. *Futures*, 1989, *21*, 396–400.

Prigogine, I. Beyond being and becoming. *New Perspectives Quarterly*, 1992, *9*, 22–8.

Prigogine, I. *The end of certainty*. New York: Free Press, 1997.

Prigogine, I. & Stengers, I. *Order out of chaos*. London: Fontana, 1984.

Putnam, L. Contradictions and paradoxes in organizations. In L. Thayer (Ed.), *Organization – communication: Emerging perspectives I*. Norwood, NJ: Ablex, 1985.

Quinn, R. & Cameron, K. *Paradox and transformation*. Cambridge, MA: Ballinger, 1988.

Randall, W.L. *The stories we are*. Toronto: University of Toronto Press, 1995.

Reed, E.S. *The necessity of experience*. New Haven, CT: Yale University Press, 1996.

Reisch, G. Chaos, history, and narrative. *History and Theory*, 1991, *30*, 1–20.

Ricoeur, P. *Time and narrative*, Vol. 1. Chicago, IL: University of Chicago Press, 1984.

Rorty, R. *Contingency, irony, and solidarity*. Cambridge: Cambridge University Press, 1989.

Salomon, G. Editor's introduction. In G. Salomon (Ed.), *Distributed cognitions*. Cambridge: Cambridge University Press, 1993.

Schauer, F. *Playing by the rules*. Oxford: Clarendon Press, 1991.

Schon, D. *The reflective practitioner*. Aldershot: Avebury, 1983.

Shackley, S., Wynne, B. & Waterton, C. Imagine complexity: The past, present and future potential of complex thinking. *Futures*, 1996, *28*, 201–25.

Shannon, C. & Weaver, W. *The mathematical theory of communication*. Urbana: University of Illinois Press, 1949.

Shapin, S. *The scientific revolution*. Chicago, IL: University of Chicago Press, 1996.

Shaw, G., Brown, R. & Bromiley, P.G. Strategic stories: How 3M is rewriting business planning. *Harvard Business Review*, 1998, *50*(3), 41–50.

Shotter, J. *Conversational realities*, London: Sage, 1993.

Smircich, L. & Morgan, G. Leadership: The management of meaning. *Journal of Applied Behavioral Science*, 1982, *18*, 257–73.

Smith, R. *The Fontana history of the human sciences*. London: Fontana Press, 1997.

Soros, G. *The alchemy of finance*. New York: Wiley, 1994.

Stacey, R. *Complexity and creativity in organizations*. San Francisco, CA: Berrett-Koehler, 1996.

Stewart, I. (1993) Chaos. In L. Howe & A. Wain (Eds), *Predicting the future*. Cambridge: Cambridge University Press, 1993.

Stonum, G.L. Cybernetic explanation as a theory of reading. *New Literary History*, 1989, *20*, 397–410.

Taylor, C. *Philosophy and the human sciences* (Vol. 2). Cambridge: Cambridge University Press, 1985.

Taylor, C. To follow a rule . . . In C. Calhoun, E. Lipuma & M. Postone (Eds), *Bourdieu: Critical perspectives*. Cambridge: Polity Press, 1993.

The Price Waterhouse Change Integration Team *The paradox principles: How high-performance companies manage chaos, complexity, and contradiction to achieve superior results*. Chicago, IL: Irwin, 1996.

Toulmin, S. *Cosmopolis: The hidden agenda of modernity*. Chicago, IL: University of Chicago Press, 1990.

Tsoukas, H. Introduction: From social engineering to reflective action in organizational behavior. In H. Tsoukas (Ed.), *New thinking in organizational behavior*. Oxford: ButterworthHeinemann, 1994.

Tsoukas, H. The firm as a distributed knowledge system: A constructionist approach. *Strategic Management Journal*, 1996, *17* (Special Winter Issue), 11–25.

Tsoukas, H. Forms of knowledge and forms of life in organized contexts. In R. Chia (Ed.), *In the realm of organization*. London: Routledge, 1998.

Tsoukas, H. & Papoulias, D. Creativity in OR/MS: From technique to epistemology. *Interfaces*, 1996, *26*, 73–9.

Twining, W. & Miers, D. *How to do things with rules* (3rd ed.). London: Weidenfeld and Nicolson, 1991.

Van Maanen, J. *Tales of the field: On writing ethnography*. Chicago, IL: University of Chicago Press, 1988.

Varela, F., Thompson, E. & Rosch, E. *The embodied mind: Cognitive science and human experience*. Cambridge, MA: MIT Press, 1991.

Vickers, G. *The art of judgement*. London: Harper & Row, 1983.

von Foerster, H. On cybernetics of cybernetics and social theory. In G. Roth & H. Schwegler (Eds), *Self-organizing systems*. Frankfurt: Campus-Verlag, 1981.

von Foerster, H. On constructing a reality. In P. Watzlawick (Ed.), *The invented reality*. New York: Norton, 1984.

von Glaserfeld, E. An introduction to radical constructivism. In P. Watzlawick (Ed.), *The invented reality*. New York: Norton, 1984.

Waddington, C. *Tools for thought*. Frogmore, UK: Paladin, 1977.

Waldrop, M.M. *Complexity*. London: Penguin, 1992.

Webster, J. & Starbuck, W. Theory building in industrial and organizational psychology. In C. Cooper & I. Robertson (Eds), *International review of industrial and organizational psychology*, Chichester: Wiley, 1988.

Weick, K.E. *The social psychology of organizing*. Reading, MA: Addison-Wesley, 1979.

Weick, K.E. *Sensemaking in organizations*. Thousand Oaks, CA: Sage, 1995.

Weick, K. & Browning, L. Argument and narration in organizational communication. *Journal of Management*, 1986, *12*, 243–59.

Weick, K. & Roberts, K. Collective mind in organizations: Heedful interrelating on flight docks. *Administrative Science Quarterly*, 1993, *38*, 357–81.

Westenholtz, A. Paradoxical thinking and change in the frames of reference. *Organization Studies*, 1993, *14*(1), 37–58.

White, H. *The content of the form*. Baltimore, MD: Johns Hopkins University Press, 1987.

Wilkins, A. Organizational stories as symbols which control the organization. In P.J. Frost, L.F. Moore, M.R. Louis, C.C. Lundberg & J. Martin (Eds), *Reframing organizational culture*. Beverly Hills, CA: Sage, 1983.

Woolgar, S. Reflexivity is the ethnographer of the text. In S. Woolgar (Ed.), *Knowledge and reflexivity: New frontiers in the sociology of knowledge*. London: Sage, 1988.

EDITORS' DISCUSSION OF THE READINGS IN PART THREE

- Chia, R. (1998) From Complexity Science to Complex Thinking: organization as simple location, *Organization*, 5(3): 341–370.
- Stacey, R. (2003) Learning as an Activity of Interdependent People, *The Learning Organization*, 10(6): 325–331.
- Tsoukas, H. and Hatch, M. J. (2001) Complex Thinking, Complex Practice: the case for a narrative approach to organizational complexity, *Human Relations*, 54(8): 879–1013.

We met at the home of one of us in North London on a grey day in late November 2004 to talk about the three readings in Part Three. What these readings have in common is the central focus they place on the social sciences. Here complexity is not to be understood simply in terms of the application of natural sciences concepts to human action. Instead the distinctiveness of the social sciences is emphasized, especially the matter of human agency.

Transferring findings from the natural sciences to the social sciences?

Doug: At one time, for instance in Descartes' era, or even in Kant's, there was no distinction between the natural sciences and the social sciences. You were a scientist. Quite recently, when elements of the natural sciences were brought into social theory, for instance around cybernetics and systems thinking, there was a general enthusiasm for this. Why is it, then, that there wasn't this reaction to bringing in elements of the complexity sciences? Is it so threatening? It's interesting that in terms of organizational management thinking there was an immediate reaction against notions from the natural complexity sciences which is brought out in what Chia and Tsoukas and Hatch do in their two articles. They both say that you can't simply transfer thinking from the natural sciences to the social sciences and that man is in the unique position of having a body, which is part of the natural sciences, and a spirit, soul or whatever, which is not a part of the natural sciences. They do different things with this point. Tsoukas and Hatch, for instance, turn to what they are calling second-order complexity, obviously with reference to second-order cybernetics, talking about it as being the human experience while first-order complexity is in the domain of the natural sciences.

Ralph: But they're not taking the same position as Chia, which is an outright rejection of the usefulness of the complexity sciences in understanding human action. He argues that all natural complexity scientists have an attitude to complexity which is actually one of simplification and reductionism. But I think he bases his argument on only one example, namely, the work of Gell-Mann. What Chia says does seem to apply to Gell-Mann. I think you can say much the same for Holland. But you couldn't say that Kauffman,[1] Goodwin and Prigogine, for example, were simplifiers and reductionists. They take a very different kind of view. What I think Chia is pointing to, and here I would agree with him, is that the project behind the work of some of the natural complexity scientists is the traditional scientific project of control. But others, very notably Prigogine, problematize this. So for me that's the big thing. Many of those who take up complexity ideas in relation to organizations, particularly those who make direct application, simply sustain and maintain the traditional project in management and organization, which is all about being in control.

Donald: But in that sense is Chia saying that complexity in human settings isn't so much a scientific category but an aesthetic one?

Robert: What do you mean by that?

Donald: That complexity in human settings doesn't really fit into the traditional project with its concern with control, reduction, prediction, formula, efficiency and so on; it's an artistic thing.

Ralph: Well, that's a way of gaining awareness of human complexity but it presents a different idea of experience, which Chia gets from Bergson.[2] What he's talking about, as experience, is the continual impingement on our bodies of the enormous variety of everything around us as we interact with each other in a wider environment. So complexity for humans is then this great flux and flow of experience, where everything's always changing. What we then do, and I think this is quite an individualist perspective, is that we punctuate the continuous flux of complex experience, we puncture it and chop it up, in order to, in some sense, control it. So experience is an unknowable flow that each of us operates on, making categories of meaning. Chia then sees organization as necessarily controlling this flow of experience and therefore necessarily alienating us from some kind of sense of true experience. Is this how you would see what he is saying?

Doug: Yes, I think that is what he does. He objectifies his subjective experience. By contrast, in Berger and Luckman's version of social constructivism there is a move to the subjective pole.[3] What I think we are trying to get at is a view of experience which is subject and object at the same time.

Ralph: So in our concept of process, of experience, which we rely on very heavily, we avoid any notion of some unknowable, virtual stream of experience which we then operate on. Instead, we understand experience as the temporal processes of human bodies interacting with each other, co-creating the patterns of their interaction. So there is no idea, here, of something impinging on each of us, which each of us then has somehow to structure through chopping up, or punctuating. All there is is the patterning of our interactions with each other and it is we who are doing the patterning together. If you want to, you can describe this patterning as chopping up, punctuating or categorizing, but that is all there is. There is only the activity of categorizing, not also some other thing that is being categorized.

Donald: I think James says there is no stuff of experience for later reflection.[4]

The tendency to reify

Robert: That's why, at the opening of your article, Ralph, you talk about this habit of reifying organizations. If we take the readings from Part Three of this book and compare them to the ones in Part One, where people are just directly applying concepts from the natural sciences, would you say that the readings in Part One of the book do reify organizations?

Ralph: Well, I think that all of those readings do reify organizations because they all understand organizations as systems. As soon as you start talking about an organization having objectives you are into reification.

Doug: Well, I wouldn't say that thinking in terms of systems necessarily implies reification. Someone could mathematically model an organization as a system, remaining aware that this is a model without moving to equating it with the organization itself. But most people do tend to move from the modelling to the reification of the model. And then there comes the further movement to reification, I think, when people start talking about living systems.

Ralph: You are right, Doug. I think the Chia article, my article, and also the one by Tsoukas and Hatch, all avoid reification and talk much more about processes, although in very different ways. So when Tsoukas and Hatch bring in the idea of narrative knowledge, they present a more processual understanding of what we're doing, even though they think in terms of systems.

Donald: Could you say what you mean by processual and what you mean by reification? What is it about their stance that makes it more process orientated? What is a process?

Ralph: Because they all bring in time, in some way, I think they are all talking about process. Of course, there is also a notion of process in systems thinking, exemplified by the readings in Part One, but it's an idea of process as the interaction between parts, which might be individuals, to create a whole, to create something outside their interaction, which it then becomes possible to reify, that is, treat as a thing that actually exists, quite independently of the parts. Whereas, in Chia's article, and in mine, there is the notion of temporal process. In the Chia version, people are interacting over time, they are impinging on each other, producing a great variety of flux and flow over time, which each of them then has to puncture and punctuate. This is the unknowable, complex flow of experience which each of us then has to simplify in order to make sense of it. In my article, I talk about temporal processes in which people are interacting together to create further patterns of interaction. You get patterns of interaction which are yielding nothing other than patterns of interaction rather than creating something outside the interaction which must be operated on, such as a whole in the case of systems thinking and a flux and flow in the case of Chia's thinking.

Donald: Do these patterns feed back onto the interaction?

Ralph: No, because they are the interaction, so you don't get any feedback, whereas in the systemic notion, the individuals create the system and the system then acts back upon them. In Chia's view, people partly create the flux and flow and then they have to operate on it to make meaning. In what I am saying, the patterning of interaction is continually emerging in the patterning of interaction and this patterning is itself meaning with nothing outside it.

Defining complexity

Robert: Can we take that point and connect to other issues that come from the Tsoukas and Hatch article, and the Chia article, about definitions of complexity? I guess one of the things that readers of this book might be interested in, is how complexity is defined. It's interesting that both articles cite the Gell-Mann definition of complexity as the shortest possible description of a system. This is a mathematical definition. In the Tsoukas and Hatch article, I've noticed that they have five characteristics, or properties, which would allow you to identify something as complex or not. So, for example, you get complexity when systems are non-linear and exhibit sensitivity to initial conditions, where small changes are escalated through feedback loops. Yet you are saying that, from your perspective, it is meaningless to talk about feedback loops.

Ralph: The approach that I would take is one which asks this question. In the work that is done in the complexity sciences, particularly the theory of complex adaptive systems, what insights might be taken up as being analogous to human action? Such insights then have to be translated in the human domain, in terms of the essential features of being human, such as consciousness, self-consciousness and choice. This means that you would take important insights, like emergence and self-organization, and then ask what they mean for human action. It doesn't mean that you take over all the features of complex adaptive systems, like feedback. The approach in my article in this part is much more selective and I don't really see the point of trying to define what human complexity is, in terms of mathematics and models.

Robert: So going back to your article in the first part, there I think you say that organizations are complex systems . . .

Ralph: And now I would say, no they aren't, because that's just a way of thinking and that to do this direct application, as I was doing then, isn't very useful. Instead, I now take a much more selective view of the complexity sciences, and ask what it is, in terms of insight, that is attractive and then ask why it is exciting in terms of an analogy for understanding what humans are doing.

Donald: Does it follow then, in your view, that there is any such thing as non-complex responsive processes in human interaction? Is there any such thing as a simple organization, for example?

Ralph: As opposed to complex?

Donald: Yes.

Ralph: I guess that I would probably say no.

Doug: You make a point about Chia's article that the opposite of complex is not simple. Tsoukas and Hatch move to second-order complexity as human thinking, appealing in the end to a better application of the natural sciences. They don't appeal to human freedom. And Chia, in moving to the sense of process in Bergson's and Whitehead's terms,[5] also does not appeal to human freedom. But human freedom is the main argument, for me, in that it is what ethics would be about.

Ralph: Just let's go back to your question, Donald, about whether there is anything that is not complex in human action. One of the insights in the natural complexity sciences, which you'll find Kauffman expressing, for example, is that all life evolves to the edge of chaos, which I understand to be a paradoxical dynamic, a paradoxical pattern of movement in time, which is both stable and unstable at the same time. So then, in that sense, all human interaction would be paradoxically stable and unstable at the same time, which is what we are arguing when we say human interaction is always continuity with potential for transformation as a form of causality. We are defining complexity as this paradoxical dynamic of stability and instability, forming and being formed by, at the same time.

Donald: But this means that not all systems are complex.

Robert: This also picks up on Peter Allen's chapter in Part Two because he classifies progressively more complex systems, doesn't he? So he has simple mechanistic systems at one end of the spectrum and complex evolutionary ones at the other.

Donald: Yes, but these are models of something, not the something itself. So you can have more and more complex models. In Ralph's article in Part Three, complexity is seen, not as some classification of a system that may have implication for the dynamics, but as the paradoxical nature of human experience.

Robert: So is complexity an intrinsic quality of systems . . .

Donald: It's not about systems but about intrinsic qualities of human interaction.

Ralph: Yes, that's right; complexity refers to the process of human interaction which is necessarily continuous and potentially transforming, repetitive and potentially changing at the same time, that is, paradox. But the potential for change and transformation is not always realized and then you find, in human action, that there is very little fluidity. Instead, there are the highly repetitive, stuck patterns of interaction which I would call mental illness. For example, neurosis is a form of highly repetitive interaction, in which there is very little variation. Now that doesn't mean that social interaction has suddenly become simple, because being depressed and neurotic isn't simple, even though it is characterized by a very high degree of repetition. What you have, then, is experience which is denying, defending against, awareness of experience. So, aspects of human experience may well be unconscious, often unconsciously blocking consciousness of experience.

Robert: In your article, Ralph, there is a section where you say that human action is not deterministic and therefore we cannot say that it is chaotic. So would you say that neurosis is chaotic because it is deterministic . . .

Ralph: It's not deterministic. It's stuck rather than that, hopefully only temporarily. Human action is not deterministic because any relationship that is deterministic cannot evolve, and that means it is impossible to learn.

Paradox

Donald: Can I just develop another theme? There is a major distinction now between the readings in Part Three and those in Part One. In Part One readings, complexity refers to mathematical concepts such as algorithmic compressibility while in Part Three readings it refers more to paradox. Could you say a bit more about paradox, Ralph, because I think that your take on paradox is very different from the take in the other two readings, if they actually deal with paradox at all?

Doug: I think we can see where paradox is important in terms of modern science by going back to Kant.[6] At the beginning of modernism, he stated the fact that the problem with trying to continue after the collapse of the Middle Ages and metaphysics was the problem of man being, on the one hand, a part of deterministic nature as a body and, on the other, being a spirit with free will and so not part of deterministic nature. For Kant it was a problem to think of this as a paradox so he tried to find a way to eliminate the paradox. This is where he came up with systems thinking. The interesting thing is that in suggesting the terms system and self-organization, he explicitly reintroduces paradox, saying, 'What I'm observing is paradoxical'. In other words this is the first time that paradox is brought back into the natural sciences. It was revolutionary. What's interesting in terms of Tsoukas and Hatch, and also Chia, is that they insist on Kant's elimination of paradox, when they say that you have to go one way and not the other, or otherwise you will end up in irresolvable paradoxes. So they choose going the one way of second-order complexity in the case of Tsoukas and Hatch and in the case of Chia, process grounded in terms of Whitehead and Bergson. Prigogine, on the other hand, holds the paradox of order and disorder at the same time.

Donald: I suppose my question is this. Is Prigogine actually saying what you are saying? You are saying that paradox, in some sense, is the generative process, simultaneously stable and unstable.

Doug: Interestingly enough, Whitehead said the same thing in one of his books, I think it's *Process and Reality*, which is a series of lectures that he gave on the main thinkers at the beginning of modernity. He said if you go back to any one of them you will find that what we have received from them, displayed in the way we talk about them or their work, is the reduction of extremely complex thinking, the essence of which was very paradoxical, and it is the paradox that defines what was generative in their thinking.

Donald: Right, but that's what I'm coming to. Does Prigogine say what you are saying about this generative dimension paradox? Or is he simply saying that it is confusing?

Doug: I think he does see the generative nature of paradox and that it means a new dialogue with nature.

Ralph: I think this is quite important to remember, given that Chia identifies only one strand in the thinking of complexity natural scientists represented by Gell-Mann and Holland, representatives of the project for control and certainty. Prigogine explicitly talks about how complexity means the end of the project of control and certainty. It therefore requires a new dialogue with nature. There are these very different positions that get taken up, so that you can't possibly lump them together. They are opposites. If we take insights from the Prigogine strand of the complexity sciences, we have to place great emphasis on unpredictability and unknowability and then consider how we would think about human interaction from this perspective.

Donald: This is the link which I have to say has, to some extent, eluded me until now. The key is the end of certainty and the end of certainty is closely tied up with the expression of paradox. Therefore paradox, uncertainty and novelty are bound up with one another. You can't have novelty without uncertainty.

Are experience and thinking separate?

Doug: But interestingly enough, as soon as anyone says that we have to talk first of all about ontology and epistemology, they are immediately in the Kantian perspective. This is because, if reality is hidden, a statement on ontology, then the central, logical question is how we know reality, a matter of epistemology. Reality is something out there and the problem is how we know it. It's the same for Whitehead. For him, the experience is out there and we somehow break it up or something. But then the essential question is not about process but once again about epistemology and ontology, in other words, how we know about this experience and what the ontological status of this experience is. Gell-Mann and Holland remain completely in the Kantian perspective of hidden reality, which is the title of Holland's book, so the essential project is epistemology.

Ralph: That view is expressed in Chia's article, where you get the unknowable flow and flux of experience that we operate on to categorize it.

Donald: But the question I would have to ask you, Ralph, is this. You say that the Chia article indicates a separation between our experience as undifferentiated flux and our human processing of it and that this is a difficulty. I want to ask you about what I think is a different version of a similar approach in your own writing. When you talk about the process of reification, are you not talking about a separation between thinking and experience? It's quite clear in the Tsoukas and Hatch article, and maybe the Chia one, that they say there is complexity out there in the world, including the complexity of our interaction, and then the problem is how we think about it. You say no to this and claim that there is only experience as interaction between people. But then, at certain points you say that some ways of thinking abstract from direct experience, as when people reify their experience or when they conceptualize things in a particular way that does not reflect a direct engagement with their experience. You seem to be saying that they, somehow or another, depart from their direct experience. My question is how can you depart from experience if your experience is something you are continually co-creating rather than being something out there?

Ralph: Because in your thinking about your experience, if you postulate a construct, such as an organization, actually being a thing or a system, you are abstracting from your experience of interaction. Where in your experience would you find this thing?

Donald: But the act of postulation is in itself an experience, according to your definition of experience, and you're introducing a conceptual separation between that category of experience and some prior experience . . .

Ralph: No, I don't think I am. Suppose we are thinking together and talking to each other about our experience of a particular organization. Suppose in this discussion we are postulating that this organization actually exists as a thing outside of our interaction, just as physical objects exist in nature outside our interaction with each other. I would say that in such a conversation we are using a process of reification. The theme emerging in the conversation is reification. Having this reifying conversation is certainly experience, not another category of experience but the same process of experience as that in which we have a conversation in which we talk about an organization in some other way that does not involve reification. But in the experience of the reification conversation we are talking about another experience, the experience of the organization, which is not about the direct interaction with others that we have in an organization. Instead we are talking about an interaction with the 'thing', a physical object in nature, called an organization. I would say that we are then talking about something that is an abstraction because it is not in our direct experience. If we sit here and talk about the University of Hertfordshire as some 'thing' that actually exists then where is it? I say it does not exist as a thing. What indubitably exists, as organization, in my experience is patterns of relationship with the people I meet when I go there.

Doug: This immediately links to the issue of ideology and alienation. We necessarily create conceptual wholes, such as a university or any other organization. People create often highly developed fantasies of what is going on, what is causing what, why they are doing what they are doing and then begin to act upon the fantasy. I think it's the necessary basis of human experience that we constantly create wholes that makes sense of our experience. In fact these wholes constitute our ideologies, the basis on which we act. But these ideological wholes must be constantly negated, that is challenged, explored and negotiated with each other, otherwise they become the ground of the alienation of our experience. In such negation we move to the next whole. We're constantly caught up in an ideology and it is the essential human responsibility to keep negating such ideological wholes.

Ralph: I think this is the important point. If we talk together about an organization actually existing as a physical thing outside our interaction with each other then we are engaging in an act of imagination. We are constructing imaginative wholes and in believing that they actually exist, and acting on that basis, we are acting on the basis of belief, of ideology. This ideology exists in our experience, and in that sense is as real as anything else in our experience. But this real ideology is now based on an abstraction from our experience, and it is an abstraction because it is based on an imaginative construct of a whole, the imaginative nature of which is being covered over by the postulate that the whole actually exists as a thing. When Doug talks about the ongoing need for negation, I think he is referring to the need to constantly question this 'reality' postulate and keep exploring the nature of our imaginative construct and what it means for the ethics of what we are doing.

Donald: But that's precisely my point. As an act of imagination, the organization, as thing or system, does exist as an imaginary phenomenon and therefore we must accord imagination some status.

Doug: But that imaginative whole is an ideology. If it doesn't exist as anything other than an imaginative whole, then it is an ideology.

Ralph: So, there are some explanations holding that what we construct in our experience as an organization is a thing or a system that exists outside our interaction. There are others, reflected in my article in this part, which hold that the organization exists only as an ideology, as an imaginative whole constructed in our interaction, or I would say as themes patterning our experience of being together which we can find in our experience. The imaginative wholes, or fantasies, we construct in our experience can quite easily alienate us from that experience, just as we may experience unconsciously blocking consciousness of our experience. For this reason we need to continually negate our imaginative wholes. We can find the imaginative construct of the university in our experience as the experience of value, which involves an imaginative construction of a whole. This isn't an illusion, it's as real as anything in our experience, but what's not real is a 'thing' outside of the imaginative construct. Now to me, those are different explanations. Reification is sort of fantasy of a physical thing existing when it doesn't.

Donald: And is that problematic?

Doug: I would say it's destructive because it posits an ideology as a thing in itself and not something to be constantly negated.

Donald: I thought you were going to say it was problematic because it ascribes intention to something that can't possibly have it. I'm asking these questions because all the readings in Part Three make distinctions about what is out there, what we experience and think about that experience, and take slightly different positions on it.

Ralph: And of course that's a big distinction from the readings in Part One where these questions don't really arise. This is the kind of discussion you start to have when you try to approach the explanation of human action from the social perspective and you no longer take it for granted there's something real, the natural science of complexity, that applies to something real, the organization. So we move into something that all these readings are bringing up, something like reflexivity.

The issue of power

Donald: Can I switch topics and ask what the various readings say on the issue of power? Ralph, in your article you regard power as the patterning of interactions that exclude and include people in group processes.

Ralph: Well, our theory of experience as temporal process is very much a theory of power because interaction is the experience of enabling and constraining each other.

Doug: That's the essence of relating.

Donald: I think this is a major difference between the readings in Part Three compared to those in Part One. We go from thinking about complexity in mathematical terms, such as algorithmic compressibility, to thinking about complexity as paradox. We also move from a kind of power-neutral landscape to one where power is at the heart of everything and that's a major step forward, I think, in theorizing about organizations in complexity terms.

Robert: Yes, any talk about power asymmetries is absent from the readings in Part One.

Donald: In strategy we are concerned with order, not just as symbolic order which to a large extent is the realm of language, but also political order which has to do with the allocation of scarce resources, many of which are material, that is, not socially constructed but out there, regardless of our experience. So how do the various readings weave these two things together in a way that acknowledges power when it comes to resource allocation?

Ralph: Well, I don't think any of the three readings in Part Three are explicitly dealing with that.

Doug: You could argue that if you take the experience of not knowing as a motivation to negotiate what is going on and how resources should be allocated, this provides an indication of how you would think about resource allocation.

Ralph: If you regard power as central and focus on processes of enabling and constraining relating, then the power asymmetry you mentioned, Robert, is tilted more towards some than others, and it's tilted on the basis of need. And if you think about the nature of need, it can be emotional need so that if I love someone more than they love me, the power balance is tilted towards them. But it can be on the basis of the control of resources which has emerged in patterns of inter-action in the past. So if you have a resource I need, the power ratio will be tilted to you. I have to do what you require me to do in order to get some of that resource. Then we see the allocation problem, not as a rational calculation, but as a matter of power figuration.

Doug: And in terms of narrative, it is about who can tell the most powerful story about who we are and what's going on. This becomes the basis for making the allocation.

Donald: How would this manifest itself in theories of strategic management? For example, Tsoukas and Hatch see narrative knowledge as second-order com-plexity. Is narrative a better way to deal with the political dimension of strategy and organizations?

Ralph: Well, I think that both Chia and Tsoukas and Hatch make sharp distinctions between particular forms of knowledge. I wouldn't think in terms of such a split, saying that propositional knowledge is useful for one purpose and narrative for another.

Doug: Tsoukas and Hatch talk about Ricoeur's work on emplotment. At the heart of what Ricoeur does in his book, *Time and Narrative*, is mimesis.[7] He talks about mimesis one, mimesis two and mimesis three. This third one is very close to what Mead is saying when he talks about gesture and response. Ricoeur then says that the meaning of a narrative is in its reception just as the meaning of the gesture is in the response. I think Ricoeur is talking about narrative emergence. The focus is not on the individual telling the story but on the meaning emerging in the interaction between the narrator and those to whom the story is directed. The narrative is forming meaning and being formed by it at the same time. I think this then becomes the basis of what strategy would be about. Strategy becomes this process of forming and being formed at the same time, rather than simple intention.

Ralph: You see then how the Tsoukas and Hatch article deals with the narrative aspect in one way and we deal with narrative in a rather different way. We are saying that narrative isn't simply a form of knowledge but that it is the very patterning of our interaction with each other. Our interaction is thematically patterned in narrative form.

Doug: Mead uses the term 'conversation'. He would say that the essence of human interaction is conversation.

Ralph: So we are using narrative more in the conversational sense, in which there isn't a beginning and an end and in which the plot, the theme, is emerging. We are constructing it.

Donald: I get this. I agree that it is tremendously helpful to think about organization and strategy in terms of 'emergent' meaning in 'power relating'. The bit that I'm left wondering about, in all the readings, is how this relates to the decision to close a hospital or to allocate three hundred thousand pounds to this project rather than that project. How does the material dimension of power manifest itself in these theories?

Ralph: If you take a social perspective in relation to these matters, you are trying to understand the narrative of the political interaction that is going on, which leads to the point where somebody says 'close the hospital'. When you look at that story, it's not a simple rational calculation but a pattern of negotiating different interests. There are many different stories reflecting these interests, usually about what led up to the hospital closing. So what's important is the conversation. There will always be conversation in which there is negotiated this action which closes down the hospital.

Doug: In a sense, the meaning of that hospital is constantly in flux. It's always expanding or closing, to some extent, as it moves on. But people focus on this one moment of a decision being made, in a sense cutting that out, trying to define that as the nature of human decision making or strategy, whereas it's simply an aspect of the ongoing meaning of what this hospital is about.

Donald: Right, that's a good point, but I am interested in the practice of strategic management in the light of scarce physical resource endowments. How does your theory inform our practice rather than just explain it afterwards?

Ralph: A theory focuses your attention on particular aspects of a practice. Some theories of strategic management focus your attention on analytical calculating activities. We are saying that there are much more complex processes of interaction going on in which people are negotiating to do this or do that in this interest or that interest, negotiating what it means to serve that interest and not another interest. So what this kind of theorizing is doing, is focusing your attention on, not just a rational calculation, but on much wider processes of interaction of which a rational calculation may be part and may be serving all sorts of interests other than rational calculations. The rational calculation may be a big front for something else.

NOTES

1 See for example Kauffman, S. (1993) *The Origins of Order: self organization and selection in evolution*, Oxford University Press, Oxford.

2 Bergson, H. (1977) *The Two Sources of Morality and Religion*, University of Notre Dame Press, Paris.

3 Berger, P. L. and Luckman, T. (1966) *Social Construction of Reality*, Doubleday, New York.

4   James, W. (2002) *The Varieties of Religious Experience: a study in human nature*, The Modern Library, New York.
5   Whitehead, A. N. (1978) *Process and Reality (Gifford Lectures Delivered in the University of Edinburgh During the Session 1927–28)*, The Free Press, New York.
6   Kant, I. (1934) *Critique of Pure Reason*, Dent, London.
7   Ricoeur, P. (1984–88) *Time and Narrative*, 3 vols, University of Chicago Press, Chicago, IL.

CONCLUDING REMARKS

This book has represented one 'run through' of summarizing the field of complexity and organization for newcomers to what has proven to be an exciting and provocative body of research. Theories of complexity point to new possibilities for understanding human interaction in general and organization theories in particular. At the same time the content of the book has implicitly pointed to the myriad alternative possibilities for such a 'run through'. Ilya Prigogine, in answering the question 'What is complexity?', often answered that the direction taken by the complexity sciences was in essence saying that the object of research was 'not simple' – the type of response you can easily give when you have attained the recognition that Prigogine had in his later years.

There is, however, something important in the 'not' of the 'not simple'. This is similar to the enthusiasm about drawing attention to the shift in emphasis from the linear to the non-linear. In a sense what we have presented in this book is one argument that the answer to the question about complexity cannot be given in the straightforward way expected by many coming from other scientific paradigms. As mentioned in our introduction, Peter Allen argues that any system is complex which has the capacity to respond to its environment in more than one way. Thus, complex systems tend to self-organize, producing emergent new order. Self-organization is at the core of the difference those speaking of complexity are trying to draw attention to. We have presented one of many possible broad pictures of what trying to think about this and find one's own position might entail.

Responding to complexity and organization in different ways

There is an important link between responding and the negation mentioned above. In presenting a hypothesis, a position, we build on the work of others by presenting a response which negates others. It is by negating that we are able to focus on difference. The question is then: what do we expect in making this difference? Are we negating simply to present a position as true in itself? Is the negation merely the presentation of another view which may be correct for those who find meaning in it? Considering these two extremes of dogmatic positioning and scepticism is important for the questions which the readings and conversations in this book raise in terms of complexity and organization.

Many questions have been raised and formulated in such a way as to point to making a clear decision for either dogmatic positioning or scepticism. These include, among others, the differing understanding of self-organization and emergence; the question of whether the insights of the complexity sciences have metaphorical, analogical or literal meaning for the social sciences; whether complexity thinking is simply a further development of second-order cybernetics or a radical shift of paradigm; whether, in the end, the object of scientific research will remain complex or will prove to be simple, having been previously only coarsely perceived; whether humans can be taken as the agent components of a system or whether this would deny human freedom; whether the procedure of programming simple rules in computer simulations can be helpful in understanding social interaction or whether this is reductive, again denying human freedom. We have presented this book as an aid for newcomers – to help them explore their own positions on these matters and the implications of arguing one side or the other. Perhaps even more importantly, readers will have become aware of how they are approaching the discourse around complexity and organization.

Debates of such an 'either–or' character emerge as unavoidable, as has been seen over the last few years of research on complexity and organization. It is important not to diminish the role of such debates but also not to take them out of the context of the ongoing discourse. Continued movement in this direction, however, could open the way for the sceptical argument that the nature of such discourses is that they are 'open' in the sense of appreciating or recognizing the 'truth' of each contribution. This is to be respected and each accorded a world of meaning of its own, not to be diminished by others.

An alternative would be to view the role of such polarizing and negating either–or debates as an emergent and key aspect of an ethics of responding. Because of the complexity of the capacity of various responses, attention is focused on the importance of understanding and recognizing the difference in the response. The ethical motivation and obligation is for researchers to present as clearly and forcefully as possible the position they find themselves taking on the basis of taking seriously the work of others which has been presented and working toward the further movement of thought. The basis for such thinking can be found in the work of American pragmatist thinkers, specifically in the concepts of 'the community of scientists' and 'truth in the long run'. To understand these, perhaps it would be helpful to first consider the role of imagination, as developed by John Dewey.[1]

Awakening imagination

We have presented these readings and conversations in the hope that newcomers will be struck by one or many of the ideas around complexity and organization. Many of the articles document how the authors were struck by the ideas around chaos and complexity theories, most dramatically in the early 1990s, producing a wealth of enthusiastic responses. Wittgenstein has emphasized the contextual nature of this experience of being struck,[2] and Dewey, in his work focusing on imagination, insists that it must be understood as a social process. It is important to have such concepts in mind in moving to understand the pragmatist concept of the 'community of scientists'.

Those struck by the new ideas presented in the complexity sciences often articulated very different responses, as the articles in this reader have documented. To understand these differences as differences it is important to think about the nature of these responses as imagination. For Dewey, the imagination is the intellectual capacity to form and think in wholes, but this is not simply an individual process but a social one. On the basis of their past experience and study in complexity and organizations, many engaging with the new ideas have creatively formulated new wholes of theory as a way of moving thought which they had experienced as 'stuck'. Such wholes are powerful social constructions and they can be experienced as both exciting and threatening because of the intensity by which the will can be possessed by such an imagined whole. It thus becomes a forceful expression of values. Engaging in the necessary either–or polarization and negation of such wholes is the source of the emergence of wholes and the prerequisite for the further movement of thought. We see this as the ethics of working with difference and it has been our prime motivation in the process of preparing this book.

Working with difference

There are a number of concepts developed in American pragmatism, such as Dewey's concept of imagination and Mead's concept of the 'I–me dialectic', which not only support the concept of emergence but also include an emergent concept of the individual which allows for human freedom.[3] We hope to have presented a compelling argument for the engagement with difference. We urge readers to reflect not only on the positions stated but also on their own positions which they may now find themselves better able to articulate. In this sense we would welcome them to the community of those focusing in disciplined discussion of complexity and organization, playing responsible roles in the emergence of truth 'in the long run'.

NOTES

1   Dewey, J. (1925/1958) *Experience and Nature*, Dover, New York. See also Eldridge, M. (1998) *Transforming Experience: John Dewey's cultural instrumentalism*, Vanderbilt University Press, Nashville, TN, and London.

2   Wittgenstein, L. (1968/1980) *Remarks on the Philosophy of Psychology*, vols I and II, G. H. von Wright and H. Nyman (eds), Basil Blackwell, Oxford.
3   See especially Mead, G. H. (1934) *Mind, Self and Society*, University of Chicago Press, Chicago, IL, pp. 152–222.

Index